Secession AND Separatist Conflicts
IN POSTCOLONIAL AFRICA

AFRICA: MISSING VOICES SERIES

Timothy Stapleton, Professor, History, University of Calgary
ISSN 1703-1826 (Print) ISSN 1925-5675 (Online)

This series addresses issues and topics that have been overlooked in political, social, and historical discussions about Africa.

No. 1 · *Grassroots Governance?: Chiefs in Africa and the Afro-Caribbean*
Edited by D.I. Ray and P.S. Reddy · Copublished with the International Association of Schools and Institutes of Administration (IASIA)

No. 2 · *The African Diaspora in Canada: Negotiating Identity and Belonging*
Edited by Wisdom Tettey and Korbla Puplampu

No. 3 · *A Common Hunger: Land Rights in Canada and South Africa*
By Joan G. Fairweather

No. 4 · *New Directions in African Education: Challenges and Possibilities*
Edited by S. Nombuso Dlamini

No. 5 · *Shrines in Africa: History, Politics, and Society*
Edited by Allan Charles Dawson

No. 6 · *The Land Has Changed: History, Society and Gender in Colonial Eastern Nigeria*
By Chima J. Korieh

No. 7 · *African Wars: A Defense Intelligence Perspective*
By William G. Thom

No. 8 · *Reinventing African Chieftaincy in the Age of AIDS, Gender, Governance, and Development*
Edited by Donald I. Ray, Tim Quinlan, Keshav Sharma, and Tacita A.O. Clarke

No. 9 · *The Politics of Access: University Education and Nation-Building in Nigeria, 1948–2000*
By Ogechi Emmanuel Anyanwu

No. 10 · *Social Work in Africa: Exploring Culturally Relevant Education and Practice in Ghana*
By Linda Kreitzer

No. 11 · *Secession and Separatist Conflicts in Postcolonial Africa*
By Charles G. Thomas and Toyin Falola

Secession AND Separatist Conflicts
IN POSTCOLONIAL AFRICA

Charles G. Thomas and Toyin Falola

Africa: Missing Voices Series
ISSN 1703-1826 (Print) ISSN 1925-5675 (Online)

© 2020 Charles G. Thomas and Toyin Falola

University of Calgary Press
2500 University Drive NW
Calgary, Alberta
Canada T2N 1N4
press.ucalgary.ca

This book is available as an ebook which is licensed under a Creative Commons license. The publisher should be contacted for any commercial use which falls outside the terms of that license.

LIBRARY AND ARCHIVES CANADA CATALOGUING IN PUBLICATION

Title: Secession and separatist conflicts in postcolonial Africa / Charles G. Thomas and Toyin Falola.
Names: Thomas, Charles G., 1979- author. | Falola, Toyin, author.
Series: Africa, missing voices series ; no. 11. ISSN 1703-1826
Description: Series statement: Africa: missing voices series, ISSN 1703-1826 ; no. 11 | Includes bibliographical references and index.
Identifiers: Canadiana (print) 20190214708 | Canadiana (ebook) 20190214775 | ISBN 9781773851266 (softcover) | ISBN 9781773851273 (Open Access PDF) | ISBN 9781773851280 (PDF) | ISBN 9781773851297 (EPUB) | ISBN 9781773851303 (Kindle)
Subjects: LCSH: Secession—Africa—History—20th century. | LCSH: Africa—History—Autonomy and independence movements.
Classification: LCC DT30.5 .T56 2020 | DDC 320.1/5096—dc23

The University of Calgary Press acknowledges the support of the Government of Alberta through the Alberta Media Fund for our publications. We acknowledge the financial support of the Government of Canada. We acknowledge the financial support of the Canada Council for the Arts for our publishing program.

Copyediting by Peter Enman
Cover image by Magharebia, used under the Creative Commons License Attribution 2.0 License (https://creativecommons.org/licenses/by/2.0/deed.en).
This image has been lightly altered from the original. Original image can be found at https://commons.wikimedia.org/wiki/File:Le_Mali_entame_le_dialogue_avec_les_Touaregs_(6972875286).jpg
Cover design, page design, and typesetting by Melina Cusano

Contents

List of Maps	vi
Introduction	1

Part I: The Civil Secessions — 23

1. The Secession of Katanga, 1960–1963 — 39
2. The Secession of Biafra, 1967–1970 — 67

Part II: The Long Wars — 99

3. The Anomaly of Eritrean Secession, 1961–1993 — 115
4. The Secession of South Sudan, 1955–2011 — 157

Part III: The New Wave of Secessions — 189

5. De Facto Secession and the New Borders of Africa: Somaliland, 1991–Present — 203
6. Transnational Communities and Secession: The Azawad Secessionists, 1990–1996 and Beyond — 231

Conclusion: Secession and the Secessionist Motive into the Twenty-first Century	263
Notes	287
Bibliography	327
Index	341

List of Maps

All maps by Nathan E. McCormack and Charles G. Thomas

Map of Africa—Secession Case Studies Shown in White	*vii*
Map of Congo and Katanga	*37*
Map of Nigeria and Biafra	*65*
Map of Ethiopia and Eritrea	*113*
Map of Sudan and South Sudan	*155*
Map of Somalia and Somaliland	*201*
Map of Mali and Azawad	*229*

Map of Africa—Secession Case Studies Shown in White

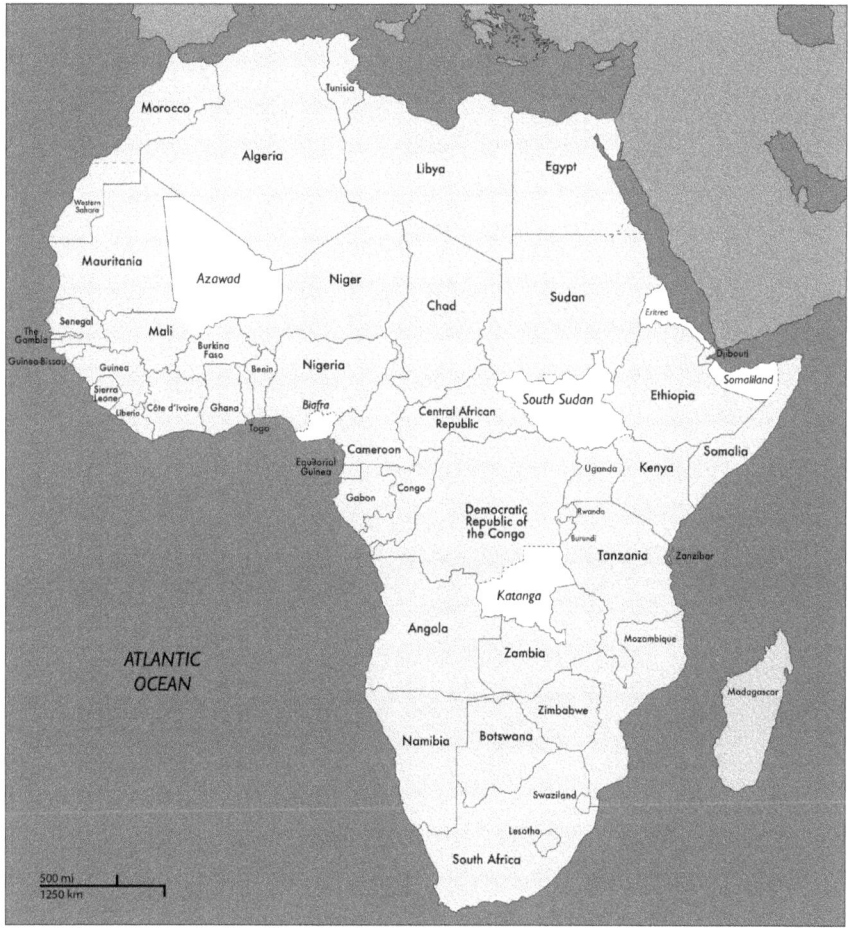

Copyright © 2014 Nathan E. McCormack and Charles G. Thomas

Introduction

The African secessionist conflicts of the postcolonial era remain rare and in many ways exceptional phenomena, that have blended politics and violence in ways unlike any other struggles on the continent. The structure and goals of these conflicts have evolved over the course of four decades of independence and been continually shaped by the experience of the preceding separatist wars, the international reaction to their prosecution, and the broader global political trends. The main undertaking of this volume is to explain the historical context and precedents that have shaped the concept and practice of secessionist conflicts in Africa from independence to the present day.

To accomplish this goal, this introduction lays a foundation for the history of secession in Africa. It begins with an explanation of the natural intertwining of politics and warfare on the African continent in terms of both external and internal state conflicts, including a discussion of the exceptional and evolving form of secessionist wars, and then proceeds to a general overview of what secession itself entails as well as its related terms of separatism and irredentism. Following this is a brief summary of the main theoretical conceptions of the motives behind secession in the world, with an eye toward what drives this form of violence against the state. Next is a basic discussion of the relative absence of the secessionist motive in Africa and the proposed reasons for this. Finally, the introduction ends with a description of the structure of the book and how it uses the historical arc of secessionist conflicts in Africa to explain the anomalous structure of secession and separatism in terms of the African state.

War and Politics

As clichéd as it may be to begin with a quotation from an eminent voice from the past, it seems appropriate to start this section with Clausewitz's famous observation that "war is the pursuit of politics by other means." War is the ultimate expression of political violence, an organized effort to drive forward a political ideal, supported by a political body and carrying forth a conscious or unconscious ideology. Therefore, a war must of necessity carry a political goal within its execution, the grand strategy of the aggressor that then defines the rhetoric, structure, and execution of the violence, whether it be one of external projection of power against another state or an internal conflict advancing a particular political objective. Viewed in such a way, it is no surprise that Africa, which has seen such political turbulence beginning with its rapid decolonization, has also seen a subsequent abundance of conflict. The African state, like any other state, creates and maintains its prerogatives by control of the means of violence, and in this sense all conflicts can and must be viewed in their political relation to the states involved.

This relation is readily apparent when one examines the various major conflicts that have dotted the continent since independence. The most obvious of the struggles within Africa are those of state against state, which despite their visibility are generally rare upon the continent. These include the formal conflicts between Ethiopia and Somalia over the Ogaden in 1977–78, where two centralized and powerful states fought a conventional war over territory historically claimed by both nations. This conflict was followed in short order by the often overlooked struggle between Uganda and Tanzania in 1979, where the Tanzania People's Defence Force drove Amin's Ugandan Army from the Kagera salient and toppled the dictator's regime. Beyond these eastern conflicts, the multiple wars between Libya and Chad in the 1970s and 1980s fall into this category. Qaddafi's conventional Libyan forces were attempting to claim a strip of Chadian territory and were ultimately frustrated over the course of multiple incursions. The Horn even saw what might be termed a continuation of an earlier conflict in the recent Ethiopian-Eritrean War of 1998–2000, where the borders of the recently separated states became the subject of a violent disagreement. Of course, dwarfing all of these, in both political meaning for the continent and scale, were the wars waged between the white settler regimes in southern Africa, including South Africa and Rhodesia, against the Frontline States.[1] Beginning with the earliest liberation struggles in the 1960s through to the massive Battle of Cuito Cuanavale,[2] these wars featured the military efforts of multiple independent African countries, including Tanzania, Zambia, Angola, and Mozambique, in a decades-long concerted conventional war against multiple South African and Rhodesian incursions. Despite the often-fragile state structures of Africa, these states are more than capable of prolonged conflict in pursuit of their political ends.

In state confrontations these political goals vary, but they still serve as the guiding principle of the struggle. In fact, in these struggles it is always primarily a clash of opposing political beliefs or needs that drive each side into the conflict. For the Ethiopia-Somalia struggle it was competing political claims for the Ogaden, an Ethiopian region filled with ethnic Somalis. For the Tanzania-Uganda War it was the political struggle for control of the Lake Victoria region and the stability and security of either regime. Amin needed a war and conquests to cement his increasingly tenuous control of his state, while Nyerere's Tanzania could never achieve its goals of security and peace with Amin's regime at its borders. The Chad-Libya wars were fought for the glorification of Qaddafi's Libya at the expense of the Chadian government and for the sovereignty over the Aouzou Strip in northern Chad, which Libya claimed due to a previous unratified colonial treaty. Within the clashes between the Frontline States and the settler regimes, it was the political question of decolonization and majority rule versus South Africa and Rhodesia's desire to secure their minority regimes that drove the conflict. All of these conflicts were the extension of frustrated political goals of the aggressors clashing with the status quo of their opponents. What mainly sets them apart from the greater proportion of African conflicts is their method of prosecution. Whereas the vast majority of African conflicts involve one or more stateless actors, out of definition these state confrontations involved developed logistical systems and complex political structures on both sides. This altered the conflict from one involving a protracted guerrilla struggle to a conventional war between two developed regular militaries. The simple fact that it is an external conflict for two states determines both the nature of the conflict's interaction with the states and the methods of its waging. This dynamic alters considerably when one considers the wide variety of internal state struggles, which radically outnumber the external struggles since independence.[3]

Let us examine one particular family of conflicts that have emerged in Africa in the past decades. This specific strain of conflicts is best viewed as the liberation struggles of the former colonies that had not yet been granted their own self-governance. Perhaps the first in this category was the Mau Mau in Kenya, an insurgency meant to advance the political goals of the Kikuyu in the face of an unfair system of colonization. The scale would only increase from there, including the brutal struggle in Algeria that began to unravel the French Empire in Africa, although the French sphere of influence was somewhat preserved due to their own political manoeuvring. The greatest of the decolonization struggles took place in the regions administered by the Portuguese, where the colonies of Guinea-Bissau, Angola, and Mozambique all saw protracted struggles against a formal colonial power. These wars lasted from the early 1960s until 1974, when the Carnation Revolution overthrew the Portuguese government. The trailing conflicts of this sort were those of the anomalous former British colonies of Rhodesia and apartheid South Africa. Rhodesia first committed its own act of political violence in its Unilateral Declaration of Independence in 1965, severing itself from the British sphere of influence. From this point on, a struggle was waged by the white settler population against the black African popular fronts of ZANU and ZAPU, both of which clamoured for majority rule, the last step in decolonization, which finally came in 1980. As for South Africa, the struggle itself is hard to categorize because of its strange history. While the struggle of the ANC and Pan-African Congress groups against the apartheid government may be viewed as the struggle against the colonizers who had created an oppressive imperial state, they may also be viewed as reform struggles, which will be covered shortly.[4] In either case, the political aspirations of those involved were clear and the struggle was tailored to attain those goals.

In the liberation conflicts in Africa, the political goal that defined them was obvious: the national self-determination of a colonized people, free from either the control or even nominal influence of their former colonial power. Put simply, these were struggles for freedom from an established foreign state structure, and as such the struggles were often conducted against an opponent superior in arms, capital, and training. This meant that the primary method of waging war was what would be defined by Mao Tse-Tung as a protracted conflict, one where the nascent nationalist forces avoided direct confrontation with the superior foe and instead concentrated on sapping the latter's will to fight until political circumstances forced an end to the conflict or the balance of power had shifted so as to allow a conventional war of manoeuvre to commence. To effect this struggle, the liberation movements needed to create a political framework that would serve as an alternative to the colonial rule and use this limited example as a symbol to gain popular approval. The political goal had to be compelling enough to draw in the populace in sufficient numbers to affect the protracted struggle and to eventually place that political structure into power over the newly freed nation itself. In short, liberation conflicts are defined by the political goal of freedom from an outside colonizer and are structured in such a way as to promote a domestic national government as both the basis for struggle and the end goal itself.

A second prominent strain of internal conflict on the continent is those conflicts waged to alter the ideology or form of government in control of the state. These wars have happened all over the continent, with the most common examples often following in the wake of the decolonization itself, as internal groups seek their own advantage in the new power structure. The radical Lumumbists of the Stanleyville faction in the Congo in the 1960s stand as an excellent example of these, rejecting the central Leopoldville government's sovereignty and demanding acceptance of their own power. In addition, the long civil wars faced by both Angola and Mozambique following their independence struggles may be characterized as reform conflicts, as RENAMO in Mozambique and UNITA and the FNLA in Angola all were fighting against the domestic power structures that had ascended following the liberation struggles in those lusophone countries.[5] Within the greater struggles in Ethiopia in the late 1970s through the 1990s, there were a number of reform conflicts that became embroiled in the greater Eritrean conflict against the ruling Derg, most notably the struggle of the Tigray People's Liberation Front. As a final and perhaps the clearest example, there are the myriad groups that struggled within Uganda after the fall of Idi Amin, with groups as diverse as Alice Lakwena's Holy Spirit Mobile Forces and Yoweri Museveni's National Resistance Army all seeking a hold on the domestic power structure. As long as there have been independent domestic political power structures in Africa, there have been armed groups willing to dispute these structures.

Much as with the liberation struggles, the political goals of the reform conflicts are fairly obvious. These struggles are defined by the involvement of groups seeking the reform or replacement of the recognized state apparatus. In many ways, they are the cognate of the liberation struggles, except that they are political violence aimed at the postcolonial state as opposed to the colonial empire. As such, the same structures and practices are often required of them as of the national liberation movements. Due to the 1963 Organization of African Unity charter, which placed the sovereignty of the recognized government above reproach, the reform movements were often cut off from external aid and thus were at an even greater disadvantage than the liberation fronts had been (although there are exceptions, such as RENAMO and UNITA's aid from South Africa). This made the protracted struggle even more attractive following the international acceptance of the freed African nations and their sovereignty. Still, just as in the liberation struggles, the political goals of the reform movements needed to be compelling enough to enlist popular support, although as can be seen by the examples, the results of both the political programs and the military operations behind them varied considerably. However, to put a simple definition on them, the reform conflicts were internal popular struggles intended to alter the domestic political situation to one preferred by the aggressors, whether they were identified by ethnicity, ideology, or religion.

Both of these forms of conflict, along with the other plethora of conflicts featuring violence of the populace against the state,[6] feature a variety of commonalities. Both, obviously, must take the form of stateless mass movements. This is because the participants of the struggles already exist within a state that they wish to politically control and transform as opposed to dismantle. With the success of their goal, they move from mass movement to state government. Both enter the realms of African wars when the political goal may only be reached with the application of violence, and as the violence spreads, it moves from protest to conflict to war. As the previous world independence struggles had shown, the most efficacious method of pursuing these wars was that of a protracted guerrilla struggle. As such, both of these types of conflicts, having similar origins in mass discontent with the state structures and similar goals of overthrowing these structures, took on similar forms and similar methods and often saw similar outcomes: the independence of African states or the protracted struggle between an African state and its dissidents. However, there was a third major struggle throughout this period that involved internal violence against the state, one that took on its own form and own unique structures, and one that was affected far more by international context and events than either of the previous two. These were the secession struggles of Africa.

The secession struggles must be viewed separately from the other types of internal African conflicts for a variety of reasons. The first must be that their political basis is distinctly different from that of their two internal compatriots. Whereas, as mentioned, liberation and reform conflicts looked to seize the control of the state apparatus and thereby gain sovereignty for their faction, secession conflicts looked to sever it completely and form their own sovereign body separate from the original. Whereas the previous two looked for state domination, secession struggles looked for state division. Of course, since the conflict itself is simply the pursuit of the political goal by other means, the alteration of political goals meant an alteration in structures and methods of conflict. One may look down the list of liberation and reform conflicts and see stateless mass movement after stateless mass movement, each pursuing its own protracted guerrilla struggle against the state itself. These may exist and may pursue their goals through those methods because their success means they take on the newly conquered state's legitimacy and sovereignty in the global community. It is not so simple for secessionist movements. Secessionist states are dependent upon diplomatic recognition of their existence for success, something that does not happen simply with a proclamation of independence. As such, their relationship both with their "host" state and the community of states at large is even more complex than that of liberation or reform struggles. They must pursue their conflicts in such a way as to gain the local control over the populace or territory they wish to rule and at the same time exist as a recognizable state that may be accepted into the greater global community. This is an extremely ambitious and difficult political goal, and the importance of the resulting structures and methods of secession take on increased dimensions.

It is in these structures and methods that we see the second major divergence from the other internal African conflicts. The liberation and reform conflicts within African states could look to previous conflicts around the world that achieved similar goals. For liberation struggles, the Indochina wars and the struggles against the Japanese in Southeast Asia during the Second World War gave an obvious example, one of supposedly undeveloped people besting the industrialized world through the use of guerrilla and protracted warfare and a strong conception of national identity. For reform conflicts, the same examples offered inspiration, as did Mao's victory over the Nationalist Chinese despite the massive amount of American aid given to Chiang Kai-Shek's government. The postwar anti-colonial struggles allowed all colonized people to see the possibilities of resistance and revolution. However, for secession there was little precedent established. The European examples such as Belgium happened in a completely different century and in very different circumstances that bore little resemblance to the postcolonial world. The rest of the world offered no parallel secession examples at the time. As such, the African secession conflicts were pursued in a disjointed and evolving way, changing their form as the circumstances altered and the political goals the protagonists sought proved impossible to attain. It is this changing form that this volume is intended to address, by mapping both the attributes of the secessionist struggles and the contexts that shape them.

Secession Itself

To begin, it is perhaps most appropriate to discuss in depth exactly what secession itself is. To further refine the earlier definition given, secession is a group or territory's political removal from a sovereign and recognized state and establishment as a distinct sovereign body. What is especially important within this definition is the creation of a new and recognized sovereign body, which is the key component of understanding secession within the greater body of separatist initiatives. While secession may be achieved through a variety of means, it is rare for peaceful secessions to occur, as even those such as the separation of Somaliland occur within the context of a greater struggle within the original sovereign body.[7] This is generally unsurprising, as the removal of any members of the populace or body of territory diminishes the state and may be viewed as violence against the state itself. It is in this complete removal that secession separates itself from the concept of separatism, of which it is a subcategory and related concept.

Separatism seeks the separation of a demarcated group, be it ethnic, cultural, religious, or racial, from the pre-existing political body, but not necessarily its own recognized sovereign body completely divorced from the previous state. Instead separatism may simply seek limited or full autonomy under the existing political group without going so far as to seek total separation. This is a far less extreme option in the eyes of the existing state from which the group seeks to separate, and it means that separatism has the far greater potential of success, as the original host state may actually find the new arrangement advantageous compared with its previous system, or at least less harmful than the whole secession of a people or region. Interestingly enough, while all secessions themselves are separatist in nature, all separatisms are not necessarily secessions. They are simply defined by the end relationship between the state and the separating region.

Lastly, in terms of secession and separatism, it is important to discuss the related concept of irredentism, which is a specific form of separatism that seeks the total cleavage of a people or region from a pre-existing political body but does not create a new distinct sovereign body. Instead, the separating group is attached to or absorbed within another pre-existing political body, often one that can claim ethnic, religious, racial, or even political commonalities. Therefore, while irredentism seeks the extreme measure of complete withdrawal from a state, it does not meet the conditions of secession as it does not form its own new sovereign state and instead acquires the legitimacy and sovereignty of its new host state. Irredentism has been especially prevalent in recent years where ethnic nationalism has re-emerged and the idea of greater ethnic homelands and nation-states have become acceptable. It often takes the form of claims of a greater homeland of peoples containing the ethnic community the presumed host state represents.

Of course, all three of these concepts intersect in a variety of ways. As noted, secession is itself separatism with the distinction simply being the establishment of a new political body in the wake of the separation. Irredentism is also separatism taken to the level of complete withdrawal but without the founding of a new sovereign body. Even ideas of irredentism and secession can intersect in a variety of ways, with perhaps the most common example being that of a transnational community which itself has no state. In these instances it often becomes common for the dispersed community to harbour desires for all of their constituent parts not only to completely separate from their current host states but also to found a new sovereign state based upon their common identity. The problematic idea of a greater Kurdistan serves as perhaps the most accessible example of the phenomenon, although it has occurred throughout the world.

While all three concepts are addressed within this volume, the majority of the focus is upon the full secessionist motive. While this is not to say that separatism and irredentism do not play their own part within the struggles discussed, it is the conflicts fought for secession and their attendant dynamics that offer the most fruitful explorations, while it will be seen that separatism and irredentism are often the byproducts of the more extreme secessionist stances. Of course, with these definitions in hand, the question must be asked, why do groups seek secession? What motivations lie behind the complete cleavage of a state and its constituent groups?

The Secessionist Motive

Numerous studies have been written upon the general secessionist motive in the postwar era, with political scientists debating the underlying motivations of secessionist and separatist motives. These studies often took the recent separatist or secessionist groups and examined their commonalities within the context of the strength of their separatist impulses. The early work was done by Donald Horowitz, who examined separatism within the intersection of ethnic identity, group development, and regional development. He sought a connection between separatist impulses and the relation between advanced and backward groups and regions. In terms of advanced groups, he defined an advanced group as appearing to have "benefited from opportunities in education and nonagricultural employment. Typically it is represented above the mean in number of secondary-school and university graduates; in bureaucratic, commercial, and professional employment; and in per capita income."[8] Those he defined as backward appeared to lack these opportunities or at least the benefits of them on the whole. His examples of these groups ranged from the "advanced" Tamils in Sri Lanka and Igbo in Nigeria to the "backward" Karens in Burma and Kurds in Iraq. These groups were then cross-referenced with the comparable regional economic development, with per capita income being used as the main variable. This then allowed each group to be viewed within the matrix of one of four categories: an advanced group in an advanced region, an advanced group in a backward region, a backward group in an advanced region, and a backward group in a backward region. Horowitz then compared the frequency of secessions within each category to determine the effects of ethnic anxiety and economic opportunity on secession frequency and timing, determining finally that "backward" ethnic groups are the more frequent separatists while "backward" regions hasten the process of secession and separatism.

He contends that the reasons for this are rather self-evident. His "backward" groups are almost without fail separated from any positions of power or opportunities for advancement within the state. With the state structures as they exist offering little advantage to the less developed group, they see little advantage to maintaining their presence within the state itself. Meanwhile "advanced" groups are continually offered advantages and advancement within the state structures, giving them a strong inducement to remain within the state itself, although they may not always do so. When these groups do attempt to secede, it is often because of the persecution of their status by the less advantaged majority, such as Baluba in the Congo. In terms of regional advancement, Horowitz maintained that groups within less developed economic regions were offered few advantages in staying within a more advanced state and therefore would seek their separation more quickly. Inversely, those in economically advanced regions were given greater aid and inducements to stay within the state structures that offered them economic advantages and therefore would take longer to develop any sort of separatist motivations. By drawing these demarcations, Horowitz was able to trace the frequency and speed of development of secessionist motivations within a group to the advancement opportunities of the constituent groups and economic development of the regions they inhabited. However, these were purely material reasons buttressed by ethnic identity and would serve only as a stepping stone for more complex views on the secessionist motive that would emerge with the dissolution of the Soviet Union.

One of the few complete syntheses of the increasingly complex models of secession emerged solely as a study of Soviet sovereignties following the end of the Cold War. The author, Henry Hale, argued that the dissolving Soviet Union served as a perfect petri dish for observing the increasing calls for secession, separatism, and sovereignty within an unstable region. His study, "The Parade of Sovereignties: Testing Theories of Secession in the Soviet Setting," identified seven separate material and cultural factors purported to be involved in the creation and maintenance of secessionist motivation and searched for their actual effects in the new states emerging in the Eastern Bloc. These seven factors included regional wealth, regional autonomy, ethnic distinctiveness, group skill sets, elite upward mobility, regional historic precedents, and regional demonstrations of secession and separatism.[9] While regional wealth and group skill sets had already been covered by Horowitz's exploration into the secessionist motive, the rest were drawn from the theories of such prominent political scientists as Michael Hechter, Paul Brass, and Ted Robert Gurr. By looking at the relative characteristics of the splitting republics within these categories, Hale felt he could determine which factors were the most influential and in what way, that is, whether relative wealth of a region mattered, and if so, whether it was the richer or poorer regions that sought autonomy.

The results of his survey proved to be shocking: those factors previously thought to be influential often turned out to be of far less importance, or even to produce the opposite effect. Those factors that had the most impact upon the separatist motive were regional wealth, previous levels of autonomy, ethnic group distinctiveness, and regional demonstrations of secession. Even these proved to be slightly different than the earlier Horowitz hypotheses, as Hale discovered that as regional wealth increased, so did the chance of separatist activity, as opposed to Horowitz's contention that poorer regions tend to hasten the development of secessionist ideologies. Meanwhile, factors such as group education, elite mobility, history of independence, and past victimization proved to be statistically insignificant in the creation of separatist sentiment. These conclusions, although backed by statistical evidence, can be disputed, but serve as an interesting jumping-off point for the discussion of separatism and secession in the greater world and Africa in particular.

Accepting Hale's data as correct, ethnically distinct areas with high wealth concentrations, relative autonomy, and surrounding regions containing their own separatist sentiments should produce a relatively robust number of secessionist movements and subsequent conflicts within a greater region. Africa over the past forty years would therefore seem to be a region ripe for such movements. Ethnicity in Africa has always been considered especially strong due to the artificial colonial state constructed to take advantage of both ethnic identities and artificial separations of ethnic groups, such as the Somalis or Yoruba. Even now the ethnic fissures in African states are often credited with the relative lack of development within African states. As to high wealth concentrations, the extremely uneven economic exploitation of Africa's natural resources has created extremely uneven economic zones, with extremely rich areas such as the province of Katanga, the diamond-producing regions of Angola and Sierra Leone, and the oil-rich regions of Cabinda and the Niger Delta existing side by side with some of the least developed regions on earth. Relative autonomy has been in constant flux as the African state has gone from a robust centralized creation modelled on the colonial blueprint and supported by the global economy to an often divided and weakened state. Lastly, with the principle of self-determination having been the keystone to the liberation of Africa from colonialism, and autonomy from external control having been seen as the central tenet of all African nations, one can definitely see the drive for self-rule and sovereignty on the continent. As such, one would expect secessionist conflicts to make up a significant portion of the wars that have wracked the continent over the past four decades. However, this conclusion could not be further from the truth.

The Absence of the Secessionist Motive in Africa

Despite the seeming abundance of factors promoting the spread of separatist and secessionist conflicts in Africa, that continent maintains the smallest percentage of secessionist conflicts of any developing region of the world. As the well-regarded research of Pierre Englebert and Rebecca Hummel notes:

> Most other regions of the world display a greater propensity for separatist activity: since 1960, 44 percent of domestic

conflict years in the Middle East and North Africa, 47 percent of those in Asia, and 84 percent of those in Europe have had separatist content, as against 27 percent in sub-Saharan Africa.[10]

So why, despite the majority of African states playing host to an internal conflict in the forty years since independence, has there only been a handful of secessionist conflicts waged against the generally heterogeneous, young, weak, and youthful countries of Africa? The answer lies within the propensity for the disgruntled political entities to accept central governmental reform or at least modest separatist goals as opposed to outright secession, looking for an ethnic or regional autonomy within a weak state structure. This preference results from a combination of two factors, the lack of international legitimacy and the structure of the weak state within Africa.

In terms of the lack of international legitimacy, the root of the idea rests with the outcomes of the earliest attempts of secessionist struggles: those of Katanga and Biafra. As the upcoming case studies of these conflicts amply illustrate, the lack of international support or recognition for the separatist regimes as mandated by the United Nations' actions in the Congo set a precedent in favour of the African state structures in the international community. This precedent set during these first waves of was that the pre-existing state was the sole legitimate power and that any separatist movement was an internal disruption. This became codified within the Organization of African Unity (OAU) Charter and continued to bedevil African internal conflicts of all stripes for the remainder of the Cold War, where even such liberating insurgencies as Yoweri Museveni's were denied any and all outside aid because of the precepts adopted by the African nations. Without access to outside aid, recognition, or even diplomatic channels, secession became an impossibility on the African continent, and attempts to achieve it slowly disappeared.

The second factor has to do with the advantages offered within what is now known as the "Weak State" in Africa.[11] Whereas state structures remained relatively robust throughout the Cold War because of outside aid and the lack of credible threats to their sovereignty, following the collapse of the Soviet Union the states faced a lack of foreign support and an increasingly turbulent world outlook. This combination produced the paradoxical weak state, which continues to be reproduced throughout Africa due to the advantages it affords elites. With the state being the sole provider of international legitimacy and therefore international support, it becomes theoretically impossible for the state to disappear completely, and therefore it is able to be continually diminished by the ruling elite and yet persist. This possession of legitimacy also may be leveraged for personal and foreign capital aid with little oversight due to the weak regulatory structures inherent in its weak structures, while at the same time it shields personal ambitions under the thin umbrella of national sovereignty. Lastly, due to the structure of African sovereignty, it is the state and only the state that has legitimate access to markets for export, a vital attribute in the majority of African states that depend on extracted commodities for their economies. Simply put, the weak but sovereign state structures serve as a conduit to domestic and foreign aid, capital, and development that is exclusively available to those with access and is not in any real way regulated or overseen. Therefore, the weak state structure continues to be an ideal structure for elites' personal enrichment and continued control.

This combination of weak state structures, easy exploitation, limited international sovereignty and legitimacy, and tacit rejection of formal secession within Africa has produced the tendency for limited separatist or reform conflicts among the currently dispossessed or discontented political groups of Africa. Whereas ethnic Georgians could splinter themselves off from Russia and gain the international recognition and connections needed to survive, individual ethnic groups in Africa such as the Kongo or Oromo would be separating themselves from their only source of international markets and influence while not gaining even the chance of a separate sovereign nation. African dissident groups have thus found it far more practicable to struggle for autonomy under the sovereignty of a continuing weak state or even control of it, thus tapping themselves into the weak state's legitimacy at a local level while maintaining regional decision-making capabilities. This compromise tends to favour both sides of the equation well: the central state may co-opt a militant separatist movement by bringing them into the redistributive system of the state, thus relieving the pressure to project their limited power. Meanwhile, the separatist movement gains limited autonomy and self-determination while still remaining a part of a sovereign nation with all the advantages that that entails. Within the constraints of the limited African state and conceptions of legitimacy, separatism is simply the more effective and attainable solution for ethnically distinct populations.

Of course, the question then becomes how have the secessionist conflicts of Africa come to exist in this form, and this is the greater question of the present volume. The structure of legitimacy of African states, their inability to support secessionist goals, their resistance to ethnic nationalism and other varieties of sub-nationalism, and the current resurgence of ethnic autonomy movements may all be explained through the context of the greater arc of secessionist movements and the subsequent lessons learned in their wake. This volume, then, follows the general thematic construction of the modern African secessionist conflict and how it came to take its current form, to chart out the unique structures of African insurgencies, how they came to be that way, and where these secessionist and separatist movements may proceed to.

Contents

To continue this study of the development of secessionist conflicts in Africa, the general evolution of their prosecution, and the specific cases that altered the pursuit of secessionist or separatist goals, this work splits the conflicts into three thematic areas and offers two specific case studies of each that illustrate the specific turning points in the history of African secession. Each of these thematic eras will be presented in a section with an introduction laying out the premises of that theme with the case studies to follow. Part I, "The Civil Secessions," offers an incisive view into the early attempts at secession in Africa. These were secessions that were imposed top-down upon pre-existing political entities and which generally featured a conventional struggle for the seceding territory. In particular, the introduction to this section focuses on four major points of commonality in the manifestations of Civil Secession. The first is the structure of the seceding groups, which took the form of pre-existing state governments, often already constructed as the administration or elected government of the seceding region and therefore already existing as a state framework. The second is the leadership driving these secessionist movements, which comprised almost exclusively members of the postcolonial bourgeoisie that filled the ranks of the increasingly Africanized civil and military services following the departure of the colonial regimes—the "New Men of Africa." In particular, the introduction to this part explores their competing nationalist goals with those of the host states' New Men. The third major point of convergence is the legal justifications for their separation, something that proved to be an extremely important idea within the struggle for international recognition. Specifically, the legal justification was seen as the key to the legitimacy of the separatist state and therefore to its existence under international law. The final point explored within the general overview of Civil Secessions is the general strategy of their pursuit of independence. To put it bluntly, the forceful separation of an administrative region from a pre-existing nation could only be effected by a skillful combination of military force and diplomatic manoeuvring to gain the acceptance of both the host nation and international community. This section addresses the combination of conventional warfare and global lobbying that was tried in this type of secession. In addition, there is a brief overview of the international reactions to and ramifications of the Civil Secessionist wars.

Chapter 1, "The Secession of Katanga, 1960–1963," deals with the first major attempt as secession in postcolonial Africa, that of Katanga from the Congo. It will explore not only the specifics of the state structure of Katanga, the hybrid leadership of Tshombe and his Belgian advisors, the political and military tactics adopted by the CONAKAT and their mercenary officers, and the colonial legal justification for Katanga's separation, but also the legal precedents the Katangese Secession set in terms of secession in Africa. In particular, Katanga proved to be a defining moment in international law in terms of African sovereignty, with the United Nations creating a series of binding resolutions that defined how the international community would respond to the chaos of secession in independent Africa and a secessionist movement's arguments in favour of self-determination following decolonization. This chapter also covers how the Congo Crisis and Katangan Secession in particular then shaped the founding precepts of the Organization of African Unity, which established "Non-interference in the internal affairs of States" and "Respect for the sovereignty and territorial integrity of each State and for its inalienable right to independent existence"[12] as the central tenets of the organization. These precedents set in international law then served to radically alter the trajectory of secessionist struggles in Africa.

Chapter 2, "The Secession of Biafra, 1967–1970," follows much the same formula as the previous case study. The story of the secession is told in brief, followed by a delineation of its constituent parts. The administrative and general ethnic structure of the state, the military and administrative leadership of Ojukwu and his Igbo compatriots, the military and propaganda underpinnings of the Biafran state, and their reasoning for secession from an already divided Nigeria are discussed to maintain the commonalities established already within the overview. Following this, the more anomalous features of the secession are explored, specifically the general international denial of Biafra's legitimacy, which effectively killed the ideal of Civil Secession in Africa. From here the chapter also discusses the ramifications of this denial, including the paucity of arms, equipment, and personnel available to the Biafran state, the limitations this set on their diplomatic initiatives, the establishment of a siege mentality within the Igbo population, and the final consensus against secession on the continent of Africa.

Part II, titled "The Long Wars," examines the parallel developments of several long-term struggles at the same time as the more conventional Civil Secessions. These conflicts, explored conceptually in the introduction to this part, are not as easily defined as the Katangan and Biafran secession attempts but proved far more influential in terms of the future pursuit of separatist goals than their civil counterparts. Instead of building their struggles around pre-existing state structures, the protagonists in these wars fought on the conception of national identity and self-determination along mass movement lines. Prime examples of these are the Eritrean People's Liberation Front, the Sudanese People's Liberation Movement, and less successful but still extant groups such as the *Mouvement des forces démocratiques de Casamance* in the Casamance region of Senegal and the *Frente para a Libertação do Enclave de Cabinda* in the Cabinda exclave of Angola. The introduction to this part examines the theoretical formation of this identity among the disparate populations of sub-Saharan Africans and the general alterations this would create in the nature of the conflicts they pursued. Of specific note is the decisive switch from a conventional campaigning war to a Maoist idea of a protracted war, which depended on the flexible boundaries of population as opposed to the rigid borders of a state. Of course, just as was seen in the protracted conflicts in China and elsewhere, the formation of national identity as a necessary product of waging the war meant that the identity itself would evolve as the mass movement grew and evolved to effectively pursue its goals. As such, the introduction to Part II also explores how the Long Wars' length and demographic dispersal allowed for a diverse amount of political ideologies and goals to become expressed within the conflict, which in turn altered both the structures and methodologies of the separatist forces. In total, it introduces the reader to the framework of the political development of the Long War mass movements, the structure and methodologies these movements engendered, and finally the often complex manoeuvrings that were required to support these bottom-up insurgencies, as opposed to the direct paths of the Civil Secessions.

Chapter 3, "The Anomaly of Eritrean Secession, 1962–1993," explores what is currently the first successful secession in postcolonial Africa. The case study narrates the ebbs and flows of the thirty-one-year Eritrean struggle for independence, which serves as an exceptionally pertinent example of the protracted struggle in Africa. Beyond this, the chapter explores the various popular movements within Eritrea and their specific enunciations of Eritrean nationalism, their strategy and tactics during the war, their ideological grounding, and their eventual fates within the greater struggle. Of specific interest within the case study is the eventually dominant Eritrean People's Liberation Front, which eventually effected the detachment of Eritrea from Ethiopia. Following the examination of the EPLF and its struggle, the chapter offers the four reasons for its success in securing independence. The first is their successful implementation of Maoist theories of protracted warfare on both a strategic and tactical level, allowing for a husbanding of strength until a switch to a war of manoeuvre was advantageous. The second was the intense social revolution that the EPLF undertook within their occupied zones, altering the societal structures of their population to bring them into a modern and participatory public society and thereby creating both a national identity and logistical base. The third was the unique historical context of the Eritrean struggle, where the EPLF was able to use the anomalous nature of its connection to Ethiopia to argue a new precedent of self-determination within international law. The last was their pragmatic relations with the other groups in conflict with the Ethiopian state, particularly the Tigrayan People's Liberation Front. These relations proved decisive when the TPLF seized power in Ethiopia and allowed for the unique situation of a legitimate sovereign government to bestow legitimacy and sovereignty upon a secessionist state.

Chapter 4, "The Secession of South Sudan, 1955–2011," is so named because the case study of the Sudan offers the best vantage point on the complexities engendered by the Long Wars template of secession and separatism. The chapter follows the multiple revolts in the Southern Sudan against the authority of the North, making particular note of the leadership, membership, and structure of each rebellion and the consequent alteration of their political goals and military methods of pursuing them. This approach allows for the exploration of the complex and evolving values of secession, separatism, reform, and even inter-ethnic conflict that both emerge and submerge as the Southern Sudanese movements change from the Anya-nya days to those of Anya-nya II and the SPLA. In particular, the benefits and limitations of the amalgamation of ethnic ambitions inherent in the SPLM are explored, along with the identity fostered, its fracture along Dinka/Nuer lines, and the components of its final achievement of secession from the North.

Part III, "The New Wave of Secessions," moves the narrative forward in time to study the massive geopolitical changes wrought by the end of the Cold War. The introduction to the thematic section explores two simultaneous developments in Africa beginning in the 1990s in the greater context of global politics. The first was the weakening of African states following the fall of the Soviet Union. So many states of Africa had been bolstered as proxies of either Soviet or capitalist ambitions on the continent that they existed in their current robust form only so long as outside aid was offered to support them. With the ending of the Cold War these states, from Mobutu's Zaire to Mengistu's Ethiopia, began to weaken and lose their ability to hold their own populaces in check. The second was the re-emergence of the nation-state as both a desirable and acceptable goal. Since the terrors of nationalism gone awry in the world wars, the idea of states based upon ethnic identity had fallen out of favour in international quarters and the idea of ethnic self-determination had been laid by the wayside. However, in the 1990s the United States' enthusiastic acceptance of the breakup of the former Soviet Union into ethnically self-determined states brought the idea back into mainstream acceptability and the forces of ethnic nationalism re-emerged on the world stage. While these ideas would be tarnished by the bloody clashes within and between the successor states to Yugoslavia, the genie of ethno-nationalism had been let out of the bottle. The combination of weakened states and resurgent ethnic nationalism set off a wave of secessionist and separatist movements in Africa, of which the general structure, again including general ideology, mannerisms, methodology, and composition, will be examined in the introduction to this part. This introduction also explores the interaction of this new wave of African secessions, the weak states, and the existing precedents of state sovereignty to trace the increasing predilection for separatism and de facto autonomy instead of de jure secession on the continent in light of the continuing paramountcy of the existing state structures in terms of international relations. While the ensuing chapters will explore the role of autonomy in keeping together the de jure state in Mali and Somalia, this phenomenon has also been seen within the increasingly weak Zaire/Democratic Republic of the Congo and even in a novel form in Northern Nigeria.

Chapter 5, "De Facto Secession and the New Borders of Africa: Somaliland, 1991–Present," integrates the unique experience of the breakaway republic of Somaliland into the greater narrative of the new wave of secessions. Since 1991, Somaliland has been separated from the failed state of Somalia and in that time has established itself as a stable and democratic country with a constitution that manages to combine both traditional and progressive elements. However, despite the existence of a functioning state apparatus for nearly two decades, Somaliland has yet to be recognized by any other nation. The inclusion of this case study is necessary insofar as it allows the discussion of the continued pitfalls for the concept of secession in the regional, continental, and global contexts. Therefore, beyond the examination of the structures of the separatist government and its popular roots, this chapter focuses primarily on both Somaliland's example of a successful and thriving state within a turbulent region and the international difficulties of statehood that the case continues to illustrate.

Chapter 6, "Transnational Communities and Secession: The Azawad Secessionists, 1990–1996 and Beyond," is the last case study of the book and illustrates the culmination of the limitations set on secession in the 1960s and their interaction with the current ideas of ethnic self-determination and secession in Africa. The case study expands on the general structure, ideology, and methods used by the transnational Tuareg communities to attempt to establish an ethnically Tuareg state out of the Azawad region of Niger and Mali. In addition, the case study of the Azawad conflicts explores not only the increasingly important conception an ethnic nation-state but also the complex mixture of goals and ideologies involved in the attempt to make such a state a reality. In addition, the Azawad movement illustrates the transnational character of ethnic separatism and the increasingly transnational character of secession, separatism, and irredentism. Finally, by looking at the final settlement of the Azawad conflict and its subsequent resurrection, the case study examines the interaction between ethnic separatist ambitions with the weakening states of Africa and the limits of ethnic nationality in the face of regional power structures.

The Conclusion then brings the reader full circle and reiterates the historical evolution of African secession and the actions and contexts that have shaped it throughout the past five decades. Of especial importance are the trends moving from the secession of a state to the secession of a nation and the increasing recourse to separatism as opposed to secession. The Conclusion also discusses how the emergent US-led Global War on Terror has reimposed many of the structures that had propped up weaker African states during the Cold War, eroding the gains that secessionist and separatist groups had seen during the initial post–Cold War years. Finally, it ties together the various political, economic, social, and cultural aspects of the past secessionist conflicts and weaves them into the greater history of postcolonial Africa and its future.

PART I

The Civil Secessions

The idea of the Civil Secessions was one that had relevance within a very specific time and place in Africa and involved an ideological framework that no longer really exists. As such they are a concept that is no longer extant. This is not to say that they are no longer important to study— the absolute opposite in fact is true. The arc of the Civil Secessions, including their birth, their existence, and their extinction, does just as much to inform us about the historical dynamics of secession in Africa as any of the still-existent long-term conflicts or even the small ethnic separatist insurgencies still occurring on the continent. In fact, they may prove more informative by showing us, at a scale rarely matched since, the factors that have shaped the idea of secession and made it such a contentious and rare issue on the continent of Africa. As such, this overview will outline the general historical arc and characteristics of the Civil Secessions, allowing for a theoretical look at the context in which they occurred before giving way to the case studies of Katanga and Biafra that allow for specific exploration to be done.

History and Self-Determination

The central point in understanding the historical context of the Civil Secessions is the idea of self-determination and its evolution in the postwar world. Prior to the Second World War, the idea of self-determination had found limited support within the Great Powers that defined the international community. The rise of liberals such as US President Woodrow Wilson had helped define self-determination as an international goal, with his Fourteen Points being largely agreed to in principle by other global powers during the First World War. However, following the signing of the Treaty of Versailles and the turn to isolationism in the United States, the Fourteen Points, including their conception of self-determination, largely fell by the wayside. The idea re-emerged during the Second World War with the circulation of the Atlantic Charter, the formal statement of the Allies' war goals. Among the shared listed goals of the United States and the United Kingdom was the statement that there would be no territorial changes made against the wishes of the people, a statement in support of self-determination. However, Prime Minister Winston Churchill was not pleased with such an inclusion, leading to significant questions as to whether all of these postwar goals would be pursued with equal vigour.

Following the end of the Second World War, the remaining powers were left uncertain where to proceed in terms of economic and diplomatic relations. While the majority of the developed world was rapidly framing itself into camps around the two rival superpowers of the United States and Soviet Union, it became obvious that the old interwar practices of closed borders and isolationism had been disastrous. It had not lessened the desperation of the Great Depression and had not prevented any power from becoming embroiled in the general conflict. As such, the idea of "interdependence" became the watchword in postwar diplomatic relations, and structures began to be put in place to facilitate the desirable international connections. While there were scattered organizations either still in existence following the collapse of the League of Nations, such as the International Labor Organization (ILO), or newer groups intended to facilitate the increasing interdependence of the states such as the International Monetary Fund (IMF), there still was no unified political instrument to bring these states together. It was in this context that the major international powers convened at San Francisco in 1945 and on 24 October formally signed into existence the United Nations, creating a political framework for the interactions of 50 of the 51 nations present at its drafting.[1]

The Charter of the United Nations was to prove a decisive document in the processes of both decolonization and secession in Africa. The former was specifically due to chapters I, XI, and XII. Chapter I, article 1 specifically spelled out the idea of Self-Determination, noting under the purposes of the United Nations the intentions "to develop friendly relations among nations based on respect for the principle of equal rights and self-determination of peoples, and to take other appropriate measures to strengthen universal peace."[2] Thus, the signatories of the new organization, including the major colonial powers such as Britain and France, were suddenly obliged to respect the ideology of self-determination being demanded by their colonized peoples. However, a small loophole was evident within the differentiations of chapters XI and XII. Chapter XII explicitly called for the UN to "promote the political, economic, social, and educational advancement of the inhabitants of the trust territories, and their progressive development towards self-government or independence,"[3] which would seem to call for decolonization in terms of the independence of the states involved. However, chapter XII only dealt with the trustee territories, which were those territories that were either Mandate Territories (which were generally those ex-colonies of Central Powers lost to the Allies in the First World War), those detached from the defeated Axis powers (as such mostly just Japanese-held islands), and those explicitly given to UN trusteeship by their colonial controllers.[4] As to the remainder of the colonized world, these fell under chapter XI, which only stated the political goals as "to develop self-government, to take due account of the political aspirations of the peoples, and to assist them in the progressive development of their free political institutions, according to the particular circumstances of each territory and its peoples and their varying stages of advancement."[5] No mention of independence was given, simply the idea of self-governance. As such, there was the possibility of a much lengthier period of control by the former colonial powers.

However, the writing was increasingly on the wall as the colonies of Africa emerged from the Second World War with robust economies and an increasing awareness of their political situation. The populations of most colonies had been rising over the previous decades and had also been increasingly urbanizing. These trends helped foster increasingly educated and organized mass movements that would agitate for better living conditions, better labour conditions, and increasing access to political power. Following the war there were demonstrations and increasing attempts to claim the self-determination promised within the United Nations charter. The first regions of decolonization were the ex-Italian possessions in Libya and the Horn,[6] with Tunisia and Morocco following shortly after. It was also in this early period that the Sudan was finally relinquished by Britain under pressure from the increasingly radical Egyptian government.[7] However, the first real stone to fall in sub-Saharan Africa was Ghana, which, under the leadership of Kwame Nkrumah, asserted its self-determination over several years and finally claimed its independence on 6 March 1957.[8] This was to prove a milestone in the minds of Africans, a moment when the most prominent spokesperson of Pan-Africanism emerged at the head of Africa's first formally decolonized nation. Finally, a sub-Saharan country that was part of article XI and not article XII, one that had been a colony and not a mandatory territory, had been released after its own homegrown agitation and lobbying. After this the French Empire in Africa began to follow suit, with the autonomy and independence of its long-time colony in Guinea in 1958.[9] Following these initial decolonizations, the floodgates truly opened in 1960, which has been dubbed the "Year of Africa" due to the independence granted to seventeen separate African states, including such notables as France's Senegal, Britain's Nigeria, and Belgium's long-tormented Congo. In the decade following this massive step, the entire British African empire and the vast majority of the French colonies would gain their independence. By 1970 the only major formal colonial presence in Africa was the Portuguese, who under the *Estado Novo* fascist government founded by Antonio Salazar in the 1930s claimed that their holdings were not colonies at all but overseas provinces of Portugal proper.[10] In this single decade the concept of self-determination was grasped as an essential right and advanced by the colonized African states until they were granted the control of their own political destinies.

Nature and Character of Civil Secessions

It is no coincidence that it was this same decade from 1960 to 1970 that spawned the Civil Secessions. These secessions attempted to follow the example of the decolonized states of Africa, claiming their right of self-determination to emerge as fully functioning states with international rights and recognitions. At the time this claim of statehood was not necessarily an impossible idea: the UN charter specifically stated that it recognized and supported the self-determination of peoples, with little specific definition of the term. Beyond this, there was at the time no specific mention that the already determined (and possibly illegitimate) political boundaries that had been in place since the Berlin Conference of 1885 were necessarily those of postcolonial Africa.[11] As such, the general idea of the Civil Secessions was that the secessionist governed territories could and would fulfill the role of the state and in doing so gain the recognition required to join the international community while separating themselves from what they considered a disadvantageous (or even genocidal) connection with their previous colonial collective.

In each case it is clear that the Civil Secessionist conflict was about the secessionists attempting to maintain the theoretical and practical functions of their separated "proto-state" in the face of the aggressive actions of their previous host states to reintegrate them. In maintaining these functions, they hoped to both keep domestic legitimacy with their populations and gain the international recognition that would give them the material and diplomatic support they needed to complete their political and territorial separation from their host states. These theoretical and practical functions the secessionists were attempting to fulfill can be brought forth from a variety of texts delineating the concept of a state. An earlier definition works off the idea that "the State as a person of international law should possess the following qualifications: (a) a permanent population; (b) a defined territory; (c) government; and (d) capacity to enter relations with other states."[12] It was enough, then, that the states had seceded and had entered into attempted diplomatic relations; however, one can argue that the denial of formal recognition of the Civil Secessionist states meant they never fulfilled the full requirements of statehood, while the military struggle meant that one by one the other attributes were swept away.[13]

Perhaps a better delineation of the attributes giving legitimacy and existence to a state may be found in the more theoretical realm of academics such as Charles Tilly, Max Weber, Perry Anderson, Ali Mazrui, and Crawford Young. By linking their theories of the functions of a state together, we may get a list of attributes that a state fulfills. When taken together, these authorities' concepts can be listed as follows:

1. A State defends its nationals or citizens from external enemies through the use of an effective army.
2. A State regulates crime and disorder through the use of a police force.
3. A State develops an effective civilian bureaucracy to administer the functions of the state.
4. A State raises revenue and creates an economic infrastructure to pay its army, its police force, and its civilian bureaucracy.
5. A State resolves disputes through a system of law and a judiciary that enforces the law.
6. A State creates laws through a legislative process.
7. A State provides public services such as safety, education, health care, transportation and roads, and postal service.
8. A State acquires and sustains political legitimacy, which allows the state to govern with lower attendant social costs.[14]

Given this list of attributes, one can easily see the structure of the Civil Secessions, leaving one to only conclude that the Civil Secessions indeed were attempts to declare a state and then garner recognition.

Of course, in attempting to create a politically separate but yet viable African state, the Civil Secessions created a series of parallel practices that let them fulfill these requirements of legitimacy both domestically and internationally. These practices were the separation of a pre-existing political unit that was both multi-ethnic and with assumed legal legitimacy for self-rule, that is, a historically justified civil nation; a leadership created out of the "New Men" of Africa, the Western-educated and wealthy bourgeoisie of the state; a standing professional army and/or gendarmerie; and conventional military tactics based around the taking and defending of territory. Each of these would in its own way parallel the existing African states and at the same time serve as an attempt to establish or maintain the new secessionist state.

In terms of standard African statehood, those states emerging from decolonization were granted legitimacy and recognition based on the same list of attributes enunciated above. Their borders were fixed by the earlier 1885 Berlin Conference, to which the majority of the newly independent states formally agreed in the mid-1960s. Within these borders was a multi-ethnic population, which was the only acceptable option in the postwar anti-nationalist ideology of the colonial powers. Their legislative processes, systems of taxation, and public services were all also inherited from their colonial structures and then built upon by their African administrations. Britain left parliamentary democracies and efficient civil services in states as diverse as Nigeria, Botswana, and Kenya. France left a legacy of republicanism and Gallic public service in their own former colonies as well as general regional structures of cooperation. While these were then altered or simply evolved under African leadership, at the time of decolonization, the states were defined by their inherited state functions. In addition, their formal separation was built upon the legal idea of the voluntary renunciation of colonial agreements and the idea that they now assumed their own rightfully self-determined autonomous statehood.

The Civil Secessionist States built along these same lines. While the decolonized African states inherited the colonial systems of governance, taxation, and public services, the Secessionist State inherited these attributes from its host state, usually in regional form. Katanga and Biafra had both had their own regional administrations reaching back into colonial days and thus had a legacy of these structures that allowed them to define their statehood.[15] Beyond this they too defined themselves as a multi-ethnic Civil State, not a nation-state, on the assumption that a nation-state would not be granted recognition in the postcolonial Cold War environment they found themselves in.[16] Lastly, to parallel the legitimacy of the accepted colonial boundaries, the new secessionist states needed their own accepted international boundaries. In their case they often argued historical precedent, such as in the case of Katanga's separate administration from the rest of the Congo or the Sudan's separate administration of the North and South.[17] In each case the Civil Secessionist state attempted to assume the proper structure of African statehood and thereby also assume the acceptance given to the postcolonial African state.

Of course, these systems of taxation, legislation, and public works were not mechanical creations within the decolonized African state; they were run by the newly emergence professional African bourgeoisie, the "New Men" of Africa with Western educations. Kwame Nkrumah, whose efforts were pivotal in both the decolonization of Africa and the creation of a Pan-African identity, serves as a central example of these figures stepping into the leadership of these new states. At age seventeen he was already serving as a student teacher and by age twenty he had earned his teaching certificate at Achimota College.[18] From here he pursued his studies in the United States, earning a bachelor of arts degree in economics and sociology from Lincoln College in 1939 at age thirty, a master's of science degree in education from the University of Pennsylvania in 1942, and one in philosophy at the same university in 1943.[19] While he did not earn any more advanced degrees, he completed the majority of his work for a doctorate of philosophy in Pennsylvania, read law at Gray's Inn in London, and studied economics at the London School of Economics. He emerged as a well-rounded intellectual who then bent his intellect toward the nationalist movement in Ghana, eventually emerging as the leader of the Convention People's Party (CPP),[20] which would win the general elections in 1951 under colonial auspices and eventually emerge as the dominant party in independent Ghana.[21]

His story is echoed in the national leadership of other African states during the decolonization period. Jomo Kenyatta graduated from Thogoto Mission School in Kenya and eventually studied at the University of London's School of Oriental and African Studies, completing graduate work in anthropology under the noted Professor B. Malinowski.[22] After earning his master's he stayed on as a teacher of the Kikuyu language and had his manuscript published as *Facing Mount Kenya*. It was while he was involved with his studies that he became increasingly tangled in Kenyan nationalist politics,[23] eventually being jailed for his suspected connection with Mau Mau activities in 1952.[24] When he was finally released from his detention in 1961 he was a national hero and emerged as the head of the Kenyan African National Union,[25] which attained power in the 1963 general elections and went on to lead the Kenya during its emergence as an independent nation. Even Julius Nyerere, before emerging as the first president of Tanganyika (and then Tanzania), earned a master's degree at Edinburgh College in 1952 before returning to spearhead the nationalist movement in his state.[26] Throughout sub-Saharan Africa it was these Western-educated elites who emerged as the leaders of the nationalist movements and the administrators that ran the state following its independence.

Again paralleling the decolonized African states, the Civil Secessionist states' systems of taxation, legislation, and public services were run by these "New Men," who emerged first in the regional politics of their territory within the newly independent state. It was generally, then, these figures who took advantage of their regional authority to initially agitate for the secession of their region and its populace.[27] With their elevated positions they were often in the best possible social situation to take advantage of these cleavages within society. When the secession was declared it was then these figures who were in positions of running the independent state and determining its structures. Of course, much as it was the Western-educated elites who agitated for and found legal and moral justifications for the decolonization of their states, it was then these regional "New Men" who discovered and advanced their own legal justification for the separation of their state. With the separation underway, this secessionist bourgeoisie took their traditional places in the positions of leadership and administration in their separatist proto-states and served as the most visible figures of the secessionist conflicts.[28]

In terms of a standing professional army, one was obviously necessary for the new African nations, and it often fulfilled the first and second functions of the state as given, as well as covering the Weberian base of a state monopoly on violence. These structures were, much like the other pieces of state apparatus, often inherited from the previous colonial regime.[29] The Ghanaian Army, for example, was initially the Gold Coast Regiment of the Royal West African Frontier Force, although this in turn was descended from the earlier Gold Coast Constabulary. Formally incorporated under the Colonial Office in 1901, the Gold Coast Regiment served in the Yaa Asantewaa War, the First World War, and the Second World War with distinction before becoming the national armed forces of Ghana following independence.[30] During the run-up to independence, its officer corps was increasingly "Africanized" to prepare the army for its new role, and access to formal military educational institutions such as Sandhurst in Great Britain or St. Cyr in France for the officers allowed for a new route for a rising military bourgeoisie. Analogous examples exist on the other side of the continent, where the militaries of Kenya, Uganda, and Tanganyika were all members of the King's African Rifles before independence and had given sterling service in the colonial as well as international conflicts.[31] In both the East and West African forces, the soldiers were long-service professional soldiers who served their purpose well in terms of forming a stalwart, if later on politically volatile, military structure for the newly independent nations.

Again the Secessionist States copied these structures, forming their own professional standing militaries. While often these were initially created around a core of previously national forces that rallied to the secessionist cause, there were often insufficient numbers of these troops to truly maintain the security of their proto-state in the face of the aggressive reaction of their host state—and these initial forces were thus unable to fulfill the first function of the state. To supplement these forces the secessionist states resorted to a variety of initiatives. It was in the initial secessionist conflicts in Africa that mercenaries achieved a high profile.[32] With a strong enough economic base, a secessionist state could hire itself a good number of foreign veterans of the various brushfire wars occurring across the globe to bolster its military capability. Another option would be the limited or wholesale recruitment of the secessionist state's population.[33] While this was of course dependent on the popularity of the secessionist leadership and the perceived legitimacy of the state, in the right circumstances it could provide a large number of motivated troops. The secessionist state would then mould this mixture into a distinct, professional, standing military to enforce the monopoly of violence for that state within its borders, fulfilling the function of a truly national military.

Lastly, this national military for the newly independent nations of Africa was intended to protect the territorial sovereignty of its home state. It was a military trained to be not only a visible symbol of the monopoly of violence that was embodied in the state but also one that could press the territorial claims of the state if needed. As such, these armies were trained primarily in conventional military tactics that called for the most resource-efficient methods of taking and holding territory as inherited from their colonial military doctrine. These same tactics served to prepare for an internal security role, something many of these forces undertook with regularity. Taken in combination with the general form of the inherited forces, that is, generally a core of light infantry with limited artillery and little to no air force or armoured arm, this meant that the African armies generally employed a limited, out-in-the-open campaign with little theoretical capacity to either outgun or outwit their opponents.[34] Direct column marches and simple flanking manoeuvres were favoured on the strategic offensive, while digging in to fixed positions was generally preferred on the strategic defensive. These doctrines fit the limited manpower and resources of the inherited African militaries, allowing them to get the most out of a force that had been trained initially to both engage in limited external campaigns as a part of a larger whole and to serve as an oppressive force against their own populace. Simply put, the African armies were rarely a complete force meant for combined arms actions, and their tactical doctrine did not stray far beyond fundamental strategic considerations of deploying infantry to take-and-hold or to defend their home territory until such time as international aid could be deployed.[35]

As can be guessed, since the general conventional structure of the military was inherited by the secessionist region, its general tactical and strategic doctrine was inherited as well. Indeed, the two primary functions of the military were perhaps even more essential, as it was needed to both suppress dissident/loyalist elements within the newly independent state and defend the declared borders of their new country. With the necessity of recognition and therefore legitimacy in the eyes of the world, both of these goals were amplified tenfold. The suppression of dissident opinion both muffled the voice of and controlled the potential violence of disadvantaged groups within the new state.[36] As both of these factors could lead to a denial of legitimacy in the world order, the military's capacity to minimize them was key in the establishment of the secessionist state. In addition, as defined earlier, the state has to both have a defined territory and defend its nationals or citizens from external enemies, and if it is unable to do so, or as Weber would define it, if it is unable to maintain its monopoly on violence, then it loses its legitimacy as a state regardless. With this in mind, the tactical and strategic doctrine adopted was perhaps even under greater pressure to ensure the territorial integrity of the new state as well as safeguard the populace and (to the extent it was capable) their property. The inherited conventional tactics were thus infinitely more suited to the needs of the Civil Secessionist state than to the possibility of a guerrilla struggle.[37]

WHY CIVIL SECESSIONS?

By examining the arc of these early attempts at secession, it is then possible to see the influence that the initial wave of decolonization had upon them. The growing and increasingly urbanized and educated populations of colonial African states agitated for their right to self-determination. Following this the African states were granted recognition on the world stage as legitimate states based upon their possession of all the characteristics of a nation, embodied in their territorial existence, their multi-ethnic population, their educated administration, and their ability to defend their population and borders. With decolonization mandated by international law and the ascension of independent governments leading the existing states, there was no question of the emergence and acceptance of the postcolonial African states.

The Civil Secessions attempted to follow the same story and mirrored the actions of their decolonized host states. First, calling upon the same privilege of self-determination, the Civil Secessionist state declared itself separate from its original parent state, usually based upon a historic administrative division within the host itself. Then the Civil Secessionist state attempted to display all the characteristics of a fully functioning independent state: definitive territoriality, a heterogeneous population, educated and enlightened political leadership and administration, and a military or gendarmerie to secure the safety of their new borders and population. The assumption was that the seceding state, upon fulfilling all the necessary characteristics of a state and making the legal arguments for its existence to the world, would be granted the same legitimacy as its previous host state. And why not? In many cases these proto-states exhibited exceptional characteristics and had solid arguments favouring legal separatism if not outright secession. As will be seen, the same arguments that could be levelled to allow the Congo its independence would apply to secessionist Katanga: it shared a defined territoriality, it was home to a blended population of Africans and Europeans, and it had its own administration and military. In some cases, a secessionist power like Katanga could even claim a more able administration than its parent state![38] Of course, the parent state could not be counted on to simply accept the partition of its territory and the removal of its people and resources. The most common response for the parent nation would be to take aggressive action to prevent the secession, using their often superior military and international connections. In this case, the seceding state tended to put its faith in the idea that the logic of its self-determination would be apparent to the world and the international recognition it would garner would enable its survival and preservation.

While this seemed to be unassailable logic at the time, there arose a number of complications and counter-arguments over the course of the decade that would render the recognition or even forbearance of the secessionist state an impossibility. These complications would begin with the previously mentioned secession of Katanga from the Congo in 1960, where the existence of the secessionist state was dealt its first blows under international law due to the decision of the United Nations to classify Katanga as a security threat to the Congo as a whole.[39] The position of the Civil Secessionist movement continued to erode with the formation of the Organization of African Unity in 1963. The OAU not only then served as a buffer between the greater international community and African affairs but also roundly rejected any threats to the territorial integrity of the inherited colonial borders. The final death blow was evident in the case of Biafra, where the refusal of the vast majority of the international community to offer recognition of any kind doomed the philosophical underpinning of the "decolonization" model of the Civil Secession. This denial of international legitimacy, coupled with the displayed capability of Nigeria to deal with its own affairs, effectively destroyed any hope for the concept, and Civil Secessions have not been attempted since.[40]

Map of Congo and Katanga

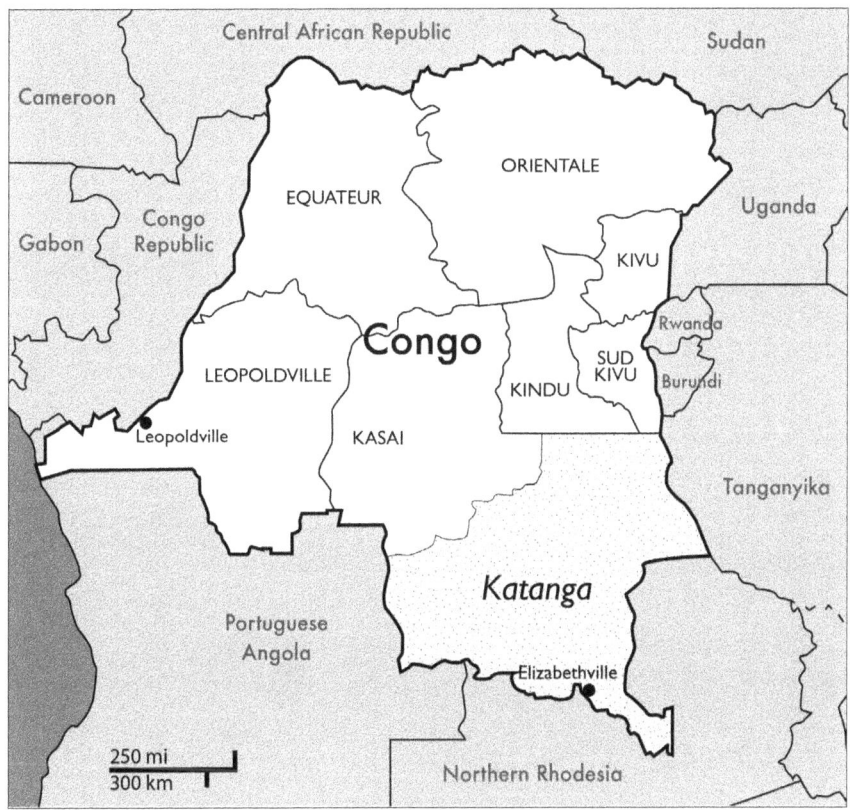

Copyright © 2014 Nathan E. McCormack and Charles G. Thomas

1

The Secession of Katanga, 1960–1963

The transition to independence was not easy for the majority of African nations. Army mutinies, ethnic struggles, parliamentary challenges, even brutal liberation struggles marked the birth of the nation-state for most of the former colonial possessions. Even taken in this context, few underwent the trials of the Congo upon its independence from Belgium in 1960. Liberated into the world with little infrastructure and less preparation, the Congo began to fragment almost immediately. This was to be the turbulent period known as the Congo Crisis, which would take centre stage in the debates on decolonization and in the development of the United Nations' responses to global crises. Over the next five years, the central government of the Congo fended off Cold War intrigues, parliamentary strife, ethnic troubles, rebel governments, an army mutiny, a coup, and even the attempted secession of its most resource-rich province, Katanga. The mutiny of the Force Publique (later the *Armée nationale congolaise*, or ANC) was the first army revolt in free Africa. Colonel Mobutu's first coup, launched on 14 September 1960, was designed to place the College of Commissioners in power and was one of the first on the continent. The secession of Katanga was the first secession movement of the independent era. The Congolese government would deal with all of these crises by processes of trial and error. Processes that would be all too common in later times would slowly take shape in the chaotic environs of the splintered Congo.

The secession of Katanga was one of the central issues involved in the Congo Crisis, and its defeat would be a vital step in creating a stable central regime. At the same time, the after-effects of the secession set numerous precedents in international law and helped to show the members of the

African community the steps they would need to take in order to avoid such a problem themselves. The Katangan secessionist movement revealed several patterns that would recur in the future secessions, and also exhibited anomalous characteristics that were not repeated in later separatist conflicts. While the patterns of creating what White would term a "civil nation,"[1] being led by the "New Men" of Africa, establishing a standing and professional military, and waging an essentially conventional war were standard within the wave of secessions immediately following independence, the massive amount of direct external intervention by individual nations and international organizations that was seen in the Congo was never replicated.

The Roots of Katangan Secession

The seeds of Katanga's secession were actually planted in 1958, with the emergence of the CONAKAT political party. It had become obvious to all onlookers that independence was on the horizon for African nations and national consciousness was beginning to take root within the black populations of the colonies. Despite these dynamics, Belgium did little or nothing to prepare the Congo for independence, instead hoping that its continued underdevelopment might delay any demands for independence or make the Congo completely dependent upon Belgium in the likely event of independence. The Belgians did not offer any advanced schooling to the masses, did not set up a local Africanized administration, and did not attempt to further develop the local economy. The Belgian administration in the Congo held independence back for as long as it could, but even the underdeveloped state of the black bourgeoisie could not prevent the rising tide of nationalism. Various political parties emerged within the provinces of the Congo, with Joseph Kasavubu's ABAKO party and Patrice Lumumba's MNC emerging as the two most widespread parties. Smaller parties emerged with support in various regions, and of these perhaps the most influential and powerful was CONAKAT of Katanga Province.[2]

Katanga was already an anomaly among the provinces of the Congo. Nearly 50 percent of the tax revenue of the Congo came from mineral-rich Katanga.[3] The province held large deposits of copper, cobalt, silver, platinum, uranium, and zinc, and had been extensively developed by the Belgians and the *Comité spéciale du Katanga* (or CSK) during their period of colonial rule. Of all the provinces, it held the closest relationship to the Belgians, and the majority party, CONAKAT, reflected this. CONAKAT (short for the *Confédération des associations tribales du Katanga*) was founded in 1958 in Elisabethville, the capital of the region. Led initially by Godefroid Munongo, in 1959 it absorbed the Union Katangaise, a party composed of the Belgian and other European expatriates who held the majority of wealth and power within the province.[4] The party extolled a vision of a federal Congo, with each province having a great deal of autonomy within its borders and being guided generally by a central government. In addition, at the time of its founding, the party wished for union with Belgium, believing that the central government of the colonizer would give direction to the new state. Finally, the party believed in the idea of an "authentic Katangan," an individual who, regardless of race, had been "integrated into the province" and who would protect "the legitimate rights of the original residents of this province."[5] With these goals in mind, CONAKAT may be seen as having been a semi-nationalist organization, with the goal of keeping the running of the Katangan state within its own central control. This was to have dire consequences following independence in 1960.

The elections of 1960, although meant to set the stage for Congolese independence, instead began the process of the splintering of the state. The two largest parties, ABAKO and MNC, both gained significant power within the government but neither could claim sole control of the government. This led to a coalition government, with Kasavubu claiming the presidency while Lumumba was appointed the prime minister. However, despite the forming of a political partnership, the two still had considerable disagreements that would undermine the government of the Congo from day one. In terms of Katangan political aspirations, CONAKAT won eight seats in the lower chamber of the Congolese parliament and seven in the Senate, but it was denied any ministerial appointments within the newly formed government of Kasavubu and Lumumba. This slight was compounded by Lumumba's electrifying speech at the 30 June Proclamation of Independence, which invoked the images of "magnificent mansions for whites in the cities and ramshackle straw hovels for blacks" and "the cells into which the authorities threw those who no longer were willing to submit to a rule where justice meant oppression and exploitation."[6] This had a negative effect on the large European population of Katanga, which backed

CONAKAT and its new leader Moïse Tshombe, as well as the watching audiences in key Western nations such as the United States and Belgium. Since the province was already unsteady in its support of a unified Congo state and had only narrowly been talked out of proclaiming secession a few days before independence,[7] it would not take much for the province to go its own way. The tipping point came mere days after independence.

On 5 July, the Force Publique mutinied in Léopoldville and other locations across the country, beginning what over the next five years was called the Congo Crisis.[8] The soldiers of the military had assumed that independence would open new avenues of promotion for them, allowing long-service soldiers to finally rise to commissioned ranks. However, these hopes were quickly dashed by General Émile Janssens, who starkly explained to the soldiers that they would continue to serve Belgian officers, leading to an eruption of violence by the rank and file of the Force Publique.[9] Belgium responded quickly and on 10 July transported an additional 5,600 troops to join the 3,800 who were already in the country, ostensibly to protect its citizens who still resided in the Congo and to restore order. This was not acceptable to the newly independent state, and the situation was made worse by an incident a day later in Matadi where at least a dozen Africans were killed by Belgian troops.[10] In the midst of the chaos, Moïse Tshombe declared independence for Katanga, proclaiming:

> This independence is total. However, aware of the imperative necessity for economic cooperation with Belgium, the Katangan government, to which Belgium has just granted the assistance of its own troops to protect human life, calls upon Belgium to join with Katanga in close economic community.
>
> Katanga calls upon Belgium to continue its technical, financial, and military support.
>
> It calls upon her to assist in re-establishing order and public safety....
>
> To all the inhabitants of Katanga, without distinction of Race or Color, we ask that you gather around us to lead our country and all its inhabitants forward to political, social, and economic progress, to the betterment of all.[11]

With this statement, the first secessionist conflict in Africa began. Although the central government opposed the secession, it was powerless to enforce its will while the mutinous army was rampaging throughout the nation. The same day, Kasavubu and Lumumba turned to the United States for aid. This request was promptly rejected by President Eisenhower, who instead suggested they appeal to the United Nations.[12] The requests on 12 and 13 July proved to be the beginning of a grand experiment for the United Nations and its place within international law.

The Beginnings of External Intervention

The United Nations' response to the Congo's requests spurred the body to take direct action to reimpose order and peace within the beleaguered state, with the initial step being the passing of United Nations Security Council Resolution 143. This resolution, passed on 14 July, gave a broad mandate to the United Nations armed forces that were to play such a great part in the secession crisis. It called upon the Belgians to remove their troops from the Congo, while simultaneously providing for "such military assistance as may be necessary until . . . the national security forces may be able . . . to fully meet their task."[13] The next day, troops from various member states began to arrive in the Congo to restore order, and within a week they had deployed to every major centre in the nation. Katanga, however, would not accept the United Nations troops within its borders and refused to expel the Belgian forces. United Nations Resolution 145 was passed on 22 July, reaffirming the legitimacy of the United Nations presence within the borders of Katanga and urging the removal of the Belgian forces. While the situation was deadlocked, a further resolution (Resolution 146) was passed on 9 August, assuring the Katangans of the UN's resolve to enter Katanga but not to interfere in the Katangans' current disagreement with the central government. This was accompanied by a further demand for the withdrawal of the still substantial Belgian forces within the province. Tshombe fired back at the UN force with ten demands, including a demand that none of the troops would be from Communist or communist-oriented nations and a demand for a reaffirmation of the UN's statement that it would not interfere with the internal workings of the state.[14] These demands were accepted, and the UN troops finally entered Katanga. Shortly afterward, a new constitutional crisis struck the Congo and effectively halted any attempts to reintegrate Katanga until 1961.

It is necessary to provide a brief description of this crisis, because of its effects upon the actual secession conflict itself. Chaos still reigned and the Congolese army was still an unstable element. In the midst of this, the already considerable tensions between President Kasavubu and Prime Minister Lumumba publicly erupted, with each trying to remove the other from power on 5 September. The UN seized the radio station in Léopoldville and forbade all air traffic, effectively neutralizing Lumumba's base of support. At the height of the confusion, Colonel Mobutu of the ANC staged a coup on 14 September, replacing Lumumba and Kasavubu with a committee of young, educated, and nonpolitical Congolese.[15] Both had been rapidly losing their international standing due to their actions, but Lumumba in particular had managed to alienate a great deal of support. He had already been viewed as unstable and a dangerous leftist by the United States, Belgium, and members of the opposition parties, all of whom had been searching for a reason to remove him.[16] This hostility had been exacerbated by Lumumba's response to the attempted secession of South Kasai, a province in the Congo, during the early days of the Congo Crisis. Lumumba had sent in ANC troops, who had responded with widespread and sustained brutality to the local Luba dissenters, further undermining the prime minister's position and helping legitimize many of the efforts to remove him. Meanwhile, Kasavubu was largely seen as blameless and would eventually be invited back into the government.

In the days following Mobutu's coup, Lumumba was confined to his house under the protection of UN troops, but he escaped in December and attempted to reach Stanleyville, the base of his support. He was recaptured and held briefly by the Congolese central government, but was considered too dangerous to the Congo to be held. Already his political followers in the Stanleyville region were arming themselves and could likely threaten the Leopoldville government, particularly while said government was also dealing with the Katangan conflict. To prevent further threats from Lumumba himself, the former prime minister was flown to Katanga with two of his associates. All three were beaten, tortured, and then executed by the Katangan Gendarmerie, with Lumumba's death being reported on 17 January 1961, to be greeted with shock all over the world.

This event must be mentioned because of the immense changes it forced on the dynamics of the conflict. Despite the earlier demands for his removal and the shock at his actions toward South Kasai, following this political murder Lumumba became a martyr, and none were painted more harshly than the Katangans for their slaying of the former prime minister. A new government of Lumumba loyalists set themselves up in Stanleyville and declared themselves the legitimate executive of the nation.[17] These claims were greeted eagerly by those who regretted the death of the fiery nationalist. The United Nations was excoriated for its inaction in the event, with several member nations withdrawing their contingents in protest. In the near future, on 21 February, the UN Security Council would pass a resolution to bring a final end to the Congo tumult.[18] The Council of Commissioners in Léopoldville immediately reached out to try and patch together an alliance between the warring factions and end the strife that was tearing the nation apart.

In his capacity as president of the de facto state of Katanga, Moïse Tshombe attended several of the attempted peacemaking conferences over the next four months. Although Tshombe would miss the first, all four meetings involved one or more of the factions currently dividing the Congo between them. The first took place at Léopoldville beginning on 25 January; the second in Elisabethville in February; the third in Tananarive, Madagascar, in March; and the final conference in Coquilhatville on 24 April. The Léopoldville conference's aim was to constitute a representative government for the Congo, but due to his absence, Tshombe declared it invalid. The Katangan government demanded at least nominal recognition from the Léopoldville government, which was not forthcoming. The conference in Elisabethville was in response to the UN initiatives of late February. These initiatives were the first steps toward authorizing the use of force by the UN troops to prevent the broadening of the conflict. On 28 February, Tshombe entered into a military alliance with the central government and that of the secessionist South Kasai Province. Ostensibly this was aimed at the "Communists" of the Stanleyville government, but in effect it was a preventive measure taken against the increasingly aggressive United Nations. The next meeting, at Tananarive from 8 to 12 March, was an overwhelming success for the Katangan government and Tshombe. They entered the conference with three objectives and achieved them all, partially due to the continued panic instilled in the factions by the UN resolution of 21 February. All the parties agreed on a denunciation of the UN resolution of 21 February, the idea of a federal government structure with each region having general autonomy, and the concept of each region having its own gendarmerie and police at its disposal.[19] In this way, Katanga had effectively won the beginnings of recognition. This recognition, however, was not to last. The Léopoldville government realized its error and reached out to the UN and the Stanleyville government in an attempt to reclaim the balance of power. By the time of the Coquilhatville conference of 24 April, opinion had hardened against the Katangan initiatives and Tshombe was actually arrested and imprisoned by the Congolese government inside a military villa in Leopoldville.

During Tshombe's imprisonment, new negotiations were undertaken by the other factions, and the parliament began to reassemble to serve as a representative government for the Congo. By June, Tshombe was promising to send a Katanga delegation to join in the process and pledging an end to the separate Katangan state. However, upon his return to Katanga he rejected his earlier statement, and he celebrated the first anniversary of Katangan independence on 11 July 1961. Secessionist Katanga was still a going concern, but events were rapidly catching up with it. Already the UN's Resolution 161 of 21 February had caused a realignment of the Congo that would lead to the downfall of Tshombe's government. Aside from authorizing the UN forces to use force and repeating the demand for the removal of foreign soldiers and technical assistants, the resolution had two major effects on the Congo. First, the resolution increased the military tension between the UN and the various armed forces within the borders of the Congo. The Katangan Gendarmerie clashed with the UN forces on 30 March, beginning a running series of skirmishes that eroded the position of Katanga vis-à-vis the international community.[20] Second, the resolution led to the realignment of the diplomatic stances of the various factions, with Tshombe, Kasavubu, and the separatists of Kasai coming together to form an alliance of sorts for their protection. However, Tshombe overplayed his hand, which led to the rapprochement between Stanleyville and Léopoldville. With three of the four political forces now aligned against Katanga, these factions formed a government during the month of July while Tshombe continued his defiance. By the time the president of

Katanga attempted to intervene, the government had been formed, rendering him impotent. On 2 August, the new coalition government led by Cyrille Adoula took power and pledged to end the secession of Katanga. Belatedly Katanga sent a delegation to take part in the government, but the beginning of the end was upon the breakaway state.

The United Nations as Peacemaker

Of course, it must be stressed that initially the United Nations was not trying to suppress the Katanga secession. The UN did not have the authority to do this and thus never attempted a forcible disarming of the Katangan government. The UN's mandate, however, included the removal of the foreign elements of the Katangan Gendarmerie and government, and it was under this mandate that the initial exercises of force were carried out. The prologue to the larger operations of the latter half of 1961 was the expulsion of Georges Thyssens. Thyssens was an "ultra," a hard-line advisor to Tshombe and Munongo, who had frustrated all attempts by the United Nations to apply pressure on the state.[21] Under increasing pressure from the UN, the Belgians produced a list of those foreign advisors whose expulsion would be appropriate. Thyssens was one of these. On 7 July, Thyssens was detained by UN peacekeepers, after a brief struggle, and forced onto a plane. His forcible repatriation was an indication of the methods by which Katanga would in future be bent to the will of the United Nations and the central government. The Tshombe government even made nominal efforts to provide names of individuals to be expelled, creating a list of eleven names of people who could be repatriated safely, while declaring that list exhaustive. Again the demand for the replacement of foreign nationals in the Gendarmerie was made, but France and Belgium pleaded their lack of control over the mercenaries. This stated inability worked for the Katangan government, which used these foreign mercenaries as trainers and officers for their locally recruited Gendarmerie. With its central control already shaky and in face of mounting pressure to deal with the Katanga problem, on 24 August 1961, the central government formally requested UN aid in the removal of the foreign personnel. This was the beginning of the actual shooting war between the United Nations and the Katangan Gendarmerie.

However, the first clash between the two was bloodless. The UN forces under the direction of Dr. Conor Cruise O'Brien began Operation Rum Punch on 28 August, with the intention of rounding up the foreign soldiers and mercenaries staffing the Katangan Gendarmerie in Elisabethville.[22] The surprise was complete and the majority of the Belgian nationals were rounded up and expelled from the Congo. No casualties were sustained in the course of the operation. Unfortunately, a key component went awry. The Belgian consul had assumed responsibility for ensuring the surrender and expulsion of the foreign nationals, but at the beginning of the operation he revealed he had no authority over any of those who were not Belgian regular officers. This left the UN forces flat-footed, while a large number of foreign mercenaries were left to their own devices. These men blended into the civilian population or disappeared over the Rhodesian border, simply to return after the conclusion of the operation. By 9 September, over a hundred officers were still unaccounted for. Between the hollow statement of Tshombe declaring the termination of the mercenaries' services and the duplicitous actions of the Belgian consul, the operation was hamstrung and achieved only a fraction of its hoped-for success. The United Nations continued to insist on the repatriation of the mercenaries, but this only resulted in a final refusal by Tshombe to aid in their expulsion. This led to Operation Morthor in early September.

In theory, Operation Morthor ("Smash" in Hindi) was intended to expand on the success of Rum Punch. O'Brien had obtained warrants for the arrest of four prominent Katangan ministers and intended to use their detention in combination with the final expulsion of the mercenaries to bring a negotiated end to the state of Katanga. Plans were laid to seal off Tshombe's residence in Elisabethville and seize the town's post office and radio station, thereby stripping the Katangan government of most of its methods of communication. On 13 September, the operation began and almost immediately ran into complications.[23] The post office was heavily guarded by Katangan paracommandos led by mercenary officers. This led to a general firefight for possession of the building, which claimed lives on both sides. Meanwhile the UN forces never managed to seal off Tshombe, who promptly fled across the Rhodesian border and pledged resistance to the utmost. With the element of surprise gone, the operation degenerated into a series of firefights across Elisabethville between ill-equipped UN forces and the Gendarmerie. While this dragged on into 14 September, an isolated UN garrison of Irish troops was surrounded in the mining town of Jadotville. While offering a heroic defence, the Irish troops were subjected to withering fire and strafing from the lone Fouga Magister jet fighter the Katangan forces had, and the Irishmen finally capitulated on 17 September.[24] These UN soldiers served as hostages in the ceasefire negotiations that were being set up. Unfortunately, the plane carrying UN Secretary-General Hammarskjöld crashed on its way to Ndola for a meeting with Tshombe, killing all aboard.[25] In response to this tragedy, the UN forces patched together a ceasefire on 20 September, bringing the debacle of Operation Morthor to an end. Conditions for a permanent ceasefire began to be suggested, much to the disapproval of the central Congolese government.

As a reflection of this disapproval, in late October the Adoula government attempted an invasion of Katanga which failed, further weakening the government's authority within the nation. This invasion stirred up the Gendarmerie, which repeatedly provoked the UN forces left in Katanga in early November. These actions served to convince the UN under the new leadership of U Thant that the only way that the Congo might find stability was the reintegration of Katanga into the Congo proper. This led to the resolution of 24 November,[26] giving the UN forces a mandate to use force to remove the mercenaries if necessary. Tshombe and Katanga were incensed and called for resistance to the utmost against what they characterized as UN aggression against their sovereign status. Katangan gendarmes constructed roadblocks, despite warnings from the UN forces, and on December 2 began a minor engagement against the UN forces that were attempting to clear one of several blocked roads.[27] By December 5, this skirmish had escalated into a general conflict, called Operation UNOKAT, or Round Two, by the UN forces involved. In contrast to their earlier operations, the UN forces were no longer restricted in their mandate and had built up effective airpower to cover their operations.[28] On December 6, the United Nations bombed multiple Katangan airports and positions and the UN's ground forces continued their strikes into Elisabethville. By the middle of the month, the UN forces held the majority of strategic locations within the province and Tshombe called for negotiations. On December 17, he was told that negotiations would only take place under the framework of the Basic Law concerning the structure of the Congo, which did not recognize

Katanga as a state. While Tshombe agreed to these terms and signed the Kitona accords on December 21, he reneged on this agreement, claiming that he did not have the sole authority to make such a decision. Katanga remained insistent on its independence but continued diplomatic wrangling with the central government for months to come.

Although under considerable pressure, the Katangan government prolonged its negotiations both with the United Nations and the Congolese government. Throughout 1962, various incidents and provocations took place, involving UN authorities and Katangan forces. By 20 August, the United Nations had had enough and released the U Thant Plan for National Reconciliation.[29] It was not open to negotiation and had to be accepted by Katanga within ten days or sanctions would be applied. The Katangans protested against the provisions of the plan, which called for the subordination of Katanga and all its resources to the central Congolese government, but they had little leverage to fight against it. In an untenable situation, the Katangan government accepted it under protest on 2 September.. Throughout the next three months, the Katangans dragged their feet over adherence to the plan, while beginning another mercenary recruitment drive. In addition, during this period, Tshombe succeeded in adding nearly twenty military airplanes to his air force, despite warnings that the recruitment drive and the purchase of the planes endangered the successful implementation of the U Thant Plan and that Katanga would pay the penalty for any failure to adhere to its precepts.[30] By December 10, the United Nations had resolved to impose sanctions in response to the provocative actions of Tshombe, which included the blockading of UN supplies and the detention of UN troops in Katanga. Finally, on Christmas Eve, the dam broke and Katangan gendarmes became involved in a five-hour firefight with Ethiopian UN troops at a roadblock. Despite several demands for a ceasefire by the UN forces, the conflict continued, leading again to a general engagement. On December 28, Operation Grand Slam, also known as Round Three, initiated a UN offensive across the breadth of the separatist Katangan state. Multiple air sorties destroyed the interior defensive lines and logistical bases of the Katangan Gendarmerie, and the UN troops, reinforced over the past year, achieved great success on all fronts. By December 30, all meaningful resistance had ended, and by 3 January 1963, Jadotville was captured. Tshombe continued to demand a scorched-earth policy from his new base in Rhodesia, but he was finally convinced to return to Elisabethville under the terms of an amnesty. By 21 January, the secession of Katanga had ended and the U Thant Plan had been put into effect.

Katanga as Archetype

The attempted secession of Katanga offers several areas of comparison in terms of the trajectory of African secessionist conflicts. The fact that it was the first of its kind in the post-independence era would have a profound effect on its course and nature and in turn would create several precedents in the international community in terms of that community's opinions about self-determination and in terms of the process of self-determination within the new nations of Africa. Katanga came to be seen as a typical secession of its period due to its formation of a civil (as opposed to an ethnic) state, its leadership by "New Men" of Africa, its formation of a structured standing army, and that army's prosecution of a conventional conflict to try and ensure the independence of its home state. However, it also served to set the most important international precedents in terms of dealing with issues of African sovereignty. It is this set of precedents and the consequent international legal structures set up by both the United Nations and the emerging Organization of African Unity that continue to shape the process of sovereignty, legitimacy, and international relations of all subsequent African separatist movements.

The continuities of the separatist state will be dealt with first, before moving on to the far more lasting and important international ramifications of the Katangan conflict. In looking at the general nature and structure of the fledgling Katangan state, it is easy to see that it was typical of the first wave of secessionist conflicts that aimed at creating a "civil nation." In the immediate postwar period, there had been a subtle redefinition of the idea of the "nation." This transferred the focus of nationhood from an ethnic group effecting its own administration, which had been the common focus of the "nation-state" since the nineteenth century, to the idea of an administration that would oversee multiple ethnic identities and endeavour to foster them all equally. This created the distinction between *ethnic* nations, which as a concept fell out of favour until the 1990s with the end of the Cold War, and *civil* nations, which were seen as the new favoured form of the state. Katanga was undoubtedly among the ranks of the civil nations, with representatives of numerous races and ethnicities represented within its borders and administrations. CONAKAT, which formed the ruling party throughout the existence of the separate Katanga, was itself a product of the union between the original *Confédération des associations tribales du Katanga* and the *Union Katangaise*, which contained the majority of the wealthy white settlers of the region. CONAKAT expounded among its goals the desire to effect "the Union of all the original residents of the province of Katanga, black and white, without racial discrimination, who show by their behavior that they have been integrated into this province."[31] In this effort, they were most likely attempting to create a separate and binding Katangan identity above and beyond the pre-existing ethnic identities of the inhabitants of the province. The senior members of the government of the separate state were all from differing ethnic groups, while they were aided by European advisors, which ensured the attempt to represent and foster a unitary identity and agenda. Although there was intergroup strife during the period of the separate state, this was almost entirely aimed at the repression of the Luba, who were seen as non-Katangans living within the borders of the nation and constituting a threat to Katanga itself.

The state of Katanga also had legislative precedent on its side when making its arguments for its separate nature. This continues to be a common argument in favour of international recognition in each movement—the ability to show a historical antecedent to the state being proposed, in order to make the case that the separatist state is justified in its existence. In the case of Katanga, its case rested upon the history of the *Compagnie du Katanga* and the *Comité spéciale du Katanga*. The Compagnie was a private concern that was granted several concessions across Katanga by Belgium in 1891, giving the company a free hand to develop its territories as it saw fit to achieve profitability. It worked hand in hand with the Congo Free State, Leopold II's created personalist colonial state that claimed the entirety of the Congo River Basin, to develop the province and solidify Leopold's claim on the region. In 1900, the Compagnie made a pact with the Free State, setting up the *Comité spéciale du Katanga*, which was granted the undivided management of the region's assets. Although by 1910 the administrative and political roles were taken away from the Comité, it still remained a potent economic force up to and beyond independence.[32] Meanwhile, from

1910 to 1933, Katanga enjoyed a special administrative status, separate from the rest of the Congo. It is this history as a separate administrative and developmental zone that Katanga proposed as its precedent first for a federal system of governance in the unified Congo and later for Katanga's secession from the central government. This historical sleight of hand has since been put to use in the secessions of Biafra, South Sudan, Somaliland, and Eritrea. Although the strength of each case must be evaluated on its own merits, the Katangan experience was the first in postcolonial Africa to propose the idea of a precedent for separatism.

Also typical of the secession conflicts was the leadership of the New Men of Africa and their top-down leadership and administration of the secession. As the inevitability of independence became increasingly obvious through colonized Africa, there had been in general a push to "Africanize" the administrative services of most colonies. At the time of independence, Belgium was woefully behind in this process in the Congo, with only twenty university graduates within the indigenous population. However, this did not mean that there was no rising African bourgeoisie to take the reins of leadership within the state. Patrice Lumumba and Joseph Kasavubu each rose to prominence within a nascent middle class within the Congo. The same group produced the dissenting leaders of the rebelling states. All the major figures of the CONAKAT regime were what the Belgians referred to as *évolués* (or "civilized"), their term for the members of the newer generation who were integrated into the administrative and economic policies of the Congo. Three key figures in particular represent the New Men in CONAKAT and the independent state of Katanga: Moïse Tshombe, Godefroid Munongo, and Jean-Baptiste Kibwe. CONAKAT in turn provided the intellectual and ideological drive toward the independent Katangan state.

Moïse Tshombe was born in 1919, the son of a wealthy Lunda trader in Katanga. His father had established his business by buying the stock of smaller agriculturalists in the Sandoa district and reselling the products to the workers in the copper belt of Katanga. His firm, Tshombe and Sons, was profitable enough to enable him to educate his sons and send his family members abroad to visit Europe. Moïse himself was taught at a Methodist mission school, completing his primary schooling and earning a teaching certificate. He went on to earn a degree in accounting and establish several business ventures before entering into politics. He rose to the position of president-general of CONAKAT in the second half of 1959 and headed the party's delegation to the political and economic roundtable discussions leading to the independence of the Congo.[33] While Katanga was still part of the Congo, he was elected as a provincial deputy for the Elisabethville region and after secession became president of the state of Katanga. Coming from one of the wealthiest families of the nation and having a solid education placed Tshombe squarely in the new *évolué* class of the Congo.

Godefroid Munongo was born in 1925. He was a Yeke and a descendant of the legendary nineteenth-century paramount chief Msiri. This immediately gave him high standing in the traditional power structure of the Congo. However, he quickly added to this prestige, spending two years in a seminary before switching to more worldly pursuits and earning his degree from the School for Administrative Sciences. After this, Munongo rose through the Belgian administration, working first as a court clerk and rising to the level of a territorial agent by 1958. It was Munongo who helped found CONAKAT and was in fact its first president.[34] However, there was a conflict of interest between his administrative career and the political party, and for this reason he stepped aside in favour of Tshombe in 1959. In 1960, he was elected to the position of provincial deputy for Elisabethville and upon Katanga's secession became its minister of the interior. Munongo, having risen into the new middle and upper class, was the firmest "ultra" and ideologue of the Katangan secession.

This last of the major figures is Jean-Baptiste Kibwe, a Tabwa who was born in Katanga in 1924. Kibwe completed his primary education and went on to four years of high school, then further studies in law, political science, and sociology. He served with the *Comité spéciale du Katanga* and the Banque du Congo Belge.[35] Already well placed within the administrative organs of colonial rule, Kibwe also served with the territorial administration in the mid-1950s. Kibwe served with Tshombe at the political roundtable in 1960, being CONAKAT vice president that year. Upon the secession of Katanga, Kibwe served as both its vice president and its minister of finance. Kibwe, like Tshombe and Munongo, had firmly entrenched himself within the administration and politics of Katanga before and during independence. By using the rising prominence allowed to the Congolese as independence approached, Kibwe climbed into the class of the *évolués* and became a leader of the Katangans in the new Congo state.

It was these men and their companions who formed the core of CONAKAT, which in turn served as the central party and administrative command structure for the secessionist Katanga state. It was CONAKAT, especially its militant "ultras" from the Union Katangaise, that led Katanga into secession and served as its guiding force in terms of international relations, foreign aid, and legal arguments for the existence of the separatist state. As such, CONAKAT and its leadership served as a central player in the top-down imposition of the secessionist state and its ideological structures as proposed in both CONAKAT's initial goal for an autonomous Katangan state run by "authentic Katangans"[36] and the *Union Katangaise*'s calls for an "awakening of a Katangan national conscience."[37]

To defend that national consciousness, Tshombe, Munongo, Kibwe, and others assembled the Katangan Gendarmerie. Constructed out of the remnants of the ANC in the region after the mutiny, it was supplemented by recruitment among the Lunda and the Yeke and staffed initially by Belgian officers seconded to the Katangan state. This force was supplemented by mercenaries hired en masse to bolster the military power of Katanga.[38] It was originally constituted to secure the borders of the Katangan state, to control the uprising of the mutinous ANC, and to police the Luba of northern Katanga, who were separated from the larger population of the Luba by the secession of Kasai and were assumed to be an internal threat. Of course, as continued international pressure was brought to bear on Belgium, it slowly withdrew its officers and replaced them with mercenaries to provide a strong leadership for the fledgling force. It is estimated that the Gendarmerie had approximately 8,000–10,000 troops and was originally led by 114 officers and 117 other ranks of the Belgian army.[39] These were supplemented by approximately 300 Belgian, South African, Rhodesian, and French mercenaries hired to replace the Belgian army officers who were slowly but surely forced to leave.[40] Around 100 of these mercenaries were placed in leadership positions within the Gendarmerie, while the other 200 or so were placed in an all-white "International Company."[41] The training of the Gendarmerie was generally held to be average in quality, although its paracommandos were noted as being extremely tough and disciplined, having been trained by Commandant Roger Faulques, a French officer discharged from that army after his central involvement in atrocities during the Algerian struggle for independence came to light.[42]

A key factor in the success of the Gendarmerie, in addition to its leadership, was the high standard of its equipment. Above and beyond the small arms with which the men were largely equipped, the troops were well supported by mortars, artillery, and air power. During the siege of Jadotville, all three had a considerable effect and allowed the Gendarmerie to capture the Irish UN force guarding the mining centre. Captain Pat Quinlan, commander of the Irish contingent, repeatedly mentioned the mortar bombardments his men endured, although he also took pains to mention the ineffectiveness of these strikes. In addition, while describing the preparations of the Gendarmerie in encircling Jadotville, Quinlan noted the presence of a heavy gun, assumed to be a French 75 mm artillery piece.[43] Quinlan's accounts also mention numerous jeeps and trucks and most notably the French-made Fouga Magister jet airplane that would wreak such havoc among the reinforcements who attempted to relieve the Irish company. The Fouga had been purchased by the Katangan government through a French firm and gave a decided edge to the Katangan forces, while the UN was bereft of air cover. At the time of the ceasefire that ended the secession, the Indian Brigade confiscated large numbers of weapons, including several dozen machine guns, over a hundred mortars of varying sizes, an armoured car with a 37 mm gun, and several locally manufactured armoured personnel carriers.[44] Overall, the Katangan Gendarmerie was admirably equipped for conventional operations within the Congo and performed reasonably well.

Katanga as Anomaly

Despite the continuities between the Katangan secession and the rest of the first wave of secessionist conflicts in Africa, there were several unique aspects to the Katangan conflict. The most obvious of these were the open and decisive interventions by both national and international groups. Belgium played a central role in the secession of Katanga, just as its final rejection of Katanga would lead to that state's dissolution, while the United Nations acted first as peacekeeper and then as aggressor in dismantling Katanga. For the first and last time in African separatist conflicts, widespread international intervention played a major part, with the final legal framework set up by the United Nations establishing what continues to serve as the precedent in terms of African secessions, as well as the framework of the Organization of African Unity, which continues to be a deterrent to the recognition of secessionist movements.

Belgium's interests in the secession of Katanga were all too obvious. The massive mineral wealth of Katanga was the crown jewel in the holdings of the *Société générale du Belgique*. The *Union minière du Haut Katanga* held the vast majority of mineral extraction rights within the state. This represented a large proportion of the $750 million of the general "Congo Portfolio" held in Belgium.[45] Of course, these mining industries also employed nearly 10,000 Belgian citizens within the province, giving the Belgians another reason to interfere with the inner running of the fledgling state. This intervention took the form of both military and administrative aid to Katanga during its years of secession.

With the mutiny of the ANC on 5 July 1960, the Belgians quickly moved additional troops into the Congo, raising their numbers to 8,600. Although the majority of these began to be removed on the arrival of the UN force, they were not removed from Katanga. Tshombe rejected the imposition of the UN force and instead leaned heavily on the Belgian troops seconded to his forces, while at the same time accepting some seven to nine tons of armaments provided by the Belgians.[46] Although eventually the United Nations was able to negotiate the insertion of forces into Katanga, the Tshombe government refused to abide by UN resolutions 143, 145, and 146, requesting the removal of all foreign troops and personnel. When Resolution 161 was passed on 21 February 1961, it caused a stir, as it empowered the UN to use force to remove the foreign nationals.

This cut to the heart of Belgian interference with UN policy in Katanga, and Belgium refused to remove the Belgian officers of the former Force Publique until suitable replacements were found. The Belgians did remove a minimal number of the Belgian officers seconded to train Congolese forces, but those Belgian troops functioning as mercenaries could only be asked to leave.[47] Indeed, to make good on the losses incurred, the Belgian government worked closely with the Katangan mission to hire mercenaries, offering them the resources of the Sûreté (the military secret police) in vetting prospective soldiers. The advent of the Lefèvre ministry in Belgium changed the outlook somewhat, with negotiations being carried on with a view to replacing the Belgian troops with those of the UN force.

This was known as the Egge plan, but it was unfortunately interrupted by the tribulations of operations Rum Punch and Morthor. While the Spaak government was to remove all regular Belgian forces by November 1961 by withdrawing their passports, Rum Punch had been hamstrung by the inability of the Belgian consul to remove the mercenary soldiers, and thus Belgian mercenaries continued to serve in Katanga.

In addition, Belgium offered significant technical assistance to the Katangan separatists. Although refusing to offer recognition to the breakaway state, the Belgian government did send the Belgian Technical Mission, or Mistebel, which was to provide invaluable support. Over the course of its mission, Mistebel provided the backbone of the administration of Katanga as well as organizing Belgian support for the Gendarmerie, warning the Belgian personnel about UN attacks, attempting to rally the West to support the Tshombe regime, and overall helping guide Tshombe and the Katangan state. Although it was recalled to Belgium in October 1960, it is not too far of a stretch to say that the Technical Mission offered vital support to the secessionists at a critical juncture in the history of Katanga. It was the withdrawal of this support that began to slowly eat away at the Katangan state. Once its military and administrative components were withdrawn from Katanga, all that remained for Belgium were the financial aspects of its interests. Once these were assured, Katanga was on its own.

In fact, Belgian disengagement truly began following the 21 February 1961 resolution, which began the proactive attempts of the United Nations to remove any outside interference from Katanga. While the Belgian government protested against operations Rum Punch and Morthor, the fact remained that by that time the majority of their formal interactions with the Tshombe regime had ended. Despite the Belgians' protests against the United Nations' Round Two, they began to support the UN initiatives to bring the Katangans to heel and even joined in the economic sanctions of 1962. In fact, their help in this case was invaluable, as cutting off the financial payments from the *Union minière du Haut Katanga* resulted in the crippling of the Katangan economy and ensured the dismantling of the separatist state.

Belgium was not the only state whose removal tipped the balance within the Katangan Secession. Following the initial breakaway of the secessionist state, the United States under the Eisenhower administration found itself wondering what role it might play in the Congo Crisis. While they hoped for a unified and effective Congolese state, the influence that Lumumba had over the nationalist elements of the government and his reputation as a leftist left the United States uncertain of their path forward. In addition, Lumumba's insistence on the removal of all influence by NATO ally Belgium made the United States even more concerned about rising spectre of Communism in the Congo. The emergence of the Western-oriented Katanga offered a chance for a local locus of allied influence, while the increasingly strident Lumumba made demands for US support. Ultimately the Eisenhower administration would find itself in the position of actively trying to undermine Lumumba's position within the Congo while musing about the role the Katangan forces might play in central Africa. This policy found its apex with the US support for Colonel Mobutu's coup and arrest of Lumumba, which led directly to his murder on 17 January 1961.[48]

However, the shocking assassination of the former prime minister happened to occur three days before the accession of the Kennedy Administration, who took office to find the present Katanga policy anathema to their goals in central Africa. Although they were as stridently anti-Communist as the Eisenhower administration, they placed a higher priority on the emergence and development of the decolonizing world as independent allies. While they could support Mobutu as a strongman bulwark against the assumed communist aggression, they could not countenance a fractured Congo. As such, the United States quickly reversed course and played a role in clearing out the remaining Belgian interference while providing considerable supplies and air cover to the central Congolese government. This was done largely in the hopes that a singular, centralized independent Congo would find alignment with the United States agreeable as opposed to retaining ties with the neocolonial powers and possibly leaning closer to the Soviets. While the Kennedy administration ultimately would not play a direct role in the fall of Tshombe's Katanga, the *volte-face* of American foreign policy toward the secessionist state undercut any remaining international support for the breakaway state.

The United Nations also played a central role in the Katangan secession, taking on initially the role of mediator and eventually that of antagonist to Tshombe's state. UN aid was requested by Lumumba and Kasavubu in 1960, in response to the mutiny of the ANC and the reinsertion of Belgian troops into the Congo. A series of UN resolutions gave the UN force its mandate to keep the peace and request the removal of foreign personnel, beginning with Resolutions 143 and 145. Upon the refusal of Katanga to allow the entrance of UN troops, Resolution 143 was passed, asserting the right of the United Nations force to be present within the boundaries of Katanga. At this point, the UN troops existed solely as peacekeepers and to prevent any aggressive action toward civilians within the Congo. Their mandate was solely self-defence, and they had no right to interfere in the internal difficulties of the Congolese state.

This all changed with the passing of Resolution 161 on 21 February 1961, which emerged as a response to the death of Patrice Lumumba and the apparent chaos descending across the Congo. This resolution empowered the United Nations to "take immediately all appropriate measures to prevent the occurrence of civil war in the Congo."[49] This included the use of force as a last resort. Although once again not actually allowing any proactive measures to be taken as far as the Katangan situation was concerned, Resolution 161 altered the entire situation within the Congo and caused a rapprochement between the Léopoldville and Stanleyville governments. This in turn isolated the Katangan separatists and left them as the sole targets of the UN peacekeepers. The 21 February resolution also reinforced the demand that all foreign personnel leave the Congo, which was finally acted on with Rum Punch and Morthor several after several months of delay, when the Katangans still had not removed the foreigners. Unfortunately, it was the debacle of Morthor that led to the death of Dag Hammarskjöld and a complete change in the UN's views on the Katanga situation.

Following Hammarskjöld's death, U Thant rose to the secretary-generalship and began to take decisive steps to end the secession of Katanga. The 24 November 1961 resolution effectively ended any hopes for a separate state of Katanga by recognizing the central authority of the Léopoldville government and condemning the separatist activities of the Tshombe regime. At this point, the secretary-general was empowered to use force to remove any and all foreign personnel and take any measures necessary to make certain they remained absent. This not only provided a belated approval of the activities of Rum Punch and Morthor but also gave a reason for the offensives of December following the provocations by the Gendarmerie. With Round Two (Operation UNOKAT) and Round Three

(Operation Grand Slam), the United Nations had effectively transformed itself from a passive peacekeeping force into an aggressive power with the mandate to dismantle the Katangan state.

The thought process behind the transformation may be seen in the progress of the resolutions passed over the two-year period of 1961–1962. Initially, the United Nations sustained the hope that the central authority of the Congo would reassert itself after a brief period of chaos. This would hopefully then lead to negotiations between the various factions and a settlement of the crisis. As time passed, it became increasingly obvious that several factors were preventing this from occurring and therefore the mandates were provided to remove these factors. At first the strategic thinking was that the Katangan state would fall into line without foreign intervention. This led to aggressive moves against the foreign elements as opposed to the state itself, as shown in such heralded operations as Rum Punch. However, as the Congo factions realigned themselves and isolated Katanga, it became increasingly obvious to the United Nations that the Katangan state itself was an impediment to the unity of the Congo. This resulted in the 24 November resolution, which announced the recognition of the Léopoldville government and the rejection of Katangan sovereignty. At this point, any and all members of the Katangan state's apparatus became unlawful combatants and could be repressed by the UN force. It was the final alignment of the Léopoldville and Stanleyville governments that gave the United Nations the justification to dismantle the Katangan State.

Katanga as Precedent

This series of actions by the United Nations in 1960–62 created an entirely new precedent with regard to the application of force through that august body. As Trevor Findlay notes in his work on the UN force in the Congo, the mandated force was originally constituted as neither a peacekeeping nor a punitive force, under either chapter VI or chapter VII of the UN charter, respectively.[50] Hammarskjöld had established a force without a necessarily defined purpose within the Congo, instead relying on his own powers, as delineated in article 99 of the UN charter, to "bring to the attention of the Security Council any matter which in his opinion may threaten the maintenance of international peace and security."[51] This was done to avoid the invocation of articles 41 (sanctions) and 42 (direct force) in chapter VII, which would have required the naming of Belgium as an aggressor in the occupation of Congolese territory. Following the 9 August 1960 and 21 February 1961 resolutions, Hammarskjöld still had not invoked either of the articles involved in the application of direct punitive measures, and yet he had implicitly sanctioned actions normally under the purview of article 42 of the charter. This created a hybrid mandate for the uncertain force, one that Findlay argues was neither a peacekeeping nor a punitive force and instead fell under what he refers to as a peace-enforcement mandate that offered extralegal flexibility to the actions of *Opération des Nations Unies au Congo* (ONUC), a mandate that was finally exploited to its full extent by U Thant in Round Two and Round Three when finally bringing Katanga to heel.[52] This expanded mandate involved actions such as the continued application of force both to prevent civil war and to expel the mercenaries from Katanga, which fell under the quasi-legal stance taken by Hammarskjöld and were later justified under a rapidly expanded mandate for self-defence and freedom of movement within the UN force's area of operations. This expanded conception of freedom of movement and self-defence allowed for the aggressive pursuit of the policies of the UN, which, following the 21 February resolution, was ever more determined to support the territorial integrity of the Congo and was therefore geared toward the eventual downfall of the Katangan state.

    The precedent set by the actions of the United Nations was one that would alter international participation in African secessions. As mentioned, the 21 February resolution explicitly set the UN's conception of the maintenance of territorial integrity of the Congo as a precondition for the peaceful resolution of the Congo Crisis. It thus involved an implicit condemnation of secessionist struggles as threatening to both domestic and international peace and security. While this initially might not seem to be such a worrisome development, given the previous necessity for the Security Council to agree to actions under article 42, Hammarskjöld's efforts to create a mandate for his international peacekeeping and peace-enforcement force under articles 39 (determining threats to peace), 40 (provisional measures), and 99, without the direct invocation of 42, meant that now an international force could be created and wielded against secessionist threats with little difficulty, especially under the more aggressive leadership of U

Thant. The precedent of the UN's actions in the Katangan Secession set in place the idea not only that secession movements would be viewed as threats to international peace and order but also that the UN could enforce its mandates against such a threat.

Beyond the central international authority of the United Nations, another transnational organization came into being informed by the experiences of Katanga and the foreign agitation that maintained it. This new international body was the Organization of African Unity (OAU), and its own core values would alter the trajectory of African secession struggles. The initial idea behind the organization was found in the dreams of the early Pan-Africanists, who had hoped that the shared historical experiences of the African people would help them come together and create an international organization that could both defend the sovereignty of the newly decolonized states and help better the lives of all Africans. While there were varying conceptions behind what form this organization would eventually take, with a more radical bloc called the Casablanca group looking for a strongly integrated federation while the more moderate Monrovia Group wanted a looser, more decentralized organization, a compromise was struck throughout the discussions in early 1963, and all thirty-two initial member states combined their efforts to formally create the OAU. The organization's charter, signed on 25 May 1963, promised in article III both "non-interference in the internal affairs of states" and "Respect for sovereignty and territorial integrity of each State."[53] This effectively recognized the authority of the central government of each member state and pre-emptively established the unlawfulness of any attempt at partition. From the signing of the OAU's charter onward, any overt outside interference in any secession process became a prohibited action under the OAU agreements. This meant that even any separatist group would have to make do with its own limited resources and what little covert aid could be offered to it by sympathetic parties. So, while the processes of leadership, structure, army building, and the prosecution of conflict would repeat themselves and evolve as the circumstances changed, the intervention of outside forces, either for or against the secession of a region, became unheard of.

This combination of the UN's forceful rejection of Katanga's right to self-determination and the OAU's enshrinement of the existing state's sovereignty would set a twin precedent severely hampering any future attempts to separate from a recognized African sovereign state. Any further attempts would have to do without any significant outside assistance from either a continental or global ally, and even the recognition of any separatist government was cast into doubt as a result of the Congo Crisis. Because of all this, the international legal parameters set during and after the Katangan secession would affect every subsequent secessionist struggle on the continent.

The Congo Crisis, of which the Katangan secession was part, introduced the problems of postcolonial Africa to the world. Between a repressed bourgeoisie, inadequate infrastructure, Cold War manipulation, ethnic violence, and unstable governments, the Congo represented the worst experiences of the emergence of the independent African nations, while at the same time offering a testing ground for the international difficulties that would accompany widespread decolonization. The secession of Katanga offered several unique difficulties for both the African state and the international community. These difficulties would be echoed through the coming decades, and it was the experience of the Congo Crisis that informed the future decisions of the international community. The Katanga secession established the precedents to be used with regard to future separatist movements in Africa and the responses to them. As such, the trial by fire of the Katangan separatists would set patterns of secession that would last until the thawing of the Cold War, the return of the idea of the ethnic nation, and the collapse of both the international order and the stability of the African nations.

Map of Nigeria and Biafra

Copyright © 2014 Nathan E. McCormack and Charles G. Thomas

The Secession of Biafra, 1967–1970

The Nigerian Civil War, fought in an attempt to secure the secession of its breakaway eastern region known as Biafra, is remembered primarily by the world as a human tragedy of epic proportions, one where countless lives were lost when hunger became a weapon against the besieged Igbos. However, the case of Biafra was to have far more wide-ranging effects on the world, although they would prove more subtle than images of starving children. The war confirmed the supremacy of the Nigerian federal government, but it also signalled the end of the traditional power structures in the new multi-state nation. It also brought forth the understandable African cynicism of the motives of the greater world in their affairs, as arms poured into Nigeria from a multitude of would-be patrons but food and medicine was far less forthcoming. And finally, although none would notice at the time, the death of Biafra marked the final end to any hopes of Civil Secession on the continent of Africa.

THE CONTEXT OF BIAFRA

The Nigerian Civil War, like all civil wars and certainly the majority in this volume, did not exist in a vacuum. One may trace the earliest roots of the conflict back to the British administration, which welded three distinct regions into Southern Nigeria, administering the West, the Mid-West, and the East all as a coherent unit. These three regions were dominated by two majority ethnic groups, the Yoruba in the West and the Igbo in the East, with the Mid-West being inhabited by a mixture of these groups and a variety of minority peoples. There was a delicate balance between the regions, and as each were developed under the British "Dual Mandate,"¹ they became economically linked and yet still culturally distinct. British racial conceptions at the time led them to believe that the more Westernized and Christianized Igbos were the more promising material, and they quickly began developing the East as a centre of education and administration. While this did not please the Yoruba, the balance was maintained. However, this began to change in 1914 when Britain connected the previously separate Northern Nigeria to the South, making a single colony united under a single administration. At the time, the North was far less developed and remained a very conservative Islamic society due largely to Britain's policy of Indirect Rule, which had left traditional Islamic rulers and social systems in place. This, along with the size of the region, immediately set it as an imposing entity within the newly minted unified colony. However, this did not come to a head until Nigeria began to press for self-determination, with the Federal Republic of Nigeria gaining its independence on October 1, 1960. It was in the newly elected parliament of Nigeria that the size and monolithic leadership of the North stepped to the fore, allowing the conservative North to often dictate the course of the nation, even as Igbos had spread over the nation to function as necessary administrators.²

These feelings of the Easterners that they were subjects as opposed to citizens were exacerbated by the resource distribution within the nation. While the North was easily the largest of the regions, it consisted largely of grasslands that were used for herding and agriculture. While these provided an economic base, it was the West and the East that provided the true engine to the Nigerian economy. The West, while also agrarian, held the city of Lagos, which was the capital and also primary port of the nation, bringing with it considerable trade and economic activity. However, even this economic power was dwarfed by the East, where oil had been discovered in the Niger River Delta in 1956. The discovery of commercially viable oil deposits and their development by Shell–British Petroleum, Mobil, Texaco, and Gulf Oil, quickly caused the value of the region to skyrocket. However, despite the massive oil wealth of the region, upon independence much of that wealth fell under the control of the Northern-dominated government despite the environmental costs and local involvement in the East, with the soaring production eventually providing nearly half of the revenue of the whole country. This led many Eastern leaders to question the rights of the

North to control what they saw as their resource, especially as they watched much of the wealth drawn forth leave their region to enrich the other parts of the country.[3]

It was these essential political and economic tensions between the large, conservative North and the small, developed East that would form the backdrop leading up to the Civil War itself, but it would be first a pair of failed coups that would rend the nation apart. The first coup occurred on January 15, 1966, when a small group of young army officers who were predominantly Igbo struck across the nation in an attempt to seize power from what they argued was a corrupt system of governance.[4] The final straw for this movement was the Western regional election, where mass confusion, corruption, and irregular reporting led to hotly contested results and over 300 persons were arrested for various electoral violations. In the end, Chief Samuel Akíntọ́lá was elected premier of the West and his party, the Nigerian National Democratic Party, was awarded the majority of the seats, but the fiercely contested election became symbolic of the decay of the Nigerian democracy.

Despite their stated goals of overthrowing corrupt elements of the government, the young officers' coup itself failed, succeeding only in spilling a large amount of blood and driving the country into the control of the ranking senior army officer, Major General Aguiyi-Ironsi,[5] who had rallied the loyal troops into a counterweight to the mutineers and secured the surrender of the young dissidents. However, it was not so much the success or failure that was notable, it was the blood that was spilled: the political leadership of the Northern power bloc. In a single night the officers of the coup killed Sir Ahmadu Bello, the Sardauna of Sokoto and chief political power of the North; and Sir Abubakar Tafawa Balewa, the Federal Prime Minister and also a northerner; as well as Akíntọ́lá, premier of the Western Region and a key political ally of the Sardauna. Beyond these political casualties, the plotters also managed to slay Brigadier General Maimalari and Lt. Col. Largema, two senior officers and both Northerners themselves. While there were several other casualties, in the wake of the failed coup and the arrest of the plotters these losses were sorely felt in the North.[6] In one night the majority of their political and military leadership had been slaughtered by a handful of Southern junior officers, and there were few if any likely candidates to replace them. It did not escape the notice of the

Northerners that of the plotters, five of the six were Igbos and that General Ironsi, himself an Igbo but a political neutral, did nothing worse than imprison them. However, despite organized acts of violence against the Igbos in the North, Ironsi was able to keep the fragile nation together under four regional military governors, one for each region and representing its interests along with the regional administrations now under military control. The nation seemed to be stabilized and perhaps even on the road to a restoration of a renewed democratic government. Then on 29 July a second coup attempt rent the fragile nation apart a second time.

The reasons for the second coup attempt were far more straightforward than the supposed motives of the first. The North had been marginalized and the majority of its citizens were confused and angry at the losses of their leadership and the non-punishment of the youthful mutineers. Stories and theories of an Igbo plot to control the nation began to make their way through the North and the halls of the military.[7] It did not help that while a large percentage of the enlisted and non-commissioned personnel of the army were Northerners, the highest ranks of the military were from the South and a plurality of these positions were held by Igbos.[8] With the government now run by the military and with a majority of the army's leadership and potential leadership from the South, the North found itself in a difficult and dangerous position. It already hungered for revenge for the losses of its traditional leaders, and now the government seemed to be slipping further and further from its grasp. The final straw was General Ironsi's well-intended but politically tone-deaf declaration of an abolishment of the federal system of government.[9] He had intended to place the nation under a unitary government that would control the nation as a whole without the worry of regional interests. Unfortunately, this only confirmed the hysterical fears of dominance that were driving the North further from the central government and sent the Northern elements of the Army into revolt.[10]

When the coup erupted on that July evening, it unleashed a torrent of bloodshed that far surpassed the earlier deaths of the first coup. Unlike the January coup, which narrowly targeted the political and military leadership the plotters saw as corrupt, the July coup wrought indiscriminate violence upon any and all Easterners in the military. General Ironsi and his host in Ibadan, Lt. Col. Fajuyi, were both beaten and killed by a young Northern officer and his men.[11] At army garrisons in Abeokuta, Ibadan, Ikeja, Lagos, Kaduna, and Kano, Eastern troops and officers were arrested, tortured, and killed by their Northern colleagues. The final toll was reported as 43 officers and 170 other ranks killed.[12] However, much as in the first coup, the young officers in charge could not seize total power and were finally brought under the control of the military governors, and Lt. Col. Yakubu "Jack" Gowon was placed into the position of head of state. Although Brigadier General Ogundipe was the senior officer of those remaining, he refused the position and instead endorsed Gowon's ascension, which was also supported by Commodore Wey of the Navy and Lt. Col. Adebayo as the smoke cleared over the fractured military. In the end, the coup was brought to heel with two major demands still hanging in the air: that the republic be split into its constituent parts and that both Northerners and Southerners be repatriated to their regions of origin. Neither of these was to be accomplished, although the North did reportedly come within a hair's breadth of declaring its own secession.[13] Instead, on August 1, Gowon took to the airwaves to assure the nation that he would do "all in my power to stop any further bloodshed and to restore law, order, and confidence in all parts of the country."[14]

Unfortunately, this proved far more easily said than done. While Gowon attempted to bring together an ad hoc constitutional conference in September, the North would only accede to a loose federation before turning a neat about-face a few days later. While the delegates were still dealing with these developments, news of a new outbreak of violence interrupted the proceedings. However, this time it was not the military but the civilian populace of the North, which began a massive wave of organized violence against the Igbos still living there. In the towns of Makurdi, Gboko, Zaria, Gombe, Jos, Sokoto, and Kaduna the communities of expatriate Easterners were beaten, robbed, and killed with abandon.[15] This set off a massive exodus of the Northern Igbos who wished to return to their home region. As they arrived, even greater tales of cruelty and malice emerged. Young women had been accosted and forced to watch their children killed. Men were beaten to death in the streets. A lifetime's worth of possessions were stripped and burned out of sheer hatred. In the end, estimates of the dead ranged anywhere from 3,000 to 10,000 and there were anywhere from 500,000 to 2 million Igbos driven from their homes, but the numbers past a certain point were immaterial.¹⁶ While initially the North looked to be a potent source for secessionist sentiment, now their feeling of marginalization had passed and instead the East burned with rage at both the North for their violence and the central government for not intervening to end the pogrom.

This was not the first time violence had broken out against Easterners living in the North. Following the first coup there had been riots targeting the Eastern communities, with hundreds of casualties, that had also sparked a wave of migration back to the East. However, in the weeks following the coup the military governor of the East, Lt. Col. Odumegwu Ojukwu, prevailed upon the Igbos to return to their Northern homes for the good of the nation's economy.¹⁷ Now, as the leader of the dissenting and increasingly separatist Eastern state, Ojukwu could not countenance such violence again. When the ad hoc Constitutional Committee reconvened in October there were no Easterners present. The leadership of the Eastern region had decided that a united Nigeria held nothing for them and were already on their way to secession. While there was some delay in the process due to a meeting between Gowon's federal government and Ojukwu in Aburri, Ghana, in January 1967 that seemed to produce a confederal solution, the agreement itself was later rejected by the federal government as unworkable. While both sides still attempted to hammer together an agreement, the North, West, and Mid-West fell into line behind Gowon's initiatives to withdraw Northern troops from the West and create a number of new states within the federation to spread power more evenly throughout. However, for the East this plan had many problems. The Eastern government saw this as an attempt to partition their areas of control and divide their power. In addition, this would have removed the valuable oil-producing areas from their control, a complete non-starter as far as the Enugu government was concerned.¹⁸ In the end, diplomacy could be taken only so far, and on 27 May 1967 the Consultative Assembly in Enugu declared the Eastern region "a free sovereign and independent State by the name of the Republic of Biafra."¹⁹

The Biafran War

The war did not start immediately, but by this point it was inevitable. The first shots fired on 6 July must have come almost as a relief for both sides after waiting so long for the final shoe to drop. While the Federal forces still looked upon the conflict as a limited police action, the Biafrans were in deadly earnest. However, it was the Federals who would take the initiative, seizing Ogoja, Nsukka, and the valuable port terminal of Bonny in the first two weeks of the conflict and seeming to be firmly in control of the military situation.[20] Unfortunately for the Federal cause, these early gains were to be answered in shockingly short order with the eruption of the boldest stroke of the war on August 9. Biafran forces mounted in a column of more than 100 vehicles began a lightning dash west across the Niger and into the Mid-West state. A simultaneous mutiny of Mid-West officers gave the Biafrans control of the region with hardly a shot being fired, and the column continued its hasty advance toward the Western seats of power at Ibadan and Lagos.[21] In their wake a Mid-Western separatist regime was already being put into place, further fracturing the Federal government. However, there was no parallel uprising of Yorubas in the West and the column itself was halted by the hastily assembled Federal 2nd Division outside of Ore and forced to turn back.[22] Their retreat was hastened by the collapse of the separatist Mid-Western government in a cloud of political infighting and the region's reoccupation by Federal forces on the 22nd of September.[23] The military situation did not get any better for the Biafrans on the other fronts, as Federal amphibious operations claimed the port of Warri and in the North the 1st Division of the Federal forces threatened Enugu, the Biafran capital. The Biafran military and political administrations subsequently were moved to Umuahia. The only offsetting victories the Biafrans could claim were a series of counteroffensives that recaptured Nsukka and Opi, which had previously fallen to the Federals.

October brought only worse news for the beleaguered Biafran forces, as Enugu finally fell on October 4 to rapturous applause in Lagos. Eleven days later the important port of Calabar fell to another amphibious operation. By the end of the year the Federal troops advancing from the southern coast and Northern command had captured Ekong, the last remaining gateway the region had to Cameroon. Meanwhile, the Biafran forces managed to hold the important town of Onitsha on the Niger River, but only barely, and they were slowly being squeezed out of the border regions and cut off from the rest of the world. The beginning of 1968 did not prove to be any different, although the Biafrans carried out several counteroffensives and won a surprising amount of territory back from the advancing Federals. The Biafrans announced the recapture of Opi and Adaru and fell into a fierce fight for the industrial centre of Akwa. However, these gains were rapidly overshadowed by the Federal offensives in late March. Onitsha was again their objective, and this time the Federal forces were successful after a five-hour battle on 21 March 1968.[24] However, no matter how low morale might have been after this loss, the Biafrans were rejuvenated on 13 April when Tanzania officially recognized the state of Biafra. This was followed by recognition by Gabon on 8 May, the Ivory Coast on 14 May, and finally Zambia on 20 May.[25] This was an extraordinary step, one that set off peals of joy in besieged Biafra, as with international recognition they might actually be given their sovereignty by the greater international community. This was unfortunately not to be, as the intentions behind these nations' recognition were certainly not to break the internal dynamics of the war or the Federal government's prerogative in waging the war. Instead, each did so for political reasons that will be dealt with in the following sections. And despite this brief period of exultation, the war continued to be lost one battle at a time. By 19 May, the vital port and oil refining facility of Port Harcourt fell to the Federal 3rd Marine Commando Division.[26] Not only did this deprive the Biafrans of their best refinery, but with the loss of Port Harcourt Biafra was now completely isolated from the outside world. The only way outside aid could enter was by being airlifted, a tenuous lifeline given the Federal side's marked air superiority. The Biafran side had begun the war at a marked disadvantage in terms of both manpower and equipment, and the loss of these lifelines essentially closed the door on any chance of evening the scales.

Despite now being in what militarily was an untenable position, the Biafrans refused to end their struggle. In June they launched another series of counterattacks that retook several towns along the Imo River and drove the Federal forces five miles back. These counterattacks were the last major operations before a lull in the war centred around the peace talks being held in Niamey, Niger, under the auspices of the OAU. When these talks collapsed in July, both sides returned to their previous states of aggression and the Federal troops began operations aimed at dissecting the Igbo heartland. Drives toward Nnewi and Aba met stiff resistance but were not halted, and on September 4 the Federal forces captured both Aba and the rail junction at Oworo. The capture of Owerri on the 16th reduced Biafra to a small rectangle of territory that was supplied by two makeshift airports on opposite sides of the state. All signs pointed to a collapse of Biafra by the end of 1968. However, as often happens in war, the circumstances altered and the conventional wisdom was upended.

Until this time Biafra had been depending largely on sparse shipments of outdated small arms and large quantities of locally fabricated ordinance, most notably the homemade mines known as *ogbunigwe*. It was not unusual to see sentries handing their relief their own rifles, as there were not enough arms to fully equip the whole army.[27] Meanwhile they were facing a Federal army that was well equipped with state-of-the-art arms bought from the international market. Britain continued to supply small arms and munitions in what they considered their traditional role. When they refused to provide larger ordinance or aircraft, the Nigerians turned to the Soviets, who leapt at the chance to gain a greater toehold in Africa's most populous state and access to the oil of the delta once the conflict was ended. Before long, large quantities of Soviet arms, along with Czech Delfin fighters and Russian MiGs, were streaming into the Federal armouries. While it cannot be said that the differential in armaments was solely responsible for the Biafran reverses, it is impossible to contend that it did not have a considerable effect on the conflict. This concept was driven to the fore when in late 1968 a large shipment of modern arms arrived at Uli and immediately changed the tenor of the conflict. With these new materials of war, the Biafrans surged forward again and recaptured Okigwi and threatened the Federal hold on Onitsha and Owerri.[28] A subsequent advance on the Aba front threw back Federal forces but could not capture the town. Several local counteroffensives forced the Federal forces back on their heels, and the year ended with the Biafrans having risen from near collapse to seize the initiative from the Federal Nigerian forces.

The early months of 1969 passed without any significant changes in the battlefronts. The Biafran forces seemed to be marshalling themselves for another effort while the Federals were continuing their now-frequent air raids in an attempt to further weaken Biafran logistics and morale. It took until April for either side to be ready to move, and then it was again the Federal forces that leapt forward. Now using tracked armour for better off-road capability, the Nigerian forces thrust toward the provisional capital of Biafra at Umuahia.[29] The Biafrans could slow but not stop the assault and began to evacuate the town. With the fall of Umuahia, the only connection left with the outside world was the radio transmitter at the Uli airfield, and the remaining territory of Biafra was about to be split in two. In this desperate situation, the Biafrans again launched an offensive hoping to stave off final defeat, and yet again they succeeded. They retook Owerri and drove back the vaunted 3rd Marine Commando Division several miles, badly damaging the Nigerian Division's morale and reputation. They also launched a successful offensive north of Umuahia and smashed a significant number of Federal formations, halting yet another Nigerian "Final Push" on Biafra. By May 1969 the situation was still dire for the Biafrans, who had been reduced to 10 percent of their original territory, but they had again staved off the Federal forces, which halted to reorganize and reshuffle the leadership of the three divisions engaged while the rainy season caused a general halt to the conflict.[30]

However, by mid-1969 the writing was on the wall. The Biafran forces were reduced to a single airstrip for supply, and even the humanitarian relief flights from Joint Church Aid were arriving with less frequency than ever. The Federal military had established a fierce blockade of all food and military supplies since the beginning of the war, and since the fall of Port Harcourt the only supplies for Biafra came via limited air flights. Their nation was starving and running out of any and all necessities of conflict or even life. In this dark hour Ojukwu, still the supreme leader of Biafra and the embodiment of its struggle, issued the Ahiara Declaration, which demanded an alteration to what he claimed was the "Biafran Revolution."[31] Property was to become communal, the administration was to be stripped of its fat and indolence, and the military was to be transformed into a "Peoples' Army" to better pursue the goals of revolutionary Biafra. More than this, Ojukwu's pronouncement lambasted the perceived corruption in Biafra, declaring that some were profiting from the peoples' misery, taking bribes or living expansively while others suffered. Ojukwu declared that the revolutionary principles he laid down would transport Biafra beyond these ills and allow a final victory.

While revolutionary fronts had been tasting success in Africa for years, by the time of his declaration, Biafra did not prove to be revolutionary. Instead the Ahiara Declaration became a *cri de coeur*, a last unrealistic demand from a leader who had led his people into ruin in a fight against their larger hosts. It would also become emblematic of Ojukwu's overall leadership of the secession, wherein impossible demands had already been placed on his people and only excuses offered for the failure against a stronger foe. Six months later the final collapse of Biafra began and none of the Ahiara principles had come to pass, the battered secessionist state too weary and beleaguered to bother with creating a revolution while they continued to starve. The November 17, 1969 offensive of the Federal troops met little resistance, and the first major breakthrough began on the Southern front, where the 3rd Marine Commando Division shattered the fragile Biafran lines. The 3rd Division captured the Aba-Umuahia road and pressed on to link up with the 1st Division in Umuahia itself. Owerri fell to the Federal forces for the last time on January 9, 1970, and their forces continued advancing toward Uli and the last airstrip in the nation. It was captured on January 12, but this was essentially an afterthought. Ojukwu and several members of his cabinet had flown out the previous day and left General Philip Effiong, his chief of staff, to conclude the war. On the 12th, in the face of continuing Federal advances on all fronts and the withdrawal of the central leadership of the struggle, General Effiong broadcast an announcement of Biafra's surrender. On January 14 he made his way to Lagos to seal the unconditional surrender of Biafra, and on the 15th the Republic of Biafra ceased to exist and its territory was formally reintegrated into the Federal structure of Nigeria.

As a coda to the conflict, it must be noted that despite the acrimony with which the war was waged and the widespread fears of genocide harboured by many of the Igbos, the aftermath of the conflict was surprisingly gentle. General Gowon decreed that in this war there were "No Victors and no Vanquished"[32] and that the nation must be made whole again. To promote this reconciliation, the Federal government promised no "Nuremberg Trials" and a general amnesty was declared for all of the secessionist combatants. While several Biafran senior army officers and administrators were detained for a period of time, there was no further action taken against them except for the occasional barring from further government employment. Further down the chain of command, the Nigerian forces in general behaved well. While there was looting and violence on the part of many occupying troops initially, this regrettable action still paled in comparison to the normal aftermath of such civil wars. For the most part, it has been reported that throughout the conflict the Federal forces had behaved well within the "Code of Conduct" that had been established by General Gowon at the start. Overall, it was a very mild way to end the war, despite the widespread starvation and bombing and the deep pathological fears of annihilation held by the Igbos. In fact, the only true anger displayed by the victors was toward the outside powers who rushed in offering humanitarian aid following the collapse of Biafra. To the Federal government, this offer of aid by such nations as France and Portugal following their integral roles in prolonging the conflict was insulting and crude. As will be discussed, overall the world at large had not altered the course of the conflict so much as prolonged it. It was Nigerian arms that began and ended it, and they now wished to reconcile themselves without the continuing interference of the outside world.

Civil Secessions Compared

It was increasingly common during the Biafra conflict to compare it to the previous attempt at secession by Katanga, if for no reason than temporal proximity and the fact that they both occurred on the continent of Africa. Biafran commentators and those sympathetic to their cause aggressively opposed these comparisons, as the case of Katanga was anathema to the other African nations and any comparisons to this earlier case could only hinder the attempts of the Biafrans to gain vital foreign recognition of their struggle and sovereignty. In the details these commentators were indeed correct. Whereas Katanga nakedly courted hated neo-colonial powers such as Belgium and Rhodesia, Biafra was engaged in a struggle for the self-determination of an oppressed region.[33] Few could argue that the Katangans were exploited economically within the Congolese system,[34] no matter what their political difficulties, but the Igbos and the many peoples of the East could argue that their struggle was about security and the failure of their host state to provide it.³⁵ In these differences the Biafrans were indeed correct, and while the Katangan ideology was abhorrent to the states of Africa the Biafran one found sympathy; nevertheless, their methods and structures of secession had many parallels—hence their grouping in this volume under the heading of Civil Secessions.

To begin with, like Katanga, Biafra existed in the form of a state before the secession began. The Eastern region had existed as a constituent state within the federation well before the coup attempts fractured it, with its boundaries having been established with the earliest political divisions of the country and official limited self-government codified in the Regional Assemblies set up in 1946.³⁶ By Nigerian independence in 1960, control of this state was placed in an administration and government that were democratically elected and put into place by the people of the region—although again this changed following the coup attempts, when Ojukwu was put into place as the military governor of the region.³⁷ However, even then the administration of the region existed in its pre-set form; it simply functioned under a different chief executive until the day the secession began. Even after secession this same framework was retained, although now the region took on even more sovereign duties. This was made easier by the large number of skilled administrators and politicians who fled to the Eastern regions following the pogroms in the North. Thus, at the time of secession and throughout the majority of it, Biafra was a civil state, with set borders and a pre-set administration defining its existence. Put simply, it was a state in search of its sovereignty, not a nation seeking a state.

However, this pronouncement and this volume's opposition of the ideas of a state and a nation might need clarification in terms of Ojukwu's definition of Biafra as "Africa's first Nation-state."³⁸ In this he obviously had Biafra in mind as a state of the Igbos, constituted for their protection and the promotion of their economic and political goals. However, this is problematic for a simple reason: Biafra at the time of its secession contained a number of minority ethnic groups, such as Ibibios, Efiks, and Ijaws.³⁹ These groups were even represented within the higher ranks of the secessionist state, such as Philip Effiong, Ojukwu's chief of staff. In fact, it was even these marginal peoples that felt the horrors of the war first, as they tended to live in the border regions of the Eastern State and their homes were battlegrounds long before the Igbo heartland was. Of course, it was also during this period when the paranoia of the Igbo leadership cast away the minority groups, as they blamed the rapid Federal advances on sabotage by their minority neighbours, only to have the same military failures happen in the Igbo heartland where a supposedly loyal populace would have made them impossible.[40] In any event, the conception of Biafra as a nation-state only applied following their losses of 1967 and early 1968, when indeed Biafra was reduced to simply the Igbo heartland and the fears of an ethnic genocide forced the populace into a siege mentality. This does little to change the fact that the original formation of Biafra remained one of a pre-existing civil multi-ethnic state that only changed during the long, psychologically torturous struggle for the Igbo lands.

In addition, much as Katanga argued its case for sovereignty based on the original separate administration of the *Comité spéciale du Katanga*, the Biafrans also pointed to colonial administration and boundaries to justify their separatist goals. The Eastern Region, much like the other regions of Nigeria, had essentially been administered separately until their being joined first with the Lagos Colony into Southern Nigeria in 1912 and then combined with the North to form the state of Nigeria in 1914. With this in mind, the Biafrans argued that they had always been a separate state within a federation and now that that federation no longer was able to provide safety to their region, they were free to remove themselves.[41] This sentiment was compounded by the confusion following the two coups of 1966. While the civilian government had been corrupt, it had been the sovereign government of the Federation of Nigeria and embodied the constitution that held that union together. Following the first coup, General Ironsi assumed power in what can be at least thinly painted as a legal assumption of authority—while there was no constitutional provision for the military assumption of power, it was granted to him by the federal government, which saw him as the lone figure able to control the situation.[42] Ironsi was in the process of reforming that central government when he was slain in the July coup that overturned the system—and here is where the crux of the argument lies. Whereas Ironsi was invested with his power by the constitutional government of Nigeria, General Gowon never was.[43] In the wake of the July coup Gowon was simply placed at the head of the government by a military that was already bucking the constitutional government. As such, the Biafrans could argue that their secession from the state of Nigeria was historically correct: the federation they had belonged to had ceased to exist upon the military seizure of the government. In the absence of any future agreement (such as the failed Aburri Agreement) the Eastern region returned to its own separate sovereignty. Again, and as will be witnessed repeatedly throughout secession attempts, the historical legitimacy of the secession was stressed and argued throughout the military campaign to win that sovereignty.

Much like in Katanga as well, the leadership of the Biafran secession was composed of "New Men" of Africa and the idea of the state was imposed in a "top-down" method. The primary figure of the secession and the one who would come to dominate the struggle was Lt. Col. (later General) Emeka Odumegwu Ojukwu.[44] There are few figures who inhabit the history of their struggles as much as Ojukwu, who from the first to the last was the motive power of the rebellion and remains a controversial figure in Nigerian history. Emeka Ojukwu was born in 1943 to a self-made shipping millionaire who had been knighted by the Queen of England. He grew up in a world of privilege, receiving an exceptional education both in Nigeria and abroad and finished his schooling at Oxford. He served in the administration of Nigeria for two years but then found what he felt was his true calling, in the Army. He joined in 1957 and underwent officer training at Eaton Hall, earning his commission shortly after. Ojukwu served in the UN force in the Congo like most ambitious young Nigerian officers of his generation and proved himself an excellent officer. During the January 1966 coup attempt he was serving in Kano and quickly took control of that northern city and declared its loyalty to the federal government shortly after. For this loyalty he was declared the military governor of the Eastern Region under Ironsi's government. It was during this time that he urged the refugee Igbos to return to their homes to repair the economy of the North. In the aftermath of the July coup, he refused to rejoin the new central government, and thus sparked the secession of Biafra.

Throughout the secession Ojukwu controlled all aspects of the state. Throughout the conflict a series of official and unofficial peace talks were held, in which Ojukwu's vision of Biafra dominated whether he was present or not.[45] In terms of the military he determined to a great extent where men and material were allocated, as was extremely apparent in the case of his period of favouritism toward mercenary officer Rolf Steiner, who saw his command grow from a company to a brigade during a period of a little over a year.⁴⁶ As the conflict began to look more hopeless, Ojukwu entrenched himself further, and in a final attempt to turn the tide issued his "Ahiara Declaration," a last-ditch attempt to create a revolutionary state that could withstand the growing tide of the Federal military. Even in the end it was deemed necessary that he should flee the failing state to allow it to surrender. The stated reason was that he was leaving "in search of peace."⁴⁷ It seems far more likely that he indeed believed his statement that "I did this [fleeing Biafra] knowing that whilst I live Biafra lives."⁴⁸ Seeing how completely he embodied the state, it is hard to argue with either his contention that Biafra as an idea would live on or the connection between his leaving and the East's relatively peaceful reintegration into the federation.

This is not to say he was the only major figure of the Biafran state but simply that he overshadowed the rest to such a degree that they seem to have had far less import in the state itself. However, several leading figures, both in the military and without, indeed embodied the new bourgeois elite of Africa. General Philip Effiong, Ojukwu's chief of staff, had also served as an officer in the Nigerian military before the coups wracked the nation. He was connected by the old ties across the forces and considered General Gowon an old friend. Beyond this, he embodied the old Sandhurst training–based class-consciousness of the military, with one reporter noting, "Until the very end Effiong looked like a British Staff general—a polished Sam Browne belt, a sword for ceremonial occasions and a chauffeur-driven, khaki-coloured English Humber car bearing a General's flag."⁴⁹ In many ways, he reflected the bourgeois nature of the militaries on both sides. As far as the administration of Biafra, a large number of the senior administrators had been the educated elite of Nigeria before the breakup. Such figures as Dr. Kenneth Dike, Dr. Michael Okpara, the renowned author Chinua Achebe, and N. U. Akpan all served within the Biafran state. Admittedly this was easier for the Biafrans, as they had made up the majority of the trained administrators and middle management of the old federation before the split, but the fact remains that militarily and politically, the ideology and programs of the state of Biafra were an elite project from beginning to end, guided by the pre-secession officialdom of the region and peoples. While Ojukwu's Ahiara Declaration did make grand gestures toward mass nationalism and a "people's war," these concepts never arose, with the Biafrans' army at that point simply unable to continue the struggle.

Although it did eventually give way, the Biafran army performed acts of untold valour and nearly impossible bravery. This was even more astonishing given the ad hoc basis of its training and founding, which had its roots in the initial surge of nationalism and the employment of the high number of Igbo army officers who chose to serve the Biafran cause.[50] Recruitment proceeded at a brisk pace from the time that secession seemed probable, and by the high point of the war the army most likely had 30,000 to 40,000 men under arms.[51] These in turn were organized into five divisions that consisted mostly of infantry. There were also a number of special formations, including the Biafran Organization of Freedom Fighters (BOFF), a force hand-picked and trained to serve as a behind-the-lines guerrilla force.[52] They were mostly active in the latter years of the war and had little effect overall on the conflict. Perhaps the other major "special" force to emerge in the conflict was the 4th Commando Brigade, commanded by the German ex–Foreign Legionnaire Rolf Steiner. These fighters were recognizable by the death's head patch their commanding officer chose as their unit insignia and were trained to mostly fight as light infantry and skirmishers, with quick raids and ambushes being their forte.[53] Unfortunately the unit, which eventually reached reported numbers as high as 10,000, took high casualties in a number of engagements where it was committed to frontal assaults, including outside of Onitsha and Owerri. Steiner himself was eventually arrested after getting drunk and striking Ojukwu in a rage after one such headlong attack was ordered. After he was deported from Biafra the unit passed from the notice of history. Still, overall the Biafran army was notable for its high morale and endurance, with its members obviously fighting on and even counterattacking long after the war itself was strategically unwinnable.

Unfortunately for the Biafrans, throughout the conflict they had to deal with shortages and inadequacies of equipment. At the outbreak of the conflict the Biafrans had only what arms those soldiers deserting the Federal Army for the Biafran cause had brought with them and the sparse equipment held in the Eastern region's arsenals. While immediately arms-buying expeditions were sent out across Africa and Europe, all too often the Biafrans were sold substandard equipment or even just plainly robbed of their funds by untrustworthy gun runners. There were reports of artillery that had been bought ending up rusted beyond repair, of planes purchased whose wings were lost in transit, and of agents simply drawing money from accounts and disappearing.[54] That Biafra ended up armed at all was primarily due to two reasons: clandestine French intervention and the magnificent ingenuity of the Biafrans themselves. On the matter of the French, they drifted into semi-support of Biafra in 1968, coming extremely close to recognition but never quite crossing that line.[55] What they did do was begin to filter arms and ammunition into Biafra through their francophone African allies in the Ivory Coast and Gabon. At its high point the stream was reported to be 200 tons a week of arms and ammunition airlifted into Biafra.[56] These went a long way toward equipping the secessionist forces with modern weaponry and were almost entirely responsible for the stiffening of Biafran resistance from 1968 on. As to the natural ingenuity of the Biafrans themselves, this was readily apparent in the massive amount of fabricated arms that made their presence known on the battlefield. Although the Biafrans had no armour to speak of, jury-rigged armed cars were made out of tractors and large trucks with armoured plates welded to them.[57] Their ordinance was certainly not ever anything magnificent, originally consisting of a battery of 105 mm howitzers and several 81 mm mortars. This was quickly supplemented by a mind-boggling variety of homemade weaponry, often taking advantage of the large amount of petroleum available to the Biafrans at the beginning of the war.[58] Shops made their own rockets fabricated from old pipes. Grenades were put together from scrap metal. Perhaps the single most well-known weapon of the Biafrans was the *ogbunigwe*, the homemade landmine, made often from spare metal drums filled with explosives, old petroleum, and scrap metal for shrapnel. These deadly creations made their appearance all over the war zone and quickly became an easy and formidable weapon to use against the Federal forces. It is admirable that this late-arriving stream of imported weaponry and the hasty creation of homemade arms was enough to sustain the volunteer and amateur Biafran military for the duration of the war, especially against a Federal Army that was equipped with the best weaponry money could buy from the British, the Czechs, and the Soviets.

Of course, despite their valour and ingenuity, the Biafrans were not served well by the strategy and tactics adopted by their leadership. Given the spit-and-polish Sandhurst roots of the Biafran officer class, their adoption of static and conventional formations was not entirely unexpected, but it did not offer any advantages against the larger, better-equipped, and equally Sandhurst-officered enemy. What this matchup generally devolved into was a very strange conventional engagement, where the Biafrans would dig into defensive posts strung across the Federal line of advance. These could take any form, from quickly dug ad hoc earthworks to well-sited and well-constructed concrete emplacements. The Biafrans would fight well from these positions for a time but then generally pull back from them when Federal forces strengthened their push or increased the mass of artillery fire on the Biafran positions.[59] The Biafrans then would regroup in the next set of prepared positions to await the cautious Federal advance and the pattern would repeat itself. When the Biafrans took the offensive, it often took the form of battering frontal assaults, such as the ones outside Onitsha and Owerri. While occasionally these took the Federals by surprise and forced them back, they often proved to be very costly, in victory or defeat.

This is not to say that the war was not without imaginative tactics. The Biafran stroke across the Mid-West at the outset of the war was a masterful idea that could have altered the course of the conflict within its first few weeks. Unfortunately, after its failure there never were the resources to try it again, especially against a now wary Federal Army. The Biafrans also tasted considerable success with more irregular tactics. The ambush at Abagana by the troops of Joe "Hannibal" Achuzie was a huge boost to morale and caused severe shortages in petrol for the Federal Onitsha front for a considerable length of time.[60] Rolf Steiner's 4th Commando had several notable successes behind the Federal lines before being bloodied in the conventional struggles around Onitsha. Lastly, the aforementioned BOFF was trained specifically for guerrilla operations to hopefully harass, isolate, and destroy Federal formations in the final year of the war. Unfortunately, these guerrilla tactics never became widespread for a number of reasons, the first being that the war zone that was Biafra could never support a popular guerrilla movement nor offer it the concealment it would need to consistently operate. Successful guerrilla struggles require either wide-open spaces within which fighters can spread themselves out or challenging terrain where large numbers might be concealed; Biafra at the time offered neither. It had been reduced to a small enclave surrounded by a formidable blockade, an enclave that offered neither space nor concealment. The other major reason was that Ojukwu rightly saw a resort to guerrilla operations as a final admission of failure—that Biafra could no longer exist as a formal state and that the Federals had defeated it. In the end, the Biafran forces ended up fighting a mainly conventional war, one that they were ill-equipped to fight against a larger, better-armed, and motivated opponent. Although their tactics did not help them win it, again it is extraordinary that the conflict lasted as long as it did.

Although the basis of the Biafran secession was as different as night and day from that of the Katanga secession, it did share some of its characteristics. Like the Katanga secession, it was a Civil Secession, meaning a secession of a pre-structured state from its host political structure. While later on the Biafran struggle took on ethnic nation-state overtones, this was only after the original state was compromised to such an extent that secession on any terms was essentially impossible. In addition, this secession was offered quasi-legality by the constitutional history of the secessionist state and its relation with the host political body. The secession was also an elite project, constructed primarily by Emeka Ojukwu and shaped by his fellow educated bourgeois allies. While, as with Katanga, it did have popular internal support, its philosophy and ideology was entirely determined by the elites of its society. The army itself was a structured conventional affair staffed by professional officers. While its ranks remained generally amateur and some formations took on alternate structures, the general structure of the military was a conventional one shaped by European military tradition. Likewise, the tactics adopted were those of conventional warfare, of positional attack and defence against an enemy that used the same military philosophy. In the end, much as in the Katanga affair, these tactics were to prove disastrous against a better-armed and determined opponent.[61] Thus, while the secessions may be argued to have been worlds apart in a moral and political sense, they both bear the characteristics of the Civil Secessions.

The Failure of Civil Secession

While the conflict over Katanga began to define the limits and weaknesses of the Civil Secession in Africa, the events and ramifications of the Nigerian

Civil War rendered the practice of Civil Secession an impossibility, and none has been attempted since on African soil. This is due to a number of developments both in Africa and in the greater world political arena, but taken together they doomed the Biafran effort and established the ironclad precedent against Civil Secession—the declared secession of a governed territory with a hoped-for international recognition. The five major factors that combined to make Civil Secession impossible began with the denial of international legitimacy or a world forum for any secession attempts. The second factor was related, and it was the blanket condemnation of secession on the continent of Africa. While both of these had been hinted at in the Katanga case, the fact that they arose again in a moral case such as Biafra's set them in stone. The third was the relative paucity of military aid to the secessionists, in terms of both hardware and expertise. The Biafran war saw a mass failure of international military intervention and of the mercenaries who had been such a terror of African states since the Congo. The fourth was the readily apparent increasing ability of African states to act with strength. That the first secession occurred in the weak and anarchic Congo gave the undue impression that the average African state was unable to act swiftly in its own interest. Nigeria was a different animal altogether and altered the conception of an African state's military capabilities. Lastly, while it was easy to argue that Tshombe had been a cat's paw of the Belgian interests, Biafra and its collapse showed enough parallel weakness to close the door on the top-down conception of secession. The elite project of Biafra could no more sustain itself as a sovereign entity than could Katanga, and it became increasingly apparent that only a popular movement pushing from below could effect real change in African states. However, each of these factors is itself a complex action and reaction to the secession of Biafra and will be dealt with on an individual basis.

The international stage for secessions became very small during the course of the Nigerian Civil War. This is not to say that the world did not know of the war—it certainly did, and there are many excellent works currently in print discussing the foreign perception and projection of both the Federal Nigerian and Biafran sides to the conflict.[62] This pronouncement is also not intended to minimize the international relief efforts for the wounded and starving on both sides of the battle lines. However, one of the first major differences between the Congolese and Nigerian conflicts was the altered political role of the international community. In Katanga the international community was waist deep in the conflict. Belgium supplied copious amounts of arms, technicians, and officers to sustain the Katangan regime. The United Nations sent military formations from a dozen or more nations into the Congo to restore peace to the shattered country and bring the Katangans back into the fold. The conflict over the secession of Biafra would not see international intervention on nearly the same level. To begin with, the United Nations could only intervene directly if so requested by a member nation. This had been the case in the Congo when Patrice Lumumba requested UN peacekeepers be deployed to help quell the disturbances in his country. However, in the case of Biafra, UN intervention would require a direct request of Nigeria, a request that obviously was not forthcoming.[63] It therefore follows that the official UN policy was that it legally could not take part in the Nigerian conflict.[64] This inaction on the UN's part then left the door open for individual nations to take part in the conflict, and the Biafrans hoped for the help of one of the greater states of the world in their struggle. Such hopes were pinned on the United States, Britain, the USSR, and France, and with the limited exception of the last, the Biafrans were to be sorely disappointed.

At the outbreak of the conflict, the United States was already becoming more committed in their conflict in Vietnam and was growing increasingly concerned with Communist expansion. While they had already intervened to place Mobutu at the head of the Congolese state, they were loath to become heavily invested again in Africa. As such, they were suspicious of Biafra as a breakaway state and opposed it from the beginning, as Nigeria had always been seen as a potential US ally and a strong capitalist state. In addition, several US oil companies had interests in the region and preferred a strong central government to ensure their investments. As the conflict wore on, the Americans became more concerned with the humanitarian aspects of the conflict, but these concerns warred with the political desire to support the "One Nigeria" platform the United States had adopted from the start. In the end, although there were strong political clashes within Congress, the American position remained in support of the Federal side, and moreover that Nigeria itself was more properly within the British sphere of interest and should be left to them and the OAU.[65]

The British themselves were shocked and appalled at the bloodshed and conflict beginning in what had been perceived as a stable and economically developing Commonwealth nation. Unfortunately for their relations with all sides, this shock apparently led to a hesitant reaction on their own part, and after several sharp confrontations in Parliament the government was still undecided on what to do. Initially their instinct was to stop supplying arms to the Nigerian military, but this quickly became an impossible position to maintain, for two glaring reasons. The first was the massive amount of British business holdings in Nigeria that could be affected by such an unfriendly act. The second was the wholesale entrance of the Soviets into the Nigerian political arena, which forced Britain's hand. While initially they attempted to limit their own arms sales to the Nigerian military to what they defined as their "traditional" supply of arms such as small arms, anti-aircraft guns, light armoured cars and the like, following the whole-hog support of the Soviets in terms of arms, the British were forced to follow suit to retain their political influence in the country and also to support their access to the oil resources within the region. Despite acrimonious debate over the arms trade, the British began the war trending toward the Federal side and quickly entrenched themselves there for the duration of the conflict.[66]

Whereas the United States saw Nigeria as a keystone anti-communist state in Africa and Britain saw it as a member of its extended family of the Commonwealth, the USSR saw Nigeria as an opportunity. When the conflict blossomed into a full-scale conflagration and Britain faltered on supplying arms, the Soviets stepped quickly into the breach. In early 1967, Nigeria and the USSR signed a pact for cultural cooperation, and it was rumoured that an arms deal had been signed between the two as well. While this was denied, in short order Soviet cargo planes arrived at Kano airport bearing loads of aircraft parts and combat planes. By 1968 another agreement was signed providing for the exchange of experts between the two nations, and in 1969 Soviet warships officially visited Nigeria. Simply put, the USSR weighed its options and thought the case for Nigerian success and a future relationship was far more compelling. They supported the Federal government against the "imperialism of secession" from the start and supplied them with the materials and expertise to crush the rebellion.[67]

Lastly, of the four major powers France was the most mercurial. Initially holding themselves aloof, the French government only began issuing statements pertaining to the conflict a year after it had begun in earnest. Even these initial releases were only to inform the world that they had pronounced an arms embargo on both sides of the conflict. However, only six weeks after this statement of neutrality, the minister of information, M. Theune, enunciated a position supporting the ending of the war on the basis of self-determination for the Biafran people. The effect this had was electric, with numerous news venues clamouring for more information on the government's plans to assure this policy. On September 9, 1968, President de Gaulle himself all but recognized the state of Biafra with his proclamation, "In this affair France has aided, is aiding Biafra as far as possible. She has not carried out the act which would be decisive, the action of recognizing the Republic of Biafra, because she considers that the management of Africa is above all an affair for Africans."[68] However, despite his stopping short of outright recognition, he left the door open and was already said to be pressuring his francophone African allies to recognize Biafra themselves, as some already had. From this point on, France supplied arms, ammunition, medicine, and any other aid that they could surreptitiously ship to Biafra or route through their African allies. However, France was to be a false hope for the Biafrans. While it provided the methods to wage the war, it never provided them in the amount needed to win it. Instead French aid simply prolonged the struggle far longer than it was projected to be, for little merit at all.[69]

The remainder of the world outside Africa had very little bearing or comment on the conflict aside from humanitarian concerns. The latter became especially pronounced from 1968 on, when the Biafran propaganda began to be broadcast on the world stage. This information campaign, which was carefully coordinated and constructed to elicit sympathy, managed to bring a significant amount of global consciousness to the struggle. Especially as the struggle became one of hunger and privation on the Biafran side, the Biafran claims of genocide gained new life with the release of photos and press releases showing starving children. This in turn helped marshal a significant amount of humanitarian support for the Biafrans, although that did little to help them militarily.[70] There was some heartening of the Biafran cause when China declared its support, but this amounted to very little in terms of diplomacy or materials in the end. Perhaps the last farcical act was the recognition of Biafra by the Haitian regime of "Papa Doc" Duvalier. However, the fact remains that in the Biafran conflict there was no outside interference of the magnitude of either the United Nations or Belgium in the Congo. The most that any of the larger powers contributed to the conflict was an occasionally galling stream of armaments and, in the case of France, a maddeningly vague show of diplomatic support for the secessionist regime. As noted in the previous case, the Organization of African Unity had been founded in the interim and was generally viewed as the proper mediator of the conflict, under the assumption that African states were declared African business. So what of the OAU and the nations of Africa in this conflict?

Like many facets of the Biafran conflict, this is a question with both a long answer and a short answer. The short answer involves the Organization of African Unity, which from the outset attempted to serve as an arbiter and peacemaker within the conflict.[71] At their meeting in Kinshasa in 1967 the OAU immediately invoked article III and declared that the Biafran conflict was primarily an internal affair of the Federal Government of Nigeria.[72] Although they resolved to send a six-member consultative panel to Nigeria, they assured the federal government that they supported the territorial integrity of the state of Nigeria. This meeting was followed later by a second, in July 1968 in Niamey, which opened the possibility of lasting arbitration, but these hopes grew thinner as no real progress was made at subsequent meetings at Addis Ababa in August or the OAU Algiers summit in September. The problem at the heart of the matter was that although the OAU desired peace, they could not and would not recognize the Biafran government. Secession remained a proscribed act under the OAU charter, and the Biafrans and their struggle was, notwithstanding all other factors, illegal in the eyes of the organization.[73] This essentially crippled all hopes for either binding OAU arbitration on the matter or recognition of Biafra, both of which the secessionists had hoped for. Instead, in the resolutions adopted in both Kinshasa and Algiers, they and their struggle were written off aside from appeals for the federal government to work with them to ensure peace within the framework of Nigerian territorial integrity. The final resolution adopted following the Addis Ababa conference in September 1969 was the succinct restatement of the OAU's position: "Appeals solemnly and urgently to the two parties involved in the civil war to agree to preserve in the overriding interest of Africa, the unity of Nigeria."[74] Simply put, the OAU would not accept secession and Biafra would accept nothing less. Given this context, the OAU could only condemn the Biafrans' actions. This position was likely largely informed by other members of the OAU, such as Sudan and Ethiopia, who faced their own secessionist challenges and so did not want to legitimize Biafran ambitions.

However, beyond the OAU there were several African nations that not only sympathized with Biafra but even granted it that rarest of all diplomatic statuses: recognition.[75] Four African nations broke ranks diplomatically with their peers to formally recognize the state of Biafra, although their reasons for doing so were not all of a piece. These four were Tanzania, Zambia, the Ivory Coast, and Gabon. The latter two declared their recognition within a week of each other in May 1968. Bound together by their francophone heritage, these two were generally felt to have recognized Biafra as stalking horses for French ambitions in Biafra. Gabon in particular has been singled out for these reasons, as the Biafrans had not even lobbied them for recognition! As for the Ivory Coast, while it is true that France (and de Gaulle in particular) had considerable sway with its president, Félix Houphouët-Boigny, their reasons for recognition are often held to have been slightly more complex. Houphouët-Boigny's latent distrust both of the Muslim hinterlands shared by the west African coastal states and Soviet influence are credited with having swayed his decision, although considerable emphasis is also laid upon his humanitarian nature.[76]

In comparison to these conservative francophone states, Tanzania and Zambia were socialist anglophone states, strange bedfellows for de Gaulle's former African colonies. As might be expected, their reasons for recognizing the state of Biafra were rather different. Perhaps the best description that has been given of their actions was directed at Julius Nyerere of Tanzania: "He did the wrong thing for the right reasons."[77] Nyerere did not recognize Biafra in 1968 to help it secede; he recognized it because the terrible suffering of the Biafran people affected him deeply and he felt the only way to end the bloodshed was to give the Biafrans some leverage in their peace talks. He thought that with his recognition, they might be able to force a compromise at the negotiating table and end the looming humanitarian disaster in Eastern Nigeria. President Kenneth Kaunda of Zambia was a great admirer of Nyerere's and was often of the same mind as him. His country's following of Tanzania's lead was largely for the same reasons: the hope that recognition might offer a way to end the conflict. In the end none of the four recognitions, no matter what the reasoning behind them, made a tangible difference. What is worth noting, though, is that although Tanzania and Zambia recognized Biafra the state, they continued to condemn the act of secession; while they would recognize the people of Biafra's right to exist, they would not recognize their right to exist separately. Thus, with a few minor exceptions, the continent of Africa established a continental consensus against the act of secession that remained in force for twenty-one years.[78]

Although the recognition of the Ivory Coast and Gabon did little to aid the Biafran cause internationally, they did serve as the main conduits for arms shipments that resuscitated and sustained the Biafran struggle in 1968. However, despite the influx of arms that prolonged the conflict itself, the amount of actual international equipment and expertise involved in the conflict was a fraction of that seen in the Congo. While Katanga's secession was supported by hundreds of Belgian technicians and officers as well as a significant number of mercenary soldiers, Biafra saw just a faint echo of these previous interventions. The arms shipments from France were the most significant portion of this. Night relief flights into the Uli airport brought in an estimated 200 tons of armaments per week from French sources, often shuttled through the Ivory Coast or Gabon for a level of plausible separation between the two nations.[79] Given the paucity of heavy weaponry, modern assault rifles, armour, and planes on the Biafran side, it is perhaps best estimated that most of this tonnage was ammunition for the vast variety of weaponry the Biafran side used. In terms of other internationally provided weaponry, there was little to be had: Britain, the United States, and the USSR did not sell or provide armaments to the Biafrans, and as has been noted the black market weapons deals often went spectacularly awry. The only notable success of the independent Biafran arms search was the series of Minicon trainer planes that served as an ad hoc air force in the final stages of the war.[80] Essentially, while the Katanga mercenaries and gendarmerie were more or less directly equipped by the Belgian government, the Biafrans had much less international support in terms of supplying their armed forces.

This was borne out in expertise as well. While the Katanga struggle and the Congo Crisis as a whole lifted mercenary soldiering into the spotlight, the Biafran war served to break the reputation of the mercenary soldiers. Ojukwu's army employed a variety of mercenary soldiers and overall got a very poor return on its investment. Perhaps the best of the poor lot was the previously mentioned Rolf Steiner, who gave adequate service in organizing the 4th Commando Brigade and leading it in several irregular raids on the Federal Army. However, in the end he was criticized heavily for commandeering supplies from both the Biafran Army and the Red Cross and ended his service under a cloud.[81] As for the other major mercenary interventions, they were, with few exceptions, a disaster for the Biafran side. Colonel Michael Hoare of Congo fame made a brief appearance, but his terms were unacceptable to the Biafrans. The Federals had no intention of hiring him and he withdrew from sight. In late 1967 the French directed Ojukwu to the services of the large network of mercenaries with ties to France, mostly ex–Foreign Legionnaires. This led to the dubious employment of Captain Roger Faulques, another hardened veteran of the Congo, who promised to provide 100 veteran mercenaries to help turn the tide of the war.[82] Instead he arrived with 49 troops, who then were bloodily repulsed at Calabar with significant losses. A scant few weeks later they left, taking with them six months' pay for 100 men, a salary all out of proportion to what they had accomplished.[83] Although admittedly both sides were already loath to use hired guns, when taken in comparison with the effectiveness of the mercenaries in Katanga and the subsequent troubles in the Congo, the work of the mercenaries in Biafra was certainly a disappointment and served to close the chapter on their general use in Africa until a brief revival after the Cold War.[84]

Of course, with several of the mercenaries employed having also served in Katanga, there was something more afoot in the Biafra conflict than the local hesitation to employ outside military contractors. The two conflicts were not comparable in that while in Katanga the Gendarmerie initially faced off against a fractured and ill-trained ANC and then against a divided UNOC force with an unclear mandate, the Biafrans faced a unified and enthusiastic Nigerian Federal Army with clear goals and a sound strategy. To put it simply, the Biafran conflict illustrated the increasing ability of African states to project their power. When the conflict broke out in 1967, the Federal forces had less than 9,000 members and only 184 officers under arms.[85] While an army of this size was not uncommon in most postcolonial African states, it was hardly large enough to wage a widespread conventional war. As such, it underwent a massive recruitment and training effort and expanded itself to well over 100,000 personnel by 1970.[86] By that point its sheer size made it one of the largest militaries in sub-Saharan Africa. Beyond this, thanks to the needs of the war and the international alignments Nigeria took advantage of, this military was well equipped with the most modern military technology that it could acquire. By the end of the war Nigeria could boast of having one of the largest and most modern military forces in all of Africa. Beyond this, if outside observers occasionally remarked upon the clumsiness, the sluggishness, or even the incompetence of the army itself, the scale of its accomplishments must be remembered.[87] During wartime, the federal government expanded its armed forces tenfold (including the creation of its own air force), trained an entire generation of new officers to lead it, and managed to put down a supremely motivated opponent who was fielding 40,000 soldiers on his home ground. While certainly there were no feats of military genius, the Nigerian command managed to end the war with a mostly green army and kept the bloodshed to a minimum in the aftermath of conflict. This illustrated the increasing ability of the African state to project its strength as needed, and Nigeria emerged from the war as an African Great Power because of its exercising of these abilities. The experiences of the Federal military served to place the capabilities of African militaries back on an effective level and erase part of the embarrassing memory of the corrupt and ineffective ANC of the Congo.

The combination of decreasing external involvement and effectiveness with the increasingly potent centralized African state put an incredible strain upon the attempted legitimacy and sovereignty of the Civil Secessionist state, but in the end it was a fundamental failure of the state structure that caused its collapse. With the factors already discussed in the Introduction to Part I serving as the general framework for the existence of the Biafran State, it still was the creation and separation of a created state led by a cadre of elites and effected by the pre-existing political apparatus of the region. Biafra, like Katanga before it, was a project of the elites that founded and ran it, particularly Ojukwu himself. As has been noted, Ojukwu was essentially the heart of the rebellion and of the separatist state. His military and civilian subordinates were also elites, and it was their combined vision of Biafra as a state that served as the blueprint for the secession. The input of the vast majority of the population was not considered in its creation. This is not to say that the population at large did not share in the waging of the conflict or share the sense of being a part of Biafra. If anything, the sacrifices and heartbreak that the Biafran people, particularly the Igbos, underwent in their quest for their own state remains one of the most notable aspects of the conflict. However, it is not their participation in the general existence of Biafra that would define it as a populist movement but instead the stake that the general populace had in the definition of their state and its outlook, something that neither the leaders of Biafra nor Katanga cultivated. Instead Biafra tended to be a singular state, run by a leader who was described afterward by his fellows as "a dictator."[88] The only time that the governing philosophy of Biafra itself was questioned was in the bombastic Ahiara Declaration of June 1969, where Ojukwu made the bold statement:

> When I speak of the ordinary Biafran I speak of the People. The Biafran Revolution is the People's Revolution. Who are the People? you ask. The farmer, the trader, the clerk, the business man, the housewife, the student, the civil servant, the soldier, you and I are the people. Is there anyone here who is not of the people? Is there anyone here afraid of the People—anyone suspicious of the People? Is there anyone despising the People? Such a man has no place in our Revolution. If he is a leader, he has no right to leadership because all power, all sovereignty, belongs to the People. In Biafra the People are supreme; the People are master; the leader is servant. You see, you make a mistake when you greet me with shouts of "Power, Power". I am not power—you are.[89]

Throughout the lengthy document Ojukwu makes numerous attempts to redefine the Biafran war as a populist revolution and suggests several radical alterations in the composition of the Biafran ideology. He even attempts to position the "Revolution" as one of global populism, opposing the imperialism of outside states and seeking solidarity with the rest of the postcolonial world. However, despite these firebrand words, Biafra never actually altered its structure and remained under the unitary structure it had always assumed. By the time the Ahiara Declaration had been distributed to the populace, Biafra itself was so depleted that the remaining populace could not carry out any of its precepts, and it was only a mere seven months later that Ojukwu fled the secessionist state and the war ended.

The cases of Biafra and Katanga both show the limitations of the top-down imposition of the state. The case of Biafra is perhaps even more poignant in that it reveals the ultimate limitations of the state structure even with the full engagement of the populace. With the elites imposing the conception and idea of the state and determining the methodology of attaining the state itself, a certain inflexibility entered the struggle: the elites insisted upon a state existing and their status within it. This in turn led to the necessity for a conventional struggle that was not necessary in terms of the more flexible popular struggles. Simply put, the elite projects became limited to the idea of an existing state proving its legitimacy and thereby gaining recognition,[90] which became unworkable in the geopolitical environment of the decolonization of Africa and the creation of the OAU.

In the final accounting of the Civil Secessions, Katanga set the stage for their ultimate failure as a strategy, but Biafra proved the concept a stillborn one. The elite conception and presentation of the Civil Nation posited the existence of the state itself as the sole immediate goal of the secessionist conflict, a goal that set a generally smaller and weaker state in a conventional struggle against its internationally recognized host state. The goal of maintaining the facets of legitimacy within the secessionist state by the regime were temporarily successful in Katanga because of the massive external military aid to Tshombe's regime as well as the weakness of the Congo's response and the muddled ideological goals of the United Nations. This central attempt at legitimacy became infinitely harder to achieve in the Biafran case due to the paucity of external aid given to the secessionists as well as the strength and clear goals of the federal government. Of course, in terms of international legitimacy, the United Nations set the precedent of recognition in the Katanga case, but this in turn would be reinforced by the construction of the Organization of African Unity and its precepts. By the end of the Biafran war it was clear that the idea of the creation of a civil state and then struggling for its legitimacy and recognition on a global or even continental stage was a dead end in terms of the secessionist goals on the continent of Africa. However, parallel conflicts occurring elsewhere on the continent would take a different evolutionary path and would set the stage for more successful outcomes for separatists and secessionist groups in Africa.

PART II

The Long Wars

While the Civil Secessions, those secession attempts that involved the simple declaration of a territorial sovereign nation and then a struggle for recognition, proved to be a dead end in terms of gaining political separation, they were not the only means attempted during the years of decolonization in Africa. At the same time that Katanga was haggling with the Congolese government and the United Nations, two other secession attempts were already underway on the continent, although due to their nature they received far less commentary and attention at the time. However, these two secessions, the ill-defined Sudanese struggle and the Eritrean Revolution, not only survived the decade that saw the rise and fall of both Katanga and Biafra but continued their struggle for many years, with mixed results. These two conflicts are examples of what this work will term the Long Wars, and they existed within the same international context as the Civil Secessions. However, these struggles took a remarkably different direction in their manner of secession, which resulted in vastly different outcomes.

Revolutionary Methodology

This different methodology of secession may be traced to the intellectual context that surrounded the secession attempt. As has been established, the Civil Secessions were based on the example of decolonization. The secessionist proto-states were constructed in such a way as to attempt to gain international recognition upon their declaration. The struggles themselves ensued when the host state refused to recognize the removal of the secessionists from their state and mobilized military forces to compel the reintegration of the would-be independent polity. The struggles then generally took the form of the secessionist state being gradually overpowered while it vainly attempted to gain the recognition it took for granted following the international precepts of self-determination that had led to decolonization itself.

The Long Wars were based on a different conception of decolonization, taking their examples instead from the far-flung corners of the globe where colonialism and imperialism had not been abolished civilly by international law, but had instead been thrown bodily from the formerly colonized region. Put simply, while the Civil Secessions had taken decolonization as their model, the Long Wars looked to the global liberation struggles for their structure and ideology, resulting in a reversal of the previous model. Instead of declaring a state and then struggling to defend it and its legitimacy from external threats, the Long Wars established a precedent of mass movements struggling against the occupying forces and decisively defeating them before seeking full international recognition. While previously there had been few if any examples to bear out the efficacy or even possibility of such an undertaking, following the Second World War two prime examples leapt into prominence: those of China and Vietnam.

China had been a victim of colonialism since the nineteenth century, with the costly Opium Wars, Taiping Rebellion, Boxer Rebellion, and then the Revolt at Wuchang, which finally overthrew the Qing Dynasty, all serving to bind China further into a web of unequal relationships in terms of trade and power. Following the overthrow of the Qing Dynasty and the ascension of Sun Yat-Sen to the presidency of the First Chinese Republic under the banner of his Kuomintang Party (KMT) during the struggles of the early twentieth century, there had been the hope of a peaceful unification of the state, but it was not to be. Instead Sun Yat-Sen's government effectively ended with his death in 1925, with the country still split among warlord factions. Chiang Kai-Shek, the commandant of the recently founded Whampoa Military Academy,[1] managed to seize power and unify the country following his Northern Expedition to crush the remaining warlord-run regions.

While the country was now unified, the Chinese Communist Party (CCP) objected to the increasing corruption and continued colonialism present in the state. Beginning in the late 1920s the CCP split with the KMT and began an armed resistance to the Nationalist government.[2] Although the CCP was riven with its own internal conflicts,[3] by the mid-1930s the majority of the factions had been put down and the largest remaining group under Mao Tse-Tung was driven across China in the legendary Long March. By 1937 the Communists were at bay and the Second Sino-Japanese War had begun with the Japanese invasion of Manchuria.

The Long March and the following Sino-Japanese war thrust the previously little-known Mao Tse-Tung into the international spotlight as both a political theorist and a guerrilla leader. It would be his central ideas that built the Red Chinese into a formidable conventional and guerrilla force over the course of the eight-year-long war with the Japanese. His writings, which are still widely available today, cover both the essential military strategies needed to defeat the imperialist aggressor and the social programs needed to establish the functional state to drive forward the liberation of China. In terms of military strategy, Mao proposed a guerrilla war to wear down the Japanese in the vast and often hostile spaces of China, weakening the invaders until a decisive struggle could be won against them.[4] In terms of social planning, Mao's Communists built from within and constructed the means to continue the struggle without the external aid of the industrialized nations. By the end of the Second World War, the Communists had not only developed themselves into a powerful military force but had organized themselves into an efficient and organized society from which to launch their final campaign to "liberate" China from its corrupt leadership.

With the Japanese defeated it was only a matter of time before the still simmering conflict between the Nationalists and Communists re-erupted. Finally in 1946 the last confrontation began, with the Nationalists receiving massive amounts of military aid from the United States while the Communists still remained generally isolated from external help.[5] Despite the disparity of aid given and the symbolic KMT victory at Yenan,[6] the Communists followed the military doctrine they had established in the previous struggle to marshal their strength and gain the upper hand. Their evolution from static defensive warfare with guerrilla operations to a mobile offence marked the beginning of the final stage of the conflict, and Mao's forces slowly drove the Nationalist forces farther and farther south. As they advanced, the Communists captured larger amounts of military hardware and organized their expanding territory, finally driving Chiang Kai-Shek's government over the straits to exile in Taiwan in 1949.

The story of the Vietnamese struggle parallels that of the Chinese, but follows a more explicit anti-colonial narrative. At the time of the Second World War, the area known as Vietnam was part of French Indochina, a region that had been claimed and conquered in the late nineteenth century during the expansion of the French Empire. When France was overrun by the Germans, the colony fell under a pro-German collaborationist French government known as Vichy but was swiftly occupied by the Japanese, who intended it to become part of their Greater East Asian Co-Prosperity Sphere. However, seeing the struggle between the French and the Japanese for Vietnamese favour, the Vietnamese Communists met at a conference in Bac Bo to plan their own struggle for Vietnamese independence. The organization they formed to accomplish these goals was named *Việt Nam Độc Lập Đồng Minh Hội*,[7] or Viet Minh for short. The Viet Minh immediately set out to mobilize the peasants, workers, and bourgeoisie to oppose either French or Japanese imperialism. The mass organization that emerged was stratified under the command of a central committee, much like the CCP, and also followed their example in making it a primary goal to set up guerrilla bases in remote safe locales from which to wage a struggle against their stronger occupiers.[8] While there were immediate splits within the greater Nationalist front, the Viet Minh survived in their prepared guerrilla bases.

The Second World War ended with the Viet Minh as arguably the strongest and best organized Asian liberation front. French control had been broken in 1943 and the Japanese were finally defeated in 1945. During the waning years of the war Franklin Roosevelt had made it clear he preferred that Vietnam remain under its own administration, giving hope to the Nationalists that their history as a colonized state was coming to an end. On 2 September 1945 Ho Chi Minh spoke before a crowd of Vietnamese nationalists in Hanoi and proclaimed the independence of Vietnam.[9] However, in the aftermath of the war, the French were determined to take back their imperial possession, making conflict inevitable.

While the struggle during the Second World War had been impressive, most could write off the abilities of the Viet Minh because they had been fighting a Japanese Empire that was overextended and finally beaten by a combination of other great powers. With the beginning of the First Indochina War against France, it now appeared that the Viet Minh would be fighting a battered but still formidable imperial power. However, the Viet Minh had a strong political and social structure in place supporting their veteran guerrilla organization, as well as an effective strategy that had been tested against the Japanese aggressors.[10] The war began easily for the French in 1946 with the capture of several major cities while the Viet Minh retreated to their previous strongholds in the countryside. The French attempted to counter the political clout of the Viet Minh in 1949 by creating an opposition government, but it gained little international traction. By 1950 the war had bogged down into monotonous raids and skirmishes between the Viet Minh guerrillas and the French regulars, wearing down the French will to continue the fight. By 1954 the situation was considered a quagmire by the French public, a view that was validated by the shocking Vietnamese victory at Dien Bien Phu, which demolished any French dreams of a return to empire in Indochina.

The Viet Minh victory was seen as a remarkable feat: a non-industrialized proto-state had organized itself and waged war on an imperial power that had the backing of the United States.[11] By constructing a social and political apparatus to sustain a protracted war and avoiding direct conventional conflict with the stronger enemy, the Vietnamese won their independence and inflicted a decisive defeat upon their previous colonial overlords.[12] While the rest of the colonized world could take notice of Mao's victory in China over a Western-backed opponent and appreciate the victory, it would always be possible to dismiss it as a victory against a rotten and corrupt regime. The Viet Minh victory over the French was a direct application of concepts either paralleling or borrowed from the Chinese example. The efficacy of the revolutionary liberationist model offered could no longer be denied. The colonized world could look at the decisive Viet Minh victory in 1954 and see a possibility that had previously been considered impossible: that by fighting a slow, protracted war supported by an organized citizenry, smaller and less developed nations could drive out their colonial masters.

The Revolution in Africa

This model was not slow in its transition to Africa. Looking simply at North Africa, the *Front de libération nationale* (FLN) in Algeria began waging its own protracted conflict in 1954, following the Chinese and Vietnamese revolutionary model to wage a struggle in both the urban centres of the state and in the countryside.[13] However, sub-Saharan Africa was a different story. With the political agitation of the increasingly aware and mobilized populations of the colonies, self-government and then decolonization began in 1957, seeming to negate the need for such drastic measures as a protracted liberation war. However, not all regions of Africa were in the process of decolonization and many did not have the same dynamics as the majority of the states now being given self-rule. Portuguese Africa was held under the ideology of lusotropicalism, and the fascist government that ruled Portugal argued that Angola, Mozambique, Guinea-Bissau, and the Cape Verde islands were not colonies themselves but were instead overseas provinces of Portugal proper.[14] South Africa was held in the grip of an apartheid minority rule and also claimed a mandate over Namibia.[15] Northern Rhodesia followed the more peaceful path of decolonization but Southern Rhodesia (simply Rhodesia following 1964) resisted the calls for majority black rule and declared itself independent in 1965.[16] In all of these cases, the international call for decolonization had not started the process of self-determination, and so the alternative route of protracted liberation struggle was called for.

Portuguese Africa consisted of three major territories: Angola, Mozambique, and Guinea-Bissau, with the Cape Verde islands initially being lumped in with Guinea-Bissau. During the process of decolonization, the peoples of lusophone Africa had high hopes for their own self-determination, but these were quickly dashed as the Portuguese refused to release their colonial holdings. While initially the nationalist groups within these territories accepted this idea, assuming this meant that then they would be treated as Portuguese citizens, it quickly became obvious that this was just a conceit to allow the weakest of the colonial powers to maintain its grip on its empire. Several mass movements quickly formed to demand and eventually struggle for their liberation from the Portuguese. In Angola no fewer than three movements developed over the course of the 1960s, with the *Movimento Popular de Libertação de Angola* (MPLA), the *Frente Nacional de Libertação de Angola* (FNLA), and the *União Nacional para a Independência Total de Angola* (UNITA) all forming social bases, guerrilla cells, and international contacts to carry on their struggle for liberation. In Mozambique the *Frente de Libertação de Moçambique* (FRELIMO) was formed by the combining of three nationalist fronts under the leadership of Eduardo Mondlane. It fought for a social and military struggle for control of northern Mozambique and then spread its control slowly through the country to contest Portuguese rule. Lastly, there was the *Partido Africano da Independência da Guiné e Cabo Verde* (PAIGC), formed under the brilliant leadership of Amilcar Cabral. Cabral's understanding of the interrelationship of social transformation and military struggle in the pursuit of liberation made him a rising star amongst the African nationalist leaders.[17] His overarching philosophy and skill in enunciating it even earned him international recognition at the Tricontinental Conference in Havana, where leaders from states in South America, Asia, and Africa met to discuss their challenges and hopes in the process of decolonization.[18]

In each of these struggles the fronts made political education and mobilization their primary concern, creating safe loyalist areas that then supported the expanding efforts of guerrilla control. The developments of these fronts and their resolution to use violence resulted in protracted conflicts with a NATO-backed Portuguese military that would not accept the loss of its African territories.[19] These conflicts were long, and although the fronts had limited battlefield successes, they drained the already fragile Portuguese economy while undermining Portuguese support for the wars. The ultimate success of the nationalist fronts came in 1974 when the Carnation Revolution overthrew the Portuguese dictatorship and the new government made ending the interminable colonial wars a priority.

For South Africa, things were not so clear cut, since in theory the state had been a semi-autonomous dominion within the British Empire since its formation in 1910, had lifted the British veto over its legislation in 1931, and only been formally independent since its adoption of a new constitution in 1961. However, during this entire period the country was ruled by the white settler–dominated government, which imposed a hardened race-based social stratification on its population, with the Africans being made into a permanent underclass. Following the ascension of the National

Party in 1948, the structure of apartheid was imposed, harshly delineating the lines between races and oppressing the black majority more than even the previously insensitive white rule had done. The black majority had already had political organizations such as the African National Congress in place to try and deal with the increasingly unfavourable situation they found themselves in, but following the Sharpeville Massacre in 1960 the ANC formed *Umkhonto we Sizwe* ("Spear of the Nation," also abbreviated as MK) as an active military wing.[20] Using the pre-existing social networks of the ANC and other liberationist groups, *Umkhonto we Sizwe* launched a series of bombings across South Africa to try and weaken the apartheid government and draw international attention to the struggle.[21] However, MK did not achieve much in these initial strikes; their initial command structure was not well coordinated with the goals of the ANC, and following the 1963 raid on the Rivonia farm, their leadership was largely jailed or in exile.[22] This experience found itself paralleled with the more radical Pan Africanist Congress, or PAC, which was formed in 1959 and had initially organized itself for a more active role against the apartheid regime than the ANC. Beginning as early as 1960 the PAC had formed its own armed wing, which came to be known as *Poqo* (Xhosa for "Alone").[23] However, much like the ANC, after a series of directed clashes with white police and indigenous collaborators, the PAC and *Poqo* were largely driven into exile by the active apartheid security forces. Beginning in the early 1960s the members of the exiled leadership for both groups reorganized themselves into more politically integrated and disciplined military forces abroad and attempted to find ways for their fighters to return to South Africa and begin the fight anew.[24] However, due to the hostile regimes in Angola, Mozambique, and Rhodesia both groups experienced extreme frustrations in attempting to continue their campaigns. Even collaborating with other liberation fronts led to at best limited successes, with the ANC taking notable losses in the Wankie Game Reserve when they attempted to infiltrate that region[25] and *Poqo* being limited to mixed results in their partnership with the Zimbabwean African People's Union.

The tide eventually turned with the fall of the Portuguese Empire in 1974. The ANC was now able to move its MK forces into Angola and Southwest Africa, where they aided the local nationalist groups and managed to press their way into South Africa. The Soweto Uprising in 1976 led to a massacre of black South Africans by the apartheid government, convincing many young men to join both liberation fronts, swelling their ranks. By the early 1980s both groups were infiltrating South Africa and organizing domestic military structures to carry on the guerrilla struggle within the country.[26] A campaign of bombings and targeted killings in the cities was followed by an expansion of attacks into the white-controlled farming regions in the countryside.[27] The South African government, already reeling from its exertions in Southwest Africa, Angola, and Mozambique, began preparations for a political transition under President F.W. de Klerk in 1990, with the anti-apartheid groups being decriminalized and the political prisoners being released. The pressure of the armed groups such as *Poqo* and *Umkhonto we Sizwe*, under the direction of their political leadership, had brought the apartheid regime to heel and brought forth open elections whereby the Africa National Congress under Nelson Mandela would assume power in South Africa.

As noted, the apartheid government also had difficulties with the South West African Peoples' Organization (SWAPO), which was struggling for the liberation of Namibia. Namibia had been a German colony following the Scramble for Africa, but had devolved to South African control after their conquest of it in the First World War. Since that time the South Africans had ruled it as an occupied territory and ignored calls for its self-determination following the Second World War. As such, in 1962 SWAPO was created to organize the people of Namibia in their struggle against the encroaching apartheid of South Africa. Hostilities erupted formally in 1966[28] and continued as a protracted struggle known as the Border War, named so after the border with Angola, which was seen as the militarized region that threatened South African control. SWAPO fighters had found it increasingly challenging to operate solely within Southwest Africa and so had begun crossing the border to Angola for sanctuary from the aggressive South African forces. This in turn led to South African military interventions into Angola, sparking a regional conflict that eventually involved SWAPO, the MPLA, UNITA, Cuba, the ANC, and the South African military. Finally in 1988, following the titanic struggle at Cuito Cuanavale in Angola, the South African government agreed to recognize the independence of Namibia in the tripartite talks between Angola, Cuba, and South Africa proper.[29]

Lastly, the minority government in power in Rhodesia[30] took the radical step of declaring its unilateral independence from the British Crown in 1965 to preserve its white-dominated colonial system. While Rhodesia's neighbours and former federation members Zambia and Malawi had gained their independence upon the election of a representative government, the Rhodesian government did not wish to incorporate the majority-African population within its white settler–dominated government. Britain therefore refused to grant the Rhodesian government self-rule, leading the Rhodesians under Prime Minister Ian Smith to issue the Unilateral Declaration of Independence.[31]

At that time a liberation struggle had already begun under in 1962 the auspices of the revolutionary Zimbabwean African Peoples Union (ZAPU), which in 1964 had split to produce two rival liberation fronts, ZAPU and the Zimbabwean African National Union (ZANU). While they consistently made statements and token efforts toward a unified front, their rivalry continued to simmer even as each built their social base amongst the populace and built safe base areas in the surrounding sympathetic African nations. ZAPU took a more orthodox Marxist-Leninist line, attempting to mobilize the labouring urban Africans within Rhodesia. They largely were given support by the Soviet Union and despite attempting guerrilla actions throughout the war were often focused on building larger conventional formations to effectively combat the Rhodesian security forces.[32] Conversely, their rivals ZANU took a more Maoist perspective and focused on mobilizing the rural peasantry for the liberation struggle. They largely drew their support from China and throughout the struggle focused on widespread guerrilla warfare to drain resources and manpower from the Rhodesians.[33] While both found support within the country, increasingly the mobilization and organization of peasant cells gave ZANU a powerful constituency.[34]

Already the Unilateral Declaration of Independence had seen the Rhodesian government expelled from the Sterling Zone in 1965 and isolated from any Commonwealth ties. While the Eastern Bloc supported the liberation fronts, the Rhodesian government only found formal allies in South Africa and the Portuguese Empire, but both of these were facing their own struggles in southern Africa.[35] With the fall of the Portuguese Empire in 1974 and the withdrawal of much of the South African support in the same period, the Rhodesian government found itself isolated and facing two mature liberation fronts with broad ethnic bases of support.[36] The Rhodesian position was increasingly untenable, and despite several operational victories, strategically the war was becoming unwinnable. Finally, in 1978 the white minority attempted a power-sharing agreement, allowing the election of Bishop Abel Muzorewa in 1979, but this could not last in the face of the surging nationalism of ZANU and ZAPU. To resolve the issue, the Rhodesian government, ZAPU, and ZANU attended a British-facilitated constitutional conference beginning in September 1979. By December all parties signed an accord called the Lancaster House Agreement that reversed the Unilateral Declaration of Independence and set elections to be held under British auspices. In April 1980 the ZANU-PF party of Robert Mugabe was elected in Zimbabwe as the strong political education and social base fostered by ZANU's strategy created electoral support for the liberation parties.[37] However, it is important to note that without the exhaustion of the Rhodesian government through the protracted conflict, the liberation of Zimbabwe from white rule would never have occurred.

Secession as Protracted War

It was these models of liberation struggles that informed the structure and methodology of the Long War secessions. The factions involved recognized that their separatist states would never be given recognition without first winning a military victory over the host state. However, as may be noted in the cases of Civil Secession, the host state held all the advantages in terms of political and military power. The existing state held international legitimacy, which opened up a host of strengths denied to the secessionist bodies. The host could deal fairly and openly with other nations of the world, receiving access to both markets and international aid. They had currency to purchase military hardware, medicine, and food. They had a larger and established economic base to draw from to pursue their military goals. Simply put, as a rule the host state was larger, stronger, and better developed in pursuing the projection of violence and political power than the separatist groups. It was thus imperative for these groups to find a model that offered a chance for victory in terms of a secessionist struggle. They found such a model in the conception of the protracted struggle of a mass movement of people.

This model offered a number of advantages. The general methodology and structure of the revolutionary liberation model involved initially politically and socially mobilizing the populace, usually through intensive educational efforts. This population base would then serve as a recruiting ground for fighters, cadres, and support personnel, as well as a source of food, shelter, and intelligence during the guerrilla operations intended to weaken the enemy.[38] When a region that could be made safe from the opposition was found, whether across international borders or separated by difficult terrain, it would be transformed into a base, where a developing industrial and agricultural economy would be set up. These regions would take on increasing complexity as members of the popular front with various skills found their way to the base area, with the eventual goal being one of self-sufficiency and enough output to support the operations of increasing numbers of guerrilla fighters. In effect, at this point the popular movement would have taken on the form of a functional society within their state, and it then used the base of this society to support the campaign to harass and weaken the host society. When the enemy was weakened sufficiently and the surrounding populace mobilized enough, additional base areas would be created until a final conflict could be chanced with the enemy.[39]

These movements offered a contrasting vision to the conventional state that they existed in and took on a methodology that would attempt to counter the inherent strengths of the host state. While the host state had the sole legitimate access to the outside world, the liberation/secession front attempted to create a self-sufficient society. While the host state had a large, strong conventional military, the liberation/secessionist model offered few targets for this military and weakened it through guerrilla warfare. In effect, the secessionist groups did not need to have the legitimacy of a state (and therefore take on the weaknesses of the Civil Secessions) and therefore were free to prosecute the conflict in as advantageous a way as possible.

However, this model also imposed several of its own limitations and difficulties. To gain a large enough and devoted enough following often required a complex and often circuitous path to create a program that would sustain a protracted conflict. Class divisions often proved nearly fatal to the protracted conflicts as the goals of the peasants, the base of such insurrections according to Maoist doctrine, were often distinct from the goals and aspirations of industrial labourers, the bourgeoisie, and even the colonial elites. To create an effective mass movement the program they followed often had to address these varied goals and create a compromise that could attract enough general followers without creating a program too broad to build an attractive alternative society upon. For example, the Viet Minh were able to build an effective popular movement by creating a liberationist program against the Japanese, but they were able to sustain this program and move it forward by offering a compelling and egalitarian society to the disadvantaged peasantry and workers. However, even during the Japanese occupation, they had to soften their program of land redistribution to attract the rural landlords to their cause and sustain it in the struggle against the occupiers.

Beyond this class struggle, in Africa and elsewhere there was the difficulty of ethnic identity, which often had influence well out of proportion to its historical basis. In Angola the three fronts were often based regionally and developed their own ethnic identities. In Zimbabwe, ZAPU gained the reputation of being an Ndebele movement while ZANU was thought to better represent the Shona. Such ethnic divisions could easily tear a liberation or secessionist front asunder. As will be noted, the secessionist struggle in Southern Sudan had to continuously reinvent itself to maintain a balance in perception with respect to the various groups within it. When this balance was upset, the movement inevitably splintered into another regional or ethnic movement.

The program of the popular movements that drove the Long Wars will often be seen to change, splinter, and evolve throughout the course of the decades-long conflicts. Class, ethnic, economic, and even racial conceptions of the struggle had to be addressed and accepted by a large part of the populace to allow for the growth of a society that could foster and endure the protracted nature of the struggle. However, when a program was finally agreed upon, the struggles that ensued could bear fruit, as will be noted in the successes of both South Sudan and Eritrea.

Map of Ethiopia and Eritrea

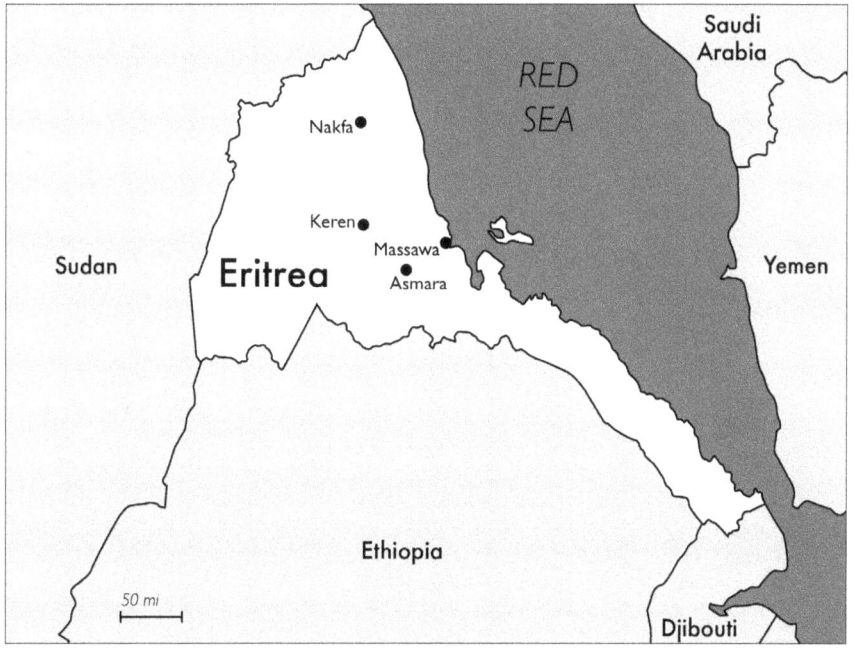

Copyright © 2014 Nathan E. McCormack and Charles G. Thomas

3

The Anomaly of Eritrean Secession, 1961–1993

It is nearly impossible to truly pin down the starting date of any of the long conflicts for secession in Africa, as one may choose the formation of the mass movement that sustained it, the pivotal action that drove the mass movement, or the creation of the context which surrounded this action. The Eritrean Secession might be said to have begun in 1958 when a group of Cairo-based Eritrean exiles met and established the earliest clandestine organization for the liberation of Eritrea. It equally might be said that those seeds were sown in the 1952 joining of the former Italian colony of Eritrea to Ethiopia or in the following years when various political factions fought to direct the impotent Eritrean Assembly. There is also the obvious jumping-off point of the Italian conquest of Eritrea in the late nineteenth century and subsequent intense development of the region following their crushing defeat at the hands of Menelik II at Adowa in 1896. Some scholars have even gone so far as to trace the validity of Eritrean sovereignty and struggles all the way back to the Axumite kingdoms of central Ethiopia and their intermittent warfare against the coastal pastoralists. However, while all of these were to prove pivotal moments in the development of the nation of Eritrea, this study marks the beginning of the war proper on 1 September 1961, when a small guerrilla band led by early dissenter Idris Hamid Awate opened fire at an Ethiopian police post in Western Eritrea.[1] From this date until the United Nations referendum in 1993 that established Eritrea as a separate sovereign nation, Eritreans fought a protracted conflict against Ethiopia and their numerous backers that featured guerrilla raids, pitched battles, a social revolution, the politicization of a population, and one of the worst famines the world had seen to date. What emerged from this crucible of conflict was the first successful secession in Africa since independence, a remarkable undertaking and one that forms the centrepiece of this volume, both as a case study of the difficulties involved in secession and the anomalous circumstances required to effect such a complete separation.

THE END OF ERITREA

When the shots were fired by Awate and his fledgling Eritrean Liberation Front guerrillas in 1961, it was in response to the rising pressures of Eritrean nationalism that had been unleashed following the Second World War. From the late nineteenth century until 1941, Eritrea had been a prosperous Italian colony, dubbed in the 1930s the centrepiece of dictator Benito Mussolini's new Roman Empire. The colony served as the staging area for fascist Italy's subsequent invasion of Ethiopia, and large numbers of Eritrean colonial troops were used to great effect against Emperor Haile Selassie's armies.[2] However, with the expansion of the worldwide hostilities to East Africa in the 1940s, the Italians were driven out of their holdings by British East African forces and both Ethiopia and Eritrea were placed under British control. While Haile Selassie was able to return to his throne in 1941, at the end of the war the British were left with the uncomfortable question of how to deal with Eritrea. In 1947 Italy formally renounced its claim to Eritrea or any of its other African territories, leaving the outcome even more uncertain.[3] While political factions were already forming in the small state and agitating for their own particular hoped-for outcomes, the case was eventually handed over the United Nations for a final verdict.[4] While the United States desired a consolidation of their ally Ethiopia's control over Eritrea, the Soviet bloc pushed for total separation between the two nations. It was an acrimonious struggle mirrored by that within Eritrea, where the Unionist Party pressed its traditional interests by supporting union with Ethiopia against those of the Muslim League and the Liberal Progressive Party, who favoured Eritrean independence. In the end, there was what might be at best termed a compromise, with Eritrea being joined to Ethiopia as a federated territory under the Ethiopian crown.[5] This of course was not much of a compromise to those favouring independence, as it still placed their foreign affairs, military, finance, and international commerce under the "federal" government of an absolute monarchy.

While the Eritrean nationalists were disheartened at the development, it was only the beginning of what would become complete Ethiopian dominance of the "federal" arrangement. Haile Selassie's government completely nullified and then dismantled the Eritrean state over the next ten years through a combination of money, informal influence, and often naked military intervention. The very year of federation was the last year that free and open elections were held in Eritrea. The constitution was suspended shortly thereafter and the jailing of dissident politicians and journalists soon followed. In 1956 Amharic was made the official language over the protests of the majority of the nation, which had traditionally adopted Tigrinya or Arabic as their preferred languages.[6] That same year the Eritrean Assembly was "temporarily suspended." Although elections followed, they were without direction or organization, leading to bitterly contested results. The nascent labour union movement that had been growing in strength and organization was essentially driven from sight by a series of crushing blows dealt to it by the federal military during protest strikes in 1958.[7] This was followed in 1959 by the leaders of the assembly voting to replace their own penal code with that of Ethiopia after one of their increasingly common visits to Addis Ababa. By 1960 the main political supports of a separate Eritrea had been dissolved, with most governmental and grassroots organizations having been reduced to irrelevancy or driven from the country. Even protests directed at the United Nations, which had created the rapidly crumbling federal system, were simply met with the response that all protests would have to pass through the federal government first—in this case the Emperor himself.[8] The final curtain fell in 1962, when the assembly was at last "persuaded" to vote itself out of existence, a process aided by armed police and jets providing air cover. Eritrea was officially no more as of 14 November 1962.[9]

The Birth of the Eritrean Armed Struggle

While the first shots of the conflict were fired in 1961, since 1958 there had been a group of expatriate notables who were already beginning their resistance against the creeping imperialism of Haile Selassie. Formed in

Cairo, the Eritrean Liberation Movement (ELM) was the first major organized dissenting group and consisted of members of the disenfranchised educated upper classes of Eritrea. Many of its earliest known members were former members of the Eritrean Assembly, driven from their homes during the increasing violence of the Ethiopian repression. Woldeab Woldemariam was a common example of the early Eritrean nationalist leadership. A newspaperman and former representative from the Liberal Progressive Party, he was driven into exile by the events of the mid-1950s. He served as an early figure to rally around and still serves as a noble example of Eritrean nationalism. Another figure who proved to be pivotal in both the ELM and its successor movements was Osman Saleh Sabbe of the Muslim League.[10] He too was a staunch nationalist and represented a consistent link of Eritrea's struggles with the greater postcolonial movements of the world, most notably Pan-Arabism. However, despite its growing organization and outreach, the Eritrean Liberation Movement was anything but a monolithic endeavour. While outreach was already beginning and underground urban organizing in Eritrea proper was underway, the movement itself fractured into several cliques and factions. While the ELM was still trying to organize itself as a party in exile, one of its splinter groups, the Eritrean Liberation Front (ELF), took centre stage and opened fire on the Ethiopians in 1961.

The decision to transform itself into an armed struggle was a momentous one for the ELF and quickly propelled it into the spotlight. Its guerrilla struggle brought it increasing attention and growth despite an incompletely articulated program, with little ideology aside from being fiercely devoted to the idea of Eritrean nationalism. This would prove to be enough as the struggle continued. The ELM, never fully organized or devoted to armed struggle, slowly came undone and during 1961–1965 the ELF made every effort to subsume or destroy its rival. By 1965 this goal had been accomplished, with the few remaining ELM cadres being absorbed into the growing power of the ELF. However, with its growth, the ELF had also inherited the same difficulties that the ELM had struggled with. Eritrea itself housed almost equal populations of Christians and Muslims, which were then even more divided amongst nine separate ethno-linguistic groups across what was now Ethiopia's fourteenth province. These divisions gave way to factionalism and competition within the front, threatening it even as the Ethiopian military began to increase its pressure upon the nascent movement. Taking their cue from the earlier success of the Algerian FLN, the leadership of the ELF decided to divide the nation into five "zones," each overseen by a different commander who often represented the majority confessional and ethnic group.[11] Unfortunately, this simply increased the rivalries, as each zone came to be run as a fiefdom and offered little cooperation to its neighbours in the face of increased resistance by the Ethiopian armed forces. While the struggle continued and the guerrilla forces increased their pressure on both the cities and the countryside, the Ethiopian forces were being rearmed by massive infusions of aid from the United States.[12] From 1960 on, the military aid alone to Ethiopia was staggering, with $10 million a year in grants and loans being offered, and from 1964 on material and logistical support continued to arrive.[13] This made the struggle all the harder on the Eritrean guerrillas, and the Ethiopian strategy continued to evolve to incorporate the massive advantages they accrued in armour, air superiority, and special counter-insurgency forces. By 1968 it was becoming obvious that the Emperor's troops were taking increased advantage of the zonal divisions, attacking each region in turn and inflicting terrible losses on the isolated forces. As the situation deteriorated, cracks began to show within the ELF, culminating in the Anseba Conference in September 1968.[14] This was to prove another pivotal moment in the struggle for Eritrea, as it established the unity of three of the zones following a largely democratic process supported by both the civilians of the regions and the guerrillas fighting in them. However, this action was not sanctioned by the ELF leadership, nor was it accepted by the remaining two zonal commands, giving rise to another rift with the united front of the Eritrean forces. However, with the increasing weakness of the ELF's position and the positive military results garnered by the united zones, it became obvious which way the winds were blowing. In August 1969 the remaining ELF leadership and zonal commanders met with the united zones' commanders at Adobha.

The Split of the Nationalists

The Adobha conference would prove to be one of the last attempts at a truly united front in Eritrea for nearly a decade.[15] While the independent-minded unified zones had seen better results in the recent struggles with Ethiopian troops, the ELF and its remaining zonal commanders still controlled the purse strings through their connections to the Arab states that offered money and weaponry. These offsetting dynamics, combined with a strong desire for unity at any cost, led to the resolutions adopted at the Adobha. All the zones were reconnected under a sole leadership council, which now styled itself the General Command. This General Command would consist of thirty-eight total members, six apiece from each of the three linked zones and ten each from the two remaining zones. This led to a structure that was inordinately stacked against the more independent and increasingly dissident unified group. Beyond this, the General Command would still serve under the previous Supreme Council of the ELF, which remained in the hands of the previously unsupportive leadership. While this arrangement temporarily re-established the ELF as a politically united force under its central leadership, it remained an untenable structure. The three unified zones continued to chafe under the current leadership and the often conservative directions in which it was taking the organization. By 1970 the General Command erupted into violence, with six members of the command itself being jailed and over 300 guerrilla fighters being executed. The progressive and dissident elements of the ELF, already dissatisfied with the politics, strategy, and leadership of the Supreme Council, began to splinter off and slowly coalesced into the second major combatant group of the war, the Eritrean People's Liberation Front.

This split of the armed forces would not be the last but was certainly the most important of the conflict. The literature since the independence of Eritrea has followed various paths to analyze the reasons behind the divergent characters of the ELF and the EPLF, covering aspects of religions, ethnicity, class, even economic backgrounds of the various member groups, but perhaps the simplest explanation is that a rising tide of student recruits in the late 1960s brought with them newer radical ideas that had been absent in the earlier leadership of the ELF. These progressive philosophies were brought to the fore as these students assumed leadership positions and participated in overseas training courses in such revolutionary countries as Cuba and China. By 1970 the rising ambitions of these younger aspiring leaders and the faltering grip of the older conservative leadership simply could no longer coexist, and the split occurred. The ELF remained a fiercely nationalist but loosely disciplined group of guerrillas and older intellectuals while the EPLF took a more rigorously revolutionary tack and began organizing a disciplined peasant base from which to grow its infrastructure. Despite their shared goals of Eritrean liberation, the two fronts immediately found themselves in military conflict, leading to a weakening of both sides as well as a reduction of sabotage, ambushes, and guerrilla strikes on the Ethiopian forces in Eritrea. The Ethiopian army launched a strong ground offensive in late 1970 that battered the ELF regions and followed this with a vigorous bombing campaign by the Ethiopian Air Force.[16] Although neither of these proved decisive, they enhanced Ethiopian control over the regions and allowed for the building of further infrastructure to maintain that hold, such as a series of roads in Western Eritrea that increased the Ethiopian influence near the Sudanese border, a vital gateway for the ELF's arms and food.

Despite the military setbacks for both nationalist movements embodied in both the Ethiopian offensives and their own civil war, the early 1970s would prove to be fruitful for the nationalist movements. The Ethiopian forces treated the "pacified" regions of Eritrea like occupied enemy territory and committed numerous atrocities and indignities on the Eritrean populace. Villagization schemes were attempted to cut back on guerrilla support without adequate food supplies or sanitary considerations.[17] Livestock and crops were simply seized. Entire populations saw their homes burnt to the ground. This had the obvious effect of inciting the populace against Haile Selassie's troops and caused a resurgence in membership in both liberation fronts. The war continued to be fought in the countryside and the cities, with fighters of the ELF and EPLF striking numerous targets during hit-and-run raids. Both nationalist fronts were showing an increased sophistication in their strategy and tactics and were slowly building their constituencies in both urban and rural settings. While neither front was charitably inclined toward its rival, signs were pointing to a détente between the two that would allow for a greater degree of organization in their activities. However, while the war ground interminably on, events were unfolding in Ethiopia that would alter the war in ways that neither front could be prepared for.

The Rise of the Derg

In 1974, Haile Selassie, King of Kings, Lion of Judah, the Elect of God, who had been Emperor of Ethiopia since 1930, was overthrown in a popular coup, arrested, and later killed by his military forces, which subsequently took control of his empire. The group behind this, the Derg,[18] was a loose council of 120 military officers who saw themselves as enlightened technocrats who could navigate Ethiopia through its current crises and restore its power and prestige. Although nominally headed by General Aman Andom, the committee was the site of several vicious behind-the-scenes struggles for power that ended with a former major in the Ethiopian Army, Mengistu Haile Mariam, as the main wellspring of power in the nation. General Andom was executed in November 1974 and Mengistu assumed one of the two chairs of the Derg, which he would dominate for the next seventeen years. However, the upshot of this activity was that the already over-extended Ethiopian military was thrown into general disarray. During the course of the year-long confusion, the two Eritrean nationalist fronts continued their slow rapprochement and patched together a ceasefire in October,[19] leaving both organizations free to focus on fighting the disorganized Ethiopians as well as reaching out to the numerous new dissident groups that sprang up in the confusion and bloodshed following the Derg's coup.

The next four years would prove crucial to the eventual success of Eritrean nationalism. The backlash against the growing excesses of the Derg (which shortly blossomed into what became known as a "Red Terror" as thousands of Ethiopians and Eritreans were summarily executed or imprisoned and tortured) drove massive amounts of recruits into the guerrillas' camps and opened new opportunities for alliance with other revolutionary groups such as the Tigrayan People's Liberation Front (TPLF).[20] The ELF consolidated its control in Western Eritrea and grew its numbers of both trained fighters and militia. The EPLF used this period to establish several "liberated zones" where an astonishing number of social programs were established, from land reform to literacy programs to gender liberation. Both fronts continued their harassment of Ethiopian forces and slowly began to drive them out of the Eritrean borders as best they could. In early 1975 the Eritrean fronts launched an attack on Asmara, which, although it was beaten back, set off an orgy of violence by the Ethiopian troops directed at the city itself, further alienating the urban populace. The military success of both fronts continued with the defeat of the incomparably inept "Peasants' Crusade" set up by Mengistu's government in 1976, where 50,000 ill-equipped and untrained Ethiopian peasants were unleashed upon Eritrea with promises of conquered land. These forces were casually picked apart by veteran fighters of both Eritrean fronts and the TPLF, with few if any Ethiopian peasants actually ever setting foot in Eritrea.

1977 saw continued confidence on the part of both liberation fronts. Early in the year the EPLF captured Nacfa and Afabet, two major trading centres on the northern Sahel province of Eritrea. These conquests were followed by Decamare and Keren, both important industrial centres. Beyond this, Keren was a natural fortress that commanded the passes that gave the easiest access to the Sudan, which continued to be both a humanitarian and logistical base for the Eritrean struggle. In the same period of time, the ELF captured the town of Tessenei and followed this feat with its liberation of Agordat, Adi Quala, and Mendefera. These successes reduced the Ethiopian presence to several isolated garrisons and the important cities of Asmara, Massawa, and Barentu. Massawa was particularly important as it was the primary port for Eritrea and therefore a primary entry point for the food and weapons that the Ethiopian forces needed to keep their flagging cause alive. The EPLF managed to cut the road between Asmara, the capital, and Massawa in October 1977, and the end of Ethiopian resistance to Eritrean nationalism appeared to be in sight. With Mengistu's Ethiopia caught between the liberation fronts in the north and a brutal war with Siad Barre's Somalia in the west over the Ogaden territories,[21] it seemed impossible that the state could last much longer.

THE DERG STRIKES BACK

It was at this point that an astonishing international realignment altered the balance of power in Ethiopia once again. Mengistu's Ethiopia had already proclaimed itself a Marxist republic since shortly after its inception, although this had always been taken as at best a philosophical stopgap for what was essentially an ideologically empty revolt and coup. However, by 1977 the ailing Ethiopia continued to declare its devotion to Marxist ideals and had completed an arms agreement with the Soviet Union. This new arms agreement, alongside the belated recognition of the human rights violations of the Derg regime, caused President Carter and the US Congress to deny any further military support to Mengistu's Ethiopia. Sensing an opportunity for a greater presence in the Horn, the Soviet Union immediately filled the military vacuum in Ethiopia, consequently abandoning its current proxy of Somalia. By July over $500 million worth of Soviet arms flooded into Ethiopia, dwarfing the previous US aid.[22] Beyond the military hardware, which included everything from MiG-21 fighters to SAM-7 anti-aircraft missiles, military personnel from the Soviet Union, the Warsaw Pact nations, Cuba, the People's' Democratic Republic of Yemen, and Libya arrived to bolster and train the Ethiopian Army.[23] During the siege of Massawa it was reported that Soviet advisors took a direct part in the fighting against the Eritreans and even that Soviet naval vessels provided shore bombardment to help drive away the EPLF advance.[24] Over 11,000 Cuban troops served openly in the Ogaden War, helping to halt their recently abandoned Somali allies and aiding in their eventual defeat over the next year.[25]

This massive aid continued, with 1978 shipments of advanced arms raising the total price of material aid to over $1 billion.[26] Tanks, rocket batteries, fighter planes, and long-range artillery were all provided, along with the expertise to effectively use them. Small arms arrived in almost obscene amounts as the Ethiopian army rose like a phoenix from its past four years of defeats. This staggering amount of military aid could only have one effect on the Eritrean struggle: strategic stalemate and eventual losses. As mentioned in passing previously, the EPLF had made a bold strike at Massawa in late 1977, driving the Ethiopian troops from the city to the fortified naval base and two small islands off shore. However, this was to be the high-water mark of the liberation struggle for the next seven years, as the EPLF could not attain complete control of the city and were then left to face the counteroffensive of the resurgent Eastern Bloc–backed Ethiopian Army, which was able to focus its energies on Eritrea following their victory in the Ogaden in 1978.

The Ethiopian counteroffensives of 1978–79 were not tactically or strategically brilliant, but the massive amount of men and material mustered meant that even a blunt series of assaults achieved significant battlefield results. By 21 June 1978 there were reportedly 70,000 Ethiopian troops massed in Tigray preparing for the upcoming offensive, and by July those numbers had risen to over 100,000, which, even if they were not superbly trained, were at least equipped with new and effective materiel.[27] By mid-July the offensive was underway, as multiple spearheads of Ethiopian armour and troops penetrated Tigray and southwestern Eritrea, with the heaviest blows landing on the ELF areas. By 21 July the ELF had been driven from the majority of their captured cities and towns in the western lowlands and the central highlands, exposing the western edge of the EPLF domains. Offensives also began from the Ethiopian garrisons of Massawa and Asmara, further sowing confusion and battering the overstretched Eritrean forces. The responses of the liberation fronts took different forms: the ELF attempted to hold its ground against the Ethiopian steamroller while the EPLF announced several "tactical withdrawals," in the process abandoning recent gains around such cities as Decamare and Massawa.[28] The results also differed: in their attempt to hold their ground against the massed Ethiopian forces the ELF inflicted great casualties against them but also sealed their own fate. Already battered by years of warfare and having been waning in prestige in comparison to the more radical and organized EPLF, the ELF was essentially broken as a military force following the Ethiopian attacks of the late 1970s, and its remaining forces were slowly absorbed into the EPLF over the next several years. The EPLF lost a great amount of territory and also abandoned many carefully cultivated base areas, but it escaped complete destruction and instead re-entrenched in Keren and the Sahel region of the northwest, which continued to serve as safe liberated base areas for the Eritreans.

    Of course, this had only been the first counteroffensive of the Ethiopian forces. The second round of attacks was directed at the EPLF stronghold of Keren in November 1978.[29] Featuring vicious struggles between veteran EPLF guerrillas and heavily armoured Ethiopian columns, the second offensive again showcased the military skill of the EPLF in inflicting significant casualties against the Ethiopian forces, but the disparity in men and materiel remained too great. This is not to say the Ethiopians simply came on in waves; since the influx of Soviet advisors and material, their tactics had evolved, and by using multiple columns of armour and advancing along several parallel paths, they forced the EPLF to spread their already meagre forces more thinly, exacerbating the disparity in numbers.

These new tactics had their effect, and on 26 November the EPLF forces abandoned Keren and fell back on their base areas around Nacfa and in the mountains of the Sahel, their last safe haven in the country. It was to prove an especially effective one, however, with the mountainous terrain and prepared logistical and defensive positions serving the Eritreans very well in the months to come.

Recovery and Victory

1979 and 1980 saw the Eritrean forces at bay but certainly not defeated. Ethiopian forces launched their third, fourth, and fifth offensives in 1979 and achieved nothing against the prepared and veteran EPLF. These strikes comprised over 50,000 Ethiopian troops supported by massive amounts of armour and artillery and yet were unable to make any measurable headway against the base areas of the EPLF.[30] In eight days between 14 and 22 July, the Ethiopian army lost approximately 6,000 men. Indiscriminate bombing against the base regions was resumed but caused little damage, as the Eritrean workshops, schools, and hospitals were generally either well camouflaged or subterranean by this point in the war. 1980 brought a general stalemate on the front while the army continued to "pacify" its reclaimed regions of Eritrea. These efforts included the return of numerous human rights violations and often indiscriminate violence, especially against the restructured villages that the EPLF had created in their previous zones of control. However, due to the popularity of the EPLF social programs which had been established, this harsh treatment simply continued the alienation of the Eritrean populace and allowed the EPLF guerrilla activities to continue almost unhindered behind Ethiopian lines.

The last major event of 1980 was the final destruction of the ELF. While its military forces had been essentially broken in the fighting and retreats of 1978–79, the last guerrilla vestiges still existed in the very western reaches of Eritrea near the Sudan border. With their strength almost gone and yet still standing astride the vital lifeline to food relief shipments, the ELF was more of a hindrance than a help to the EPLF's continued struggle. A brief conflict ensued wherein the EPLF, aided by their erstwhile allies in the TPLF, finally drove the remnants of the ELF into the Sudan where they would serve no further role in the conflict.[31] There now officially remained only one dominant Eritrean nationalist force carrying on the struggle, but it was one that had withstood years of civil and external war and had established itself as the more revolutionary and pragmatic of the two. By 1982 its strength would again be put to the test against the massive Ethiopian "Red Star" offensive.

The personnel gathered for the "Red Star" campaign (so named by Mengistu as a parallel to the contemporary "Bright Star" US exercises in the Mideast) was the largest concentration of military manpower seen so far in the conflict. The total military strength for Ethiopia at this point stood at 245,000, by far the largest army in Africa. The offensive itself saw 120,000 troops deployed against the Eritrean forces, although most of these were conscript troops with little training who were mostly used for massive blunt assaults against the EPLF positions.[32] Thus, although they outnumbered their Eritrean opponents by eight to one, the assaults often ended in bloody repulses, and by the end of the campaign over 40,000 of these Ethiopian conscripts would be casualties. By May 1982 the offensive had not even captured Nacfa, and in June the Ethiopian armed forces ceased operations. Despite it being their largest campaign to date, the Ethiopians still could not dislodge the Eritreans. With the failure of the "Red Star" campaign and its small follow-up "Stealth Offensive" of 1983, the strategic initiative returned to the battered Eritrean forces, and they began to hesitatingly advance against the spent Ethiopian forces in 1984. Although the Ethiopian forces continued to expand (topping 340,000 men in total in 1983 alone) and launched several counteroffensives in 1984 and 1985, they would never come so close to winning the war again.

The 1985 offensive was the largest yet and drove the Eritreans back from their recent gains with their largest losses to date (approximately 2,000–4,000 personnel killed and wounded), but this setback was primarily due to the Eritreans' switch from guerrilla to mobile warfare (which will be covered later in this chapter). The Eritrean repulse of the 1984–85 offensives saw the EPLF consolidate their hold on their western liberated zones and grow their forces from approximately 12,000 formal fighters to 30,000 by 1987, when their major counteroffensives began.[33] Drawing strength from their liberated areas and transforming the villages and cities they captured, the EPLF drove the Ethiopian forces back step by step and used their extremely effective social and relief organizations to help mitigate the effects of the massive famine that had been underway since the early 1980s. It was in these advances that the Eritreans began functioning effectively as conventional forces, taking and holding the ground they were traversing and forcing an Ethiopian response. The mobile warfare phase of the EPLF finally drew the Ethiopian forces into a decisive battle at Afabet on 17 March 1988, and over the next two days proceeded to annihilate the Ethiopian Northern Command.[34] Over 15,000 Ethiopian soldiers were killed and massive amounts of small arms, artillery, tanks, and ammunition fell into the hands of the ever-stronger EPLF.[35] Although the Ethiopian forces still existed in strength throughout Eritrea and would continue to struggle against the Eritrean liberation, they would never pose an adequate threat against the Eritreans after Afabet and were, despite their size and equipment, a broken force. In February 1990 Massawa fell to a rapid advance of the EPLF forces, who this time conquered the island bases with a small flotilla of rubber craft. By February and March 1991, Asmara fell to EPLF siege. The remainders of the Ethiopian garrisons of Asmara and Keren attempted to retreat to the Sudan and the vast majority of the combined force was captured en route. The struggle in Eritrea was essentially over, but one last act remained.

In January 1989 the TPLF had joined with a number of other ethnic liberation fronts in Ethiopia to form the combined Ethiopian People's Revolutionary Democratic Front (EPRDF). As the most veteran of all the organizations, the TPLF took the lead in the organization, and by February 1989 had driven the Ethiopian army completely from Tigray. Although relations had ruptured between the EPLF and TPLF in 1985, they had been restored during the successes of 1988, and the EPLF had sent a detachment to aid in the final liberation of Tigray and beyond.[36] Working side by side with the EPRDF from 1989 on, the combined force held Tigray and built its strength until February 1991. Despite the obviously growing threat from the combined forces of the various liberation fronts, the Ethiopian government found itself unable to muster an effective response. Beginning in the late 1980s, their Soviet benefactors had already been reducing their aid as internal tensions fostered by the strain of the Cold War weakened them from within. By 1989 the arms shipments and logistical support from the Soviet Union had dried up, leaving the already ailing Derg regime without its most important patron. While some smaller allies such as North Korea would offer Mengistu's regime aid until the end, it would not be enough to revive the Derg's strength.

From February on, the EPRDF launched a series of offensives, including "Operation Teodros," "Operation Dula Billisuma Welkita" (Oromo for "Equality and Freedom Campaign"), and finally "Operation Wallelign," which finally brought an end to Mengistu's Ethiopian regime when the dictator fled on 21 May 1991.[37] This effectively ended Ethiopian resistance and brought the TPLF-led coalition to power in Ethiopia. One of its first acts was to keep its previous promise to the EPLF and sponsor a resolution in the United Nations for the recognition of Eritrea as its own sovereign state. The thirty-year struggle for Eritrean liberation was over, and following a 1993 referendum, Eritrea joined the world as the first successful secession on African soil.

The Reasons for Success

Of course, the first major question that must spring to mind is: Why was this secession, of all attempts, successful? It did not have the foreign support or uncertainty regarding the concept of secession that Katanga had in its attempt. It did not have the humanitarian outcry of Biafra. The same factors that doomed all previous attempts and have since hobbled all subsequent attempted secessions applied to Eritrea: a lack of international recognition, a limited supply of arms, a finite and tenuous resource base, and an international consensus against the feared "balkanization" of African states. So what was it about the Eritrean case that allowed its anomalous success? What factors did the Eritrean conflict (and the EPLF in particular) have that set it apart from all the others so far and since? The answer is a tight combination of four interwoven factors that allowed Eritrea to achieve its successes. These four factors are (1) its unique historical development and the effects this had on the framing of the conflict, (2) the brilliant and ultimately successful application of the Maoist concept of Protracted War, (3) the simultaneous social revolution undertaken by the victorious party and its ultimate effect of forging a national identity, and (4) lastly, the pragmatic and decisive relations the EPLF constructed with the reform insurgencies going on in Ethiopia at the time of their revolt.

An Anomalous History

To deal with these factors in order, the first is the anomalous history of Eritrea in terms of its relations with Ethiopia. The historical basis of secessions has always been seen as a vital factor in separating a body politic from its host state. Katanga argued for its independence from the Congo based on its previous separate administration during the colonial era under the *Comité spécial du Katanga*. Biafra pointed to the historically separate administrations for each Nigerian region as well as their political separation from the North prior to 1914 as the grounds for both a confederal solution and their own secession. For Eritrea, their history with Ethiopia allowed for an even stronger and perhaps more effective argument. Although Ethiopia argued that Eritrea was their fourteenth province and was historically part of the Ethiopian empire, Eritrea could, would, and did maintain that their history not only placed them well outside the Ethiopian sphere of influence but that also that their development during the colonial period culturally and socially severed whatever historical ties might originally have been extant.

To begin with the history of Eritrea, the earliest connections that can be made to Ethiopia were to the Axumite kingdoms of the inland plateaus. By the fourth century CE, the Axumite expansion introduced Coptic Christianity to the highland plateaus that would form the heartland of both Ethiopia and Eritrea.[38] These kingdoms waxed powerful and even exerted a small amount of influence on the non-Christian peoples who lived along the coastal plains by the Red Sea, particularly at the economically thriving port of Adulis. However, these early links were severed permanently by the Muslim expansion of the seventh and eighth centuries CE.[39] By approximately 750 CE the Muslim influence had driven the power of the Axumite kingdoms and their Coptic faith from both the coastal lowlands and the Sudan. This spread of Islamic strength helped the nascent Beja kingdoms coalesce, and they quickly expanded their own influence onto the central plateau region, essentially severing the ancient "Ethiopian" control over whatever regions might now constitute Eritrea. In the fourteenth and fifteenth centuries the resurgent Ethiopians themselves had become recentralized and strong enough to challenge the Muslim states again and contested the central highlands, in a period that marked increased Christian influence. However, control of the lowlands still eluded the Ethiopians, and these plains would continue to be both an alien region and a staging ground for invaders for the next five centuries.[40] Throughout the sixteenth century the various Islamic empires of the region, especially the Ottomans, would give military aid to the Muslim coastal groups, leading to a contested existence for the fertile plateaus. By the end of the century a variety of sources referred to the region encompassing the coastal plains and the central plateau region as Medhi Bahri and viewed this nascent Eritrea as politically and culturally separate from Ethiopia.[41] In fact, from Eritrea's growth as a regional economic hub to its sublimation into the Egypt of Muhammed Ali and his successors from 1823 to its eventual fate as an Italian colony, Ethiopia could only claim partial control of the region for a period of nine years between 1880 and 1889.

Even following this partial control, in 1889 the Italians claimed full sovereign rights to the territory, as stipulated first in its recognition by the other European powers at the Berlin Conference of 1885 and later by Ethiopia itself in the Treaty of Uccialli in 1889. Admittedly the Treaty of Uccialli was and remains a controversial document. While the Amharic translation signed by Menelik II was written as saying that the Ethiopians "might" use Italy as intermediaries to the rest of Europe, the Italian version essentially suborned Ethiopian foreign policy to Italy.[42] However, despite this argument of interpretation, the treaty still clearly demarcated the boundaries of Eritrea and recognized the Italian sphere of influence over the Medri Bahri. Tellingly, even after the destruction of the Italian army at Adowa in 1896, Menelik did not conquer Eritrea as an Ethiopian possession. Instead the Treaty of Addis Ababa (signed 23 October 1896) reaffirmed Italian hegemony over an expanded Eritrea.[43] From this time until their defeat in 1941, the Italian occupation would serve to physically and culturally develop Eritrea as a separate and distinct entity far different from the feudal empire that Ethiopia remained.

Italian development played a decisive part in the creation of Eritrea. While admittedly the Eritreans themselves were seen as second-class subjects, the development of the Eritrean colony would have far-ranging implications for their culture and society. The displacement of previous notables in favour of Italian elites was perhaps the first major change, altering the traditional power structure of the region.[44] Mass plantation farming and wage labour was introduced, as large farms producing cotton, fruit, sisal, and coffee were set up and large numbers of Eritreans were recruited to work these fields to grow and harvest the produce for Italian consumption.[45] Mining was also introduced and continually expanded to produce the raw materials that the developing Italian state needed. Gold, iron, nickel, chromium, and other minerals were found and an effort was made to increase the exploitation of Eritrea's mineral wealth all the way into the 1930s and 1940s.[46] To help support this economy and develop other forms of it for their benefit, the Italians introduced improved medical and veterinary practices. In addition they instituted secular education for young men up to the fourth grade. The introduction of heavier industries and economic development also meant an expansion of infrastructure to take full advantage of the growing economy. A railway was built between Massawa, Asmara, and Agordat in 1922. An intricate network of all-weather roads was completed in 1935, primarily to aid in the military mobilization taking place in the colony. Telephone and telegraph lines were laid, and eventually airports were built to connect the burgeoning cities to the rest of the Italian Empire. Even the cities were expanded, as row houses were built to house the workers of over 300 small-scale workshops and industries around the major urban centres of Massawa, Asmara, and Assab, where increasing numbers of young Eritreans moved to earn wages to pay the new taxes being levied on them.[47] By 1935, the year that thousands of Eritrean soldiers invaded Ethiopia along with their Italian colonists, Eritrea no longer resembled its highland neighbour socially, economically, or culturally.

From 1936 to 1941, Ethiopia and Eritrea were briefly linked, but this was under the domination of Benito Mussolini's fascist military forces following the driving of Haile Selassie from his kingdom. This five-year period saw Eritrea continually used as a logistical base for the further expansion of the Italian Empire in East Africa, an empire that would be contemptuously dismantled by the British East African forces in 1941. While Ethiopia was handed back to Haile Selassie, Eritrea remained under the rule of a British military commission, which continued to use it as a light industrial centre for the war effort in the region. The United States used the former colony as a depot for its regional shipping and even constructed an airplane assembly plant at Gura. Britain leaned even more heavily upon the former colony, using its facilities to create trade goods for markets in the Horn that had been isolated by the closure of the Suez Canal to Italian trade early in the war. The Eritrean economy experienced a boom as it produced soap, matches, hand tools, beer, wine, and paper for regional trade. Simultaneously, Eritrean social structures were experiencing an "Eritreanization" under British auspices. Lesser administrative positions were opened to the Eritreans and the colour bar was slowly lowered on a variety of social functions. Education was again revitalized, and Arabic, Tigrinya, and English were taught in over sixty schools.[48] Public health services again became available and the colony continued its modernization.

Following the war the boom dried up, but the social and cultural changes remained. However, there was still the sticky question of what must be done with Eritrea. The outcome of this question has already been dealt with at the beginning of this narrative, but the import of it to both sides remains the key issue here. While Ethiopia can and did point toward the earnest desire of large swathes of Eritrean society that did indeed wish for union with Ethiopia, those who dissented had a powerful argument against union and one that they continued to use to support the cause of secession. That argument was a simple one: at no point could Ethiopia point toward a historic connection between the two nations, at least not one that was of recent enough vintage to truly matter. Even the brief periods of late nineteenth-century influence were themselves either not indicative of any formal connection or, as in the terms of the Treaty of Uccialli, formally renounced under international law. Furthermore, the Eritreans could and did argue that their separate evolution both socially and culturally in the decades of colonialism certainly put themselves outside any Ethiopian state that had existed throughout those decades. Whereas Ethiopia remained a largely feudal agricultural state that was run by a small aristocracy living off masses of downtrodden peasants, Eritrea was a semi-industrialized state with light industry, cash crop plantations, wage labour, and a flourishing administration, including a burgeoning political system made up of educated elites. As such, any claimed "union" between the two, whether it was historical or present, was spurious at best.

Thus, following the forced federation of the two states in 1952, and especially following the dissolution of the Eritrean Assembly in 1962, the Eritrean opposition did not see themselves as a movement of a political body separating itself from a host nation. Instead they saw themselves as engaged in a decolonization struggle against an African colonizer. This can be seen in a variety of literature, press statements, and even within the language used by the fronts themselves. Every group to emerge was a liberation front with nationalist intentions to free their nation from the control of an oppressive outside invader. The Eritreans would constantly make this argument throughout their struggle and made every effort to frame it as such. This was an important point for a very specific reason: as shown by the example of every secession struggle previous to that of Eritrea, the Organization of African Unity and the United Nations would brook no successful secession for fear of a domino effect and the balkanization of Africa.[49] Simply put, no international recognition could be expected and no international aid could be sought by a secessionist group. In fact, it would be far more likely to attract outright hostility and support for the host nation, in this case Ethiopia.[50] However, with the Eritrean struggle cast as one of decolonization, a whole new world of possibilities opened up. In terms of the OAU, which dominated any discussions of international interest on the continent, decolonization struggles were sacrosanct. Article II of the OAU Charter proclaimed that one of the primary purposes of the organization was "to eradicate all forms of colonialism from Africa," and article III, while serving as an insurmountable barrier to secession, declared "absolute dedication to the emancipation of the African territories which are still dependent" as one of the core principles of the union.[51] By casting their struggle as one of decolonization, then, the Eritreans avoided one of the key hurdles to every previous and following secession attempt on the continent of Africa. The OAU would never support the Eritrean efforts at any point during the struggle, but this recasting of the conflict as a liberation struggle did allow for legal wiggle room on what had been an airtight condemnation of any separation of African states, something that would have been doubly difficult in Ethiopia, symbol of African resistance and resilience and home to the OAU headquarters.

The Strategy of a Protracted Struggle

The legality of the secession/liberation would have been moot if the conflict waged to effect it had been crushed. Katanga and Biafra could argue their cases all they wished, but at the end of the day their states were overrun by enemy forces and their leadership was forced to declare an end to the separation. In comparison, the military campaign for the future of Eritrea was brilliantly successful. While the conception of it as a Long War has already been touched upon in the introduction to Part II, Eritrea stands out even among other secession and liberation attempts for being an exceptionally successful application of the military dictums of Mao's theory of protracted warfare, a theoretical construct that served the purposes of Eritrea extremely well with only slight modifications. In this, Eritrea's success resembled nothing so much as the previous anti-colonial struggles of both China[52] and Vietnam.[53] Their application of this theory cannot be especially surprising, given that contemporary African liberation fronts were taking advantage of it (most notably Amilcar Cabral's PAIGC against the Portuguese) and that many early figures in the EPLF leadership had received military training in China during their tenure in the ELF.[54] What is astonishing is the extremely clear application of these theories and their remarkable effectiveness against the Ethiopian enemy.

Mao laid out his military philosophy in a series of lectures presented over the period of the Chinese Civil War and the Sino-Japanese war of 1937–1945. Noting that the Communist Chinese forces were weak in comparison to both the Kuomintang (KMT) of Chiang Kai-Shek and the Army of Imperial Japan, he laid out the strategic vision necessary to effectively prosecute the conflict against these enemies for the ultimate victory of his revolutionary forces. Perhaps central to the military canon of Mao is his work "On Protracted War," which lays out the three stages that a revolutionary army must pass through during its protracted struggle with a superior enemy. The first is the period of Strategic Defence.[55] It is a given that the revolutionary forces will be smaller, worse supplied, and unable to resist the counter-revolutionary forces in the early stages of a conflict. The ability of a centrally organized and legitimate opponent to both generate its own support and gain outside aid will always outweigh that of a revolution in a semi-feudal nation to begin with. This early stage must of necessity be one of defence and retreat. The primary course of action for the revolutionary front must be that of survival while extending the enemy further and depleting his strength. For Mao this was easy given the vast distances involved in China. Without these distances, alternative methods of survival would have to be applied, as will be seen in the following analysis.[56] As the enemy reached the terminal edge of his operational distance and the threat of imminent annihilation passed, the revolutionaries could transition into the second phase.

The second phase as delineated by Mao was the Strategic Stalemate.[57] This occurred when the enemy had extended himself to his current limit but the revolutionaries were not yet strong enough to take the initiative. In this phase the revolutionaries then had two primary goals: the prosecution of guerrilla warfare and the mobilization of the populace. In terms of the prosecution of the guerrilla war, it was assumed that it would still be impossible to combat the counter-revolutionary forces directly, but yet it was necessary to continue to reduce his strength, in order to both safeguard the revolution and create the factors necessary to transition to the third phase. The countryside would become the home of guerrilla bands, sent to harass and damage the enemy's extended supply lines and communications. The counter-revolutionary's food and ammunition were to be hijacked or destroyed, his ability to transmit information disrupted, and his security outside areas of concentrated strength compromised as much as possible. A simultaneous objective was the mobilization of the populace, which was to take place in several safeguarded base areas. These areas, made secure by remote location, strong defences, or secrecy, were to serve as centres of production, education, and social transformation. By offering a strong alternative to the currently unpopular counter-revolutionary government, these base areas would grow the strength of the revolution by mobilizing the populace to either directly serve the revolution as fighters or indirectly serve it by producing the logistical necessities for the prosecution of the conflict. Thus, during the second phase a process of the simultaneous weakening of the enemy and strengthening of the revolutionaries would take place until the balance of power had firmly tipped in the favour of the revolution, when the final stage of the protracted conflict would begin.

This final stage was that of the Strategic Offensive.[58] Having weakened the enemy, harassed his communications, taken the security of the countryside from him, and mobilized and organized its own strength in terms of both quality and quantity of forces, the revolution could now transition from its combination of guerrilla and defensive warfare to one of guerrilla and offensive mobile warfare. While the guerrillas could continue to exist and pursue their missions throughout the countryside, the main force of the revolution would now fight in mobile conventional formations, seeking to stalk, confront, and destroy the now inferior counter-revolutionary forces. The entire purpose of the transition to mobile warfare was to use the greater agility of the revolutionary forces (who were not hampered by the great distances of communication or a hostile countryside) to concentrate an insurmountable force against the isolated enemy formations and force a decisive confrontation that would see the destruction of the opponent. With this achieved, it was simply necessary to repeat the process in the strategic offensive until all enemy formations were destroyed or driven from the revolutionary state. This would conclude hostilities and secure peace on the terms of the revolutionary front.

A key concept within this theory of protracted conflict (and one that we will see was decisive in terms of the Eritrean case), was Mao's enunciation and acceptance of the Strategic Retreat. While this was implicit in "On Protracted War," he had more fully delineated the concept in his earlier lecture "Problems of Strategy in China's Revolutionary War," where he began his exploration with the pronouncement "The objective of strategic retreat is to conserve military strength and prepare for the counteroffensive. Retreat is necessary because not to retreat a step before the onset of a strong enemy means to jeopardize the preservation of one's own forces."[59] This retreat would follow a number of strategic precepts to ensure the maximum benefit was to be gained even as the forces pulled back from a superior enemy. The first precept was that the retreat should always take advantage of prepared interior lines to safely fall back on prepared base areas from which the revolutionary forces could derive strength. The second was that the retreat should always be undertaken unless at least two of the following conditions could be met, if not more: the revolutionaries had the active support of the populace; the terrain was favourable for operations, all of the main revolutionary forces were concentrated, the enemy's weak spots had been discovered, the enemy had been reduced to a tired and demoralized state, or the enemy had been induced to make mistakes. When two of these conditions had been met, it would signal the opportunity to switch from the strategic withdrawal to the offensive yet again.[60] However, it must always be remembered that Mao intended the strategic retreat to create these favourable advantages, and thus to both preserve the revolutionary forces and enable their future success.

Finally, underpinning all of these concepts was Mao's stated Principles of Operation, as enunciated in his lecture "The Present Situation and Our Tasks."[61] These were a list of ten operational concepts that would serve as the philosophical basis for the greater strategic thinking of the Protracted War. The first was to prioritize attacking dispersed and isolated enemies, leaving concentrated enemy strong points for later operations. The second instructed the revolutionaries to occupy large rural areas and small and medium-sized cities first, leaving large urban areas for later. The third directed the combatants to focus their efforts on the reduction and demolition of their opponent's effective strength before all other things; when the enemy's strength had been broken, cities, towns, and other strategic areas would fall far more easily. The fourth exhorted the revolutionary forces to only fight when absolute numerical superiority was on their side (at least double their opponent's strength) and then, when fighting, to seek to encircle and annihilate their foe—use their numbers and mobility to complete dismantle their enemy and avoid costly battles of attrition. The fifth instructs the revolutionaries to fight no battle unprepared and without absolute surety of victory. The sixth instructs the combatants to be selfless in combat and ignore fear of sacrifice and fatigue and be accepting of the necessity of fighting several successive battles. The seventh points to the advantage of using mobile warfare to overcome the enemy but advises not to neglect positional tactics when reducing the enemy's fixed points. The eighth commands the revolutionary front to resolutely seize all strong points if a city must be attacked, taking care to use timing and aggression to overcome them and waiting for opportune moments if one must attack the defences of a large city. The ninth addresses the material strength of the revolutionaries: they must "replenish [their] strength with all the arms and most of the personnel captured from the enemy. [Their] main sources of manpower and material are at the front."[62] And the final principle explains the necessity of using intervals between fighting to rest, train, and consolidate, but also to not let these intervals grow so long as to let the enemy relax. These ten main principles served as the basic tactical thinking in the greater scheme of the strategic thought of the Protracted War.

Now, if we examine these concepts in terms of the Eritrean struggle, it is striking how often they align with the key events of the war itself and its eventual successful conclusion. The three stages of the Protracted War can be clearly seen, with the conflict actually repeating part of the evolution of the struggle to adapt to the changing situation. The strategic retreat was to prove a decisive factor in the determination of the dominant liberation front. The base areas that were to provide so much of the logistical strength are obviously in evidence, so much so that an entire section following this one will be devoted to them and the social revolution they housed. And lastly, although documented evidence for all of them is certainly not forthcoming and sometimes the principles were ignored (often to the detriment of the cause), a great many of Mao's principles of operation can be seen quite plainly in the Eritrean prosecution of their struggle.

In terms of the protracted struggle itself, the experience of the ELF and (to a far greater degree) the EPLF reflected the Maoist thought at work in African liberation struggles of time. The Strategic Defence period can originally be seen in the early days of the struggle, specifically from 1961 to approximately 1968. During this time the ELF had fled from the urban centres that had originally been its political bases to the western Sahel region while its leadership existed in exile in Cairo. As pressure from the Ethiopian military drove them farther from their original base areas, they often found themselves retreating to new base areas across the border in the Sudan, where the new waves of university-educated recruits found them.[63] It was during this period of limited guerrilla activity and cross-border withdrawals that the liberation front husbanded its strength until it was ready to begin formal expansion within Eritrea proper.

After this limited example of the ELF facing an initial Ethiopian effort, the conception of the strategic defensive and retreat is seen far more clearly in response to the Soviet-backed offensives of 1978, where the EPLF found itself facing a massive resurgent Ethiopian army that had tipped the balance of power back in favour of Mengistu's state. The EPLF leadership determined that any attempt to hold on to their hard-won gains against the steamrolling Ethiopian forces would endanger the survival of the revolution itself. The EPLF therefore abandoned what they considered "secondary" objectives such as Massawa and Keren in order to consolidate their forces and attempt to bring about a future situation where the balance of power might be more equal. Their forces retreated in a series of holding actions all the way back to their base region around Nacfa, which had been prepared for a prolonged static positional defence. Tellingly, EPLF fighters even referred to this withdrawal as their "Long March," equating it with the 1934–35 long strategic retreat of Mao's own forces to the vast spaces of western China. Once ensconced in Nacfa, the EPLF forces were able to bring about far more advantageous conditions, including better fighting terrain, a consolidation of forces, and a completely loyal and enthusiastic general population that would serve as an excellent logistical base. By the time the Ethiopians had prepared their next offensives, the Eritrean forces had already created the conditions to transition to the strategic stalemate and to begin dismantling their pursuers. On the other hand, the fate of the ELF over the same period perhaps does even more to reflect the efficacy of the Maoist strategy. Although they faced a far greater concerted assault than the EPLF, the ELF leadership refused to enact a strategic retreat and instead chose to fight the Ethiopians from their newly liberated areas. Within weeks the ELF lines were broken and they were retreating in a panic.[64] In the aftermath of the Ethiopian offensives the ELF was spent as a military force and the vast majority of its fighters were absorbed into the now safely entrenched EPLF.

As to the strategic stalemate, again several periods of the Eritrean conflict fit within the Maoist framework. From 1968 to 1974 both the ELF and the emerging EPLF were establishing those regions that would serve as their base areas and slowly expanding their guerrilla operations. During this time Haile Selassie's army was under constant harassment and could not effectively deal with the swarming raids that were taking their toll on communications and logistics. It was also during this period that both fronts established their social programs, which defined the Eritrea they each hoped to bring about following the conflict. In spreading these ideals and social frameworks, they also established their base areas from which further expansion of their forces could come. Frontline fighters and militia were recruited, workshops and medical services were established, and new political organizations were formed. It was this process of winning over the populace that again created the conditions for the transition to the next stage of combat.

The strategic stalemate was also illustrated in the Nacfa period following the strategic retreat of 1978 and lasting until approximately 1984. Much as the "Long March" of the EPLF better illustrated the conception of the strategic retreat, the Nacfa period better shows the idea of the strategic stalemate, reflecting the increasing maturity of the EPLF military command. As mentioned, the retreat to Nacfa accomplished a number of strategic objectives: it preserved the nationalist front's armed forces, it consolidated them in the face of overwhelming enemy forces, it established them closer to their own base of support in Nacfa and northern Eritrea, it established their forces in far more advantageous terrain, and it also forced the Ethiopian forces to extend themselves and their lines of communication even farther into rugged Eritrean territory. With these factors established, the Eritreans needed to accomplish two simple military goals: grow their own strength while reducing that of the Ethiopians in preparation for a strategic counteroffensive. To accomplish these goals, the Eritreans resorted to a combination of positional and guerrilla warfare.[65] The guerrillas wreaked havoc on the extended Ethiopian lines of communication, while the fortified lines of the Eritreans withstood four separate offensives in 1979 alone. These offensives cost the Ethiopians massive amounts of men and materiel, while the Eritreans reaped a large amount of captured arms and ammunition.[66] The lines were again tested in 1982 by the "Red Star" campaign, which again did little more than waste massive amounts of men and armaments while increasing Eritrean morale and arms caches. With this the Eritreans felt they were ready to enter the counteroffensive stage by 1983, but a series of local counterattacks by the still massive Ethiopian forces, including one of comparable size to the "Red Star," took place during 1983–1985, delaying but not denying the inevitable shift in strategic initiative and strength that signalled the beginnings of the final strategic offensive stage of the war.[67]

However, the strategic offensives of 1987–1991 were not the first of the struggle. Following the strategic stalemate period of 1974, the downfall of Haile Selassie and the confusion and excesses of the Derg led to a tipping of the scales in terms of power and strategic initiative. Both the ELF and EPLF, flush with recruits and captured weapons, went on the offensive and slowly but surely expanded their territory to control the vast majority of Eritrea. This was the period during which Asmara was cut off from Massawa in the standard practice of isolating the cities and saving them for last. Local superiority allowed the EPLF to capture Keren in an astonishingly brief assault.[68] During 1974–1978 both liberation fronts did their best to liberate the countryside, educate and mobilize the populace, and then slowly envelop the cities. This course was only reversed when the unexpected military intervention of the Soviets suddenly altered the balance of forces again and made the conditions supremely unfavourable for the strategic offensive of the Eritreans. This left 1978 as the high-water mark of the struggle until the reopening of the strategic offensive in 1987 by the EPLF and its allied liberation fronts.

The final counteroffensives beginning in 1987 were due to a combination of factors that weakened the Ethiopians severely and at least kept the EPLF from suffering the same fate. The failed offensives of 1979–1985 drained the Ethiopian forces of men and weapons and emboldened the large number of guerrilla fronts now actively fighting within Ethiopia itself. Beyond military overreach, Ethiopia was in the midst of one of the most severe famines the world had ever seen. Although food aid was diverted to their military, Ethiopia was slowly starving, and popular support of the Mengistu regime was almost nonexistent. In opposition to this the EPLF was as strong as it had ever been. It had absorbed what was left of the ELF's armed forces, it had captured a vast amount of military hardware from the Ethiopian forces over the course of their failed attacks in the north, it had fostered several of the now mature guerrilla fronts that were tearing their enemy apart from the inside, and while not well stocked with food by any means, their base areas produced some amount of food and their efficient social programs such as the Eritrean Relief Association ensured that they were at least not in as bad a shape as the Ethiopians.

The balance of power had shifted for the last time, and the strategic offensive began in December 1987 as the EPLF forces overran the Ethiopian defences outside Nacfa. Their mobile conventional forces sought out local advantages against the weakening Ethiopian forces in an attempt to obtain a decisive victory and on 17 March 1988 secured one. The Battle of Afabet raged for three days and saw the complete destruction of the Ethiopian Northern Command. There were over 15,000 Ethiopian casualties and the EPLF again captured vast stocks of arms and vehicles, including over fifty tanks. Whereas the Eritreans compared their earlier withdrawal with the famous "Long March," now the world took notice and compared Afabet with Dien Bien Phu, the decisive Vietnamese victory over the French colonial forces in the first Indochina war.[69] From this point the offensive was essentially unbroken and the Eritrean forces could even feel the momentum on the ground level.⁷⁰ The crushing loss, combined with the drying up of Soviet support for Mengistu's regime, sapped the strength of any Ethiopian resistance. The countryside was overrun, in 1990 Massawa and Decamere were recaptured, and by 1991 Asmara and Addis Ababa were taken in the final offensives of the liberation struggle.

By holding true to Mao's conception of protracted warfare and not being afraid of adopting a defensive or even withdrawing pattern, the Eritrean Liberation movements endured the worst that an opponent alternatively armed by the two superpowers could throw at them. The idea of withdrawing from an enemy's strength until advantage was regained was internalized within the EPLF in particular and proved to be a decisive lesson. Without the outright defeat of the Ethiopian forces, no doubt the political separation of the two countries would have been an impossibility. However, Mao's lessons revolve around the idea of base areas and the loyalty and support of the people—the peasants and proletariat that provide the raw material for the struggle.⁷¹ Without these men and women, the armed forces would never win their victories and the guerrillas would be fish attempting to swim in a hostile sea. As such, the military victory of the Eritreans, again the EPLF in particular, stemmed ultimately from the social revolution they effected in the countryside and cities, which created an Eritrean identity and mobilized the populace. This mobilized populace in turn not only formed the base areas that offered succor and strength during the conflict but also served as the strong foundation for the emergent Eritrean nation.

A Social Revolution

While both fronts stressed the social transformation of Eritrea as a component of the struggle, the ELF was not as radical as their brethren in the EPLF and consequently did not effect such a startling transformation. While the ELF did establish medical and relief services under the Eritrean Red Cross–Red Crescent society, they did not expand the medical services well beyond this. In terms of their village restructuring, they tended to establish village committees but leave them in the hands of traditional powers of the village. While they did establish several mass organizations such as the General Union of Eritrean Workers, the General Union of Eritrean Students, the

Eritrean Women's General Union, the General Union of Eritrean Peasants, and the Eritrean Democratic Youth Union, these and the subsequent contributions to the struggle itself were more in the nature of reactions to the more radical political transformations going on in the EPLF.[72] This was a pattern that was all too familiar, as the ELF tended to view the struggle as paramount and the social revolution as a secondary objective that could be handled after the war had been won. The ELF was forced to then react when the more developed and mature social programs of the EPLF began to draw in much greater support from the populace. To put it simply, the social programs of the ELF were generally shallow and reactive and consequently only generated shallow support for their cause. The effect of this policy can then be seen again in the aftermath of the 1978 reverses, where the ELF was displaced and shattered by the Ethiopian advance, whereas the EPLF had prepared loyal base regions to retreat through that welcomed them again when they returned to the offensive.[73]

To create those loyal base regions the EPLF initiated an entirely transformative program and ideal for the emergent Eritrean consciousness. By building on a basis of five major mass organizations (for workers, peasants, women, students, and youth, just like the reactive organizations of the ELF) that began to operate openly in 1977 after years of clandestine organizing, the EPLF enunciated a completely transformative program that would alter the very fabric of Eritrean society. This program's stated goals would completely rebuild Eritrea in terms of agricultural production, industrial production, education, health care, and even gender relations.

In terms of agricultural production and relations, the Eritrean general program for reform called for a socialized agricultural sector with control placed back in the hands of the producers. In theory the program claimed its goals as including the nationalization of the lands expropriated by the Ethiopians and their feudal collaborators and revising this into larger collective farms for the use of the masses. It also sought to introduce more modern farming methods, including the use of machinery and modern fertilizers to help increase the productivity of the peasant class. For the still existing pastoralists, veterinary and breeding aid would be provided as well as financial aid to help them become sedentary and successful animal breeders. Beyond all these (and several other small provisions) it purported to allow for the amicable and fair resolution of land inequality and ownership disputes while providing for the organization and collectivization of peasants so they might look after their own affairs.[74] For the most part these goals were reached. Self-sustaining cells of peasant organizers set up village committees that represented all strata of agricultural life. In such model villages as Zagher they oversaw the redistribution of land that had been monopolized by richer farming families and settled disputes within the community.[75] While this was a long process, by the end of the land redistribution large numbers of peasants who had never had land had plots of their own to tend to. Often surplus land could then be farmed collectively by the newly created farmers' association, the produce of which then went into a cooperative shop. The individual plots as well were allocated along the lines of the association membership, which organized them so as to allow the easier introduction of new farming techniques. The front even trained "barefoot veterinarians" along the lines of China's famous barefoot doctors to offer free veterinary services to the pastoral and agricultural population's animals.

Under the EPLF's guidance, similar alterations were made to the structure of industrial production and relations. Much as with the Ethiopian- and collaborator-owned land, the industries held by these proscribed groups would be nationalized along with the vital large industries of the nation itself, such as the ports, mines, public transport, and power. Meanwhile foreign-owned industries of a small scale would be allowed as long as the owners were from nations that had not opposed Eritrean independence.[76] To aid growth in the industrial sector, urban land would be made state property along with excess urban housing. The rent for this housing would then be set at a reasonable level for the standard of living in the region by the managing government. The citizens whose property was thus nationalized would be duly compensated for their losses.[77] In terms of the workers themselves, their rights were to be strictly safeguarded, partially by the organization and politicization of the workers themselves. These stated rights included an eight-hour work day and at maximum a six-day work week, as well as social safety nets for age and disability. The nationalized urban property would be made available to these organized workers to assure them decent living conditions. Most tellingly, the politicized workers would be given the right to "participate in the management and administration of enterprises and industries."[78] By offering the workers organizations, security, and strong interest in the continuation of the national industries, the EPLF theoretically offered a complete revolution to the working class. Again, much as in the agricultural reforms, the EPLF were able to implement the vast majority of these programs while the struggle was still going on. During their administration of Keren in 1977 they retained the status of the previously nationalized housing but slashed the price of the rents, particularly the lowest rents, to further aid those distressed by the conflict.[79] They also changed the pay scale for workers, lowering those that were highest while dramatically increasing those that had been lowest.[80] As to the industries themselves, even as early as 1975–76 the EPLF liberated zones had a plurality of small cottage industries sustained by and sustaining the revolution. Woodworking collectives altered weaponry while machine shops fabricated parts for everything from weaponry to generators and agricultural machinery. The collective work, reform, and politicization of the industrial base of the revolution played a vital role in the conflict.

In every sector the greatest emphasis was placed on education. Free compulsory education, grants and scholarships, the establishment of more primary schools and institutes of higher education, and most importantly the pledge to "combat illiteracy to free the Eritrean people from the darkness of ignorance"[81] were central to the educational revolution that the EPLF insisted on for their nation. While it might be thought that most of these goals could only effectively be pursued in peacetime, perhaps more than any other sector of its revolution the EPLF made education a ubiquitous part of their struggle. The EPLF demanded that all members serving in the front be literate in Arabic or Tingrinya and established this training for the both the older members and the "Vanguards," the youth who were inducted into the struggle initially in non-combatant roles until they reached adulthood. These new inductees were also given education in history, political theory, first aid and public health, and other basic subjects. In the EPLF-run refugee camps and liberated towns, classes were given in political theory, the history of Eritrea, and most of all literacy. These same literacy courses were run out of the hospitals for those rehabilitating from injuries, as well as courses in geography and elementary math.[82] Astonishingly these same sorts of courses were also provided to Ethiopian prisoners of war, the vast majority of whom were illiterate conscripted peasants and often from marginalized ethnic groups like the Oromo. Beyond the training in the field, the EPLF established and ran over thirty-six schools in 1976 alone.[83] While it cannot be said that the education was given for entirely selfless reasons, as a cynical observer can easily claim that such education is better labelled indoctrination, it cannot be denied that the mass teaching of literacy altered the entire philosophical base of the nation and helped spread the conception of Eritrea as more than a collection of nine separate nationalities.

Hand in hand with education was the complete overhaul of public health services. The EPLF sought to establish a system of free public health care that not only treated the populace at large but served as a basis for locally manufactured medicines and as centres for the eradication of contagious diseases.[84] Public health was paramount, and by focusing their energies the EPLF made remarkable headway. Two tiers of medical training (a basic and an intermediate) were established to produce a greater number of qualified medical personnel to man the expanding programs as the movement gained maturity. As of 1977 alone the EPLF was operating four major hospitals with a combined capacity of nearly 1400 patients.[85] These facilities were equipped with basic medical necessities such as microscopes, refrigerators, and X-ray machines. Beyond these central hospitals, the front operated over twenty intermediate clinics established in liberated or semi-liberated areas to deal with regional patients, and even had limited in-patient capabilities. To supplement these formal facilities, teams of doctors were trained to travel the largely rural areas, in the mould of the "Barefoot Doctors," to inoculate the populace as well as offer free medical care to the villages. Over the course of their struggle the EPLF extended medical services to the populace at large where there had been essentially no formal health services previously.

Lastly, and perhaps the most radical step taken in their social revolutionary program, the EPLF obliterated the previous conceptions of gender roles in their liberated areas. Whereas Eritrea had long been an extremely conservative and patriarchal state regardless of region, the EPLF explicitly stated their goals for women's rights. Women were to be freed from domestic confinement and assured full rights of equality in representation, pay, and participation, and progressive marriage and family laws were to be established.[86] Beyond this the EPLF promised to respect the right to maternity leave, to provide maternal services, and even to try and eradicate prostitution, which they viewed as a violent act against women. It would be right of an observer to be skeptical, though, as it is common for revolutionary movements to exalt women's rights and yet do little to attain them.[87] However, as with all other provisions within its programs, the EPLF did a remarkable job in attaining its goals under the pressures of wartime. First and foremost, women were organized as an important part of the front and were always given equal representation within the political structure of the EPLF itself. They were not barred from serving in any capacity within the front, and women commonly took combatant roles, with women constituting 13 percent of the army by 1977.[88] The education programs offered by the front were perhaps even more revolutionary for the women involved, as literacy had been even rarer amongst women than men before the conflict. However, the alterations to women's rights did not stop within the boundaries of direct service to the front. In liberated areas the land reform was just as open to women as men, and women were amongst those who claimed plots of land in Zagher and other model villages. As the EPLF's programs became more ingrained in the social fabric of communities, they often began trying to redefine the traditional practice of marriage to offer more egalitarian roles. This was a revolutionary step, as marriage was a defining characteristic in traditional Eritrean society, where it essentially relegated women to a servile role.[89] With the new laws being put into place, concepts of mutual consent for marriages became common, as well as a woman's right to divorce. Beyond this, ages of consent began to be established, doing away with child marriages, which had the effect of opening up a whole new world of independent adolescence for young women, transforming their possibilities in education, employment, and even newer ideas of courtship. Although this is not to say that all communities accepted these changes quickly or easily, the balance of sexual power was altered by the social revolution of the EPLF and women were to a great degree liberated from their previous servitude.[90]

The social revolution altered Eritrea irrevocably and even at the time was noted for its far-reaching consequences. No less a scholar of revolutions than Gérard Chaliand wrote that "the EPLF is by far the most impressive revolutionary movement produced in Africa in the past two decades."[91] This complete social revolution would prove to be vital to the success of the Eritrean struggle for two primary reasons. The first was that the revolution and the acceptance of its precepts more than anything else helped the Eritrean cause overcome the regional, linguistic, and confessional barriers to national unity. While earlier attempts in Katanga and Biafra both faltered when ethnic differences helped fracture efforts of secession, following the adoption of the social revolution there never was a credible threat of ethnic or religious divisions within the Eritrean front. Even later attempts at secession that will be discussed constantly found (and still find) themselves hobbled by the disunity often flippantly referred to by the press as "tribalism." The South Sudanese efforts, as will be discussed, were consistently riven with Dinka and Nuer conflicts within the larger struggle, often leading to suboptimal military results in the field. Other subsequent efforts such as the Azawad movement or the Casamance separatists have been hobbled not so much by ethnic divisions as by their lack of an overarching ideology that can transcend their narrowly defined nationalisms and attract a wide enough base of support to succeed. By adopting a social revolution and using it to advance precepts that created a national ideology and identity which was accepted and proliferated by the populace, the EPLF created a nation in the process of liberating it.

The second major reason for the importance of the social revolution has already been discussed in the previous paragraphs: the creation of loyal and productive base areas are a necessity for the pursuit of a protracted conflict. By instituting large-scale agrarian reform, workers' rights, women's rights, education, and healthcare, the EPLF created a popular front that earned the peoples' loyalty and efforts. More than this, in the model villages and towns and amongst the workshops and hospitals in the remote regions, they created a popular society that then had a vested interest in seeing their revolution succeed in the only way that mattered: the military overthrow of the oppressive power. Thus the EPLF's social revolution created areas that were loyal and productive for their efforts and which turned barren for their opponents.[92] Put in Maoist terms, strategically they always had one of the necessary conditions for advantage, and tactically the guerrillas always had a deep popular sea to swim in. Put simply, the implementation of the social revolution created the conditions necessary for their military triumph.

Pragmatic Alliances

Last of the decisive anomalous factors that allowed the successful political separation was what has been termed the EPLF's pragmatic relations with other liberation fronts. Given the long duration of Eritrea's conflict and Ethiopia's autocratic governmental structure from shortly after the Second World War until 1991, it was inevitable that other resistance movements would have come into being. A particularly large number were constituted shortly after the coup against Haile Selassie and the beginning of the Derg's oppressive Marxist turn in 1974. Although most of these never grew to a size where they could be considered a significant ally in the larger anti-Derg struggle, one in particular would prove to play a deciding part in the success of the secession of Eritrea. The Tigray People's Liberation Front began their armed struggle against the Ethiopian government in 1975 and quickly established relations with the two working Eritrea fronts, the ELF and EPLF.[93] Both Eritrean fronts offered aid to the fledgling group, with which they shared linguistic and educational ties. Although ties were severed with the ELF in 1976 due to disputes over boundaries between Eritrea and Tigray, the TPLF established a strong relationship with the EPLF.[94] The two fronts shared a Marxist viewpoint and a common goal of self-criticism to keep their movements ideologically pure. The EPLF even offered aid in material and training for the Tigrayans, with between three and four thousand Tigrayan fighters being sent to the Sahel for training with the Eritreans. These troops were to prove decisive in blunting the Ethiopian offensives in the early 1980s directed against the Eritreans.[95]

This is not to say that the two fronts always saw eye to eye. There was widespread disagreement between the two as to the tactics to be employed for the struggle. In 1980 the EPLF had transitioned into a conventional and increasingly professional military structure in their strategic stalemate with Ethiopia, fighting battles from fixed positions and holding their liberated territory in open battle.[96] The Tigrayans felt that this distanced the fighters from the populace as well as increasing needlessly the losses inflicted on the front. The TPLF remained adamant that a guerrilla war from the countryside was the only method that would allow success against the Soviet-backed Derg. Beyond this, there was a fundamental difference in their goals. While the EPLF was a secession insurgency, looking to physically separate their nation from the state, the TPLF was a reform insurgency, intent on using the state apparatus to carry out a social revolution in all of Ethiopia. As part of the TPLFs goals, they embraced the concept that each separate ethnic group of a state can and should form its own front and have the right to self-determination. This concept was unthinkable to the EPLF, which fought for the centrality of a nation and denied the concept of ethnic self-determination.[97] This fundamental difference led to deep tensions, exacerbated by the Tigrayans' insistence on denouncing the Soviet Union due to its support of the Derg versus the Eritreans' continued pursuit of an alliance.[98]

In 1985 the two fronts formally severed diplomatic ties due to these continued tensions, with the TPLF going so far as to offer support to a minor rival opposition front in Eritrea.[99] However, the TPLF continued to support the concept of Eritrean independence, which left the door open for a rapprochement that was not long in coming. This new agreement was hastened by Ethiopia's settlement with Somalia over the Ogaden region in 1988,[100] which freed up massive numbers of troops to continue the conflicts against the regional insurgencies. From 1988 on the TPLF and EPLF formed a coordinated front with agreed-upon goals and aims for their partnership. This united front between the Eritreans and the Ethiopian People's Revolutionary Democratic Front (the multi-ethnic coalition that the Tigrayans welded together and headed) launched a series of offensives that finally caused the Ethiopian regime to crumble in 1991. This was the deciding moment for both insurgencies.

One cannot overestimate the importance of the common goals and aims adopted between the Eritreans and the Tigrayans. Initially the two provided shared intelligence and logistics to pursue the protracted struggles that would bleed the Ethiopian regime dry. By broadening the base of the conflict, the two fronts working in combination crushed attempts by the Derg to bring an end to the conflict for over a decade. The so-called "Ethiopian Peasant Crusade" was destroyed with little fanfare in 1976. The two fronts also worked together to stymie the efforts of the Ethiopian "Red Star" campaign in 1982, the defeat of which essentially doomed any further efforts by the Derg to crush either front. Beyond this military coordination was the decisive nature of their relationship. By maintaining relations with the Tigrayans and aiding in the success of their reform insurgency,[101] the

Eritreans ensured their own reward at the completion of the campaign. With a sympathetic government now in power over their previous colonial oppressor, the Eritreans claimed their share of the spoils: a declaration of recognition of their independence in 1991.

The importance of this declaration of recognition is especially critical given the political difficulties that had been established in terms of secession in Africa. For the OAU to recognize a seceding region would require a motion to be brought before it by a member state. However, not just any member would do—as the case of Biafra amply shows. If an external power tried to bring forward a motion to recognize a separatist or secessionist movement, the "host nation" could invoke article III and argue that it was their own internal business and their sovereignty in such matters must be respected. It was this dynamic that made the alliance with the TPLF and their greater organization the EPRDF so vital. Without the EPRDF driving out Mengistu's forces and achieving their own sovereign rule over the nation of Ethiopia, there would be no guarantee of recognition at all. It was only through their effective and pragmatic relations with the now-ruling party of Ethiopia that the EPLF was able to gain the sponsorship of their own host nation for their separation and the agreement to allow a referendum two years later to determine the future political status. With the ruling regime in Addis Ababa giving their blessing to the actions within their own territory, there was little that the international community could see wrong with the formal separation of the two states in 1993. Simply put, without the simultaneous reform insurgency within Ethiopia, the secession of Eritrea would have been an impossibility.

Eritrea: Secession or Liberation?

There is one final matter to discuss on the case of Eritrea, one of classification and its place as a case study in this volume. Eritrea, and the EPLF in particular, offer a remarkably anomalous case—one where there was a vast social revolution and reconstruction and where the struggle itself was fought and discussed as a liberation. In fact, the secession of Eritrea in its historical roots and practical applications often bears a far greater resemblance to such notable liberation struggles as Guinea-Bissau or Namibia, a comparison that might be well to the Eritrean fighters' liking. So then, given its historical argument of a struggle against an African colonizer and its strategic characteristics of a revolutionary liberation, can we actually classify Eritrea's case as secession? Does it actually fit within the scope of this volume?

The answer to the former question is still being argued within the contentious realm of Eritrean and Ethiopian scholarship. There are compelling arguments on each side, and this volume does not want to wander into minefield of "Greater Ethiopianism versus Eritrean Nationalism" so familiar to all sides of the discussion. Instead, what is important in this case is the answer to the second question, that of its place within this volume. The answer to the second question, regardless of that to the first, must be that it remains a central case study in the arc of secession in Africa. Whether or not one classifies the Eritrean struggle as a formal secession, it remains the first instance of a recognized political separation in Africa, and one can't help but look at the circumstances that brought it about and feel that these circumstances are indeed necessities for the separation to occur. By this fact alone it must be included in this volume, if only to show what was necessary for a separation to take place and why any other successful subsequent separation has seemed to follow much of the same blueprint.

Map of Sudan and South Sudan

Copyright © 2014 Nathan E. McCormack and Charles G. Thomas

4

The Secession of South Sudan, 1955–2011

The longest self-determination conflict in Africa lasted for over fifty years, with only small pockets of respite marking periods of either compromise or exhaustion on the part of its combatants. Over the course of this time, the struggle of the South Sudan against the Khartoum-based, Northern-dominated government underwent radical changes that make it uniquely suited to this study. Although at its core the struggle has always been about the self-determination of the people of the South Sudan, the goals have altered throughout its prosecution, alternating between representation, separatism, and secession as different generations involved in the struggle were brought to the fore. Given that the final result has been a referendum and formal secession of South Sudan from the North, it might be easy to simplify this long conflict into a singular secessionist event. However, the history of this struggle is far more complex and the years of conflict offer an excellent in-depth case study of the cross-ethnic alliances, the fluid political ideology, the pursuit of a protracted guerrilla conflict, and finally the flexible and complex end goals of the mass movements involved in the secessions.

Early History

The beginning of the first Southern Sudanese struggle for self-determination is, like many of the separatist struggles in Africa, inextricably bound to the colonial era and the decisions made during the process of decolonization.

In fact, it is within this initial period of colonization that the implicit separation of the North and South was established, along with the antagonistic relations between the two. Egypt was the first power to expand into the Sudan. Muhammed Ali, the Albanian adventurer placed in control of Egypt by the Ottoman Empire, expanded his realm into the *Bilad al-Sudan* (the Land of the Blacks) in 1821.[1] Fuelled by dreams of greater empire and personal power, Ali quickly and firmly established Egyptian power along the riverine North. Using this region as a base for further expeditions, Ali's men penetrated further south in search of resources and, above all, slaves. The black Sudanese were renowned as military slaves and were seen as a precious resource by the ambitious pasha. His slavers agreed and rapidly expanded slaving operations not just for the military but for sale abroad.[2] While Ali died in 1849, these practices did not end. Even as Egypt drove itself further into debt in its own modernizing campaigns of the mid-nineteenth century, the Sudan remained lightly developed. While the riverine North received light development, it remained economically dependent on the slave trade drawn from the completely undeveloped South. The debts owed by Egypt occasionally obliged them to try and reform the south for the comfort of their European creditors, but the numerous European "governors" assigned by the khedive rarely made any lasting difference. By the late nineteenth century the North remained lightly developed while it preyed on the completely undeveloped South, with expansion downriver still blocked by the trackless morass of the Sudd.

The catalyst for changing this system began in Egypt as a wave of nationalism inflamed the army in Cairo and Colonel Urabi of the Egyptian Army seized control of the government in 1881. Fearing the loss of the strategic Suez Canal, the seizing of their financial investments in the country, and even the undermining of Britain's global standing, the British landed an invasion force under Sir Garnet Wolseley, who decisively defeated Urabi's army at Tel El-Kebir on 13 September 1882. The debate over the continued sovereignty of Egypt lasted for months, but when the dust settled the British remained firmly entrenched within Egypt and would essentially run Egypt until its independence following the Second World War. However, when Britain occupied Egypt it also inherited all of Egypt's holdings and difficulties, including the Sudan. Already concerned with the slave trade that sustained the Sudan, the British continued to send governors to the Sudan, this time backed by larger-scale military forces to aid in the anti-slaving operations. While these efforts seemed poised to take effect, they were swept away by the Mahdiyya, the powerful Islamist movement led by Muhammad Ahmad bin Abd Allah, the self-proclaimed Mahdi.[3] The Mahdi's army dealt the British-led Egyptians several defeats, including the annihilation of William Hicks' Egyptian army at the Battle of El Obeid in 1883. The Mahdi's advances culminated in the much-romanticized death of General Charles Gordon during the fall of Khartoum in 1885, leading to the British abandonment of the whole of the Sudan for the next thirteen years. However, when they returned in 1898, they were far more prepared for the struggle, and the Mahdi had died in the interim. The result was the crushing of the young Mahdist state at the Battle of Omdurman and the reimposition of the Anglo-Egyptian administration over the whole of the Sudan, where it would remain until 1956.

It was under British Rule, from 1899 to 1956, that the very real division of the Sudan occurred. While there had always been a cultural and geographic separation, the Arabic language had begun to bridge the gap and trade had existed to continue to process of cultural integration. Both of these processes were arrested under the British administration, with a conscious decision having been made to develop the North while keeping the South in a suspended state—a practice that would be called the Southern Policy amongst the British functionaries who would govern this newly divided land.[4] As early as 1917 the British founded the Equatoria Corps, an all-Southern Sudanese military unit, to remove the need for Northern troops in the South.[5] This effectively removed one of the only major areas of cultural interaction between the two regions. The remaining contacts were slowly severed over the next decade, with the 1922 Passports and Permits Ordinance allowing the British administration to deny Northerners access to certain regions of the South.[6] This was taken a step further with the 1925 Permits to Trade Ordinance, which gave the British the sole right to grant trade access to the South, effectively making them the final arbiters of the relationship between the South and North. By 1930 the separation of the administration of the two regions was formally declared, with the North remaining a primarily Islamic, Arabized, and slowly developing society that looked north to Egypt while the South, it was hoped, would develop into an Anglicized, Christian buffer area between the Muslim north of Africa and the British holdings in East Africa.[7]

These hopes were dashed with the advent of nationalist sentiment that coalesced before the Second World War. In 1938 a number of intellectuals joined together in the North to form what they called "the Graduate Congress," an organization that signalled the rise of Sudanese Nationalism in the modern era.[8] These intellectuals argued for a single idea of "Sudanism," a single identity for the myriad people living within the immensely large territory under Anglo-Egyptian rule.[9] This unitary ideal held substantial appeal for the populace of the Sudan, but by effacing the difference of experiences that had occurred from the slaving period to the present, the Graduate Congress glossed over the necessarily divergent identities of North and South. This led the congress to having only a small proportion of its membership claiming Southern extraction and therefore being culturally dominated by the North. It was a cycle that would repeat itself numerous times throughout the Sudan's history, with a group claiming to represent a unitary Sudan and yet lacking in Southern representation. As it was, given the isolation of the South, during the critical wartime years Sudanese nationalism would develop with a pronounced Northern Sudanese slant, something that would haunt the South when in 1945 political parties formed in the Sudan without significant Southern participation. This was exacerbated when in 1946 the Southern Policy was reversed and the South was thrown back into contact with the North on the eve of self-determination within the Sudan.[10]

The British were not entirely unaware of the unease this reunification caused the South. For over twenty years the South had been administered completely separately by the British, and before that the dominant memory of the South was that of the brutal slaving expeditions of the North. Thus the Juba Conference was set up in 1947, wherein the British, North, and South came together to discuss the future North-South dynamics as the Sudan edged toward independence.[11] However, the South was unprepared for such discussions, with their delegates to the conference having been chosen by the British and no consensus bloc having been established. While the South successfully used the conference to articulate their fears of Northern domination, they were still corralled into a choice of conditional unity with the North. While they pushed for several safeguards against

Northern political control, none were binding and the Southern delegates were left feeling isolated. This was exacerbated by the formation of the legislative assembly the following year wherein no such safeguards were adopted and the South was left with an extreme minority of representatives and no power to enact protective measures. By the dissolution of the assembly in 1952, the South was weak, isolated, and fearful of its future within a unified Sudan. While the South was to produce its own unified political party in 1954, this party was not able to exert any recognizable pressure on either the British or the Unified Sudanese Government before the Sudan declared its complete separation from Egypt in 1955 and its full independence in 1956. However, by this point the first few steps in the Sudanese Civil War had already been taken.

The First Sudanese Civil War (1955–1972)

While the Sudan was not fully independent until 1956, the incident that is regarded as the beginning of the struggles of the South took place in 1955. At its heart was the Equatoria Corps, that body of Southern professional soldiers that had enforced British rule in the South since 1917. By 1955 the Sudan had been united and the military was in the process of its own unification. Tensions had been mounting during the previous year, with the rejection of a federal system and the rapid replacement of British administrators with often abrasive Northern officials. This was worsened in the Equatoria Corps when all senior ranks that had been filled by the British were awarded to Northern officers.[12] The Southern senior NCOs were awarded just nine junior slots within the military administration, and resentment was already boiling. It finally burst on 18 August 1955, when the Southern soldiers of the Torit garrison mutinied against their Northern officers.[13] Waves of violence wracked the Torit region as the garrison turned on its officers and seized its weapons. Other, smaller mutinies arose in the South in response, with garrison soldiers in several other regions revolting and joining the general struggle. The response of the North was immediate, with the Royal Air Force helping to transport large numbers of Northern troops to the South to put down the mutiny. With government reinforcements pouring in and the mutineers' hopes for British intervention on their behalf dashed, the conflict appeared hopeless. Following a call from Governor-General Knox for a ceasefire and his guarantee of fair trials and clemency, the mutineers' resistance collapsed. While many of the Equatoria Corps surrendered, a significant number instead took their arms and deserted, fading into the deep South or across the border into Ethiopia or Uganda.[14] These deserters did not trust the North to keep their word following the removal of British authority, and their fears proved well founded by the end of the year, when a number of those who had surrendered were executed. While the deserters, now outlaws and exiles, were not organized or even particularly politically motivated, they would form a central part of the resistance to the North that would continue to grow over the next fourteen years.

In 1956 the Sudan passed officially into its independence, with the British removing their administration and with the government of Premier Abdullah Khalil becoming the official government of the Sudan. Despite assurances that the concerns of the Southern Party would be given full consideration upon independence, the Khalil government continued to spurn the ambitions of the South, with Khalil instead touring the South demanding full recognition and obeisance to the 1947 Juba agreement. Demands for increased development of the already underdeveloped South, federal status for the South, or even a plebiscite to the held under UN auspices increased as proceeds from the bumper crop of cotton of 1956 were spent almost entirely to finance the increasing irrigation and development of the North. By 1957, the Khalil government was using increasingly authoritarian strategies to contain the discontent of the South and was faced with a more serious challenge when the Southern Political Bloc managed to form in the newly elected National Assembly with enough votes to force itself to be heard.[15] Despite views ranging from increased representation to federalism to outright secession, the bloc directed its effort specifically to driving for a federal structure for the Sudan. When this was rejected, the bloc increasingly reached out to "Africans" of the North, gaining increased support for their plans of federation and representation amongst the less represented peoples of the North by 1958. However, the political turmoil engendered by the increasing power of the South was never effectively brought to bear against Khalil's government. Already beset on all sides by economic and political failures, the Republic was swept away in a military coup led by General Abboud, the commander in chief of the Sudanese Army.

Despite the change in leadership, the neglect of the South continued, with little to no representation given to Southerners and less capital for development emerging from the central government. Incidents of violence and protests increased over the following years, leading increasingly to the arrest of Southern political leaders. In addition, the armed Southerners who remained from the mutiny continued to stage armed raids throughout the Sudan, although these were alternately characterized as acts of banditry and acts of rebellion.[16] These were accompanied by increasingly violent incursions involving old ethnic rivalries, which increased the tensions of the already fragile South and convinced the Abboud government to resort to increasingly harsh measures to suppress the populace. This crackdown served as a catalyst for the formation of a party-in-exile amongst the Southern politicians, who found the Sudan increasingly hostile to their presence. In 1962, a cadre of these politicians formed the Sudan African Closed Districts National Union, professing a platform of complete Southern independence.[17] The SACDNU hoped that its political manoeuvring abroad with the UN and OAU could force this solution on the Abboud government, which itself was already undergoing several challenges within the military itself. Unfortunately, despite several attempts to draw attention to their cause, the SACDNU (renamed the Sudanese African National Union [SANU] in 1963) could gain no traction internationally and the increasing dissent between the politicians within its ranks precluded any more forceful actions. However, while the political outlook was apparently increasingly fractured and troubled, the actual struggle on the ground was just beginning to draw serious attention.

The various groups of armed mutineers had in the intervening years managed to draw more recruits from the disaffected peoples of the South.[18] The draw usually depended on the region they were occupying, with each band usually attracting the young men whose homes were nearby. By 1963 these groups had begun to slowly pull themselves into a cohesive whole, calling themselves the Land and Freedom Army (LFA). Led by General Emilio Tafeng and divided into different regional commands under local leaders, the LFA became the first concerted military resistance to the Sudanese government. However, it was not generally known as the Land

and Freedom Army, and by the end of its struggle it was simply identified by its adopted name, "The Anya-nya," meaning snake venom in several of the regional languages.[19] In 1964 the first true Anya-nya attacks occurred and rapidly grew into a vicious guerrilla struggle between the Sudanese armed forces and the Southern insurgents.[20] While initially the LFA seemed to hope simply to attract international attention, with the failure of this strategy the two sides dug in for a prolonged conflict. The North responded to the initial attacks by increasing the strength and presence of its armed forces and cracking down on the remaining Southern police, prison, and military personnel. Subsequently the Anya-nya's ranks were bolstered by the almost en-masse desertion of these personnel to their side.[21] The Northern troops then settled into a pattern of responding to the uncoordinated attacks of the Southerners with harsh reprisals,[22] which, coupled with the Anya-nya's efforts to curb the banditry in their own ranks, increased the popularity of the insurgents significantly. This pattern was to repeat itself until the end of 1964, when the government of General Abboud was finally toppled by popular protests and a power struggle between Abboud and the premier of the caretaker government that had been placed around him to bolster the state. By the beginning of 1965 Premier al-Khatim al-Khalifa was in control of the government and Abboud had resigned.[23]

Khalifa had already managed to calm the cycle of reprisals in the South and now was attempting overtures to what he understood to be the political leadership of the struggle, SANU. SANU had begun to exercise authority over the Anya-nya movement and managed to get a ceasefire of their own implemented over elements of the LFA in an attempt to win concessions from the now more reasonable central government. Khalifa's government offered amnesty and autonomy for the South under a federal structure for the Sudan in late 1964, but these terms were rejected by SANU, who had been emboldened by the struggle to insist on complete secession from the North. A series of abortive and piecemeal negotiations was attempted, with the government finally suggesting a complete round table meeting for 15 February 1965.[24] Due to the inconsistent nature of the SANU leadership and the political struggles within Khalifa's own government, the meeting was postponed until 16 March. While SANU attended the Round Table Conference in Juba, Anya-nya activity around the city remained consistent and violent, undermining the attempts of SANU delegates and the emerging Southern Front party.²⁵ By the end of the conference on the 29th, no decisions had been reached and the only lasting legacy of the conference was the final splintering and demise of both SANU and Khalifa's government. The disparate goals, philosophies, and egos of the leadership finally shattered the Southern political coalition, with the main splinter group being the Azania Liberation Front (ALF). Over the following months ALF would absorb most of the remnants of SANU and the smaller splinter groups and proclaim its own leadership over the Anya-nya. Khalifa's government, meanwhile, lost its support base in the elections of 1965 and was replaced by that of Mohammed Ahmed Mahgoub.²⁶ The demise of both leaderships was to thrust the country away from diplomacy and bring the fighting (which had never really stopped) back to the fore.

The following four years would bring little change to the situation. Protracted guerrilla warfare continued in the South and was met by limited and mostly unsuccessful counter-insurgency campaigns by the North. While a few major operations were attempted, such as a sweep of the Sudanese armed forces into Equatoria in May 1966, these rarely yielded effects commensurate with their effort, much less proving decisive. By September 1966 the remnants of the round table committee produced a resolution that a central form of government was no longer tenable for the Sudan, but this had even less effect on the conflict; the North would not give up its central control and the Southern guerrillas were already effectively ignoring the manoeuvrings of the "paper cabinets" of politicians that claimed to command them. This was just as well, as Southern leadership continued to splinter, with ALF and SANU remaining but with the creation of the Southern Sudan Provisional Government in 1967.²⁷ The new SSPG contained much of the long-standing political leadership of the Southern struggle and as such claimed leadership of the Anya-nya, but the distances involved and loose networks of allegiance amongst the disparate insurgent groups meant that only nominal direction could be given. It seemed that the war had somewhat dissolved into a general conflict blending together old regional rivalries as well as hopes for reform, autonomy, or even complete separation for the South, among both the political and military leadership of the South.

1969 was to see a radical change come over the conflict, dispelling the confused political and military pattern in the South. On the 25 May the

Maghoub government was overthrown in a bloodless coup by the "Young Officers" led by Colonel Gaafar Mohammed al-Numeiry.[28] The new Revolutionary Council tacked to the left of the political spectrum as opposed to embracing the Islamic parties that had wielded so much influence in previous administrations. Soviet military advisers appeared for the first time in the Sudan and questions were raised as to the effect these new players would have on the struggle in the South. However, Numeiry had already proclaimed that there was no military solution to the rebellion of the South. This did not mean that he brought the war to a close, but instead that he saw the military assistance brought to him by the Soviet mission as a means of bringing more coercive power to bear on the South.[29] His military embarked on a series of offensives against the South, which were disrupted only by the continuing upheavals he had to deal with within his own power base. However, by the time Numeiry had safeguarded his own position, the chance to cow the remaining splintered Southern factions into an agreement had passed. By 1970 the Southern factions had been mostly welded together on a military level by a Southern commander named Joseph Lagu, who had been associated with almost every one of the various Southern movements before consolidating his own base.

Lagu was able to bring together all of the remaining military factions through the simple expedient of having become the sole source of outside arms for the struggle. Israel, having been already dissatisfied with the Islamist tendencies of the Sudan central government, finally in the late 1960s had begun to filter weapons and expertise to the South. Lagu, already having created his own power base in Eastern Equatoria, managed to make himself the recipient of their largesse.[30] By drawing on his own base and supplying those who allied themselves with him, Lagu managed to pull together the various struggling bands and command them through their needs for materiel. Perhaps his second decisive move had been to effectively shut out the political leadership that had existed since the start of the struggle. Time and again various political groups, both within and without the Sudan, had claimed leadership of the military struggle, but none was able to truly aid in the consolidation or arming of their military manpower. Instead, each claimed the credit for the ongoing efforts while generally staying aloof from the fragmented war and manipulating the selection of military commanders for their advantage. Lagu himself had been spurned for command by the SSPG, and so it is not surprising that he rejected the continual calls for political affiliation from the various groups. Instead, Lagu was strong enough and centralized enough in 1970 to absorb his neighbouring group, the Nile Provisional Government, and then continue to consolidate his hold over the remaining Anya-nya National Armed Forces (as the military had been known under the SSPG). By 1971 his singular power and control led him to declare a unitary command known as the Southern Sudan Liberation Movement (SSLM) and set about the business of directing an armed resistance.[31] The melded command was able to more effectively fight the Northern offensives and blunt the new Soviet edge of the Sudanese forces. Slowly Lagu built a social administration amongst his forces, and by 1972 several challenges of rivals had been beaten off and Lagu was in complete control. This was just in time to receive the offer of a ceasefire from the Numeiry government on 3 March, which Lagu accepted on the 6th, marking the successful completion of heretofore unheralded diplomatic efforts. The representatives of the SSLM and the central government had been meeting since 1971 in Addis Ababa under the auspices of Emperor Haile Selassie. While diplomacy had already been tried throughout the conflict, this time there were no rival movements strong enough for Khartoum to deal with to split the Southern base, leading to far different circumstances.

The ceasefire, when finally implemented by both sides in early 1972, led to the widespread application of the Addis Ababa Agreement and the first lasting peace the Sudan would know in sixteen years. Both Numeiry and Lagu hailed it as a triumph for their side, although it was in the end a flawed agreement that continued many of the same tensions that had drawn the South into war in the first place. In terms of a political settlement, many of the most ardent of the Southern combatants were disappointed. Even from the outset the hopes for complete separation had been abandoned, with a federal solution between the North and South as the primary goal of negotiations.[32] However, the South had to settle for even less than this, gaining their own regional government but no guarantee of power sharing in the central government, which remained staunchly Northern in character.[33] The North still had essentially unopposed power in the overall state. In addition, the military settlement was again a disappointing compromise. The initial hopes of the South for its own military were flatly rejected by the North, who feared a consolidated and independent Southern force.

Instead a generous portion of the Anya-nya military formations would be integrated into the Sudanese military.[34] These forces would be based in the South and be mixed into a matching number of Northern troops who would be based throughout the regions.[35] While this offered employment for a great number of the combatants, it still left a number of fighters out in the cold following their service to the South. In addition, the integration was pushed at a much faster pace than the South had anticipated, leading to increased tensions between the Southern soldiers and their new comrades, who had barely stopped shooting at each other before they were placed in the same units. Finally, the question of economics was left off of the table, as the SSLM delegation was too limited to deal with the question at the time. However, for all of its flaws, the Addis Ababa Agreement was the first binding accord between the North and South and at least assured a certain amount of autonomy for the Southern regions. As the covenant went into effect, the country slowly began to piece itself back together.

A Troubled Interlude

From 1972 to 1983, the North and South were officially at peace with each other. However, this often only meant that there was no sanctioned military action currently occurring,[36] as the balance of political power still meant that the South was in a considerable amount of economic distress. Having gained no particular control over their own economic situation in the Addis Ababa Agreement, the South was generally a spectator to such decisions as the central government investing much of its capital into mechanized farming in the central Nile region. This left the South further behind in terms of development within the nation. In addition, the political situation continued to deteriorate. While the South could indeed elect its own regional government, the Northern-dominated central government could and did influence the elections. Often in the tightly contested elections for the presidency of the High Executive Council of the South, Numeiry's influence would prove to be key in the success or failure of a candidate, meaning that Numeiry essentially had veto power over the leadership of the mostly autonomous Southern region.[37] Finally, while the integration of the military had been completed in the prescribed five years, the process had not been a smooth one. Violent confrontations between former enemies occurred with startling regularity, and even when these were absent the Southern soldiers often felt ill at ease in their new military structures and many still held grudges both for the previous conflict and the low ranks they had been given upon integration.[38] Thus, three primary areas of the state, those of politics, economics, and security, all were under increasing strain throughout the first decade of the peace. Even before the shooting officially started again in 1983 there were desertions and increased insurgent activity in the South, with an increasing number of both Northerners and Southerners becoming disillusioned with the current situation. Finally, in 1983, the dam burst again and the Second Sudanese Civil War had begun.

The Second Sudanese Civil War (1983–2005)

Although, as mentioned, there had been low levels of violent resistance, including the continued desertion and armed struggle of Southern troops from the army, the Second Civil War is formally held to have begun with the mutiny and desertion of the 105th Sudanese Battalion, which was stationed at Bor, Pibor, and Porchalla.[39] In an echo of the original Torit mutiny in 1955, the Southern battalion protested violently when ordered to transfer its station to the North. The 105th considered this a contravention of the Addis Ababa Agreement and asserted that the government did not have the right to order it to leave its home region of the South. The commandant of the Sudanese military academy, a Southerner named John Garang, travelled to Bor on the pretext of negotiating with the protesting unit.[40] However, upon his arrival, Garang instead followed the prearranged plan to lead the unit from protest to desertion, and the 105th and its sister unit the 104th both went over to join the already brewing insurgency in the South.[41] However, while all previous units had begun their new struggle under the sobriquet of Anya-nya II, Garang welded together several of these units along with his own command to form a group called the Sudanese People's Liberation Movement (SPLM), with its armed wing taking the name the Sudanese People's Liberation Army (SPLA).[42]

Garang had been a lower-ranking officer in the Anya-nya at the end of the first struggle, where his formal education and military skill had seen him rise rapidly in the ranks of the insurgency and postwar integration of the armed forces.[43] However, this service had also made him aware of the numerous flaws in the Anya-nya structure responsible for the deep divisions and indecisiveness that had prolonged the struggle against the North. Garang was adamant about not replicating these patterns within this new conflict and quickly established himself as the sole head of the SPLA and the font from which the military and civilian aid would flow via his relationship with Mengistu's Derg in Ethiopia.[44] While several of the more veteran commanders from the Anya-nya period who had themselves taken up arms protested Garang's elevation over themselves, their Ethiopian allies were adamant about his status as head of the new SPLA. As such, dissenters were forced to either subordinate themselves to Garang or strike out on their own without patronage as another band of Anya-nya II.

This unity of command and purpose showed impressive results within the first several years of the struggle. The leadership of the SPLA was conscious of several other dissident groups throughout the Sudan and made active efforts to join their efforts to the other anti-Numeiry groups, not only within the South but within the North and West of the Sudan as well. Garang, echoing the strategy used by Lagu in the First Civil War, used his plentiful military supplies to continue to reach out and integrate further armed dissident groups in the South. However, unlike Lagu, Garang insisted on their being integrated into the SPLM itself as opposed to simply placing them under the loose authority of his movement.[45] This saw the SPLM/SPLA rapidly grow to be the strongest of any of the dissident movements, even as it brought it into conflict with the existing Anya-nya II forces that rejected SPLM hegemony in the South. However, despite conflicts with both uncoordinated Anya-nya groups and the Sudanese military, during 1983–1986 the SPLM consolidated its armed forces and managed to create several civil administrative regions throughout the South through battalion-sized "task forces" of SPLA fighters.[46] Newer regions of the Southern half of the country, such as the Nuba mountains, were added to the territorial control and civil administration of the SPLM.[47] Increasingly the SPLA was even able to reach out even to Anya-nya groups and integrate them into their structure.

The successes and increasing expansion of the SPLA had far-ranging effects on both the government of the Sudan and how it prosecuted the struggle. Counter-insurgency measures had never completely halted even throughout the interlude between civil wars, and with the advent of the

SPLA the Numeiry government attempted to redouble its efforts. However, the regime had already been facing increasing challenges to its reign. In September 1983 the Sudanese government had promulgated the "September Laws," which introduced certain aspects of Sharia law into the legal framework of the Sudan,[48] and this was followed by increasing attempts at Islamization of the laws in July 1984. These efforts made the central government increasingly unpopular, as the failure of these measures incited the Islamicist elements and Numeiry's championing of them aggravated the more secular elements of the government. In early 1985 he began to arrest political opponents of his regime, including over 100 members of the Muslim Brotherhood in March. This proved to be the last straw. In April his government was formally overthrown. In 1986, Sadiq al-Mahdi, the Islamist leader of the Umma party, was selected as the new prime minister of the Sudan. The coalition he came to power under shared the goal of an Islamic Sudan and the continued inevitable conversion of the state to Sharia law.

This alteration in government had two major consequences for the conflict in the South. The first was that the members of Sadiq's coalition by and large did not endorse the earlier Koka Dam Declaration, which had been born out of a meeting between the parties of the North and South (including the SPLM) in the period after the fall of Numeiry. The declaration had called for a constitutional convention to deal with the difficulties of the Sudan overall and was seen as a step forward in terms of resolving the conflict.[49] However, neither the Democratic Union Party (DUP) or the National Islamic Front (NIF, the Muslim Brotherhood), key supporters of Sadiq, attended the meeting or agreed with its goals. The Koka Dam agreements were thus essentially moot in the wake of the election of 1986. The second major alteration was Sadiq's increasing reliance on local militias to prosecute the war.[50] While this was not an entirely new development, the level to which Sadiq's government armed the tribal militias, especially of the Baqqara, was unprecedented.[51] These militias immediately began to raid their economic competitors in the South with abandon, committing numerous human rights violations. From their initial widespread usage in 1986 until the cessation of the conflict, the militias would represent a central dynamic of the conflict, often working alongside the formal armed forces. However, it was also their indiscriminate violence that often turned public opinion in the South away from the central government, and this image problem would have severe consequences in the direction of the conflict.

In fact, as early as 1987 the militias had grown to be such a problem that the SPLA was finding ready allies in regions outside what had formally been the South and thus found themselves in the position to move the struggle beyond the region where the first war had been fought. SPLA units began to draw the struggle into the regions of the Blue Nile, Kordofan, and Darfur, all of which had been outside of the First Civil War.[52] In addition, with the militias becoming increasing threats throughout the South, Garang's movement found diplomatic solutions with a number of the fragmented Anya-nya II forces suddenly plausible, which allowed the SPLM to continue to successfully institute a civil framework over its home base areas, clear the border with Ethiopia, and even establish themselves within the Equatoria region, which throughout the conflict had been hesitant to accept the SPLM, for reasons that will be discussed later. These gains again drove the North to the negotiating table in 1989, with Sadiq facing increasing pressure from his military to both find a solution to the conflict with the South and attempt to halt the now dozens of small-scale local conflicts occurring across the Sudan. Sadiq acquiesced and, now again in a coalition with the DUP and his own Umma party, began the peace process anew with the SPLM. While progress was underway, the increasingly radical NIF denounced the proceedings and broke from Sadiq, eventually backing several radical Islamic officers in a coup that halted the peace process, removed Sadiq, and brought Omar al-Bashir to power.[53] The war would go on.

The Collapse of Ethiopia

A great deal of the unitary success of Garang and the SPLM was due to the material and logistical support offered to them by the Ethiopian Derg. Much as with Lagu's Israeli patrons, the Ethiopian aid meant that Garang could exercise a great deal of control over his subordinate commanders, since the continuance of the struggle in its current incarnation was dependent upon his patrons. However, by 1990 the Derg regime that had sustained the SPLM was rapidly crumbling.[54] Already the SPLA had been called upon numerous times to help the Derg combat the various insurgencies that were threatening to tear their government apart, specifically the Oromo Liberation Front (OLF) and the Gambela People's Liberation Front (GPLF), which were supported by the Sudan.[55] However, while the SPLA was able to help contain these guerrilla movements, the far more organized and motivated Tigrayan People's Liberation Front and Eritrean People's Liberation Front were annihilating the Ethiopian military in the field. Even as they began their final advance against Addis Ababa, Garang refused to treat with these powerful insurgencies, meaning that once the defeat of the Derg was final later that year, the SPLM found itself isolated and in the position of needing to rapidly evacuate its numerous training camps and rear bases in Ethiopia.

In addition, the removal of Ethiopian support had far-flung political consequences for Garang and his movement. The SPLM had relied heavily on coercive power to maintain a unitary vision for the struggle. Throughout the war there had been little fragmentation of the movement, despite its extremely diverse and expanding membership, primarily because Garang could call upon Ethiopian security forces as well as Ethiopian supplies to back up his leadership. On several occasions challengers to his leadership had been arrested or otherwise dealt with by his Ethiopian patrons. Now, this security too was gone. In short order, challenges to Garang's sole control of the SPLM/A arose from within.

Two of the regional commanders in the Upper Nile, Riek Machar and Lam Akol, declared against Garang in August 1991. Their faction quickly became known as the SPLA-Nasir after the town around which they were based, and they sent out a call to all other regional commanders to overthrow Garang and join their cause.[56] Specifically, they included a message of their intention to fight for secession, something that the SPLM had not done up to that time, given Ethiopian sensitivities. However, despite their initial hopes of drawing a large contingent of allies with their pronouncement, they found that most of the SPLA regional commanders either stayed loyal to Garang's faction (which became known as SPLA-Torit) or at the most stayed on the fence to see how the struggle would play out. Violent confrontations were the general rule between the Nasir and Torit factions, which, due to the regional affiliations of Machar and Akol and the nature of the troops of Garang's SPLA nearby, led to what has been viewed as a Nuer civil war.[57] However, very swiftly it became apparent that Garang's faction remained a viable force in the field and maintained the allegiance of most of the SPLM. In fact, although Machar and Akol were able to draw in many of the pro-secession elements of the Anya-nya II, they found themselves quickly on the shorter end of the equation in terms of manpower and equipment. This development brought an unexpected element to the fore in even the earliest days of the internal struggle: the SPLA-Nasir faction was being supported and armed by the Khartoum government it was trying to secede from.[58]

The SPLA-Nasir was certainly not the only Southern dissident group being supported by the Sudanese government as a "spoiler" against their main antagonists. Between the numerous Anya-nya II, SPLA-Nasir (later rebranded SPLA-United when they incorporated more Southern elements), and other forces, Bashir's government had many unexpected allies already in place during their counteroffensive of 1992. This offensive saw the Sudanese armed forces push Garang's group out of many of their newest gains, including parts of Equatoria, and forced their withdrawal from Juba, the Southern city at which the SPLA-Torit had launched a partially successful offensive at the end of 1991.[59] However, the government's offensives were halted in 1992–93 by concerns over the imposition of no-fly-zones during the Somalia crises, and by 1994 Garang and the SPLA had recovered their footing in part because of the sea change in the diplomatic context of the conflict.

With the final end of the Cold War in 1991, the Sudanese conflict took on a much altered nature in the eyes of the international community. The Cold War binary that had defined the struggle between an SPLM that was supplied by Marxist Ethiopia and a capitalist/Western aligned Sudan was no longer applicable. Instead the Sudan found itself within a newer context of being part of an axis of Islamist extremism under the control of a military dictator, while the SPLM could legitimately point to their efforts to reach out to other dissident groups in the struggle for reform. In short order the North found itself isolated amongst the global powers, while their opponents had a raised profile.[60] The SPLM had been able to sustain itself largely through the effectiveness of the social structures they themselves had built in the first decade of the struggle, but now they found themselves as welcome participants in the political dialogue surrounding the Sudan and its neighbours. This was hastened by the Sudan's seemingly unlimited ability to alienate the countries around it, with previous allies Eritrea and

Ethiopia both finding themselves rejecting the NIF government and its efforts to supply Islamic insurgents in their states. In a mere four years after the fall of the Mengistu government, the former combatants in the Horn were working together against Bashir's government and subsequently offering the SPLM succor.

This renewed diplomatic status for the SPLM/A also meant that there was increasing pressure to come to an understanding with the SPLM-United faction. Garang's forces, christened SPLM-Mainstream, remained the much stronger faction, and although they made overtures and continued to open up their leadership structures, the SPLM/A-United refused to formally overcome their differences. However, United's failures to sustain their strength even in their home areas led the faction to rebrand itself the Southern Sudan Independence Movement in 1994 and to reaffirm its support of complete secession from the North while casting out those members who supported a less complete split. This precipitated a series of fractures throughout the organization that were only made more severe by the signing of a series of agreements between the SSIM and the Sudanese government.[61] By 1996 the majority of the splinter groups had either come to an understanding with the SPLM, had been reabsorbed, or were fighting amongst themselves. By the end of the year the SPLM/A was again effectively unchallenged as the Southern representative in what had become a greater struggle against Bashir's increasingly isolated government.

The military struggle saw continued offensives from the SPLA and an increasing emphasis on defeating the Khartoum-sponsored armed militias and what was now called the South Sudan Defense Forces.[62] However, the far more important actions were finally taking place at the conference table. Since 1994, the opposition to Bashir's government had agreed on a Declaration of Principles that established a baseline for self-determination and other reforms that would be required for a cohesive attempt at peace.[63] These had not only established a legitimate structure for the seeking of peace but also drew international attention as a means to end the conflict. While considered somewhat weak by the parties involved, they set the stage for further talks under the auspices of the governments of Ethiopia, Eritrea, Uganda, and eventually the United States.

The United States had been increasingly involved in the issues of the Sudan. Since the end of the Cold War the US relationship with the Sudan had undergone a profound realignment. While during the 1980s and early 1990s the Sudan had been seen as a strong regional ally against the Eastern Bloc, by the mid-1990s its Islamist government was now looked at with suspicion. In 1997 the United States placed sanctions against the Sudanese government as a regional supporter of terrorism and a human rights abuser. This deprived the Sudan of significant investment capital, weakening the region and serving as leverage with which the United States could exert pressure upon their putative ally. This was exacerbated by the discovery and early exploitation of oil within the Sudan in the year 2000. The oil was discovered within the notional border regions disputed by the combatants but without United States investment, and with the continued conflict between the Sudan and its Southern antagonists, it could not be effectively exploited by either side. However, this coincided with the continued efforts of the United States, wherein the George W. Bush administration was pushing the Sudan for a settlement and helping to draft the documents necessary for the agreement. This would in theory allow for possible relief from sanctions, allow for the development of the North's oil deposits, and also allow for an agreement for access to the oil within the South Sudan's boundaries. Although the definition within the proposed settlement of self-determination for the South and what forms it could take and how such a process would be decided initially caused concern amongst the SPLM, eventually a solution was found. By the end of 2004 the agreement for the ending of the Second Civil War was in place and was signed by Garang and Bashir on 9 January 2005. The signed agreement established benchmarks on government employment for Southerners, the imposition of Sharia law in the North but not the South, the splitting of oil revenues, and finally a plebiscite to be held in 2011 to determine the status of the South within or without a greater Federal Sudan. The war had ended, but the final question of secession, separatism, or federalism was delayed for six years when the South voted overwhelmingly to secede completely from the North, with the blessings of the United States and the United Nations.

Secession, Separatism, and the Negotiation of Statehood

Of course, having narrated the history of the Sudan's conflicts between North and South, it is now apparent that secession and separatism have had roles to play within the conflict, but rarely at the same time. While secession would eventually be completely achieved, it would be wrong to consider that this was the inevitable end goal for these decades of conflict. In the context of this work, it is perhaps most important to understand that the historical arc of the secessionist/separatist desires of the South is irrevocably bound to both the methods of struggle the actors had chosen and the continental and global context that each stage was taking place in.

Following the independence of the Sudan, there was little known about the actual motivations of the fighters who would become the Anya-nya, although eventually they would become synonymous with the goal of secession and complete independence for the South. On the other hand, the early Southern political representation made every effort to propose their own initiatives for dealing with what they saw as gross inequality in the political and economic development of the South. Even in the earliest days of independence, the Southern elected officials pressed for recognition of their desire for a federal structure that would see a degree of self-determination fall to the South itself.[64] This motion followed the failure to attract UN or British support for a demanded plebiscite before independence in 1955. Unfortunately, by 1957 the National Assembly declared that a federal structure was unworkable in the Sudan. Although rebuffed, the Southern Political Bloc began reaching out to other "non-Arab" groups such as the Beja and Fur for support of a federal structure. These efforts appeared to be bearing fruit in 1958 but ended up being lost in the coup that removed Premier Khalil from office.

With the change in government and increasing government repression under General Abboud, the methods of pursuing Southern representation changed. At this point it had become apparent that a political settlement into a federation was no longer a plausible option. The advent of the 1960s then saw new attempts to bring power and representation to the South. In 1962 the more prominent members of the Southern political class had removed themselves from the Sudan to avoid the increasingly widespread arrests of political dissidents. From Kinshasa they declared the creation of an opposition movement for the South, the aforementioned SACDNU, which quickly changed its name to SANU.[65] No longer relying on the North to negotiate a settlement, SANU demanded complete separation of the South into its own sovereign country.[66] However, they had no armed forces of their own and decried the methods of the "rebels" in the bush.[67] Instead, they placed their faith in transnational organizations such as the OAU and the UN. In the 1960s the United Nations was still dealing with the Katanga crisis and the OAU had just been formed, with territorial sovereignty as one of its core principles. The diplomatic calls for secession or plebiscites were made toward parties not yet willing to expend the energy necessary to support SANU.

It was coincidentally at this point that the Anya-nya formally integrated itself and began its first halting steps toward its organized insurgency.[68] However, its successes in the first years of its struggle were limited at best, and SANU tried to remain as aloof as possible from the guerrillas until such time as their own efforts failed to reach fruition.[69] At this point SANU tried to align itself more closely with the Anya-nya and therefore gain a certain amount of direct contact with the still active secessionist struggle in the South. However, given the decentralization of all Anya-nya efforts, it was always a question of exactly how much cohesion there was between the political and military arms of the struggle. By 1965 the two groups were present together as a united front at the Round Table Conference called by Premier Khalifa's government following the fall of the Abboud government, but despite agreeing to a ceasefire the local Anya-nya kept fighting. However, this conference is important in tracing the continued thread of secessionist thought. Despite Khalifa's government offering federal autonomy directly to the South, SANU and the Anya-nya insisted on secession from the Sudan itself. Interestingly, they declared "there could be no settlement of differences until separation and independence had been granted [to the South] .... Apart from posing a threat to African peace, the Southern problem has the seeds of damaging Afro-Arab relations. To avoid this, the Southern Sudan must be given its own independence if further damage is to be avoided."[70]

What can be drawn from this is the idea that the South felt that it had the political and military strength to win on the battlefield far more than it had even wanted at the outset of the conflict. However, the question may be asked, why? Why would the South feel that it could do better than federation in the critical period of 1962–1965? Put succinctly, the door had not closed on secession in Africa yet, and the South looked to be gaining strength even as the North was dealing with increasing internal dissension. In terms of international understandings of secession, Katanga had only begun its integration into the still chaotic Congo at the time and the definitive rejection of secession, the fall of Biafra, would not occur until 1967. Given the historical separation between two regions and the increasing turmoil in the country itself, it is not too far of a stretch to imagine that the South felt they could indeed achieve the complete independence they longed for. Thus there was no reason to legitimize the concept of a federal solution at the time.

However, following the Round Table Conference, the political leadership split. SANU was essentially reduced to a single representative, William Deng, while new factions such as the Southern Front (which appeared before the round table), the Sudan United Party, the Southern Sudan Provisional Government, and others appeared, and each claimed a different political goal for the struggle.[71] SANU and the Sudan United Party both now advocated for a united Sudan. The SSPG wished for complete independence for the South and attempted to align themselves with the Anya-nya, who, regardless of the political manoeuvring of the political groups, remained staunchly in favour of secession. For a brief period the SSPG held the most sway amongst the factions and had drawn itself generally into alignment with the commanders on the ground, but by 1969 they too had split. The political turmoil in the South can be somewhat attributed to the lack of coordination between the military and political sides of the struggle. All too often the political leadership proclaimed intentions of separatism or secession yet had no means to actually attain these goals. Meanwhile, those armed combatants in the field remained committed to a singular goal but rarely had any higher coordination than a regional commander.[72] This meant that no concerted efforts could be made to attain their goals either.

This dynamic continually asserted itself through the succession of Northern-dominated central governments. The North simply did not have the political or military strength to bodily draw the South into a united Sudan, but the South did not have the political or military cohesion to force the North to accept their secession. By the rise of the Numeiry government in 1969 the South found itself in essentially a stalemate. While even with the influx of Soviet military equipment and training the Numeiry government could not defeat them in the field, the Anya-nya still did not have the structure to effectively do more than survive in the South.

Two factors would alter this balance: the emergence of Joseph Lagu's Southern Sudan Liberation Movement and Israel's infusion of arms and supplies to that organization. Lagu, as mentioned, forced military cohesion through his access to Israeli arms and forced political cohesion through the simple expedient of ignoring the politicians.[73] Lagu's SSLM represented the closest the South had come to a unified front against the North, and nominal efforts to create a civil administration occurred at the same time as an increase in the guerrilla campaigns against the North. Throughout 1971 there were increasingly frequent raids in support of the secessionist agenda of the SSLM in its role as the central font of Southern resistance. And then in early 1972, the SSLM acceded to the Agreement for Autonomy for the Southern Sudan, which set the stage for an autonomous South under the Government of the Sudan.[74] The agreement was certainly not initially popular, despite Lagu's comments that he was satisfied with its provisions. Even amongst his ANAF there was widespread dissension, as most had been under the impression they were fighting for full independence. While after it was signed as the Addis Ababa Agreement it was generally followed, it was certainly not the secessionist end that most factions of the now sixteen-year-old movement had been promoting.

So despite the call for secession, why did the First Sudanese Civil War fail to achieve it? A central part of the answer must simply be that for a state to be independent it must be recognized, and for the duration of the struggle international recognition was either not forthcoming or impossible. As in the case of Biafra, post-1963 and the creation of the OAU there was essentially no chance that an African country would intercede to offer substantive recognition to a seceding Southern Sudan. Beyond this, as noted in the Katanga chapter, following the Congo Crisis and the establishment of the OAU, the international community tended to see African struggles as a regional issue and therefore within the purview of the OAU, which as noted was actively hostile to political measures to insure secession.

However, as the case of Eritrea would prove later, a military solution could force the hand of the parent state government and ensure secession via the recognition of the very government the new state was seceding from. Given the fragility of the Sudanese government and its extremely diverse populace, was a military solution out of reach? The answer must be seen as a yes due to structural reasons. Despite the weakness of the North at varying times, the Southern insurgents made several critical mistakes throughout the conflict that left them in an isolated and weak position. The first mistake was essentially in keeping the conflict a parochial one; the Southerners were certainly not the only group that was discontented within the Sudan. The multiple coups and demonstrations in the North pointed toward numerous examples of various interest groups that were often opposed to the government's initiatives. This is not to say that all or even the majority would have been sympathetic to the Southern cause, but between the large population of Southerners living in the North and the other large non-Arab populations, there were a significant number of potential allies. Yet none of these groups was seriously approached by the South after the earliest days of the conflict. This meant that the North could focus the vast majority of its security apparatus on the South, making the struggle that much more difficult.

The second error compounded the first. With the conflict concentrated in the South and with the increasingly repressive measures undertaken to control the region, the conflict seemed as if it naturally could take on the aspects of a protracted war, such as those fought in Vietnam and Eritrea. The majority of the terrain favoured it, the populace had reason to be mobilized, and the imbalance of forces would seem to point toward its logic. However, one never came about. This is not to say that guerrilla tactics were not used, but this was for the most part the fullest extent of the application. Unity of command eluded the struggle for the vast majority of its tenure, leading to fighters who would not fight outside of their home regions, uncoordinated campaigns, and overall an effect that was far more likened to "banditry" than a protracted guerrilla campaign.[75] It is the last of these that had the longest-ranging effect, as the cornerstone of any protracted liberation struggle is popular support, which is mobilized by political education and community building. These actions then create a support base for further struggles through the provision of food, information, more fighters, and sanctuary when necessary—as put so elegantly, the people become the "sea" that the guerrilla "fish" swim in. Although piecemeal efforts at education, community building, and mobilization were made after Lagu consolidated the fronts, these were never particularly widespread. Thus, the popular base for the South's struggles was never fully utilized and they remained militarily weak. In the end, the consolidation of the ANAF and SSLM and the provision of weapons and equipment from Israel were necessary steps, but they served more to sustain the conflict at its deadlocked levels than to create a decisive end. With the war still fully ongoing in the South and no further outside aid likely to appear, a military solution was impossible as well. This in the end doomed any attempts at the full secession of the Southern Sudan.

However, the same failures that bedeviled the forces of the South in the First Civil War would certainly be issues in the Second Civil War. At its start in 1983, the prevailing international attitude had certainly not changed toward the secession of a territory from an African state. If anything, the intensification of the Cold War made any tangible change in the international order almost less likely than at any point previous. The OAU had clamped down on almost all anti-statist movements and the United Nations had essentially referred such questions to the regional authorities. Even the hegemonic powers of the United States and the USSR had no interest in fostering the South's conflict. The United States backed the North for strategic reasons in the region and had not yet begun their worry about "Islamic" states. Meanwhile the Soviet Union was far more concerned with minimizing their role in sub-Saharan Africa, and their resources were already sorely taxed by what they saw as the more vital struggles for Ethiopia and Angola.[76] In addition, little had seemingly changed about the South and its structures. The leadership tended to be fragmented and parochial, the goals of the various groups tended to be at odds with each other, and finally, while there was discontent with the North, there was little else that defined the South as a strong, independent society that could stand alone against the omnipresent structures of the central government.

It was in the Second Civil War that the South would overcome each of these difficulties, but often only by the careful negotiating of the regional political context in which they were operating. The continuing issues of the South and its unity were dealt with through a variety of measures.

The first, and perhaps paramount, factor was simply the material advantage Garang and his force exhibited in the first eight years of the renewed struggle. Much as Joseph Lagu had been able to leverage his connections with the Israelis and their supplies to dominate the Southern political and military actors, Garang used his connections with Mengistu's Ethiopia to outfight and outlast the other regional fronts. Even veteran groups like the Anya-nya II could not effectively compete with an opponent that was better supplied and who had safe Ethiopian bases to retreat to when threatened.[77]

This is not to say that Garang's only initial advantage was through his weapons caches. While the Anya-nya II again articulated a secessionist creed, the SPLM/A instead called for a revolution of the whole of the Sudan.[78] This message, of an armed struggle aimed at reforming the state to represent all of its inhabitants, found greater purchase both domestically and abroad. Secession was a narrow goal and one that isolated the Southerners from the rest of the Sudan. Reform, on the other hand, not only served as an attainable goal for those already fighting but was a reasonable and even desirable goal for the diverse populations of the South and even other dissident populations in Darfur and parts of the North. Garang's forces attracted a broader coalition than the reborn Anya-nya and proved to be far more durable. Ironically, the SPLM/A's initial rejection of secession as a goal made it far more possible in the later years of the struggle.

Had the regional power balance remained the same, Garang and his front might well have won a victory as a reform insurgency. The Northern government was having increasing difficulty dealing with the SPLM/A on its own, much less with the new dissident fronts that its increasingly aggressive allied militias were fomenting. The combination of the weakness of the Northern government under al-Mahdi, the steady flow of arms from Ethiopia (who in turn rejected secession as a goal), and the SPLM/A's diplomatic manoeuvring regarding both the remaining fragments of the Anya-nya and previously neutral populations seemed to offer a way past the stalemate that Lagu and his forces had experienced. However, this was not to be: the 1991 collapse of Mengistu's regime in the face of the EPRDF and EPLF coalition effectively ended the possibility of Garang leading a united Sudan under a reform-minded representative regime. Without the logistical support and bases that the Derg had provided, Garang's movement lacked what had been a vital component of its success. Supplies became far scarcer, large populations of refugees were expelled from Ethiopia and had to be dealt with (including the families of SPLA fighters), and Garang's authority over his movement fragmented. This, combined with a newly emboldened Northern opposition, saw the majority of the gains that the SPLM had made since 1983 disappear.

While 1991 marked a significant setback to the South within the context of the civil war, it also marked a significant realignment within regional dynamics that would ultimately allow the South to secure the victory it had sought for decades. While the SPLM/A was battered during 1991–1994 it was not broken and instead found new havens within the South to ride out the new offensives from the North. Its splinter groups found that although they could call on support from their home regions, they too were underequipped and undersupplied and ultimately turned to the North for succor in their war against Garang's faction.[79] While they were able to reconcile their alliance with the North with their declarations of secessionist goals, these groups were delegitimized in the eyes of the Southerners through both their associations and their actions. This meant that by 1994 Garang's forces, while much reduced in scope and in holdings, had survived the worst of the collapse and emerged again as the sole force fighting against Northern domination in the South.

This re-emergence coincided with the dramatic change in regional and international relations. The end of the Cold War had brought about not only the collapse of Mengistu's Ethiopia but an international re-evaluation of politics in Africa. As noted earlier, the Organization of African Unity had to struggle with its role beyond the Cold War strictures that had shaped it. The ideological lens through which wars had been viewed crumbled away. Regional rivalries reignited as regimes were reshaped following the fall of the USSR. Finally, the remaining superpower, the United States, began to rethink its posture on the continent. All of these had significant effects upon the Sudanese case. Garang kept the SPLM/A ahead of the curve by insisting on a National Convention in 1994. This gathering was intended to bring a more representative and inclusive dynamic to the SPLM/A and to critique the previous eleven years of fairly autocratic leadership. While Garang and his allies emerged still at the head of the movement, its rhetoric had moved beyond that of the earlier Marxist revolutionary conceptions and now contained appeals to democracy and human rights. In addition, new structures within the movement did allow for more participation on the part of the general populace of the South. Essentially, the 1994 National Convention allowed for the reshaping of the SPLM/A into a popular democratic organization that appealed to the international community. In particular, this transformation played a large role in shifting the perception of the United States with regard to the South's aspirations. No longer stridently Marxist, and standing in opposition to a fiercely Islamist regime that was harbouring international terrorists, the South now seemed to be not only an acceptable regional partner but one that embodied much of the American rhetoric about an oppressed people fighting against an oppressive and radical regime. American support would pay dividends in the diplomatic arena in the coming years.

In addition, the recent regional realignments began to pay dividends for the SPLM/A. Shortly after the expelling of Garang's front from Ethiopia, the movement sought refuge in Yoweri Museveni's Uganda. Because of regional affinities as well as the SPLM/A's continuing conflict with the horrific Lord's Resistance Army, Museveni had offered their families refuge across the Uganda border. Over the next few years this partnership deepened and soon Uganda was offering significant aid to the Southerners. Uganda was not alone for long in their support of the Southern fighters. Both Ethiopia and Eritrea were supporting the SPLM/A's efforts against the North. Eritrea had, along with Uganda, clandestinely met with Garang in the early 1990s and pledged support against the North. The new regime in Ethiopia took time to gain their footing following their overthrow of Mengistu's government, but it also offered support in the later 1990s.[80] For both Ethiopia and Eritrea this support was sparked by Bashir's regime supporting Islamic dissident groups within their nation, causing both to turn against the Sudan in favour of the insurgent Southerners. Thus, although 1991 had seen the collapse of the Derg's support for the SPLM, by the end of the decade the new political rivalries in the region had gained Garang back significant support from several regional powers. The influx of material support helped the SPLM/A regain the initiative while the expanded border regions for operations led to a broadening of the operational space for the South Sudanese. This in turn led to a reconnection with the dissident Northern groups such as the National Democratic Alliance and the Beja Conference.[81] These allied groups expanded the scope of the struggle and put increasing pressure on the military capabilities of the Bashir government.

While 1991 had almost seen the destruction of the SPLM/A, by the end of the decade the insurgent group had undergone a complete change of fortune. Compared with the Anya-nya in 1972, the SPLM was in a far stronger position. While the Anya-nya had had a unified command structure and the support of Israel, Garang's SPLM had a unified command structure that was truly representative of the South Sudan. In addition it had multiple regional allies, several allied Sudanese dissident groups, international sympathy, and the initiative against a government that had rapidly turned itself into a pariah. However, while the conditions were set for a military victory, why would it necessarily be one that included secession? Beyond this, why would secession even be seen as a possibility now, when it had been anathema since the formation of the Organization of African Unity?

This simple answer is that the international regime that had rejected any and all secessionist causes throughout the 1960s was no longer in place. The blossoming of nationalism following the end of the Cold War was generally accepted in Africa as well. Beyond this, as noted earlier, the North had found itself isolated within the international community, with its Islamist government now regarded as an oppressive dictatorship, increasing scrutiny on its actions in Darfur, and fewer African states willing to support their actions. Thus, while it was unlikely that the SPLM/A would ever be able to overthrow the Sudanese regime, their demands for a separate regime and perhaps even complete secession would now be acceptable to the Sudanese government. This in turn would lessen the international pressure on Khartoum and allow them to pivot to their other current areas of concern in the North as well as finally fully develop their oil industry, which offered new economic possibilities for their country. With this in mind, as well as the continuation of the rivalry along other axes, Khartoum was willing to negotiate with the SPLM/A and create a delayed plebiscite with the potential of either a rejection of secession in the South or at least time to prepare for and perhaps undermine its new neighbour. Much as in the Eritrea situation, secession was conscionable now because the host state gave its permission and the international climate that had prohibited secession previously now was willing to accept it, at least in some particular cases where popular opinion allowed significant leeway toward the seceding territory.

Under these circumstances, the secession process was essentially negotiated and begun in 2005. The combatants had been drawn to the negotiating table by the internal pressure that the SPLM/A and allied dissident groups could bring to bear against Khartoum and the external dynamics that had turned international sentiment against the Northern regime. The South had endured the long wars and managed to forge a resilient social structure that carried it through to the end of the Cold War and past the collapse of its regional allies. While they would wait six more years, the plebiscite would take place and the South would become its own state, joining Eritrea as the only successful secessionist fronts in African history. This was not an easy path, but South Sudan now stands as an independent and sovereign state of Africa. However, this period has not been a pacific one, despite the emergence of an independent South Sudan. The tensions already inherent in the secessionist political and military leadership did not disappear with the achievement of their goal. Since independence, the South Sudan has been wracked with a series of internal conflicts and outright civil wars, and no singular effective political order has emerged to lead the now-independent country into the future. Its travails up to the present will be covered in the Conclusion.

PART III

The New Wave of Secessions

In 1989 the idea of secession still seemed to be a dead end. The Civil Secessions had been snuffed out with the fall of Biafra in 1970. In its aftermath, the unitary and indivisible sovereign African state was enshrined. Even for those Long Wars being waged since the 1960s, there seemed little respite. While Ethiopia was tottering under the weight of its multiple insurgencies, the question remained whether the aftermath would be a reform or a secession even if any of them did succeed. For the Sudan, there was even less hope, as the central government retained the initiative and the recognition of the international community while the SPLA was fragmenting and its factions fighting amongst themselves.

However, a massive change in the international dynamics was on its way. While the Cold War had imposed a sort of stasis upon African states and their rulers, albeit with client rulers occasionally being replaced, by the end of the 1980s the Soviet Union found itself in an increasingly untenable situation. Facing economic stagnation, massive military spending, an unpopular and unwinnable war in Afghanistan, and increasing dissent to its rule, the USSR was no longer able to sustain its competition with the United States. Reforms had actually begun in 1985 under the new Secretary General of the Communist Party, Mikhail Gorbachev. Gorbachev, noticing the economic weakness of the USSR, had tried to reform its political and economic structures, liberalizing its judiciary, its politburo, and its productive organs throughout the next five years.[1]

However, these changes would prove to be too late to save the weakened superpower. Nationalist movements pressed for more local autonomy now that they had more ability to express themselves within the political and economic spheres. Throughout the late 1980s the USSR's satellite states increasingly expressed their independence, with protests throughout the Baltic States and the Caucasus, and even more central states such as Ukraine and Belorussia slowly breaking free from the grip of the Soviet Union. While these states were not necessarily seceding yet, their actions undermined the USSR as a global actor, weakening its ability to project power abroad while at the same time sparking an internal crisis. In response, Gorbachev's government attempted to continue its internal and external reform, with the eventual goal of the conversion of the Soviet Union into a federation of independent republics. These reforms were met by the older power structures of the USSR with an attempted coup against Gorbachev, with Russian tanks rolling into Moscow in August 1991 to try and reimpose communist power over the increasingly liberal government.[2]

The coup failed due to the intervention of Moscow's populace and the swift action of Boris Yeltsin, the reform-minded leader of the Russian national government, the Russian Soviet Federative Socialist Republic (RSFSR). Following its failure, the old order collapsed, with Yeltsin quickly accruing power and marginalizing Gorbachev and the Communist Party. Over the following year the old USSR was dismantled, with its dissolution officially completed in December of that year. However, this dismantling, while agreed upon by the major states within the USSR, had been occurring already for well over a year. With the turmoil within the USSR over the previous two years, new national governments had been proclaimed in Lithuania, Estonia, and Latvia, leading these previously independent states back into their own separate realms. In addition, new states declared their separation from the USSR, with ethnic populations that had been part of the Russian state since the nineteenth century now declaring their self-determination. Georgia, Ukraine, Belarus, Moldova, Uzbekistan, and many other new states declared their right to exist and self-govern between August 1990 and December 1991. Although it had been unable to effectively project its influence for the previous several years, this final dissolution of the Soviet Union in a wave of secessions marked the end to the Cold War and the beginning of a new era not only for the global order but also seemingly for the concept of secession across the world.

The Acceptance of Secession and Nation-States

This new, post–Cold War era had several important ramifications for the nature of the state within the international order. The first half-decade of the 1990s saw the international political order upended, beginning in Eastern Europe and the former Soviet sphere. While the Cold War had continually enforced the immutable nature of the state, with the end of that conflict there were now questions about how a state should be formed and whether the postwar order was the proper configuration of states within Europe. With the victory of the United States and its capitalist allies in the long Cold War and the increasing fissures within the USSR's territories, this state structure fractured. As noted, the former Soviet satellites declared their separation from the USSR and their eventual sovereignty. While previously it might have been understood that the Baltic states would be met with acceptance in the international community, the international welcome to the new states such as Kazakhstan and Uzbekistan was something that had not been seen before. In fact, not only were these emerging states granted almost unanimous international recognition, they were swiftly incorporated into the United Nations.

This process of secession and repartition found itself echoed across Eastern Europe as the old communist order disintegrated. The state of Czechoslovakia underwent what it referred to as the Velvet Divorce, partitioning itself into its previously constituent states, now named the Czech Republic and Slovakia, in 1993. More alarmingly, the polyglot state of Yugoslavia began to tear itself apart as its constituent Slavic populations fought for their own separation from the previous state. This led into a series of bloody conflicts that roiled throughout the late 1990s as the new separatist states broke themselves apart, with the violence only halting following the military intervention of both the United Nations and NATO. However, these interventions served only to halt the horrific violence, not to intervene and put the state back together.[3] While there remained violent flare-ups until the early 2000s, the entire Balkans had reshaped themselves, with new states emerging from the shattered Yugoslav polity. In addition, following the cessation of the violence, these states were granted international recognition and were welcomed into the international community as independent sovereign bodies. By the year 2000, the former Eastern Bloc had seen the emergence of over a dozen new states, many of which had no historical antecedent or at best had thin histories of independence that were the product of romanticized legends.

Of course, what could not be ignored as well was the re-emergence of a previously frowned-upon basis for the creation of a new state: ethnicity. While civil states had been accepted since the end of the Second World War, new nation-states had been directly avoided. The conflation of nation with state had been explicitly denied within the international community, with ethnically plural states having been seen as the preferred form of political organization. However, the undercurrents of ethno-nationalism had survived even within the multi-ethnic states of Eastern Europe.[4] In fact, during the long Cold War these ethnic differences were taken advantage of by the United States, who used the nationalism of the Soviet Bloc and even the USSR's constituent states as an avenue to foment dissent and weaken their rival. With the dissolution of the USSR, and lacking any other directive force, these nations now looked to have their own states for their people: the Kazakhs wanted Kazakhstan, the Uzbeks wanted Uzbekistan, and the Georgians wanted their own Georgia. Given that, it is unsurprising that many of the new states recognized as new sovereign powers were in effect nation-states, formed around the national identities of a particular ethnic group.

The New Era in Africa

This breaking and remaking of states did not go unnoticed on the African continent. While at the end of the Cold War the idea of secession in Africa seemed an impossibility, this was partially based on the international order the Cold War had put in place over global politics. Since even before the decolonization of Africa, the international borders had been seemingly immutable. The United Nations had waged the first offensive military campaign in its history to prevent the secession of Katanga and the failure of the Congo. The Organization of African Unity had enshrined the principle of indivisible states in its very charter. While there had been some dissent from this stance in documents such as the African Charter on Human and Peoples' Rights, which enshrined self-determination in the signed draft of 1981, this remained fraught territory. Despite widespread support from its many African signatories, when secessionist groups such as Katanga were brought up, the idea of self-determination was often denied despite the plain meaning of the text.[5]

However, with the ending of the Cold War, it now appeared that the United Nations, and the United States as the sole remaining superpower, were both willing to countenance secession as an internationally acceptable phenomenon. This came into even starker focus with the initial negotiations between the new reform-minded regime in Ethiopia and its Eritrean allies.[6] With secession now openly countenanced, secessionist-minded groups on the continent could now point not only to successful international secessions in this era of fluid statehood but also to possible successes in redrawing the borders that had been set at Berlin in 1885.

Even more notable on the continent was the new acceptance of nationality as not only an acceptable goal for a state but explicitly an acceptable end-state. On the European continent this resurgence of ethno-nationalism led to new nation-states, but admittedly this was not necessarily novel within the European order. Most Western European states had been formed almost explicitly as nation-states over the modern era, with at most small ethnic minorities remaining in Germany, France, or Italy following the long process of ethnic sorting and constructing identities. However, on the African continent there were few nation-states, with Somalia as the largest example, with Swaziland and Lesotho joining it through their own complex histories in southern Africa. Instead, the borders that had been drawn at the 1885 Berlin Conference were based on the political requirements of the colonizing European powers, completely ignoring any ethnic or national divisions within these new political units. Whole ethnic populations might be divided between two or even three states, such as the Kongo of the Democratic Republic of the Congo, the Republic of the Congo, and Angola; or the Somali, who spread across Somalia, Ethiopia, and Kenya. Conversely, it meant that very few states on the continent were ethnically homogenous, meaning that issues such as representation, governance, access to state resources, and even basic rights remained contested terrain for many ethnic groups following independence.

This continued contestation meant that many of these ethnic groups, whether simply a sole minority within a single African state or a group sprawling across several, had significant grievances against their host states. These grievances led to resistance against the state that ranged from avoidance of state taxes, smuggling within their ethnic group across borders, to even occasional military actions. The Kel Tamasheq and Bedan of the Sahara continued to trace their ancestral routes through the Sahara, maintaining economic connections across their nation, often in defiance of Saharan states such as Mali, Niger, and Algeria. On the other end of the scale were groups like the Western Somali Liberation Front, who waged lengthy guerrilla campaigns against Ethiopia in an attempt to rejoin their territories to Somalia. However, despite these acts of resistance and national solidarity, the monolithic state remained the sole avenue of access to legitimacy and its international benefits, and without control or at least effective access to the state these minority ethnic groups remained marginalized with little hope of overturning this order.[7]

New Era and Nation-States

However, beginning in 1991 with the acceptance of nation-states and specifically ethnic secession by the United States, the United Nations, and the international community following the end of the Cold War, new hope arose amongst marginalized ethnic groups. For those members of divided ethnic groups, the possibility of secession or irredentism offered chances to rewrite the political order their communities existed in, especially following years of neglect or even repression under the existing states of Africa. During these years such groups had often maintained a much stronger bond with their nation than with their state, and with this now an acceptable political outcome, the larger pressing questions about the role of the state in post–Cold War Africa grew in importance.[8] Given this, it is unsurprising that the new wave of secessions that would take place in Africa would not necessarily have simply a political component but also an ethnic one, with marginalized subnational groups now pushing for a rewriting of the political order of Africa to allow them representation, if not entirely control, within a state of their own making.

Beyond the larger questions of secession and ethnic nationalism, the shifting international order would have another critical effect on the states of Africa. The Cold War dynamics had forced the globe into two opposing camps led by the superpowers of the USSR and the United States. These camps, containing a plethora of allies and proxies for the superpowers, essentially were subsidized and supported by their chosen hegemon, with the more prominent allies offering support to the emerging states of Africa and Asia as well. This led to substantial support for countries like Thailand and Iran from the United States and its allies while countries like Cuba and Ethiopia were offered substantial support by the Soviet Union and its compatriots. This support took many forms, from favourable trade deals to large-scale security cooperation, and was intended to maintain at least a balance of international power and perhaps even offer an advantage to the particular faction. The end result was the creation of two large, mutually opposing political poles that had achieved a rough political equilibrium throughout the postwar years.[9]

However, with the end of the Cold War this global construct was dismantled. The capitalist states led by the United States had achieved victory over their opponents, and the disappearance of the bipolar world forced a reimagining of the international dynamics. For those already developed states of North America and Europe, the strategic focus shifted from opposition to a communist opponent to the integration of the defeated developed powers into the global system and the fostering of democratic governance across the globe. The assumption made was that with the liberal democratic world order having proven triumphant, now the role of the United States as the sole superpower was to foster civil society, human rights, and representative government across the globe through either indirect or direct intervention.[10] For those underdeveloped states of the world, no matter their alignment or lack thereof, this meant that the political, economic, and military support they had been receiving either disappeared completely or became contingent on a very different set of objectives than those they had been pursuing. This meant, in many cases, turmoil as the ruling elites who had maintained privileged positions either were overthrown or had to make radical changes in their political stances to fall in line with the new goals of the US-led global order.

These effects were especially notable in Africa, where the development of the state had been neglected throughout the colonial era and only hastily attempted in the 1950s. During the colonial era, the state structures that had been required were minimal. There were governors for colonies to deal with local legislative issues, courts to deal with legal challenges, and the police and military to help control the local populaces. Beyond this, the level of political infrastructure varied tremendously throughout the African colonies, with the British system often relying on traditional elites for local control while the French worked hard at a lengthy but ultimately limited program of assimilating the local population into French culture and values. However, no matter the system, the highest level of administration was still overwhelmingly in the hands of European colonial professionals. This attenuation of development was also almost universally paralleled in terms of economic infrastructure. The colonies had not been conceived of as self-sufficient markets or even regional trading partners; they had been understood as sources for raw materials and commodities and markets for completed products.[11] States like Ghana and Uganda, both seen as relatively advanced politically by the mid-twentieth century, still had little manufacturing and instead produced cocoa, coffee, and other cash crops for the British market. This economic activity in turn shaped the infrastructure of the state, with railways, roads, canals, and telegraphs all being built not to integrate the colonies together but to route their goods to the nearest entrepot.

With the emergence of the African state into independence, these incomplete structures did not suddenly become whole. The ruling elite of the state instead inherited a political structure that had little capacity to do anything beyond continue its functions of extracting materials and importing the modern manufactured goods it needed. Economically this offered little chance to grow and integrate the public goods that most developed states already provided such as more expansive healthcare, education, and even local transportation.[12] Those states that attempted to pursue these goals, notably Tanzania and Ghana, quickly found themselves deeply indebted or reliant on foreign aid.[13] The result was essentially a state that had little capacity beyond the boundaries of its major cities and limited infrastructure network and little chance to improve upon that capacity. While the ruling elite could still determine the access to the outside world through their legitimacy as leadership of the state, they could do little to develop it, especially following the crash of commodity prices following the 1973 oil crisis.[14]

While the state had little capacity, it was exactly these connections to the global community that the ruling elites held that would allow the incomplete state to survive throughout the Cold War. With the fierce competition ongoing between the United States and the USSR, both superpowers or their stronger allies were more than willing to reach out to the African states in exchange for their raw commodities, their markets, and their strategic support. In return, the regimes that offered such access and support were given often massive political, military, and economic aid.[15] This bargain existed for both of the great poles, with states such as the Democratic Republic of the Congo, Kenya, and Uganda each gaining significant support from the capitalist powers in Africa while countries like Ethiopia, Angola, and Uganda[16] aligned themselves with the communist bloc. Even those countries that attempted to remain non-aligned often attempted to play the two camps off against one another to gain what material support they might from the superpowers to support their state. Regardless, throughout this period, the goods, services, and monetary aid offered by the Cold War powers often was the decisive factor in the functional capacity of the African state, which took on an increasingly authoritarian form.

However, with the end of the Cold War, the sources of support either disappeared or changed their priorities. For those states that had been aligned with the Soviet Bloc, such support, already having been drying up by the late 1980s, completely disappeared. For those that had aligned with the capitalist bloc, their patrons still existed, but with changed geopolitical goals. Now the staunch anti-communism that had served as reason enough to support strongmen like Mobutu Sese Seko in Zaire and Ibrahim Babangida in Nigeria was no longer sufficient. In fact, the global community now wished to see the governments of Africa reformed and to become more representative and participatory, echoing the long-standing demands of many of these governments' citizens.[17] For the formerly communist-aligned governments, the withdrawal of support was disastrous; for the capitalist-aligned it forced a difficult choice upon the autocrats of Africa: reform or lose support. In either case, within the new world order, there was less focus on Africa's states and less support to go around as the developing and democratizing world required assistance. The upshot was that these states now found their main source of economic, political, and military support cut off. Without this support, the African states saw a continued draining of their capacities. Countries like Mobutu's Zaire, which had slowly been dismantled throughout the three decades of his kleptocratic rule, even lost the ability to effectively control the very borders that delineated their statehood.[18]

This combination of weak states, strong nations, and apparent willingness to redraw boundaries set up the next wave of African secessionist, separatist, and irredentist conflicts. With many states of Africa having never attained or sometimes even pursued the capacity to do more than exist, the subnational fractures within their borders deepened, especially as internal or even cross-border populations turned to their own communities to sustain themselves. Now, with those states having even less power to project their control over regions, these groups sought their own access to the benefits of statehood. For some, this meant a complete split from the state and an attempt to assert their own sovereignty and connection with the global community. For many others, it meant asserting local autonomy for their community while gaining access to the global networks that the sovereignty of their host state retained. Finally, for some this meant attempting to gather together an entire border-spanning community and either create their own ethnic state from multiple African states or separate from a state where they were the minority and joining a bordering one where they would be the majority and gain access to the global networks. However, despite some subnational groups gaining (or even retaining) their regional autonomy peacefully, in most instances these assertions of local control and rule were contested by force of arms.

These new assertions of local control would emerge as the new wave of secessions. These attempts at secession, separatism, and irredentism were driven by the understood new dynamics involving the state on the African continent. As such, they would feature distinct and direct appeals to the breaking up of states along ethnic lines, often driven by the long-held grievances of populations that had never effectively been served by the postcolonial state. However, while much of the context of the state had changed, there was little change in the dynamics of these conflicts. The simple declaration of a state would not be recognized by the international community, to which the weakened but still extant postcolonial states still had sole access. This meant that when these new efforts emerged, they followed the same operational and organizational structure that had allowed the Long Wars to achieve their gains: a long-term local guerrilla struggle that would see the local populace supporting a prolonged social transformation at the same time as a lengthy, low-intensity conflict. Given that there was even less opportunity for outside aid and support with the ending of the Cold War, the way of the insurgent seemed to be the only way to prosecute any political conflict against a host nation.[19] This would be the playbook followed by the irredentists in Cabinda, the Casamance Separatists, and many other groups. In fact, many built upon earlier efforts that had blossomed before the end of the Cold War and either continued or renewed these efforts in the wake of the global realignment.

However, while these new or renewed efforts were not necessarily anything new on the continent, their opponents now faced very changed circumstances. Whereas in earlier struggles the state governments of Africa could likely call upon their patrons for the military aid they needed to suppress or defeat their internal opponents, this aid was no longer available. Beyond this, as noted, their general capacity as a state was diminished, including the lessening of their abilities to wage war, to police, to serve their populace, or even to defend their borders. The prolonged wars that the state governments had been able to prosecute were no longer tenable and in fact drained the increasingly thin resources and abilities of the state. In return, the increasingly open access to international markets meant that insurgencies could extract valuable resources and use them to fund their struggles, offering a capacity that earlier waves had not been able to take advantage of. With the states' capacity weakened and armed fronts having new avenues of support, new approaches to the conflicts and the resolutions would be experimented with throughout these conflicts, with the questions of sovereignty, secession, separatism, and ethnic irredentism having to be negotiated within the larger context of shifting concepts of statehood and nationhood on the African continent.

Map of Somalia and Somaliland

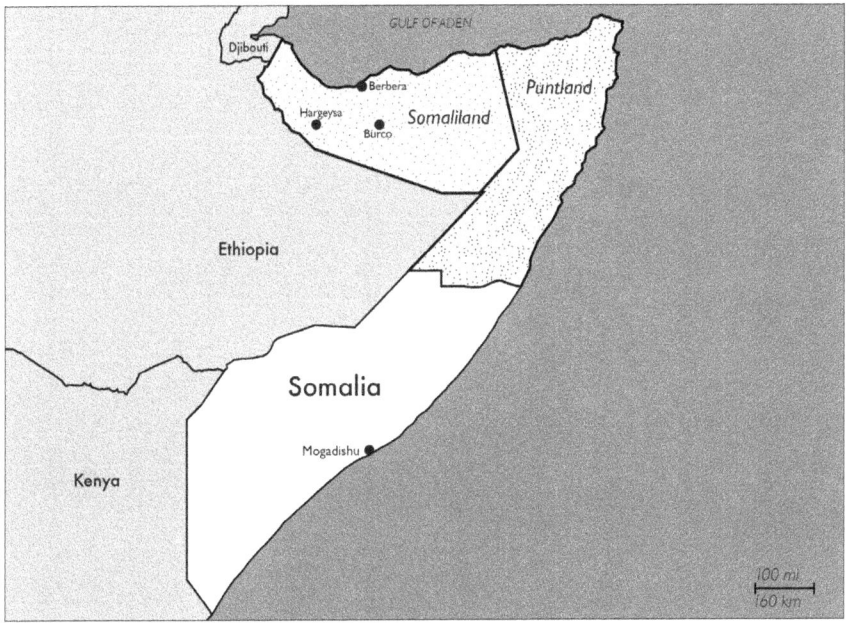

Copyright © 2014 Nathan E. McCormack and Charles G. Thomas

De Facto Secession and the New Borders of Africa: Somaliland, 1991–Present

Of all the case studies presented in this book, none is more indicative of both the legacies of past secessionist attempts and the present global political dynamics than the unrecognized state of Somaliland. The legacies of the past have imposed a continued insistence that the boundaries of all African states remain sacrosanct absent the express permission of the mother state; this has left Somaliland without international recognition despite having existed as a separate and autonomous territory for over twenty years. However, the end of the Cold War and the increasingly tenuous questions of sovereignty and the nation-state have meant that despite this lack of official recognition of its sovereignty, Somaliland has found pragmatic partners in the Horn of Africa, the Red Sea region, and across the globe to sustain itself and the increasingly capable state structures that define it. This chapter will explore the role of Somaliland in the current secessionist and separatist dynamics in Africa and how the denial of de jure sovereignty has, in the current age, not prevented its de facto existence.

The Conflict

It would be a misnomer to discuss the conflict that resulted in Somaliland as a secessionist insurgency from the outset. The separation of Somaliland from Somalia proper was not expected by the combatants, nor was it originally desired.¹ It was only the collapse of the rest of the state into a deadly civil war and its inability to effectively reintegrate that convinced the people of Somaliland that they not only could but should remain a separate political body. However, the previous reform conflict and the insurgency that drove it remain an essential component of the eventual separation of Somaliland and as such deserve discussion to contextualize the current state of Somaliland and its relations with its neighbours.

The seeds of the reform movement that would eventually coalesce into the Somali National Movement and the separation of Somaliland from Somalia were planted in 1969. In that year, the elected government of the United Republic of Somalia was overthrown by the military regime of Mohamed Siad Barre and his Supreme Revolutionary Council.[2] General Siad Barre's regime was both stridently Marxist and strongly nationalist. The former led to the state following "Scientific Socialism" as an economic path and receiving significant military and economic aid from the Soviet Union. The latter led to a call for the reintegration of a "Greater Somalia," wherein all territories that were home to Somalis would be gathered into the nation-state of Somalia.[3] It was this Pan-Somali ideology that drove the foreign policy of the Siad Barre regime throughout the next decade. While the Shifta War in Kenya, waged during 1963–1967 by ethnic Somalis with an irredentist goal, was ultimately unsuccessful, the territories there were not necessarily a high priority for the Somalis. However, not only was the Ogaden region of Ethiopia home to a large Somali population, the grazing lands of the Haud[4] had been critical to the lives of the pastoralists who made up the bulk of the Somali population.[5] This made the reclamation of the Ogaden a central pillar of Siad Barre's Pan-Somali ideology, which was increasingly buttressing the social transformation of his country.

However, at least initially the direct annexation of the Ogaden was out of reach for Siad Barre's regime. Instead, significant efforts were made to support the Western Somali Liberation Front (WSLF), a dissident insurgency in the Ogaden that had irredentist goals and its own Pan-Somali ideology.[6] Throughout 1973, the WSLF searched for a way to seize a majority of the Ogaden, and with the downfall of Haile Selassie's regime, they seized the chance. However, by 1977 Mengistu's new Derg government had begun to push the Somali insurgents back and reassert Ethiopian control over the Ogaden. It was precisely at this time that Siad Barre's Somali

National Army invaded the Ogaden in support of the WSLF and with the goal of finally annexing the region.[7] Within the first three months of the conflict, the Somalis managed to seize approximately 60 percent of the region, but at that point the tide turned against them. Their Soviet patrons had switched their backing to Mengistu's Derg, creating a critical shift in power. A series of military failures put Siad Barre's army on the defensive by late 1977, and in February 1978, a joint Ethiopian-Cuban offensive drove the allied Somali forces back. By March 1978, the last of Siad Barre's soldiers had been driven out of Ethiopia and the WSLF was on its own.[8]

While this effectively ended the hopes for a Greater Somalia for the time being, hostilities would continue back and forth between the now U.S.-aligned Somalia and the Soviet and Cuban-backed Ethiopia. However, as the formal war ended, the informal war between the two increased in intensity. Without the success of Pan-Somalism and with the loss of the economic support of the Soviet Union, Siad Barre's regime began to lose support amongst the rival power blocs within Somalia. The acceptance of structural reforms in return for aid from the IMF was a tipping point, crushing the ability of local peasant agriculturalists to compete economically and creating broad opposition to the regime.[9] Dissident fronts emerged in attempts to force alterations in the governance of Somalia. These included Mohamed Farah Aideed's United Somali Congress (USC), Abdullahi Yusuf Ahmed's Somali Salvation Democratic Front, and the primarily Isaaq clan-backed Somali National Movement (SNM). Each of these fronts was dedicated to the concept of Somalia as a whole, but wished to overthrow Siad Barre. Given Siad Barre's continued support for the WSLF in the Ogaden and his continued ambitions on the Ogaden, Ethiopia proved to be a silent haven for these fronts as they found their footing in the early 1980s.

The Somali National Movement, as noted, was founded primarily by Isaaq intellectuals in 1981.[10] While the initial leadership of the movement was based in England, it wasn't long until they, like many of the dissident groups, transferred their headquarters to Ethiopia with an eye toward northern Somalia, where their clan relations were in the majority. While the SNM's initial incursions into northwest Somalia were not especially notable, the Isaaq-dominated group began to gain support from members of other clan families and slowly build its power base. The next seven years saw a series of increasingly complex raids into Somalia while the political leadership of the SNM tried to form a more practical alliance with the other dissident fronts and also continue to grow its own popular support. However, despite its central clan identity and geographic focus on northern Somalia, there was not overwhelming support for the SNM in the region. While particular raids were spectacular, such as the 1982 attack on the Mandera Prison that freed hundreds of dissidents, the Siad Barre regime teetered but did not fall. It was not until 1988 that the equilibrium of the conflict was disrupted; both Somalia and Ethiopia, having exhausted their resources and facing numerous internal challenges, agreed to formally end their hostilities.[11] This announcement, seemingly innocent on its face, meant the loss of the SNM's safe haven in Ethiopia and the need to take drastic action.

The SNM responded to this loss of safe haven with a massive offensive against northern Somalia in May 1988. Attacks on the major cities of Burco on 27 May and Hargeisa on 31 May met with considerable success, with sections of both towns falling immediately and the SNM continuing to exploit these toeholds.[12] Siad Barre's government responded with a savage counteroffensive in the north. Heavy fighting erupted across the north in June and July 1988, with many of the original units of the SNM suffering losses to the continued air campaigns of the Somali Armed Forces. The struggle continued until March 1989, throughout which time the Somali Armed Forces made little effort to distinguish the SNM insurgents from the population at large. Over half a million refugees poured across the borders to Ethiopia, eventually settling in the Ogaden. These attacks saw Siad Barre's regime retake the major cities of the north as well, with Burco, Hargeisa, and Berbera falling completely to their forces. Meanwhile, the offensive had proven extremely costly to the SNM in terms of both trained personnel and material.[13]

Ironically, it was this disastrous offensive that would transform the war for the SNM. While the intervening year of conflict saw the loss of much of their previous fighting strength and the urban centres they had struggled so mightily to take, the response of the Somali Armed Forces turned the sympathies of the north fully toward the SNM. While many veteran fighters were lost, recruitment spiked within both the north and the newly established refugee camps in the Ogaden. In addition, whereas the SNM had previously had little to no fundraising capability or outside support,[14] now the support of the population of the north offered caches of funds both from the merchant networks that traded out of the strategic port of Berbera and the greater Isaaq diaspora. This surge in support rejuvenated the SNM, and the resulting increased military activity meant that despite the Somali Armed Forces' control of the cities, the countryside remained hostile territory, turning the counteroffensive into a quagmire. What had been an isolated and external armed group had been transformed into a popular reform insurgency.[15]

Over the next two years the SNM continued to wage its insurgency against Siad Barre's regime. While it maintained most of its activities solely in traditionally Isaaq areas, its leadership flirted with forming a united front with the other dissident groups waging war on the current Somali government. By 1990 the United Somali Congress, the Somali Patriotic Movement (SPM, a group founded in the southwest of the country), and the Somali National Movement had managed to coordinate their political goals, and on 6 August the three fronts proclaimed a united movement to overthrow Siad Barre.[16] By the end of the year, with the central government already under immense pressure from internal struggles, a failing economy, and the withdrawal of US support with the ending of the Cold War, the Somali Armed Forces could no longer hold back the insurgents. In December, fighters from Mohamed Farah Aideed's USC forced their way into Mogadishu. Foreign diplomatic personnel removed themselves as fighting engulfed the capital, and on 27 January 1991, General Siad Barre fled the city after twenty-two years of rule.[17]

While the collapse of the long-standing regime was not necessarily a surprise to the leadership of the SNM, the declaration two days later of Ali Mahdi Mohamed, one of the leaders of the USC, as the new interim president of Somalia, was. The united front of the SNM, USC, and SPM had agreed to form a joint administration, and this action on the part of a faction of the USC precipitated the collapse of an ordered transition.[18] Mohamed Farah Aideed's faction of the USC denounced this move and aggressively moved to counter Ali Mahdi's claim. Without any agreement in terms of the formation of a government, the various remaining armed groups began to jockey for power and the country began to slide toward a civil war. By November 1991 Somalia had descended into a lengthy conflict that would see multiple would-be central governments rise and fall and tens of thousands displaced or killed.[19] The following year would see the United Nations intervene to try to enforce a ceasefire between warlord factions and deliver humanitarian aid. When this mission encountered local resistance, the United Nations accepted an offer from the United States to lead a task force to complete the mission in November 1992. The US intervention would prove no more effective than the earlier UN efforts, with the American efforts to enforce peace through the capture of Mohamed Farah Aideed leading to a high-profile battle in Mogadishu in early October 1993. Domestic politics and the loss of American lives in the battle compelled President Bill Clinton to announce the withdrawal of American troops on 7 October, and the UN mission, now understood to be untenable, would be completely halted in March 1995. However, the Somali National Movement would not be a major participant in any of these conflicts; in the absence of a unified shared government, the SNM had declared the northern region politically separate from the rest of the country under the administration of the new SNM regime. Somalia was now shattered and the new Republic of Somaliland was declared.

The Trials of Governance

The declaration of a separate state did not imply that one was in evidence. While the old regime was no longer an active antagonist, the previous three years of war had left the northern region of Somali a smouldering ruin. The declaration of Ali Mahdi's faction had caught the SNM quite by surprise, and they had not intended to run a state on their own. While they had gained control of each of the urban centres and had dealt with the remaining Barre loyalists within what was recognized as Isaaq territory, the actual establishment of a government was still far from their minds. There remained questions about the surrounding territories of other clan families that had opposed the Isaaq or simply had not joined the SNM in their insurgency. How were these to be dealt with, especially with the continuing question of an eventual unified Somali again?

With these questions in mind, instead of engaging in aggression against the surrounding groups, which represented significant segments of the Gadabursi, Iise, Harti, and Darod clans, the Isaaq attempted a regional reconciliation spearheaded by its clan elders. In February, the representatives of the Isaaq, Iise, Gadabursi, Dhulbahante, and Warsengeli clans met in Berbera and cobbled together a formal ceasefire for the various clan militias in the region. This was simply the first step in bringing the north back under a pacific rule to rebuild it following the conflict. The next major step occurred three months later in Burco, where the "Grand Conference of the Northern Peoples" convened. This gathering brought together elders from the Harti, Dir, and Isaaq clans to discuss the future of the north, even as the south was caught between clan factions that were attempting to form a unity government. Hopes were initially high for the retention of the Somali Republic, but a long and often antagonistic relationship with the south, combined with improved relations with Ethiopia amongst the northern groups, brought questions about a separate Somaliland to the fore.[20] Public protests against a reunion with the Mogadishu regime finally confirmed the way the wind was blowing, and on 18 May 1991 the SNM chairman declared the creation of the independent Republic of Somaliland.[21] A National Charter was hastily drafted, with the SNM charged with the initial governance of the country under its chairman Abdirahman Ahmed Ali "Tuur."

While it seemed logical at the time to place the new state under the SNM due to the military support it had as well as the organization that it represented, the SNM was not necessarily representative of Somaliland as a whole. Not only were the vast majority of its members from the Isaaq clan family, thus marginalizing the members of the smaller populations, but even the various clans under the Isaaq family were not evenly distributed. Gaining the general support of the population seemed to be an extremely difficult goal, and without this support, governance would be almost impossible. However, this new government was rescued by the intervention of one of the traditional forms of governance: the guurtis. These gatherings of traditional clan elders and other influential members had served for centuries as the decision-making bodies of Somali groups, debating critical issues and arbitrating conflicts between both individuals and clans.[22] Following the exhaustion of war and the collapse of Siad Barre's regime, these traditional authorities were willing to place their influence behind that of the SNM in an attempt to bring at least temporary stability to the region. The clan guurtis created breathing space for the SNM and set a timeline for transition, offering two years for the creation and drafting of an actual government structure.

During the intervening years, the guurtis continued to serve a critical purpose within the new state. With the SNM still working to establish itself as a statewide political actor, these councils were institutionally revived throughout the region as an outgrowth of the new state. They dealt with issues of regional mistrust between the still divided clans under and beyond the Isaaq banner, normalizing relationships that had been frayed from years of war. Beyond this, they dealt with the issues of often mobilized but not directed clan militias that were a serious threat to the establishment of peace, as could be seen in the south. Finally, and perhaps most critically, they dealt with the issues of grazing rights and land disputes. With so much of the population displaced and the economy in ruins, the ability to return to semi-regular and regulated pastoral activity was a priority for getting the state running again.

These influential traditional authorities would be even more critical in the early months of 1992. Armed confrontation exploded in the region of Burco, where the Habr Jaalo and Garhaji clans were jockeying for political and economic authority. Burco sat along traditional clan fault lines, and when the government attempted to reclaim some heavy weapons from the clan militias in the region, a conflict was sparked. While elders of both groups managed to eventually broker a fragile peace, confidence in the SNM regime was damaged.[23]

These hostilities were followed almost immediately by another more serious conflict that flared up in Berbera in January 1992. While Burco was astride one of the major routes to the remaining territory of Somalia and thus offered lucrative trading prospects, Berbera was the major port of Somaliland and was responsible for the vast majority of customs duties paid to the nascent country. In addition, it was the source of almost the entirety of Somaliland's foreign exchange. Given its value, there was significant disagreement on how this port should be administered. While the SNM regime wanted to have significant nationalized control of what they saw as a vital economic resource, the Iise Muse clan claimed the port as their traditional territory and believed a significant portion of its revenues should go to the clan's interests and upkeep.[24] This disagreement manifested itself from January to March in a vicious struggle between SNM-backed forces that were drawn primarily from the Garhaji and Sa'ad Muse and the Iise Muse militias supported by a significant number of Habar Ja'lo.

These two struggles were particularly troubling for the nascent state. The closure, even temporarily, of Burco and Berbera crippled the economy of the state and sent shock waves throughout all the constituencies of the SNM regime. Beyond this, the warring factions exposed traditional fault lines within the Isaaq groups, threatening a splintering of the central governance of Somaliland and a possible slide into a general civil war like the south was experiencing. In fact, those groups in the eastern portion of Somaliland began looking to use the port of Bossasso, which also began to attract Ethiopian trade. Given the instability of the SNM regime, several of these groups even began to look for détente with the south and expressed federalist sympathies. With the SNM unable to assert its will over the dissident clan militias and leaders, it looked as if the Somaliland experiment was to end in failure.

The conclusion to these conflicts would come not through the government, but again through the informal traditional power structures of Somaliland. In October 1992 the elders of the Gadabursi, Isaaq, and Dhulbahante gathered at the town of Sheikh along with representatives from the religious authorities, the business community, and women's groups to broker a ceasefire and hopefully a lasting peace.[25] The Gadabursi were specifically useful within the discussion, as the Isaaq versus Isaaq dynamics of the conflict to this point allowed them the role of a third party mediator. The first order of business within the guurti was to settle the status of Berbera. It was agreed that the port should remain a public good for Somaliland, allowing the new state to have a central source of revenue for development.

However, the instability of the previous years and the danger of it reoccurring with the strictly SNM regime led this nationally representative gathering to look beyond simply settling the Berbera issue. Instead, the elders decided to settle additional questions involving state security, governance, and the political process in Somaliland. With the roles of titled and untitled traditional clan authorities having proven critical on numerous occasions already, clan structures re-emerged as at least a stopgap solution to the fragile framework of governance. Clan guurtis were given significant authority within a national legal framework, offering them both formal authority and significant responsibility. The clans and their leadership were now responsible for keeping the peace within the rural areas, with the clans now financially liable for the actions of their militia members—particularly the immediate family members of those who transgressed the agreements.[26] This led to a significant clampdown on the activities of the impetuous youth who previously had proven problematic in contested areas. This arrangement also included agreements for all clan militias to remove any impediments to commerce, such as the roadblocks that had proliferated in the recent months. These armed forces would also stay within what was agreed to be the clan's territories and disarm upon entering towns, which would be secured by nationalized Somaliland forces. It was hoped that these initial steps would set the stage for a peaceful advancement of national goals, balancing the needs of the state with the traditional authorities of clans within their regions.[27]

However, as the Sheikh conference concluded, it was hard to deny that the past two years had brought little progress. While there was now a general agreement regarding the role of clan authorities within the state, there were still significant tensions and no complete National Charter for the state. The search for a more permanent solution was carried out the following January, when the Borama Peace Conference was convened with the expansive title of "The Grand Conference of the Communities in Somaliland." This gathering dwarfed even the previous Sheikh meeting, bringing together 150 elders from all of the clans of Somaliland. While initially slated to last a month, it instead ran from January until May, allowing for a multitude of voices to be heard and to debate the central issue of the conference: a National Charter that could represent the state and its structures. In the end, a consensus was found, and for the first time, the new state had a legislative and executive framework.[28]

The agreement was a remarkable fusion of traditional Somali governance and modern parliamentary structures. The executive branch still existed in the person of the president, in this case labelled the *Golaha Xukuumadda*. The man elected to this position at the conference was Mohammed Ibrahim Egal, the politician who had been the last prime minister of Somalia before Siad Barre's coup. Despite his age and his connection with the former Republic of Somalia, he was an acceptable choice to all members of the guurti. His former service lent him some credibility as a national politician, and his position as an outsider to SNM politics meant he would not be seen as partial to the existing power structures. To balance the power of the executive, a bicameral legislature was formed. The upper house was the *Golaha Guurtida*, or the Council of Elders. This was essentially a legal foundation for the incorporation of a national guurti, which was given powers to ensure the peace and demobilize militia on top of the power to select the president and vice president. It was this group that selected Egal for the presidency. The lower house was the *Golaha Wakiillada*, the Constituent Assembly, which was to become a popularly elected body of legislators. Finally, an independent judiciary was created, rounding out the national system.[29]

With the government agreed upon, the process of nation building could proceed. Following the Borama Conference was a series of peace agreements negotiated between the clans that culminated finally in a larger peace conference, called the Sanaag Grand Peace and Reconciliation Conference. By using traditional peace-making methods involving political and religious leaders, the Isaaq and Harti engaged in a series of negotiations to settle the political, economic, and social issues that were causing regional friction.[30] This led into a series of lower-level talks between regional and even local authorities, delineating what territories would be involved and what practices would take place through and between the clan groups and diya-paying groups.[31] While slow in pace, these processes were inclusive of almost all the stakeholders and thus had an extremely broad buy-in amongst the regional authorities.[32] By October 1993, these agreements had led directly to the acceptance of the Sanaag Regional Peace Charter. The charter finally laid out a general peace promulgated through the clan structures, including provisions for freedom of movement and trade for individuals and the restoration of reciprocal grazing rights for clan lands. In combination with the acceptance of a National Charter, Somaliland had apparently overcome the initial difficulties of statehood. It had formed a representative government that was accepted as legitimate, and it had come to agreements on private property, rights of trade and movement, and sanctions against those who would break the peace.

These structures worked well for a time and bought the government of Somaliland critical breathing space as it tried to organize itself following two years of simple survival. Trust in the government and Egal as president was raised as a civil service was established, wages for government employees were set, local militias were demobilized, and the various ministries worked with internal and external authorities to aid in the continuing stabilization of the state. All of this was underpinned by two critical efforts: the removal of independent military actors and the placement of Berbera under the control of an autonomous authority answerable only to the national government. The former, which encompassed the demobilization of clan militias and local crackdowns on banditry and extortion, meant that commerce and free movement were again possible, allowing for the general administration of Somaliland's territories. These efforts were later supplemented by Egal's attempts to co-opt some of the clan militias into a formal national armed forces, something that had been avoided in the earlier years of Somaliland. Meanwhile, the creation of a Berbera Port Authority and its placement out of clan control provided a stable and direct source of revenue for the state free of local interference. The funds gained from this initiative buttressed the increasing capacity of the civil government and funded new projects such as the aforementioned national army.

Unfortunately, for all the steps being taken toward stability by Egal's government, traditional networks of power, authority, and inclusion were still critical to the formation of these state structures. While the establishment of Berbera as a public asset was a step forward, it was possible only because the clan who controlled the port was the Iise Muse, to which Egal belonged. While the representative cabinet and government often smoothed over these issues of power sharing, when exacerbated by political or economic competition this agreement was not always enough to avoid friction. Only eighteen months after Egal's government took power, a new conflict erupted. This time the epicentre was the Hargeisa airport, the primary entrance point for air traffic and trade into the country. Whereas the government had again assumed the airport as a public asset and thus under their control, the Idagelle clan asserted that per the National Charter, it was under their purview. Fractious relationships between the central government and the local militias that were providing security (and often disrupting those passing through) ended with the government seizing the airport in 1994, sparking a general conflagration between the Idagelle and the government within Hargeisa.[33] A subsequent attack at the Idagelle village of Toon brought the Idagelle further into the conflict and caused the Garhajis to take their side in the conflict. While Hargeisa was now secured, a significant rift had opened up between the government and several of the clans within the country.

Following this initial struggle, Egal's government tried to assert itself in the east of Somaliland, particularly around Burco, a location of almost constant concern since the collapse of the Siad Barre government. While the National Charter had allowed for localized control of security, now Egal's forces tried to secure several critical checkpoints along the main routes to Hargeisa and the centre of the country. This reignited the conflicts that had already been simmering within the region between the Habar Yunis and Habar Ja'lo in the region. Over the next year these fresh conflicts solved few of the questions involved in their genesis but cost the nascent country $4.5 million simply in military outlays while crippling the incoming and outgoing trade that the previous year had so methodically set into place. Given the ever-present worry about fragmentation or even the opposition choosing to join a federalist solution for Somalia, these conflicts again had drawn Somaliland into a crisis only two years after what had been hoped was a lasting solution. With internal forces so far unable to either force a military solution or engage in a peace dialogue, a solution seemed unlikely.

While an internal solution was not to be found, the diasporic Somali population took the opportunity to expand their own role in the establishment of peace in Somaliland. The Isaaq clan family had a significant network of overseas members, and as can be seen with the history of the SNM, these members often had played a critical role in the development of Somaliland proper. Their remittances had helped sustain the Somaliland economy, and now members took direct steps to halt the fighting in the country. Labelling themselves the Peace Committee for Somaliland, this group initiated discussions with the warring factions beginning in April 1995.[34] Critically, they framed the conflict not as "government versus opposition" but instead as mediation between two power blocs of clans each with its own legitimate grievances. Through the internal pressure for peace and the external initiatives of the PCS, some restructuring was carried out to increase the chances for peace: Egal reshuffled his cabinet to be more representative of the dissident factions while the Garhajis dismissed the more belligerent members of their military leadership. Perhaps most critically, despite some individuals in favour of splintering, the PCS initiatives managed to get all the stakeholders involved to agree on the common ground of a separate and sovereign Somaliland. This set the stage for the resolution of the internal conflicts without the threat of a fracturing of the state that all the clans had a stake in.

The initial efforts were a series of local peace initiatives driven across two axes, dealing with the combatants in the west around Hargeisa and in the east around Burco. From June to September 1996, clan-level peace discussions were held, bringing local ceasefires to the fore and setting the stage for larger reconciliations.[35] Additional external factors, such as support from Ethiopia for reconciliation efforts and the death of Mohamed Farah Aideed[36] in Mogadishu, helped spur the reconciliation within the framework of an independent Somaliland. With the local conflicts for the most part tamped down, the stage was set for a larger gathering to address the still significant troubles facing the state as a whole.

The war was finally formally ended at the Hargeisa Conference, which lasted from October 1996 to February 1997.[37] The formal reason for the Hargeisa Conference was the Egal regime's inability to draft and approve a constitution for the state of Somaliland, a task that had been given to it upon his election in 1993. Even with an extension of his term of service, there was little to no chance of completing this objective, and without a constitution no elections could be held. As such, the Council of Elders declared it within their purview to call a general conference to resolve this issue and to produce a constitution. It was hoped that this would result in not only a permanent buy-in from the clan members but also a final peace among those members of the state.

The creation of the constitution was by no means a simple process. Even gathering representatives proved difficult; some prominent members of clans still preferred federalism, some felt that all conflict needed to be resolved before the constitutional gathering should take place, and some felt that Hargeisa was not an appropriate meeting place for all the clans. Despite the protests the Council of Elders insisted on the meeting, which evolved into a transformative event in the history of Somaliland. Over the next five months the issues of federal power, clan representation, minority rights, the reconstruction of the east, and even the still ongoing conflicts were dealt with by the 300 voting delegates. Those clans that felt marginalized in the government were given more seats in both houses of the parliament. Those minority populations that existed within the borders were granted representation. The opposition of the east, which was centred around Burco, was granted funds specifically to rebuild the severely damaged city that would be underwritten by a national supplemental tax.[38] The end result was a general acceptance of a constitution at the end of 131 days that was slated to go into effect in February 1997. The framework would be tested for three years, after which it would be voted on through a popular referendum. In a surprise, Egal was elected for another term, this one to last five years and help continue the trajectory of his government. While this was not universally popular, his rivals accepted his election without violent protest.

With the final reconciliation between the clans taken care of and a constitution in place, Somaliland entered into a period of relative stability and prosperity. Given the continued inability of the south to coalesce around any political leadership, even with significant international support, the comparison between the two was stark. Even in light of the failing state in the south, there continued to be significant pressure on Somaliland from the Transitional National Government (TNG),[39] and even the nascent government of Puntland,[40] to rejoin a Federal Somalia. Despite two separate livestock embargoes preventing trade with the Middle East, the increased economic activity within Somaliland allowed the central government to pay off a loan that had been advanced to it by the business community in 1993, which in turn freed up more revenue for the continued development of social programs within the state.[41] By 2000, a draft of the constitution was placed before the populace for discussion and debate, with a plebiscite scheduled for the next year. On 31 May 2001, the constitution was voted on, with 97.9 percent of the 1.18 million Somaliland citizens voting in favour of the draft document.[42] This adoption did little to aid their relations with their fellow Somalis, with a large number of the eastern regions of Somaliland not voting and slowly aligning themselves with Puntland and with the Transitional National Government denouncing the constitution and refusing to recognize the Somaliland regime. However, while the other Somali populations refused to acknowledge Somaliland's success, Ethiopia remained a firm ally, with the Haud grasslands remaining accessible for the Somalilanders' use and with a significant amount of trade flowing through Berbera.

The peace and stability engendered through these firm regional relationships even allowed for the first steps toward a pluralistic democracy. With elections planned for the next year, political parties began to form. The first, *Ururka Dimuqraadiga Ummadda Bahawday* (UDUB), or the United Peoples' Democratic Party, was formed out of Egal's political group and allies. However, with the beginning of the formation of parties, the question began to be raised again about the role of the modern political system versus that of the traditional authorities within the government. Firm debates were underway about whether parliamentary seats should be apportioned by clans or a strict meritocracy enforced within them. Even as the parties began to coalesce and attempt to leverage their newfound strength, Egal passed away in a Pretoria hospital following complications from a surgery. There were immediate questions about the acceptance of the succession, but despite some tension, on 3 May 2001, his vice president, Dahir Riyale Kahin, was sworn in as president. Perhaps nothing was more indicative of the progress that Somaliland had made than the peaceful transition of power, assuring the continuance and legitimacy of the government that the citizens had made.

Since this smooth transition, Somaliland has continued along essentially the same path of stability and power sharing. The exportation of livestock continues to power the economy of the state, and there have been few civil disturbances since the 2001 constitution. The education sector has been expanding and new social roles are being explored within the state as it continues to develop. A series of elections took place from 2002 to 2005, with the district councils elected in 2002, the president and vice president in 2003, and the Parliament in 2005. While initially the district councils and the executive elections were slated to happen simultaneously, the logistics of the process proved too much, forcing them to be staggered. This was a blessing in disguise, as it allowed for both the election authorities and political parties to learn from their first election and improve upon their results. The district council elections were completed with little fanfare, but the results bore out that UDUB and its rivals *Kulmiye Nabad, Midnimo iyo horumar iyo* (Kulmiye, or the Peace, Unity, and Development Party) and the *Ururka Caddaalada iyo Daryeelka* (UCID, or the Justice and Welfare Party) had the representation to form as political parties and run candidates for the presidential and parliamentary elections to come. The presidential election in 2002 was fiercely contested. While Riyale Kahin was re-elected, it was by the slenderest of margins over his rival Ahmed Mohamed Mohamoud "Silanyo," the chairman of Kulmiye. While Silanyo and his party contested the results in court, they accepted their judicial loss and moved on to preparing for the parliamentary elections. Finally, in 2005 the Somaliland parliamentary elections took place, with UDUB gaining the largest number of seats but failing to gain a majority, while UCID and Kulmiye each gained enough to attain significant political leverage in the house. With the conclusion of these elections, Somaliland had moved itself into a new era of stable and representative government, one it inhabits to this day.

Why Has Somaliland Succeeded?

As noted early on, Somaliland has succeeded at separatism but remains in an anomalous position that is not quite secession. However, it cannot be said that Somaliland has not made the most of this situation. In the over twenty years of independent governance that Somaliland has experienced, it has established governing norms, a tax base, an education system, public services, and security within its borders, something that the remainder of the former Somalia has largely failed to do. Given the extreme difficulties so far demonstrated in secession and separatism as well as the regional circumstances involved, it is important to consider what factors underpin this success. Simply put, it must be explained how Somaliland has managed to be a success when the few other examples discussed in this volume prevailed only after decades-long conflicts.

As with many of the previous examples, the pre-independence history of Somaliland offers some significant clues as to why it has managed to succeed. In addition, the historical perspective also offers a fig leaf of justification for the separatism—much as it does for the majority of previously decided secessions. In the case of Somaliland, its separatism and success remain rooted in the intertwined histories of the Somalis, the Ethiopian Empire, and the European colonial powers. At the time of the nineteenth-century Scramble for Africa, the Somali people were spread across the majority of the Horn of Africa, which juts out eastward and results in a narrow strait connecting the Red Sea with the Indian Ocean. While the

Somali people had interacted with the Red Sea trade since antiquity, the completion of the Suez Canal in 1869 made the Horn of Africa a crucial region for the European empires, for both ready access to the Indian Ocean and stations to fuel the steamships that drove the global trade. Over the coming decades, the Somalis would be partitioned into four separate empires, none of which was under their control.

The dawn of the twentieth century saw the Horn divided among four powers: Britain, France, Italy, and Ethiopia. Britain and France remained heated rivals, with their competition fuelling their claims on Somali territory. The French claimed French Somaliland, a small enclave nestled between British territory and Italian Eritrea, with a functional port at Djibouti. The British meanwhile had claimed expansive territories east of there, encompassing most of the northern coast of the Horn itself. This gave them a significant amount of territory and, most importantly, a base from which to supply the port of Aden in Yemen, which was their primary coaling station on the Red Sea.[43] The Italians had lost their ambitions of conquering Ethiopia but still maintained a large swath of Somali territory stretching from the edges of British Somaliland and southward along the coast until it intersected with British East Africa. This territory, originally disparate colonies, was unified into Italian Somaliland in 1908. Finally, Menelik's Ethiopia had taken advantage of the multiple competing empires to secure its own expansion, often gaining agreements by playing rivals against one another. By the time the Scramble for Africa had ended, Menelik's state had not only beaten back the Italians at Adowa, they had seized the fertile Ogaden region, traditionally one of the major grazing areas for Somali pastoralists.

However, as quickly as this equilibrium was established it was upset. In 1935, fascist Italy invaded Ethiopia backed with thousands of Eritrean and Somali soldiers, toppling the government of Emperor Haile Selassie. Following the conquest, the Italian regime annexed all of Ethiopia to their holdings in Eritrea and Somalia, with Mussolini declaring a new Italian East African Empire. The rapid conquest of the region and the fascists' hostility toward British interests caused concern amongst the British colonies of Somaliland, the Sudan, and Kenya. These concerns proved to be well founded, as the start of the Second World War saw Italian forces attack and occupy British Somaliland in August 1940 following several air strikes and limited offensives on the other British African possessions. However, this occupation of British Somaliland was the high point of the Italian East African Empire, as British counterattacks from Kenya and the Sudan rapidly drove the Italians back. Following the Battle of Keren in 1941, most of the Italian resistance was quashed, and by November of that same year the last of the Italian strongholds surrendered, leaving the region in the control of Britain and its Ethiopian allies.[44]

The aftermath of the war defined the next decades for the Somali people. While Haile Selassie was returned to his throne in Ethiopia, Britain now had to deal with the former Italian colonies of Eritrea and Italian Somaliland. In addition, originally there was some question as to the Ogaden region, which seemed a natural extension of a unified Somali community. However, by 1948 the Ogaden and its rich Haud grazing regions had been returned to Ethiopia in accordance with an 1897 treaty signed between Ethiopia and Britain.[45] The next year the United Nations returned Italian Somaliland to Italian administration as a UN trust territory with an eye toward its eventual independence. Despite the disturbances caused by the war, its ending, at least on the surface, seemed to point to a return to the status quo antebellum.

However, the sweeping changes of the postwar world meant that the status quo was no longer tenable even at the time of the decisions made regarding the colonies of the Horn. Decolonization was a reality that was rapidly coming to the African continent; even if Britain wanted to hold onto its colonies, the transition of Italian Somaliland to a trust territory guaranteed its eventual independence.[46] The global realities of anti-colonial sentiment ran into the local political efforts to gain independence. The Somali Youth League (SYL) had formed in the 1940s and had played a pivotal role in securing the trust status of Italian Somaliland at the United Nations.[47] While the SYL didn't have as strong a presence in British Somaliland, the Somali National League, another nationalist movement, had established itself and was placing firm pressure on the British for independence as well. By the 1960s independence was inevitable; all that remained was the question of how the fractured Somali homeland would be disposed of following independence.

There was significant discussion about finally reuniting the Somalilands. However, this immediately began to go awry. A 1958 plebiscite held in French Somaliland affirmed its populace's desire to remain affiliated with France, although the votes are widely held to have been rigged. Britain, now regretting its gifting of the Ogaden to Ethiopia, attempted to arrange its purchase in 1956 as a way to reintegrate it with the Somali community. However, Haile Selassie had no desire to release this fertile and valuable territory and so refused to sell it.[48] This left only British Somaliland, Italian Somaliland, and the Northern Frontier region of Kenya of the Somali-majority territories able to be joined together for the creation of Somalia. Britain made it clear that Kenya would remain unified, removing one more region that could have joined. However, on 26 June 1960, Britain released Somaliland and the territory was transformed into the state of Somaliland, albeit with a resolution passed stating their intentions to join with the trust territory of Somalia.[49] When that region gained its independence five days later, the two were joined into the Somali Republic.

While the north would quickly find itself marginalized within the united state, laying the seeds for its eventual reform and separatist goals, at the time the new republic was proud of its unification.[50] Somalia fashioned itself as Africa's first nation-state, and Pan-Somalism helped drive the country forward, first under the Egal regime and then under Siad Barre. However, as with many of the other secessionist fronts discussed, the north would point to the separate administration of the territories and even their separate steps into independence as setting a precedent for their later declaration of secession. While it is true that the Somaliland Legislative Council had voted to unify with the former Italian Somaliland, this could be viewed as a voluntary agreement and one that would be terminated in 1991.[51] There was thus an argument to be made that Somaliland could and should be recognized based on its earlier recognized sovereignty.

However, this argument has carried little water with the international community. Despite its de facto existence for over twenty years, Somaliland remains officially unrecognized as a separate state. This lack of de jure sovereignty is a significant weakness on a larger scale, leaving Somaliland unable to take advantage of the official global support that might allow it to grow more rapidly.[52] This is not to say that Somaliland has no international presence, though. In fact, its pragmatic relations with its neighbouring states have actually been one of the central pillars of Somaliland's success, as it trades on its traditional economic activities and regional dynamics to gain significant external support even as it is denied official recognition.

In terms of its traditional economic activities, as far back as the pre-colonial era the pastoralists of the Horn exported livestock to the Arabian Peninsula for their primary source of income. This has continued through the centuries to the present day, and Somaliland remains a huge net exporter of livestock to the Gulf States. While there have been occasional embargoes in the region due to health concerns or livestock diseases, this trade is the economic lifeline of the Somaliland merchant class.[53] It also forms a palpable connection between the customs and trade divisions of the Somali government and the formal and informal governing structures of its trading partners. These continuing economic ties help solidify the de facto existence of Somaliland within its regional context.

Beyond the Gulf States, there has been an even more potent and pragmatic ally for Somaliland since its separation from Somalia. Ethiopia has consistently and quietly supported Somaliland in a variety of ways since the formation of its government. With the fall of Mengistu in 1991 and the rise of the EPRDF government, cordial relations were restored with the Somali National Movement. Beyond the historic ties involved between Ethiopia and the SNM, there were still significant numbers of refugees from the Isaaq groups living within Ethiopia that formed part of a transnational community which bound these two states together. Any tensions this might have caused were mostly dissipated with the renewal of some rights to using the Haud grasslands in the Ogaden to the pastoralists in Somaliland, giving them access to an economically important and culturally significant region.[54]

Of course, Ethiopia has not granted all of these conditions solely due to their good relations with Somaliland. Having a healthy and stable Somaliland serves the government of Ethiopia's interest in a number of ways. The first is the obvious benefit of having at least part of the Somali population at peace with Ethiopia. With the descent of the southern part of the country into chaos and the rise of Islamist armed fronts among the populations that border Ethiopia, the regional power has enough on its hands simply securing the borders of one part of the Ogaden. A friendly Somaliland relieves them of that security burden and limits their need for regional intervention beyond the already daunting Islamist threats in southern and central Somalia.

Even more essential to Ethiopia than regional security dynamics is access to the port at Berbera.[55] At the same time that Somaliland was stabilizing and bringing Berbera under centralized control, Ethiopia was releasing Eritrea from its forced union. While initially the ports of Eritrea were open for Ethiopian shipping, with the souring of Ethiopian-Eritrean relations in the mid-1990s, landlocked Ethiopia found itself without a secure route to the ocean. This problem was solved by the increasingly stable and robust Somaliland and its reintegrated port on the Gulf of Aden. By offering support and aid to Somaliland, Ethiopia assured itself a port from which to ship its goods and receive goods in turn. This pragmatic relationship has not extended to formal recognition,[56] but the support of Ethiopia, which has transformed itself into a general regional hegemon, has significantly aided the Somaliland national project in the years since it was formed.

In the end, though, these factors are relatively minor in terms of Somaliland's success. Two intertwined factors offer the central reasons for the endurance and resilience of the separatist state. The first of these is the strong social unity that sits at the heart of the Somaliland national project. As noted earlier, Somalia was proud of its status as Africa's first nation-state, having been formed as the political union of the Somali people, as imperfect as it was. This meant that naturally Somali cultural and social structures were held as central parts of the interaction within the new state. These social structures are extremely segmented, with the majority of the Somali people having been divided into six overarching "clan families," the Hawiye, the Darod, the Dir, the Rahanweyn, the Digil, and the Isaaq. These in turn are subdivided into numerous clans and sub-clans, with the smallest unit being the diya-paying group, which is usually anywhere between 100 and 1,000 individuals.[57] These relations permeate every interaction within the Somali world, with feuds and debts having been carried on between various segments for generations. The commonality of Somali heritage was not enough to ensure pacific relations; instead every interaction was a process of complex negotiation and competition between the interacting lineages. The complexity of these relations has perhaps been best summarized by Said Samatar, who repurposed an old Bedouin Arab saying to attempt to describe the layers involved within the Somali community:

> Segmentation may be expressed in the Bedouin saying 'my full brother against my half-brother, my brother and I against my father, my father's household against my uncle's household, our two households (my uncle's and mine) against the rest of the immediate kin, the immediate kin against non-immediate members of the clan, my clan against the other clans, and finally, my nation against the world!' In lineage segmentation one literally does not have a permanent enemy or a permanent friend, only a permanent context.[58]

Given the multi-dimensional nature of the relations between the clans and even sub-clans within the state, it was only natural that Somalia was often the location of political and economic competition between the clan families. Before the unification of the state, this competition would often lead to bloodshed. Siad Barre managed to repress this internal social fragmentation by means of his emphasis on internal scientific socialism[59] and external Pan-Somalism.[60] With the failure of both of these projects, the unifying force behind Somalia was removed, leading to a resurgence of clan-based dissent. Siad Barre did his best to suppress this dissent, but ultimately failed to stop the creation of new clan-based political organizations. These organizations included the United Somali Congress, the Somali Salvation Democratic Front, and the Somali National Movement, who were drawn primarily from the Hawiye, Darod, and Isaaq clan families respectively. The eventual collapse of Siad Barre's government led to the competition amongst the various fronts for control of Mogadishu and other valuable territories. The fronts reignited the clan struggles within the country, which continue to complicate its unity and recovery.

As noted, the Somali National Movement was primarily from the Isaaq clan family. While the other clan groups struggled for control of the southern portion of Somalia, the SNM's claimed territory was a region where the Isaaq were almost unchallenged in their regional authority. While the north had been marginalized in the 1960s and 1970s and then severely suppressed by Siad Barre's forces in the 1980s, it was essentially unified at the time of its secession. Even those minority populations living within Somaliland, that is, those members of the Darod and Dir clans who live within its borders, have long-standing relations with their neighbours. Thus, when the central government collapsed, the Isaaq were able to rally around their central identity and call upon the traditional authorities to help provide stability. Even the long, patient efforts at grassroots reconciliation were only possible due to the unitary clan-family structure of Somaliland. However, this has served as a double-edged sword, as the Isaaq clan family became firmly ensconced in power. Those Dir and Darod populations have often continued to serve as dissenting forces, with the Darod populations in the Sool administrative region near the Puntland border going so far as to at times seek greater alignment with their clan relations in Puntland.[61] However, Somaliland has generally dealt with this effectively in its most recent constitutional convention, with those minority populations being granted specific protections and representation within the government.

Even beyond the de facto recognition, the pragmatic relations, the historic precedent, or even the dominance of a single clan family, it must be said that the single most important factor in Somaliland's enduring statehood is the collapse of its previous host state. While Katanga and Biafra were brought to heel and reabsorbed by their host state, and Eritrea and South Sudan fought long and bruising wars against Ethiopia and Sudan respectively, Somaliland was born out of the failure of Somalia. Post-1991, Somalia effectively ceased to exist, with the north becoming Somaliland, the northeast splitting off to eventually become Puntland, and only a rump of a state remaining in the south. Since then, the south has experienced massive upheaval, with continued fierce fighting and little to show for it aside from increasingly radicalized Islamist elements and a de jure federal government that has yet to exercise a great deal of power on its own.

While Somaliland has had its shares of troubles since 1991, the remainder of Somalia has fared far worse. State structures essentially stopped working in the northeast, leading the local clan leadership to eventually form their own breakaway region of Puntland following a constitutional convention in 1998. Puntland remains committed to a federal solution to the issue of Somali governance, but remains separate to this day.[62] The remainder of the country, with its centre of gravity around Mogadishu, turned into a war zone as the factions of the USC and other armed groups fought over control of the city and its surroundings. As mentioned earlier in this chapter, the United Nations and other international actors attempted to provide aid to the ailing population in 1991, but this simply fuelled the conflict further as their food aid was used by the various armed groups to gain leverage in their struggle. A subsequent UN resolution deployed peacekeepers to the region in 1992, but even with the increased US intervention the conflict continued to spiral out of control. By 1995 the United Nations had completely removed their military presence in the country.

A new hope for stabilization was floated in 2000 with the formation of the Transitional National Government (TNG) and its transformation into the Transitional Federal Government (TFG) in 2004. However, this was a government in name only, as by 2006 the Union of Islamic Courts (ICU), a militant Islamist group, had seized control of most of the territory in the south. It was only subsequent military support by Ethiopia, the African Union, and later Kenya that allowed the TFG to regain much of its territory. By 2010 the TFG was largely back in control of the southern region and Mogadishu through both pragmatic relations with various warring factions and the military might offered by its regional and OAU allies. In 2012, its mandate ran out and the official Federal Government of Somalia was formed; however, despite its relatively successful formation, the government still largely relies on the support of AMISOM (the African Union Mission in Somalia) and can't effectively project force into the Puntland or Somaliland regions. Beyond this, the more extreme remnants of the Islamic Courts Union have since reformed into an Islamist group called Al-Shabaab, who have proven even more resilient and militarily adept than the ICU. Even with its resurgent strength, the Somalia government simply does not have the time, funds, or structures to effectively coerce Somaliland back into the fold. Somaliland thus endures in large part because of the fact that its host state is still ill-defined and weak, an anomalous situation within the larger arc of secessionist conflicts in Africa.

As a final note, it must be mentioned that despite the weakness of the federal government in Mogadishu, it retains the status of the formally recognized government of a unified Somalia in the international community. While it currently has placed a consulate in Hargeisa to negotiate with Somaliland, this may be viewed as a simply pragmatic move on their part. It is impossible for them to deny that Somaliland is in existence at the moment and has a regime that is not part of a larger federal Somalia. However, given its continued insistence on a federal solution, Somaliland's sustained commitment to its own sovereignty, and the complex international legal dynamics around the two territories, the future might hold additional conflict. So far no home state has countenanced the involuntary secession of any of its territory, and the international response has invariably defaulted to the pre-existing recognized state. If the federal government continues to gain strength and Somaliland cannot negotiate a solution, a struggle to maintain Somaliland's de facto secession might ensue in the future.

Map of Mali and Azawad

Copyright © 2014 Nathan E. McCormack and Charles G. Thomas

6

Transnational Communities and Secession: The Azawad Secessionists, 1990–1996 and Beyond

From 1990 to 1996, wars raged across the African countries of Mali and Niger. The Tuareg, a minority people whose traditional regions of authority spread across Mali, Niger, Libya, Burkina Faso, and Algeria, had risen up and begun a guerrilla struggle against Mali and Niger in an attempt to claim what was seen as the heart of their traditional homeland. Although somewhat fragmented in their organization and lacking significant political support even from external sympathetic groups, the Tuareg managed to sustain their struggle through judicious use of their surroundings, the weakness of their opposition, and a rough unity of their goals. While previous revolts of the Tuareg populations had been intended to force their host states to recognize their membership as citizens and access the economic facets of the state, this new rebellion brought forth a new objective. No longer simply willing to be recognized within Mali, the fragmented fronts of the rebellion now demanded their own state: Azawad. The Tuareg rebels in Mali insisted that there was no longer a reason to believe that they would be recognized as an equal community within Mali and so now sought their own nation-state in June 1990. Three months later, their brethren in Niger began their own rebellion, demanding autonomy within the state and recognition of their own unique heritage and culture. Both rebellions would continue for years, with the Tuareg insisting on their goals of recognized national and even state status. However, by 1996 all sides of the conflict were generally exhausted and peace initiatives were begun. While these would lead to an alteration in goals and relationships between the Tuaregs and their host states, the fires of secession or autonomy would not burn out so easily and embers of the conflict would smoulder throughout the following decade. Despite the failure of outright secession, the struggles of the Tuareg throughout the 1990s serve as a perfect illustration of the ethnic nationalism that pervaded the post–Cold War efforts as well as the efficacy of separatism as opposed to secession with regard to the post–Cold War state.

The Tuareg and their History

The Tuareg are a trans-Saharan people whose traditional territories stretch from regions in the south of modern Algeria and Libya to the northern areas of Burkina Faso. They are related to the Berbers of northern Africa and still maintain significant ties to those populations. Throughout their early history they had been primarily pastoralists, breeding and rearing camels, goats, sheep, and other livestock.[1] However, due to the region of their inhabitance, they also served as cross-cultural brokers and mediators across the Sahara Desert. This is perhaps best reflected in the etymology of the name Tuareg, whose disputed origin is either from the Arabic meaning "paths taken" or from Targa, the Berber name for the Fezzan region of Libya, which would denote the interior of the country. Neither of these names reflects what the Tuareg call themselves. Instead, within the Tuareg community the term used most often is *Imushagh*, although it has become far more common in recent years to use the term Kel Tamasheq,[2] "the people speaking Tamasheq," which scholars believe is also more accurate and inclusive of the people represented within the community.[3]

It is generally assumed that the Kel Tamasheq migrated to their current territory sometime around the fourth or fifth century CE. While they initially followed traditional religions, the expansion of Islam led to the conversion of the population.[4] However, like many African communities that were at a significant distance from the centre of the caliphates, the Kel Tamasheq saw a degree of syncretism at play in their Islam. Significant local beliefs were incorporated, leading to a very idiosyncratic practice of the religion. Perhaps the most noted feature is the alteration of clothing norms. Whereas much of orthodox Islam believes in the veiling of women for modesty's sake, the opposite is accepted within the Tuareg community.[5] As such, the men are veiled while the women are not. This, in combination with the indigo dye used for the clothing of the Tuareg, has led other various titles for the Tuareg, such as the "People of the Veil" and the "Blue People," the latter due to the staining of the skin that the dye sometimes caused.

Tuareg culture is itself quite complex, although much of its complexity may be understood in terms of a bipartite foundation that determines much of the socio-political organization of the Kel Tamasheq.[6] The first of these foundations is *tewsit*, or clan. These are roughly kinship groups that trace their lineage through generations and form the larger associations amongst the Kel Tamasheq. During the colonial period, these were referred to as "tribes" or "factions" by the French government, but this created a false equivalency, as although the *tewsiten* (the plural of *tewsit*) may share some of the characteristics of the archetypal tribe or faction of society, there are significant differences. The largest of these is that the concepts of *tewsiten* are not as immutable or all-encompassing as tribal associations. Instead, the relation of the Tuareg to their *tewsit* is also altered and defined by their place in the second foundation—that of hierarchy.

The hierarchy of the Tuareg was also mistakenly referred to as "feudal" throughout the colonial period, which also served to obscure how the society worked. Instead of a feudal system, the hierarchy of the Tuareg and their attached groups is akin to a caste system, a system of social strata into which one is born. This is where the initial naming of the *Imushagh* comes from; it signifies not the whole of the people but instead the noble warriors who stand roughly at the top of the hierarchy.[7] They operate within a culture of honour and shame, the *temushagha*, which binds together their caste and serves to create the social norms by which they operate. The second major hierarchical group is the *Ineslemen*, who operate by much the same norms but are responsible for religious affairs. Islamic norms are their primary guide to behaviour and structure, but as a still "noble" or "free" caste, they too operate within the strictures of traditional honour and shame.[8] Next down the hierarchy are *Imghad*, who are free but take on no claim of nobility, while trying to still maintain the *temushagha* that guides the noble castes. Due to their lack of nobility but acceptance of the social and cultural norms of the nobility, the French inadequately named them "vassals," but this simply confuses the issue. Following the *Imghad* were the *Inadan*, who were the craftsmen or "blacksmiths."[9] They were not noble, nor did they follow the *temushagha*, but they enjoyed certain benefits thanks to the roles they played in the hierarchy. These roles were not limited to the creation of goods, but also included the roles analogous to West African *griots*. Finally, at the bottom of the caste system were the *iklan*, the slaves. While this five-tiered caste system is increasingly seen as inadequate to fully describe the complexities of Kel Tamasheq society, for the purposes of this study it will suffice.

Of course, as noted, within these systems lie the categories of slaves, who are at the bottom of the hierarchy and often lack a formal lineage group. This makes the slaves themselves marginal figures within Tuareg society. Those placed into a slavery role were sub-Saharan Africans captured in the Soudan and impressed into the labour categories of the Tuaregs. They might climb to *Inadan* status, but far more either served as household slaves, the above-mentioned *iklan*, or as simple labour, the *bella*.[10] The *bella* would perform labour and pay a tribute to their master and even often travel alongside them throughout their journeys. In conflict, a *bella* would even take up arms on behalf of his master. These slaves and the Tuareg role in the slave trade were to have a significant effect on their history.

While there was in theory no intrinsic racism involved with the Tuareg system of slavery,[11] the Tuareg themselves remained significantly involved with the trans-Saharan slave trade throughout the Middle Ages and preyed extensively on the sub-Saharan African populations around them. By the early nineteenth century the main trans-Saharan trade routes ran directly through traditionally Tuareg lands and the trans-Saharan slave trade had brought wealth and status to them.[12] The Tuareg themselves often led strong raids into the surrounding African populations to capture large numbers of slaves who would be then sent along the routes north to be sold for a profit. This gave the Tuaregs a significant role in the most profitable source of wealth in North Africa in the mid-nineteenth century, expanding their power and influence. However, this would have two major effects by the end of the century. The first was that those populations that had been preyed upon would become home to a great deal of antipathy toward the Tuareg, who would be seen as a predatory threat to the more settled populations and often were targets of aggression. The second was that the imposition of colonial control by the French and their consequent destruction of the slave trade and slavery was a deeply disruptive event.[13]

Of course, the disruption was more to the economy of the Tuareg, especially with the removal of the larger routes of the slave trade. They still existed as intermediaries across the Sahara and could make a living from both trading and livestock, but had lost a larger ability to trade slaves on a large scale. Beyond this, while French rule technically emancipated the *iklan* and the *bella*, the legal transformation did nothing to alter the social and cultural structures that still held them within the caste system.[14] Thus, while the French did their best to engage the Tuareg social structures, their misunderstanding of the dynamics at play meant that at best they engaged the elite as local power brokers and left the majority of Tuareg social structures essentially untouched. In fact, throughout much of the colonial period, there was significant sympathy and empathy for the Tuareg within the ranks of the French colonial governments.[15] Their elites, the *Imushagh*, were accepted as essentially feudal lords and left relatively powerful under French auspices, leading to an alignment of the Tuareg elites with the French colonial government.

While Tuareg society was not transformed by French colonialism, many of the surrounding African societies were. Assimilation led to significant alterations in the levels of education, urbanization, social stratification, and even economic activities, which in turn led to the familiar pattern of the rise of a group of educated nationalists. These were sometimes educated members of the traditional elites, but many were "New Men" who had been educated in the French system and were now grasping at newer ideas of nationalism and liberation. These men, such as Modibo Keita in Mali, wished to gain self-determination for their own states. In 1946, Keita joined Félix Houphouët-Boigny in Bamako and other representatives of the French colonies in Africa to create the *Rassemblement Démocratique Africain* (African Democratic Rally, or RDA), a unified political party representing the majority of the peoples of French Africa.[16] Beyond this, Keita's political activities stretched all the way to the European mainland, where he served in the cabinet of French Prime Ministers Maurice Bourgès-Maunoury and Félix Gaillard. When the Mali Federation was declared independent in June 1960 after negotiations with France, it was Keita who was inaugurated as the premier of the Mali Federation and then, following its acrimonious dissolution two months later on 19 August, the first president of the Republic of Mali.

Keita and his RDA government quickly established Mali as a one-party state with a strong socialist program. While there was some interest in these programs on the part of the Kel-Tamasheq, most of their community had been more sympathetic to the conception of the *Organisation commune des regions sahariennes* (OCRS), a French project that would have seen a communal organization of the Saharan territories, which held much more promise for them.[17] With this construction of the Republic of Mali, there came an immediate attempt to build a common polity through history. The name of the state, chosen consciously to echo that of the great empire of Mali from the Middle Ages, was intended to conjure a shared glorious past that could unify a national identity through the history of the Bambara and Mande populations that would be appropriated for the populace as a whole.[18] Large investments in public art, literature, and performances were made to link together the heritage of old Mali to the present state. However, while this was not entirely appreciated by many members of other sub-Saharan groups, it completely excluded the Kel Tamasheq.

Beyond the construction of a national identity, there was also the necessity of building state capacity. Mali remained almost entirely agrarian in nature, and the new socialist regime wished to construct a modern state out of what had been a very loosely run colony. This meant stimulating agricultural production and building industry and a service sector to follow the development doctrine of the day, which in turn required a great deal of infrastructure that was not in evidence at the time of independence. Following the standard Afro-socialist path, this would begin by doing away with the "pre-modern" modes of production. The villages, so long a central social organization of Malian life, would be dismantled and reconstructed as cooperative farms wherein the methods of improved agriculture would be distributed to bring modern techniques to the people. This would also allow a cultural change, as the Africans could remove themselves from the exploitation of colonialism and instead focus on developing their own country as a communal effort.

Unfortunately for the ruling regime, most of these plans, such as building roads with voluntary labour or expecting smallhold farmers to work communally without regard to profit, proved to be wildly optimistic. To try and keep these efforts going, the government turned to coercion, conscripting young men to use their labour to build the necessary infrastructure under the auspices of the Service Civique. This led to massive passive resistance on the part of the citizens, with many avoiding taxes, avoiding party dues, and avoiding the demanded labour simply by leaving. There had always been a degree of impermanence in some regions of the country, and the attempted reforms of the US-RDA saw a mass migration of young labour to the borders of Mali and beyond in an attempt to avoid the harsh attempts at development that Keita's regime was undertaking.

For the Kel Tamasheq, this transfer of power to an independent Mali and its early years of independence were a disaster. From the beginning there was serious tension between Kel Tamasheq leadership and the leadership of the new government.[19] The issues of race, of political authority, and even of their traditional nomadic lifestyle jumped to the fore following independence. There were already significant tensions on both sides when independence was declared in 1960. For the Mande, Bamabara, and other sub-Saharan populations of Mali, the Tuaregs were horrific slavers and slave owners who had enjoyed a privileged position under French colonial rule. Suspicions ran deep, and many of the stereotypes of Tuareg culture coloured the popular perception of them. On the Tuareg side, there was the question of association with Mali at all. While Tuareg of all of the free castes and many *bella* had been involved in the discourses of self-determination in the 1950s, it had not been taken as a given that they would be citizens of Mali. Their initial inclusion in French West Africa had been the result of a voluntary treaty signed following a military defeat and their acceptance of French rule, light as it turned out to be. The independence of Mali offered them no such parallel; instead they were simply placed within the confines of the new state and expected to be productive citizens.

The first three years of living under the Malian government did not defuse the already unstable situation. The development schemes of the US-RDA were a significant irritant to the general populace, but they would prove unbearable to the Kel Tamasheq. Whereas initially the locally accepted chiefs were kept in place by the Malian government, the traditional aspects of "tribal" leadership were antithetical to the government's modernization schemes. While it was accepted as a necessary evil, the government altered the title of the chiefs themselves and even interfered in succession struggles, seeing these as government business. However, for the Kel Tamasheq this was outside interference into personal matters, irritating the situation and upsetting an accepted culture.

Beyond this, there was the simple issue of the culture itself. The US-RDA plan called for the creation of infrastructure through conscripted or voluntary labour to aid in the creation of large-scale yields of agrarian goods. The entirety of their platform was built around the conception of farming communities and the cultures they fostered. On the part of the Tuareg, there was almost no acceptance of the need for any of these things. As nomadic pastoralists, they had little need for infrastructure or permanent settlements, livestock was valued in quantity and not for yields of milk or beef, and labour beyond a few routine duties was not acceptable within their cultural strictures. While there were certainly Tuareg communities that settled for a brief while, ultimately their lifestyle was mobile and specifically oriented to their herds. When the US-RDA commissioners arrived, they perceived the impossibility of nomadic peoples taking part in the program and hit upon a simple solution: make them sedentary. Larger numbers of children were placed in schools to acquire the basis of the new Malian society, causing a clash between the new system and the traditions of the Tuareg. Beyond this, there was the simple question of labour. Whereas the new regime believed it could and should extract the necessary labour for building the state from its citizens, the Tuareg had never even been subject to conscripted labour under French rule. This was unacceptable to the Tuareg, with the Service Civique being analogous to slavery, a system that they were all too familiar with and not willing to undertake under the auspices of a regime they had equated with *iklan*.

While these events had kept tensions at a boil, the final straw was the all-too-common issue of taxes. The Malian state required a significant level of taxation, and the nomadic pastoral Kel Tamasheq were extremely difficult to tax. When told the sale of their cattle would be taxed, they simply crossed borders to Algeria or elsewhere and traded the cattle for goods or foreign currencies. To deal with this, the state instead increased the cattle tax multiple times, expecting an amount paid per head of cattle within a Kel Tamasheq's herd. While this was easier to levy, it remained extremely difficult to collect. When the collector came up empty in 1963, the government sent troops to enforce the taxation. This would lead into the first insurrection against Mali.

The Alfellaga (1963–1964)

Like many of the conflicts that erupted in Africa in the 1990s, the Tuareg revolts had antecedents in the colonial and early postcolonial period. With the heavy hand of the Keita regime seeming far worse than the colonial benevolence of the French, the Kel Tamasheq erupted in revolt on 15 May 1963.[20] Pointing to the issues of serving the Black African regime, the removal of their rights over their *bella*, the taxes placed upon them, and the abuse of the militaries, the Kel Tamasheq demanded separation from the Republic of Mali and a return to the status quo ante-decolonization. However, even with the abuses they had undergone, the fighting strength of the rebels was extremely low; perhaps only 250 men at any given time were fighting against the Malian government forces. Given this small amount of manpower, there was no way they could hope for a military victory, even against the relatively small army of Mali. With only a few thousand soldiers themselves, the Malian forces still had a decisive edge in firepower, transport, and logistics. The only strategy that made sense was that of the other revolts ongoing in the 1960s: keep the war going and hope for international aid or mediation.[21] Given the friendliness the Kel Tamasheq still felt toward both the French and the Algerians (along with the significant cross-border ties they had with the latter), there was the hope that one or both of these states would intervene to help them gain a just conclusion to their struggle.

The early days of the struggle saw significant Tuareg successes. Initially Mali only dedicated local police units and a detachment of the nomadic gendarmerie.[22] While these were fine for patrolling the region and occasionally dealing with criminals, the Malian forces were not professional soldiers and the Tuaregs had the advantage of knowing the terrain and having local support. This allowed them to consistently outmanoeuvre the Malian forces and engage only in strategically advantageous situations. The motorized vehicles for the Malian forces at least initially found themselves foundering in the rocky and broken terrain where the Tuareg consistently engaged them, and this caused the police to increasingly lean on their own camel-mounted forces. The gendarmerie, also known as the *Groupes nomade d'intervention de la gendamerie* (GNIG), were themselves already camel mounted and offered significantly stiffer resistance to the Tuareg combatants but still could not defeat them.[23] In response, the Keita regime committed an increasing amount of its regular army to the struggle. By October, a mere five months after the beginning of the conflict, the army had committed 2,200 soldiers to the conflict, supplemented by 300 vehicles and two airplanes.[24] However, despite the numerical advantage they now enjoyed, which was reaching a ten-to-one ratio, the rugged terrain of the engagements and the increasingly professional hit-and-run tactics of the Kel Tamasheq precluded a decisive victory.

By January 1964 the rebellious Tuareg were confident enough to intensify their raiding. Attacks on columns of Malian soldiers and villages were increasing in frequency. Part of this ferocity was in response to the change in the Malian conduct of the war. While early on the conflict had been characterized by raid and counter-raid between insurgent and gendarme, with the commitment of regular forces new methods of prosecuting the conflict had begun.[25] No longer was the war the sole preserve of the combatants. With the insurgents increasingly retreating into Algeria as the Malians became more aggressive, the soldiers instead turned their anger onto the members of the communities left behind. Categories of people that had been considered outside of the bounds of armed conflict—women, holy men, craftsmen—were now arrested or impressed by the Malians as sympathizers or supporters of the Tuareg rebels. Beyond this, to further isolate the rebels, large numbers of the populace that inhabited the Adagh region were relocated and much of the region was declared a *zone interdite*, or forbidden zone.[26] This meant that any civilian found within the bounds of these forbidden areas was subject to summary execution as a rebel. As this effectively cut off a large amount of the rangeland needed to water and graze the livestock that were the backbone of the economy of the Kel Tamasheq, it offered them a stark choice: obey and be ruined or disobey and risk death.

Despite the increase in raids and the fury that these new tactics instilled in the Tuareg fighters, the tide was turning against them. Diverting part of their manpower, the insurgents did their best to escort many of their people across the forbidden zones to what was seen as safety in Algeria. However, their lines of supply were increasingly strained, the army was poisoning wells and confiscating or killing the herds found in the zones, and their families were isolated from them in what was named *zones de regroupement* by the Army. These last were in essence concentrated villages where the Tuareg populace was both controlled by the Malian forces and often used as impressed labour. Above and beyond these pressures on the combatants, the hoped-for external aid from Algeria and France never materialized. France remained completely aloof from the conflict as it was ongoing, offering no support to the Kel Tamasheq in the struggle. Algeria, while initially offering a safe haven and holding a significant number of refugees, did not step in to aid the insurgency itself. Mali, cognizant of the refuge that Algeria was offering their foes, pursued a diplomatic strategy to further weaken the rebellion. By late September 1963 they had already convinced Ben Bella's government to arrest and deport several leaders of the revolt. A further diplomatic offensive directed at Morocco saw yet more exiled Tuareg leaders seized and returned to Mali.[27]

By early 1964 the rebellion had lost many of its leaders, its safe havens were disappearing, and its community was in shambles. While many in the resistance wanted to continue the struggle, those who had already been captured or surrendered were sent by the Malians to urge surrender. These voices proved decisive throughout May and June as large detachments of rebels turned themselves in. A few holdouts remained in the field or retreated to Algeria to try and reform a resistance, but these did not trouble the Malians to any great degree. The exiles remained so but were offered amnesty if they would lay down their arms. Those still fighting were hunted and in many cases killed over the next few months. By 15 August the rebellion was declared over by the Malian government.[28] A week later the triumph was celebrated on the country's Independence Day and the overall victory seen as a step forward for the forces of progress within the country.

The initial Tuareg revolt carried many of the characteristics of the 1960s wave of attempted secessions. They featured distinct groups that remained isolated from the independent state and who had lost a degree of privilege with the advent of the postcolonial state, triggering violent resistance. They hoped that this violent resistance could gain them, if not a military victory, at least international recognition and support of their claims. However, whereas Katanga or Biafra could point to firm territorial claims and a functional governance system, making them in essence a state attempting to secede, the Kel Tamasheq in Mali could not make these same claims. There was no united territory attempting to split away, but instead a cultural nation within a state attempting to remove itself from that state's authority. The end state of this removal was not well defined: would it create an amorphous state with negotiated boundaries? Would it revive the French conception of the OCRS? Would it in fact demand the reinsertion of French authority? This left even sympathetic powers unable to support their claim, as they were unable to effectively express a unified goal, bring forth centralized leadership, or even claim specific territory for their people. In fact, of the entirety of the Malian Kel Tamasheq community, only one segment had truly entered the struggle, with the Kel Adagh providing the vast majority of combatants and leaders.[29] Even though the majority of the Malian Kel Tamasheq had grievances against the Malian government, only the Kel Adagh had taken up arms in significant numbers. In the end, it was not even a unified Tuareg nation that fought for a state; it was an insurrection by some members of the Tuareg people who struggled in what amounted to an armed protest against the state of Mali. As such, the movement was a significant failure despite the initial weakness of the Malian response, and the Alfellaga, as it came to be known, was hardly recognized as a secession attempt at all. However, the resonance of the conflict and the remembrance of it would play a significant part decades later when the Tuareg again felt the call of nationalism.

THE FORMATION OF FURTHER RESISTANCE

With the cessation of the conflict and the reimposition of Malian state power, the Kel Tamasheq attempted to resume their lives. However, the targeting of livestock and relocation or flight of many Tuareg groups during the earlier conflict had left them already in an economically vulnerable position. Many had already found new homes in Algeria, Libya, or even with other Kel Tamasheq in Niger when the new wave of catastrophe occurred. Beginning in the 1960s, the favourable climate of the Sahara had already begun to reverse itself as part of an unpredictable cycle. By the early 1970s the region was entering a period of severe drought that would reach its peak in the middle of the decade. While the Tuareg and other pastoralists had enjoyed significant prosperity throughout the periods of plenty, the conflict had undermined these limited gains and left them extremely vulnerable to the climatic change. The herds they relied on perished in the drought conditions and the Tuareg themselves were pushed to the edges of their traditional territories. Without the wealth generated by the livestock, the majority of the Kel Tamasheq needed to find alternate methods of survival and alternate locations to pursue them in.

The result was what became known as the Teshumara, taken from the French *chomage*, meaning "unemployment."[30] Members of the Kel Tamasheq community were forced to urbanized regions of Algeria, Libya, Mali, and Niger, where they were left to find wage-labour employment. It cannot be overstated how devastating this was to the Tuareg communities. With their caste system as one of the central organizing principles of the Kel Tamasheq identity, the requirement of taking manual labour was a critical blow to the cultural identities of the *Imushagh* and other high-caste pastoralists. The possibility of returning to the pastoral life was undermined by a second wave of droughts in the 1980s, further reinforcing the sundering of the traditional Tuareg lifestyles. Other methods of acceptable employment were attempted, such as smuggling between the various states joined by the Sahara,[31] an updating of the traditional caravans that had contributed so much to the trans-Saharan culture in the past. However, the creation of modern states and the use of this trafficking to trade in prohibited goods and currencies made this both lucrative and dangerous, and certainly not a practice that could be pursued by even a significant portion of the Kel Tamasheq populace.[32]

The end result of this period was widespread marginalization of the Kel Tamasheq community. Those who could still live in their traditional homelands were few and far between; those who lived in exile often struggled to find permanent employment,[33] and the employment that could be found was often anathema to the traditional Tuareg way of life. As conditions in all the Saharan countries worsened, these communities faced expulsion from their new homes as the surrounding countries could not support the large numbers of refugees. The only welcoming home many would find would be in Libya, where Muammar Gaddafi proclaimed the original homeland of the Kel Tamasheq and offered them a place to find work and support for their community to revive itself.[34] This proclamation in 1982 would change the course of the political life of the Kel Tamasheq and reshape the next three decades of their relations with their former homelands.

The dislocation caused by the waves of droughts had not only forced marginalization upon the Kel Tamasheq, it had thrown their precarious political situation into stark relief for all members of the community. They still had no homeland, the Algerians had not supported their struggle, the Malians and Nigeriens were sub-Saharan Africans who had little use for them, and no outside help was available to aid them in gaining any social or political status. This solitude shaped a new understanding among many of the exiles, whether they were Nigerien or Malian Tuareg. There was now the need to create their own centralized and unified community tied to the communal and traditional space of the Tuareg. There was now the need to create both a national identity beyond the fragmented communities of the Kel Tamasheq and a state to give themselves true political and economic self-determination. While this concept of a nation-state would be struggled over, it emerged as part of the soul searching of Tuareg intellectuals, authority figures, and *evolues* over the course of the 1970s and 1980s as they found their way through the marginalization of the Teshumara.[35] This struggle to shape the conception of a Tuareg nation-state would emerge as a series of narratives that could be collectively known as the *Tenekra*.[36]

The first figures to try and overcome the segmented nature of Kel Tamasheq were the surviving leaders of the Alfellaga still in Algeria. These men, notably Younes ag Ayyouba, Issouf ag Cheick, and Elledi ag Alla, came together in 1974 under the auspices of the Algerian government and discussed what they saw as the way forward for the Kel Tamasheq.[37] Their understanding of the struggle moving forward was as an extension of the previous Alfellaga and the explanation of its import to this new generation of shattered and scattered Tuareg. This could serve as a rallying point and a way to hopefully bring together a collective identity for them. However, the discussion quickly became focused on who could be involved in this project. Was it just the Kel Tamasheq or could the other suffering Saharan pastoralists be a part of it? What of the Bidan or the Fulbe? These were groups that also had been marginalized after being split and were weakened by the disruption of the trans-Saharan communities they had belonged to. These questions led to a second meeting in 1976 involving many of the Tuareg *evolues*, which helped to further define the questions of who would belong to this imagined community and potential state.³⁸ The name that emerged from that meeting was the *Mouvement de libération de l'Azawad*, or MLA.

The Azawad is a valley formed by two wadis, the Azawad and the Azawagh, that flow between the Adagh and Air mountains.³⁹ The valley stretches between Mali and Niger and forms the heart of what had traditionally been the territory of many of the Kel Tamasheq. The call to this traditional land helped form the first territorial conception of the Tuareg state, and the remembrance of many of the scattered communities of the valley helped unify the exiles around a shared identity. By stretching the territory across Mali and Niger, it helped to assuage the divisions that had already grown within the community during its fracturing. With this choice of territory and identity, these *evolues* and Alfellaga leaders also agreed on a plan of battle, with each authority granted a different territory to organize and struggle for. This was to be a war that would not end until complete separation was achieved.

Unfortunately for the leaders of the previous Alfellaga, while they had helped bring together the national narrative of the Kel Tamasheq, they still could not claim leadership. Their support by Algeria, their foundation consisting almost entirely of Kel Adagh, and their separation from the greater issues of the younger generation of scattered Kel Tamasheq all contributed to their undoing. Algeria saw the Alfellaga leadership's inability to unify the Tuareg or direct them to service in the western Sahara⁴⁰ and began to withdraw their own support. The members of other segments of Tuareg society disliked their apparent privileging of the Kel Adagh in terms of leadership positions. Finally, the newer generation of Tuareg did not entirely trust their connections with Algeria or their plans for the future struggle against Mali and Niger. Instead, the centre of gravity for the new struggle would be found in the younger generation that was coming of age in Gaddafi's Libya.

Kel Tamasheq had been flocking to Libya since the early 1970s. There were abundant labour opportunities and Gaddafi's government was welcoming of the Tuareg even before his 1982 pronouncement. The Tuareg population fit well into his attempts to create a Pan-African solidarity movement, but one that was markedly pro-Arab and pro-Islamic at its core. Starting in 1979, Libya began to offer support and training to those members of the Tuareg population who believed in the *Tenekra*. These trained fighters were at first subject to attempts to fold them into larger movements planned by Gaddafi, but each in turn was found wanting. By 1980 the Kel Tamasheq who longed for their nation-state were being trained in Camp Al-Nasr, which at its peak was training 2700 fighters.[41] Above and beyond military training, these camps also offered basic educational instruction on subjects such as literacy and history. Although the camp would close later, hundreds of fighters gained additional instruction after volunteering to fight with the Palestinians in the Lebanon conflict.

Upon their return from the conflict, these Tuareg found two new camps constructed by Gaddafi's government, although these were explicitly for the Nigerien Kel Tamasheq.[42] Despite this bar, many Malian Tuareg managed to undertake the training offered. The fighters from this camp who served in the Chadian wars of Gaddafi earned a substantial amount of money, a significant portion of which was then shared with those Kel Tamasheq who were beginning to organize more political and military opposition to the Malian and Nigerien governments. With the broadening of the Kel Tamasheq involvement, the Kel Adagh senior leadership was increasingly marginalized, and attempts were made to create a unified front between the two major factions, Malian Tuareg and Nigerien Tuareg. The latter was not to be, as these groups were divided between different camps following the formation of a solely Nigerien politico-military group.[43] By the mid-1980s the Malian Tuareg had been trained in great numbers and many had gained significant military experience in Chad fighting for Gaddafi's ambitions. Small groups of Kel Tamasheq fighters slowly filtered back into Mali and prepared for their long-hoped-for conflict. By 1990, both Malian and Nigerien Kel Tamasheq had managed to create a unified identity and goal of statehood and a new war was about to break out, a war they were far more prepared for than the unfocused and somewhat naïve struggle of the 1960s.

The Second Rebellion

While preparations had been made for a rebellion throughout the 1980s, there was no agreement on when or how it would begin. Caches of weapons had been hidden, returned refugees were ready to rise up, but there was no spark agreed upon to launch the rebellion. While initial plans were still focused on the future, a series of catastrophes involving the locally based insurgents running afoul of the Malian armed forces created a necessary truncation of the timeline lest all of the cells within Mali be swept up. On 28 June 1990, the Menaka cell of the Kel Tamasheq rebels attacked the administrative and police headquarters of Menaka itself and seized several four-wheel-drive vehicles from the government and local NGOs.[44] This strike, although small in nature, marked the official beginning of a second rebellion against the government of Mali.

Between June and October of that year the rebellion was shaping into a rough parallel of the previous struggle. The Kel Tamasheq used hit-and-run tactics to avoid any decisive confrontation with the scattered and ill-trained forces of the Malian government. The raids provided the rebels with additional vehicles, weapons, and supplies, all while creating a confused response from the Malian armed forces. The new generation of fighters was more coordinated and far better trained than the rebels of the 1960s, leading to far more effective attacks and efficient use of the material seized in them. Their experience in Lebanon and Chad, combined with their understanding of mobile warfare, made them a formidable opponent for the less mobile and more conventionally organized Malian army. In particular, the mobility allowed by the Tuareg's technicals[45] far outstripped that of the Malians.[46] Thus, the first several months of conflict were extremely one-sided as the Malian forces were continually forced onto the static defensive in the wake of the lightning attacks of the Tuareg.

Quick assaults were not the only tactics that the Malian Kel Tamasheq employed. Radio broadcast challenges to the Malian armed forces were established, giving the location of Kel Tamasheq bases, enjoining the state's army to attack the Tuareg fighters. These led to costly losses for the Malians, as they lacked the training or cohesion to use their advantage in firepower to the fullest and instead were often repulsed after desultory bombardments and charges on prepared rebel positions. The Kel Tamasheq quickly established themselves as the far superior military force, gaining victories on the offensive against caravans and bases and on the defensive from their own prepared positions. Perhaps the most devastating of these victories was the raid at Toximine, where 45 lightly armed Kel Tamasheq rebels attacked a camp of 450 Malian soldiers on the night of 4 September 1990.[47] Using a surprise assault to initially capture the heavy weapons of the army, and then turning them against the soldiers, they routed the whole detachment while killing approximately a quarter of the enemy force.

The Malian response to these actions was initially an attempt to reintroduce the same system that had worked in the previous conflicts: the creation of forbidden zones and the suppression of local populations that were seen as possible collaborators. These methods were unfortunately well suited for descending into excess, and although they caused logistical difficulties for the Kel Tamasheq rebels, in combination with the rebels' success they created widespread sympathy for their cause, spreading the rebellion further. By late 1990 this had become a significant problem for the Malian government under Moussa Traoré. This was not necessarily because of any decisive losses, although Toximine had demoralized government forces, but instead because Traoré's government was facing several other political and economic challenges during the rebellion. With Traoré's government teetering, negotiations with the Tuareg seemed like the fastest way to settle at least one significant challenge to their rule.

Negotiations with the rebels began in October 1990 through initial contacts with traditional authorities in the Kel Tamasheq communities. By December 1990 the talks were in earnest. However, at this point it is important to discuss who was actually negotiating on behalf of whom. The Traoré government was weak and looking for a fast way to disentangle itself from this insurgency in the north to instead deal with the political restiveness in its southern heartland. It was looking for a workable solution that could lead to general stability. The traditional leaders of the Kel Tamasheq, although serving as mediators, had no formal authority over the rebels and instead were opposed to the armed uprising. The question quickly became that of who could speak for the rebels. Many of the rebels had identified themselves as being associated with the *Mouvement populaire de libération de l'Azawad* (or MPLA, sometimes alternately named as the *Mouvement populaire de l'Azawad*, or MPA), but there were deep splits in what that actually meant within the movement itself. While the peace agreement with the Traoré government was eventually mediated by Algeria and signed by a representative of the rebels,[48] the result was not peace but instead a fracturing of the rebel movement.[49]

The agreement, named the Tamanrasset Agreement after the Algerian city where it was negotiated and signed in January 1991, proved to be the seed of serious division within the ranks of the rebels.⁵⁰ As negotiated, it implicitly placed Azawad and the Tuareg within the framework of Mali, making the region of Kidal, where the Kel Adagh dwelled, a full-fledged and relatively autonomous region within Mali.⁵¹ While this gained significant freedom for the Kel Adagh, who had been at the heart of the 1960s rebellions and the kindling of Kel Tamasheq nationalism, this autonomy was not appreciated by many members of other factions of the Tuareg community. While the MPA could feel confident in their negotiated peace, the more hardline groups, which tended to be outside the influence of the Kel Adagh and the more *evolue* members of Kel Tamasheq society, rejected the new peace and continued their attacks on the Malian government. The first of the significant splinter groups was the *Front populaire de libération de l'Azawad* (FPLA), which launched a number of significant strikes at Malian military targets starting in February 1991.⁵²

The FPLA was to prove a very different group than the MPA. While the MPA was seen as a group of moderates using military force for separatist goals, the FPLA insisted on a militant separation from Mali and the establishment of the state of Azawad. Given these more aggressive goals, the attacks of the FPLA had a much further reach than those previously launched by the MPA and the initial rebellion. No longer fighting for recognition but instead for a military victory, the FPLA spread their attacks south and west, passing Timbuktu and the bend in the Niger River. Of course, the MPA was not a monolithic whole either, and by the end of the year had split into the MPA and the *Armée revolutionnaire de libération de l'Azawad* (ARLA), further fragmenting the Kel Tamasheq along social and class boundaries.⁵³

While the Kel Tamasheq combatants were fragmenting and the Tamanrasset Agreement was being broken by both sides, the Traoré regime was faring far worse. Traoré had ruled as an autocrat since overthrowing the Keita regime in 1968 and had only slightly liberalized his regime in the 1980s under pressure from the IMF. However, this window had been all that was needed for the opposition, who formed the *Congrès national d'initiative démocratique*, or CNID, in 1990. Demonstrations rocked the capital of Bamako, destabilizing the regime just as the Tuareg revolt had begun. The failure of the peace agreement had come on the heels of a suppressed demonstration that had seen 300 dissidents killed, driving the military into action. On 26 March 1991, the Malian armed forces under Colonel Amadou Touré entered the capital and arrested Traoré, overthrowing his government and ushering in a new regime in Mali.[54] This was to have significant effects upon the peace process, as although the Tamanrasset Agreement remained in force, the signatories to it had been marginalized or removed and the framework itself had been largely ignored by both sides.

However, with the advent of Touré's regime and his determination to transition to democratic rule as quickly as possible, there was also the need to finally deal with the Kel Tamasheq fighters in the north. The previous agreement had called for autonomy, many of those still fighting wished to have complete secession, and the government of Mali simply wished for the conflict to be over. This called for a unity of purpose amongst the Kel Tamasheq combatants, which was provided by the United Movements and Fronts of Azawad (MFUA), an ad hoc organization consisting of military and political representatives who claimed legitimacy from each armed group.[55] While these men were undoubtedly authorities within their spheres, there was a question as to how much they truly represented the wishes of all combatants and how much they actually represented the more central concepts of the MFUA. However, these men were able to negotiate with Touré's government and come to what was called the National Pact peace treaty, which was to define the ultimate goals of the Kel Tamasheq armed movements in terms of state, nation, and citizenship within Mali.

The National Pact peace treaty was signed in April 1992 under the auspices of France and Mauritania. The pact was intended to smooth over the long-standing grievances of the Kel Tamasheq and their isolation from the levers of the Malian state. Kel Tamasheq fighters and intelligentsia were to be integrated into the Malian armed forces and administration, meaning that there would be notable representation of their needs within the government. Funds would be made available to help approximately 160,000 Kel Tamasheq refugees return and reintegrate into society. Additional funds would be set aside to help reconstruct the north following the conflict that had erupted there for the previous two years, and a tax exemption for ten years would be granted to northerners to help them reconstruct their lives as well. Finally, the northern region would be granted a special status within the Malian administration, essentially bestowing social, economic, and administrative autonomy.[56] While all of these were renegotiated over the next several years and most were incompletely implemented at best, they offered at least the framework of a deal that was agreeable to both sides of the conflict. However, as the deal evolved and was implemented in a piecemeal fashion, the greater Kel Tamasheq community was left further outside the dealings of the MFUA and began to lose their patience.

Throughout the period, the fragmented armed fronts were already rarely obeying the ceasefire that had been called to aid in negotiations. While the MFUA was put forth as the representatives of the combatants and the community as a whole, their authority over the many armed groups was always in question and, as negotiations dragged on, began to evaporate. These groups launched raids on the settled agriculturalists throughout this period, especially on the ethnically Songhay people of the Niger Bend.[57] As refugees returned following the 1993 acceptance of the pact by the FPLA, there was increasing strain on the food resources of the region as aid was slow to arrive. This was exacerbated by the increasing infighting between various Kel Tamasheq factions in the resistance, especially between the ARLA and MPA over the shape of Kel Tamasheq society.[58] These tensions kept the struggle at a simmer, and events in Gao would soon cause the conflagration to erupt again.

The ethnic Songhay populations inhabited the north but had been left in limbo by the negotiated settlement. Already at odds with the Kel Tamasheq thanks to their raids, the Songhay formed a self-defence militia in May 1994. Called the Ganda Koy ("Masters of the Earth"),[59] these militias rapidly took on forms analogous to the Kel Tamasheq fronts, with small arms, heavy weapons, and technicals fleshing out their arsenal in a rapid burst of organization.[60] With what has been referred to as the tacit if not explicit support of the military and the local government, the Ganda Koy began to arrest and kill the local Kel Tamasheq and other Saharan nomad populations. By the end of June they had reportedly killed over 450 Kel Tamasheq and others and had stepped up their patrols both on land and with boats on the river. Large-scale pronouncements urging other citizens to drive away or kill the "nomads" were distributed, creating at least two other similar organizations that continued the conflict.[61] The Tuareg groups responded with their own raids and killings, creating more chaos in the north even as the main negotiators worked toward a solution. It was only following two outbursts of violence in Gao, one by the *Front Islamique*

Arabe de l'Azawad (or FIAA, one of the secessionist groups fighting in the north) on the Ganda Koy members and African civilians and the other the reprisals of the survivors on the remaining nomadic population in the city, that both sides returned to the negotiating table.[62] The attacks had convinced the non-combatants on both sides that the violence would have no end without their own intervention, and in late 1994 the local authorities signed their own pact to force a ceasefire in their communities.

With the state still unable to enforce the National Pact, many local conflicts were resolved over the next year locally. Communities that had used their disparate histories to create conflict now used it to try and stop the violence. Local initiatives were aided by the UN personnel who were in the region and smaller efforts to integrate the militias of both sides into the national military. While these were underway, parallel efforts by the Malian government and the local authorities were undertaken to disarm the militias and enforce local peace agreements. The efforts by President Konaré, who had won election to the presidency of Mali in a transition to a democratic administration in 1992, were considered especially important, as his rhetoric consistently defined the issue as a national Malian one as opposed to a Tuareg problem that the nation had.[63] This defined the Tuareg as part of the nation, a critical step in being able to reintegrate the fighters into the nation as opposed to defining them as an ethnic enemy of the state.[64] By March 1996 these multiple lines of effort had borne fruit, and on the 26th the stacked arms that had been surrendered were burned in the Timbuktu market square in a symbolic *La Flamme de la Paix*.[65]

Following the peace of 1996, elements of the National Pact were able to be more fully put into place and a relative calm returned to the north. The combatants on both sides were largely amnestied and allowed to resume their former lives.[66] While violence was still occurring, it was not a directed political act and instead was a reflection on the difficulties the region was still having while reconstructing its communities. The decentralization of the region, that is, the local autonomy that the Tuareg had won, had reduced the prevalence of conflict and the region had returned largely to normalcy.[67] While there would be further political ruptures a decade later, the Tuareg had at this point completed their rebellions for the purpose of gaining political concessions in Mali in the initial post–Cold War era.

The Kel Tamasheq: A Nation with an Imagined State

The revolts of the Tuareg in Mali serve as an interesting case study of the interactions of secession, separatism, irredentism, and the changing ideas of nationalism in the post–Cold War era. The revolts in the 1990s began as what could be understood as a direct attempt at secession and the establishment of a state around the conception of Azawad, the putative Tuareg homeland for what was now considered the imagined community of the Kel Tamasheq. However, local and regional events took place that would shape it into different forms, opening the possibility for secession, then possible irredentism, and finally an acceptance of autonomy under the decentralized rule of the Malian state.

Of course there is the question of the earliest revolt against Mali in 1963. Given the stated objectives of the leaders, does this not point to a continuity and establish the struggles of the Kel Tamasheq as one of the Long Wars for secession in terms of duration? There were certainly combatants who were more than willing to hold forth on their desire for separation from the hated Malian state and that their struggle was to bring that about. However, there are difficulties in linking this earlier war to the later efforts that characterized the struggles of the 1990s. As noted earlier in this chapter, while there were certainly members of the leadership of the rebels who dreamed of being separated from Keita's state, there was little to no idea of an end state after such separation was completed. Considering that much of the rancour was due to the loss of what the Kel Tamasheq saw as their deserved privilege following independence, it would seem that much of the struggle was instead somewhat paralleling the earlier Civil Secessions, with the major difference being that while Katanga had a specific civil structure inherent within its community, the Kel Tamasheq almost appeared to be looking for an outside party to construct it.[68] Whether this would have taken the form of a French enforcement of what the Kel Tamasheq had assumed would be their deserved autonomy or the final creation of an *Organisation commune des regions sahariennes* that would benefit all of the Saharan pastoral groups was never quite articulated. It is therefore difficult to say that this is necessarily a secessionist conflict without there being an understood state to be created.

Further complicating the issue is that while the 1963 revolt has been generally discussed as a revolt of the Kel Tamasheq based upon their disgruntlement with the Malian government, this is actually a mischaracterization. While many important traditional figures arose and helped coordinate the conflict, the truth remains that the leadership and fighting manpower for the struggle came almost entirely from a single segment of the Tuareg community: the Kel Adagh. Coming from the region nearest the mountainous terrain of northern Mali near the Algerian border, the Kel Adagh were certainly the most aggrieved and felt it necessary to take up arms, but they represented only one confederation of the Kel Tamasheq community. None of the other confederations saw fit to rise up or even coordinate with them on any level, leaving the Kel Adagh the lone members of the revolt. This is not to say that the Kel Adagh would not play a large role in the later revolts, but simply that they were an isolated community at the time in terms of their armed resistance. Without a fully articulated goal of a state or even the representation of the entire nation to which they belonged, it is hard to place the original struggle as a precursor of the later revolts in any fashion, aside from inspiration for the Kel Adagh themselves and an early attempt at a reform insurgency within the newly independent state of Mali.

However, the revolt that began in 1990 can without a doubt be linked closely to the reignited secession desires amongst the Kel Tamasheq of the post–Cold War Era. While the 1963 struggle had failed because of its fragmented participation, the capacity of the Malian state to project its power, and its essential lack of a practicable end-goal, the new struggle was taking place in an entirely different context. The intervening years had dramatically changed the political, economic, and military landscape, allowing for a much different outcome within this struggle. In terms of fragmented participation, those years had been disastrous to the entirety of the Kel Tamasheq community, and the Teshumara had forced large-scale changes on them. While there remained questions about exactly how the Kel Tamasheq community could or should be defined, by the end of the Teshumara there was a shared experience that had begun to draw the scattered populace together. By midway through the 1980s there was a palpable conception of a Kel Tamasheq community and shared experience that began to define a modern Tuareg nation through the narratives of the *Tenekra*.

The coalition of Kel Tamasheq fighters, both abroad and within Mali, helped define the struggle around the creation and reclaiming of Azawad, a homeland built around the conception of the traditional homeland of the Kel Tamasheq. With the initiation of the hostilities in 1990 there was initially one and then several armed fronts, each claiming to represent the now-conceived ambitions of the united Kel Tamasheq and the desires of an ethnic homeland.

This is not to say that the conceptions of this ethnic homeland or who would belong to it were monolithic. As with any process of identity formation, there were fractious struggles over the inclusion or exclusion of peoples and the conception of what social and cultural form the nation itself would take. Even the period of transition, the Teshumara, was not experienced in the same way across the Kel Tamasheq populace, and these experiences then were expressed differently when individuals and groups attempted to define their "Kel Tamasheq"-ness. When the conflict began, this was immediately seen in the fragmentation of the armed groups struggling against Mali. While all fronts were opposed to continuing Malian rule of Azawad, by the end of the first few weeks of fighting there were already four major armed fronts in the conflict, each with a separate view on how Azawad would be defined and run. The MPLA (later MPA), FPLA, and ARLA were all struggling initially for a Kel Tamasheq nation or region, and the *Front islamique arabe de l'Azawad* (FIAA), which comprised primarily nomadic Arab groups from northern Mali, also rejected the Malian government rule and also broadcast their own Azawad-focused agenda.[69]

This fragmentation of armed groups and ultimate goals led directly into the confusion following first the 1991 signing of the Tamanrasset Accords. With the fronts so fragmented and the leadership of each not entirely clear—especially with the growing rift between the Kel Adagh fighters of the previous generation and the newer rebellious groups—the accords were simply not seen as binding by the vast majority of combatants, since they also involved concessions that only a portion of the combatants agreed to. While the MPA and the FIAA agreed in theory to the Tamanrasset Accords' settling of grievances within the framework of a unitary Mali,[70] the FPLA categorically insisted on a separate Azawad and so refused to cease their struggle. The formation of the ARLA from splits in the MPA was another result of these contestations of the identity of the movement.

The MPA had been led initially by many of the same leaders from the Alfellaga generation of the 1960s who were pushing for a re-establishment of traditional Kel Tamasheq society in their traditional regions, but the ARLA included many members who felt that the Kel Tamasheq people had undergone significant transformations in the past decades and needed to reform themselves from within.[71] This same process repeated itself with the National Pact under the Konaré regime. While the MFUA was technically an umbrella group that represented the interests of all the armed fronts, the National Pact represented something far closer to the separatist desires of the MPA than those of the more radical groups. The fact that even years later splinter groups continued clashing with the government and the MPA despite the "settling" of the conflict is a stark illustration of how contentious the new nationalism of the Kel Tamasheq was.[72]

Hearkening just as closely to the themes of the 1990s waves of secession is the characterization of the peace proposals and process, from the Tamanrasset Accords to the National Pact to the eventual final ceasefire brokered by local elites. The Tamanrasset Accords were essentially a discussion between a Cold War–era regime and what had been the previous generation of Tuareg and Arab leadership, brokered by Algeria, a state acting as a third party within the negotiations. However, the wave of changes that the ending of the Cold War enabled occurred with startling rapidity within Mali and its neighbours. The Traoré Regime, which had been in power since 1968 with the complicity and support of France and other African regimes, was swept out of power through a popular uprising against the disliked government. While the failing war in the north had helped delegitimize the regime, its ailing economy and increasingly firm opposition had seen the regime teeter and finally fall to a coup led by Lt. Col. Amadou Touré, who quickly arranged for a National Conference to figure out the next step of ruling in the post–Cold War, post-dictatorship Mali. Central to this process was the settling of the conflict in the north. Whereas the independence-era states of Africa had been unbending Westphalian states in theory, the new era offered significantly more flexibility. The new state could maintain its most important attribute, its sovereignty, and still offer significant decentralization of governance and developmental incentives to the Kel Tamasheq. In effect, the new state could offer the Kel Tamasheq autonomy under their sovereignty along with integration into the political and financial networks of the state without compromising the practical functions of the post–Cold War state.[73] This allowed for the political resolution of the conflict, that of separatism and not secession, whereas the earlier era of African politics could not have offered that solution.

It is, finally, worth noting that the resolution leading to the *Flamme de la Paix* also sits within the conception of the new wave of secessions. Whereas from independence to the 1990s the state remained supreme and rarely tolerated alternative or parallel structures of influence, by the 1990s in many ways the African state had grown weaker and less able to fulfill all of the functions necessary to provide for the citizenry. The bloody conflicts between the Kel Tamasheq and other pastoralists on the one hand and the Ganda Koy and their parallels on the other were not solved by the state. The Malian military often found itself more entangled with the conflict than controlling it. Instead, the final ceasefire was the result of dozens of small local ceasefires negotiated by traditional authorities. Where the state could not bring the combatants to heel, those local authorities that represented alternative structures of authority did so.

In the end, the struggles of the Kel Tamasheq in the 1990s are extremely typical of the new wave of secessions. The struggle itself did not begin with the delineation of a state and then the conflict to defend it, but instead with the imagining of an ethnic nation-state and the beginning of the guerrilla war to compel its secession. The struggle itself rarely saw decisive battles and instead was intended to weaken the already distressed state. The conflict itself also often saw the parallel negotiation of who belonged to this new imagined state, with consequent confusion about the final goal. The democratic reforms sweeping Africa with the end of the Cold War also affected the struggle, bringing in new regimes that had other means of settling the conflict than outright military victory. Finally, the 1990 Kel Tamasheq revolt in Mali had ended with that most typical of settlements. Secession, while initially a stated goal, was still simply almost impossible to effect. However, the new Malian state was able to make use of its sovereignty to both maintain its status as a state and pursue a policy of decentralization. This let the Kel Tamasheq have their own local control of their desired "Azawad" while also giving them access to the flows of influence and capital that the sovereignty of the weak state allowed them to maintain.

However, although this system would theoretically help halt secessionist attempts, in practice this was not the case, as will be discussed later.

Whither Irredentism?

As noted, the Kel Tamasheq are not simply a Malian group. Like many ethnic groups in Africa, their population was divided multiple times by the borders drawn at the Conference of Berlin in 1885. With the advent of independence, there were sizable populations of nomadic pastoral Tuareg in Mali, Burkina Faso, Algeria, Libya, and Niger. It is the last of these, sharing a large border with Mali, where a large number of Tuareg militants were to take up arms as well. The Tuareg of Niger's struggle had many connections in its genesis and its prosecution with those of their kin in Mali. The Kel Tamasheq of Niger took up arms in the 1990s in response to the same crises, prosecuted their conflict in much the same manner, and even shared many of the same goals of secession or separatism from their host state.

While the Kel Adagh of Mali had risen up in revolt in the 1960s, the Kel Tamasheq populations of Niger did not rebel in the early years of independence. However, they both regretted the failure of the *Organisation commune des regions sahariennes* and much like their brethren were swiftly subsumed by the new state government of their host state. The new Nigerien state constitution had devolved almost all important powers to the new president Hamani Diori.[74] Quick action during the later years of independence had transformed Niger into a de facto one-party state, with Diori's *Parti progressiste Nigérien* (PPN) in firm control. Since the PPN was dominated by the Zarma/Songhay ethnicities, the political influence of other ethnicities was circumscribed, with the nomadic Tuareg left almost entirely out of the patronage of the new state.[75] While the Kel Tamasheq continued their traditional practices, tensions rose within other interest groups, culminating with a coup in 1974 led by Lt. Col. Seyni Kountché.[76] The coup was initially welcome due to the coercive nature of the PPN, but within a short time Kountché's military government proved to be no less repressive and brutal.

Little of this mattered to the Nigerien Kel Tamasheq, who continued to live within the Sahara as they always had. However, the great droughts of the 1970s that had so devastated the flocks and herds of their Malian brethren were just as harsh on their own beasts. The same crushing and scattering process led to their own Teshumara, and Nigerien Kel Tamasheq joined their Malian brethren as refugees in Algeria, in Libya, and as wage labour in the urban centres of the other Sahelian states. Many underwent the same training with Gaddafi's forces, serving in the same conflicts and forming their own units and militant groups. Several of the camps within Libya for training militants were even set aside as only for Nigerien Kel Tamasheq.[77] It was here that the first organization was created for the militants who intended to return to Niger, the *Front populaire pour la libération du Niger* (FPLN).[78] These would be many of the initial combatants in the new struggle.

Much like the Malian Kel Tamasheq, the Nigerien Tuareg were slowly repatriated back to their homeland by Algeria and Libya in the late 1980s. While the repressive regime of Senyi Kountché had been overthrown and a new republic was now in power, there remained significant ethnic tensions, and many of the aid supplies intended to help support the repatriated refugees had been stolen or sold by government officials. In May 1990 numerous protests took place against the government, culminating in the slaying of a soldier in the city of Tchin Tabaraden by Tuareg youths.[79] The Nigerien response was devastating, with a strong military expedition dispatched that undertook a violent manhunt for the perpetrators. Over 300 Kel Tamasheq men were killed, their possessions stolen, and the women of these Kel Tamasheq communities sexually assaulted.[80] This galvanized some of the Tuareg men who were already disposed to resistance, while also driving others back across borders with the movement of Tuareg being thrown back into Algeria and Mali.

It is here where the stories of the two Kel Tamasheq populations intersect. Several of the Nigerien Kel Tamasheq who fled across the border were promptly arrested by the Malian authorities at Menaka. The Malian MPLA launched a raid in June 1990 to free those Nigerien Kel Tamasheq, a raid that marked the beginning of the MPLA's formal armed revolt against the Malian government, as noted previously.[81] The Nigerien rebellion would take slightly longer to begin, with its earliest escalation after the Tchin Tabaraden massacres being in later 1991.[82] However, the hit-and-run conflicts were much more sensitive for the Nigerien government, as the main road linking landlocked Niger to the coast and the extremely important uranium mines both existed within what had been traditionally Kel Tamasheq territory. By 1993 there were four separate Kel Tamasheq fronts fighting the Nigerien government over this territory: the *Front de libération de l'Air et de l'Azaouak* (FLAA), the *Front de libération Tamoust* (FLT), the *Armée revolutionaire de la libération du Nord Niger* (ARLNN), and the *Front patriotique de libération du Sahara* (FPLS).[83] The pattern followed was much the same as that of the Malian struggle, with the Nigerien military unable to effectively come to grips with the Kel Tamasheq rebels, and several attempts were made to cordon off regions to lessen the amount of manoeuvring space the rebels had. The Nigerien government even broadcast its willingness to negotiate but found few takers amongst the rebels, who by late 1993 had formed the *Coordination de la résistance armée* (CRA), an umbrella organization for prosecuting the conflict.[84] Conflicts riddled the government as those loyal Tuareg were discriminated against and many lost their positions, further fuelling the war. By 1994 the rebels were demanding a large autonomous region as a precondition for their further negotiation.

By late 1994 these demands were seen to be largely bluster. The CRA and other armed fronts began negotiations, and although there were several false starts, by 1995 most combatants had begun to negotiate in good faith. That year marked the signing of the Ouagadougou Accords, which eventually served as the outline for a peace between the Kel Tamasheq and Niger. Although autonomy was not achieved, the Kel Tamasheq were assured participation in the government and aid in reintegrating their people into the Nigerien state. By 1998 the very last of the combatants had signed the accords and peace returned to the Republic of Niger. While the war was not as high-intensity as that in neighbouring Mali, it was extremely economically destructive, with the primary routes out of Niger and the most valuable resource-rich region both severely disrupted by the fighting. In the end, the Kel Tamasheq found it more agreeable to make a deal with the Nigerien state than to continue a conflict that was as exhausting for them as it was for their foes.

However, with the transnational linkages between the two conflicts, from ethnic solidarity to shared history to shared goals of autonomy or secession from their host states, why didn't the Kel Tamasheq of Mali and Niger form a united front to achieve their goal? Given the territory they claimed as their traditional homeland and their similar aims, an irredentist movement would have offered a shared goal for the whole of the Kel Tamasheq community. Given these factors, why did such a movement fail to emerge?

The first reason is essentially that despite the shared language and heritage within the Kel Tamasheq community, they were still not a monolithic group. The experience and identity of each of the segments of Kel Tamasheq society was unique unto itself and it took remarkable measures for even larger confederations to come together to work toward a common goal. The conception of a unified Azawad was a creation of the 1990s *Tenekra* amongst the Malians, developed during the experiences of the Teshumara and Gaddafi's Libya. While efforts were made during this period to unite the Kel Tamasheq communities, under the guise of the united *Front populaire pour la libération du Sahara arabe central* (FPLSC) or even the short-lived Kel Nimagiler movement, the community remained fractious both between Kel Mali and Kel Niger groups and within these divisions.[85] By the time the various Kel Tamasheq began repatriating, there was an almost complete separation of the communities. While Azawad was the dream of Kel Mali, it was not that of the Kel Niger, and so each went their own separate ways. This is not to say that there was not still some crossover at the local level, as at Manaka, but ultimately the two divisions of the same ethnic group had different goals for their fronts, and this was a barrier to their united front.

The second reason that an irredentist movement was ultimately impossible had to do with the differences in the territories claimed. While Mali proved to be flexible in its settlement, allowing decentralization throughout its state, this was largely acceptable due to the regions the Kel Tamasheq wished to control. Northern Mali, absent the historically and economically significant towns of Gao and Timbuktu, is largely already outside the scope of the Malian state. With the post–Cold War assumption of sovereignty and all the benefits it entailed despite lack of direct state control, it was thus not only possible but to a degree beneficial that the north would be autonomous. However, for Niger the opposite was true. The two most vital resources of the state, its logistical connection to Algeria and its strategically vital uranium mines, both fell within the territory that the Kel Tamasheq wanted to control.[86] There was no way that the government could accept the separation of this territory from central control. These were resources that required possession to maintain their benefit to the government. Given this reality, the Kel Tamasheq of Niger could not be offered any sort of separatist settlement and they could not win secession on the battlefield. This would leave any irredentist movement effectively checkmated. The ultimate result—that of a decentralized Mali giving autonomy to its Kel Tamasheq and a firm Niger offering concessions to their own rebels—remains the end expression of the political realities of the states involved in the conflict.

Coda

Despite the settlement in Mali and Niger, there were still the issues of the fragmented community and the need for both parties to adhere to the agreement. Already fragile, these efforts were also vulnerable to a change in the regional contexts that spawned them. While autonomy and integration were both possible solutions to the conflicts, new regional realities would cause another eruption of violence in the next decade, one that would again raise the spectre of a Kel Tamasheq homeland splitting from Mali and Niger. However, these outbreaks will be covered later in the Conclusion to the volume as it examines the continued legacy of past secessionist attempts and their intersections with transnational conflicts, particularly those ignited by the numerous confrontations subsumed under the title of the Global War on Terror.

Conclusion: Secession and the Secessionist Motive into the Twenty-first Century

This work has discussed a conceptual idea of three different waves of secession that have rolled across the continent of Africa since the initial independence of sovereign nations in the late 1950s. The first, the Civil Secessions, offered a unique typology that would quickly ignite a firestorm and then be snuffed out. These secessions are so named because they were attempting to create civil states, states that were multi-ethnic and constructed around a civil structure of laws and institutions. Those that had pursued such projects in Katanga and Biafra understood that international political recognition was the only possible path forward for their political project and structured their secessionist actions around this goal. However, their desires to directly declare and demonstrate their existence as independent states backfired, as in both cases recognition was denied and the perceived need to defend the borders of their nation left them in the path of far more powerful opponents.

The second wave, the Long Wars, proved far more ambiguous than their Civil Secession counterparts. Whereas with the Civil Secessions there was a direct declaration of secession as their motive and the immediate attempt to defend what was now sovereign state territory, the Long Wars drifted through secession and separatism and often blurred the lines where the contestation of sovereignty was actually taking place. Whereas the Civil Secessions were modelled after the negotiated and recognized independence of African states such as Ghana, Nigeria, and Mali, the Long Wars would find their models in the global liberation struggles of the 1950s and 1960s. These have been dubbed the Long Wars because they involved the secessionists' waging protracted struggles as they husbanded their strength and created parallel governance structures to continue their contestation of sovereignty.[1] The extended construction and evolution of these military, political, and even social structures over the long conflicts meant that not only could these conflicts be sustained, but there were at least functional governance structures to take over when these conflicts ended rather spectacularly in success.

The Long Wars found success during a period of rapid political change on both a continental and global scale, and this same changing context helped fuel what has been termed the New Wave of secessions. While structurally the Long Wars had been waged in a very different way than the Civil Secessions, they offered at least a similar vision for their end point: complete secession and the establishment of a multi-ethnic state for their people fighting for their independence. The forces unleashed by the end of the Cold War would mean that, although the New Wave of secessions would be structurally waged in the same way as the Long Wars, their end goal would shift. A combination of resurgent subnational ambitions along with the collapse of state capacity after the Cold War would mean the New Wave of secessions would instead pursue often more openly separatist goals as opposed to secessionist ones, as subnational interest groups looked for more autonomy under the umbrella of weakened state control.

However, as each wave progressed, it can be seen that the actual secessionist motive and the methods by which it was pursued in independent Africa altered over time. The way that secession and separatism were understood underwent a radical change, with the initial political demands of immediate and recognized sovereignty giving way to a more ambiguous process by which the motives often skirted the line between secession, separatism, and irredentism. By the time the New Wave had hit, the very idea of secession had to a large degree drifted away despite the signal successes of Eritrea and South Sudan. This alteration in the secessionist motive was largely driven by a combination of political changes on the continent of Africa as well as African states' relationship with the global community, but it is important to understand this evolution in order to also understand where the ideas of secession, separatism, and irredentism exist now within the context of the African continent.

The Evolution of the Secessionist Motive

The secessionist motive in Africa was born at the same time as its drive for independence. While certainly the drawing of borders of the colonies and later independent states did not help tamp down the subnational frustrations and ambitions within the states, the drive for multinational, multi-ethnic states following the Second World War meant that almost any borders that existed would see a degree of contestation of political control and sovereignty. However, the drive for independence along the lines of the colonial boundaries did inspire the initial secessionist motive within the now-independent states. The idea that there was an international body of law that demanded self-determination and that demanded respect for the concept of sovereignty meant that those subdivisions within the colonies would believe that their own self-determination and desire for sovereignty must be respected, just as the demands of the larger nationalist fronts of Africa's had been. In this sense, the early secessionist motive was modelled after the premises of international law that had granted independence to Africa over the late 1950s and early 1960s.[2]

During this time, this must not have seemed that remote a goal. Most of the nationalist movements in Africa had struggled for years in seeking political control of the colonies they had found themselves in, and following the Second World War these movements saw recognizable movement toward their desires. The major colonial powers of France, Britain, and Belgium all were severely weakened by the war, and Portugal, despite being neutral, had been in decline for decades.[3] At the same time the creation of the United Nations as an international governing body, which included self-determination for all peoples within its charter, offered hope that the emerging global order would help dismantle the colonial system that controlled Africa.[4] This combination of rising nationalist ambitions and organization,[5] weakened colonial powers, and the global acceptance of a political regime that demanded self-determination then managed to enable the dreams of the nationalists in a far more rapid manner than they had ever anticipated. While the colonial powers had imagined they had decades to slowly enact a program of decolonization, within a decade the colonial system was in its initial stages of being torn down across Africa.

Of course, these same factors drove forward the secessionist motives of subnational groups. Groups like the Moïse Tshombe's Katangans, while working with other nationalist groups for their own larger national independence, questioned whether the redrawing of the continental order could only deal with the political governance of the already-existent colonies. This came into even sharper focus as many of these subnational groups had very different relationships with their colonial powers, relationships that often made the integration into independent state political orders much more difficult. Whether because of the economic development that had occurred in the region, such as with Katanga,[6] or the privileged status the population held within the colonial order, such as with the Kel Tamasheq of the French Sahara,[7] these groups were not necessarily opposed to their political independence, but were not amenable to the new state order being ushered in by the nationalists. They were already looking for chances to assert their own political independence, especially as many of these groups already had at least a semi-functional political organization to drive forward their ambitions.

These parallel organizations were swept along with the same tides that had driven nationalist motives in the postwar period. The weakening colonial powers, while perhaps not quite as excoriated amongst some subnational groups as they were amongst the nationalist groups, offered the same opportunity for new political leadership within their homelands and real sovereignty as opposed to colonial rule. However, whereas the nationalists were focused on the political control of colonies transformed into sovereign states, this first wave of secessionists were looking at the restructuring of the colonial order into multiple sovereignties. Underpinning these beliefs was the general view that if the European colonial order was to be rejected, why should not the boundaries that system had imposed be rejected as well? This was bolstered by the wording of the new United Nations charter, which demanded self-determination for all the populations of the world. To the secessionists, this was a clear indication that the new global order would not be constrained by elements of the old. Thus, the initial secessionist motive had been informed by the idea that the political leadership of a population could help guide those people through the creation of a new sovereign state, effectively creating new, completely self-determined states on the continent.

This first wave of secessions had unfortunately been very optimistic in its assumptions that the dismantling of the colonial order had ushered in a new era of renegotiation of state boundaries and sovereignty in Africa. Whereas the state as a structure did indeed still represent the default social and political organization on the continent, no existing state accepted the renegotiation of boundaries to create new states. Instead, with limited exceptions, these new attempts to assert political sovereignty and then receive recognition were rejected by all parties involved in the process. Katanga had a brief period of international quasi-legitimacy but lost any support it had with the assassination of Prime Minister Lumumba by Katangan forces. In the rebellion's wake the international community quickly quashed the legal justifications for secession through a series of United Nations and Organization of African Unity precedents, but the secessionist motive still found a new spark with Biafra. While Biafra could not lean on international law, it had hoped that the instability of Nigeria and the violence of the coups and pogrom would generate sympathy and possible recognition for its secessionist project. However, the door had been closed on secession and the attempt was finally ended in 1970.

While the formal secessionist motive had been effectively abandoned by 1970, with the path to complete political separation on the African continent largely closed off in international legal thought and no longer within the capabilities of any aggrieved subnational group, this didn't mean that the struggles for political autonomy or separatism were over. Instead, within this new frozen international order, the secessionist or separatist motive entered a far more ambiguous and fluid realm. The states that had emerged in Africa were not necessarily fully functional, but the development of capacity within their borders was largely reliant on external exchange with the developed nations of the world. The keys to this exchange were held by the new nationalist political elite, who managed to effectively make themselves gatekeepers between their own sovereign nation and the increasingly polarized world of the Cold War.[8] However, this very ability to gatekeep allowed for the creation of circumscribed networks of patronage that controlled the flow of development within the rest of the new state. This often left marginalized groups outside the limited development taking place even as they continued to exist under the monopoly of legitimate use of violence that the new states maintained. This, combined with often increasingly undemocratic governments, led to a series of clashes with the new states by the subnational groups. However, despite the weakness of the new states, they still were more powerful than their subnational groups and could exert far more deadly firepower in these struggles than any constituent group. This capacity was of course also well subsidized by Cold War patrons that did not want to lose friendly African governments.[9] This meant that in order to persist in these clashes the subnational groups necessarily had to pursue quiet, prolonged conflicts.

It was during these prolonged conflicts that the aforementioned ambiguity was explored. While secession had seemingly been quashed as a political goal following the fall of Biafra, that did not mean that it was entirely gone. However, those groups fighting for their own political, social, and economic control locally had fierce debates within their ranks about the official end goal of their struggles, debates that could continue for as long as their struggles did. These debates in turn often meant that the stated goal of a struggle might change from year to year as new leadership or factions ascended to power. For example, the Sudanese Civil War began as a secessionist attempt that eventually saw its leadership realize that secession would be an impossibility within their political context. Instead, the question of regional autonomy and integration into the networks of gatekeeper patronage was raised, leading to separatism being achieved in 1972. However, when these networks of patronage and development failed to be fully realized, the next phase of the conflict saw the re-emergence of, at first, a desire for reform within the autonomous system that the South inhabited. During the course of the conflict, the increasing organization of the Southern fronts and the weakening of the North saw this desire for reforming the earlier agreement instead transform into the re-emergence of the secessionist motive that the rapidly changing geopolitics of the post–Cold War era had made a possibility. This sort of pattern played itself out throughout the longer, evolving conflicts across the continent, where secessionist desires might transition into reform or separatist ones and back, as the capabilities of the combatants and the context within which they struggled changed.

The crushing of the attempts in Katanga and Biafra and the precedents their loss set had largely quashed the secessionist motive as a realistic goal for those groups fighting prolonged insurgencies for their subnational rights. While the idea of secession had re-emerged from time to time throughout the 1960s, 1970s, and 1980s during these fights, as noted they often were discarded as an ideal once negotiations with the parent states were underway—or sometimes were even discarded within intergroup rivalries as more capable groups took control and fought for more moderate reforms. This often found a decent amount of success, as local groups could still fight for regional autonomy or a larger reform of the central government that would include them within the networks of development they had been left out of.

This general lack of pursuit of secession as a goal would eventually be overturned as several momentous events occurred that undid the perceptions that had stymied secession as a desired end of these struggles. During the decades of the Cold War it had become patently obvious that the international system would not recognize secessionist states, thus undermining the very reason for which subgroups would pursue secession. Without this recognition, the secessionist region would not have the access to international markets or even political support that would allow them to function for the benefit of their populace. Beyond this, thanks to their access to the international system and the military support of the Cold War blocs, the parent states could call on economic and military strength that could crush all but the most determined of insurgencies.

These perceptions would all be belied or reversed with the end of the Cold War. The idea that no secessionist state would be recognized within the international order was undone during the collapse of the Eastern Bloc. Old states were immediately partitioned and larger unions were split across Eastern Europe, with these new states welcomed into the new world order by the United Nations. For those African groups watching, this was an obvious overturning of what they had always perceived as the blanket condemnation of secession; not only was the international community welcoming secessionist states, but the lone remaining superpower, the United States, was actively encouraging more splits within their former adversaries, citing the ability of the local populations to self-determine their political fates. Perhaps just as important, the end of the Cold War meant that the support that African states had been receiving from the two poles of the struggle to maintain their security capacity was undergoing rapid changes. For those states that had aligned themselves with the Communist bloc, their patrons had now largely collapsed. The Soviet Union was no more, and its successor states had their own problems to deal with due to their own political turmoil and moribund economies. On the other side of the spectrum, those that had been supported by the United States and its Western allies saw their support become conditional not on halting the spread of Communism but now on the emergent security threats of the new global order.[10] Allies like Zaire[11] found themselves far less critical in the new security priorities of the United States, while those like Sudan found themselves rapidly transformed from allies against Communism to targets due to their ties to fundamentalist Islam. In all of these cases, the capacity of African governments to maintain their abilities to extract, provide, and control were all undermined. This opened the possibility that localized insurgencies could survive and perhaps even thrive against the now weakened parent states. In both cases, the factors that had largely undermined the secessionist motive and driven many more toward reform or separatism had themselves been largely dismantled. While this might have seemed theoretical at first, the success of the Eritrean bid for secession seemed to hinge largely on the weakening of the Ethiopian Derg regime in the late Cold War as well as the direct acceptance of its independence by the United Nations in 1993, signalling that there might indeed be something new afoot on the continent.

Beyond this, there was now another new factor to add to the secessionist motive. Whereas all previous African secessions had largely been built along what might be referred to as civil lines, the events in Europe pointed to the new acceptance of nation-states as the end state of secessionist activities. This meant that the idea of ethnic identities being the basis for whole political sovereign states was now an accepted phenomenon, something that the aversion to ethnic nationalism in the wake of the world wars had previously ruled out. Given that the majority of subnational identities in Africa were based on ethnicities and that many of the existent regimes in Africa saw the deep ethnicization of politics despite their civil state structures, this new acceptance was noted with deep interest. Suddenly, those ethnic groups that had previously been struggling for autonomy or their own access to the network of gatekeepers could instead dream on their own ethno-state, where instead of competing with the groups that had historically held power for a share of the access and networks, they could have control of them in their entirety.

Of course, this did not always mean that subnational groups would drive for their own secession, ethnic or not. Instead, much like during the Long Wars, these still-lengthy struggles would see an evolution of motives and often compromises made as both sides of the conflict often lacked the capacity to force a decisive result. However, while some groups set out for secession and ended up with autonomy under their old parent states, this did not necessarily end their secessionist ambitions, and now it was more than possible to reignite a conflict and continue to push for complete separation following a period of reinforcement and retrenchment. The signal success of the South Sudan showed this was now a potential path forward, where despite significant splintering and an earlier agreement for regional autonomy, secession was eventually achieved along the lines that the long-struggling Southerners had desired from the beginning. At the very worst, these groups could use whatever military successes they achieved to argue for a better deal with their host state—settling for separatism on better terms or a reformed regime. As such, while the new wave would now allow for possible secession, it certainly did not guarantee the secessionist motive and instead far more often saw negotiated reform or separatism as the end state, with the possibility of revision in the future. This paradigm would play itself out into the present day, as those regimes that managed to achieve separatism rarely saw themselves entirely happy with the result, while those few that actually achieved secession quickly found that it was not the answer to the challenges that had initially spurred their extended military endeavours.

Whither the Secessionists Now?

While this work has largely looked at the military conflicts that have taken place to achieve secession, it has to be noted that these are not simply episodic events that begin with shots being fired for a political goal and then end with either a crushing of the attempt or the achievement of secession. The actual driving forces behind the secessionist attempts form as ideologies and ideas long before conflict begins, and even following the cessation of hostilities the idea of secession does not simply disappear. This often is even more complex because, as we have seen, it is often difficult for a secessionist movement to have a completely coherent, accepted, and immutable political goal. Even during and after these conflicts, attempts to achieve a satisfactory end state for any or all sides can often be a far more challenging process than the conflict themselves. On top of this, oftentimes the political project of secession or separatism can intersect or be co-opted by other political projects as the situation changes, making the challenge take on additional dimensions. Given such complexity, although this work has presented six historical case studies for contextualizing secessionist conflicts, it must be asked what the eventual end state of any of them actually has been.

In terms of the Civil Secessions, there was in theory a decisive endpoint to the conflicts involved, as was to be expected of the conventional struggles they represented. In the Congo the secessionist government under Moïse Tshombe was driven from its territory and the local administration dismantled. However, while the civil government involved was removed, these were not the only actors. The Katangan Gendarmerie, that mixture of locally raised forces and expatriate mercenaries, escaped to Portuguese-controlled Angola along with some of the administration, forming another secessionist front, the *Front de Libération nationale Congolaise*, or FLNC.[12] Its armed elements continued their regional struggle by invading Katanga twice during the 1970s in struggles that became known as Shaba I and Shaba II.[13] In both cases these invasions were beaten back by Mobutu Sese Seko's government with significant international aid, including direct military intervention by the French and Belgians.[14] Following these eruptions, the FLNC kept up its agitation, but with the resources of the province being strategically critical to Mobutu's government, the drive for secession largely died away. However, with end of the Cold War there have been continual challenges from Katanga and other regions of the country seeking their own voice during the transformation of the Congo during and after the deadly Congo Wars (1996–97 and 1998–2003).

While in the Congo there was a weak state combatting at best a political rival, the aftermath of Biafra offered a very different case. The Nigerian government emerged from the civil war as the unchallenged administration of a high-capacity African state with significant international support. However, conversely, while the secessionist state of Biafra was decisively defeated, the manner of its defeat, the emotional appeal of its government during its final year of existence, and its recasting as essentially a quasi-ethnic polity created a strong ideological project that survived long after its military defeat. In the southeast of the country there has been continuing sympathy for the Biafran project and a significant mythology formed around the three years the Biafran state existed. Numerous popular groups have claimed to continue the work of the Biafran state throughout the years of military rule, with the most prominent being the Movement for the Actualization of the Sovereign State of Biafra or MASSOB.[15] MASSOB has continued agitation for the secession of the Biafran homeland and has remained a significant thorn in the side of the government of Nigeria, leading to several high-profile clashes and crackdowns, even as the country passed from military rule back to electoral democracy. While these clashes have not broken out into a formal military conflict, the idea of Biafra and its political goals remain an animating force in parts of the country.[16] There have also been newer groups that have been more active in recent years, such as the Indigenous People of Biafra, or IPOB. IPOB has largely undertaken a peaceful approach, offering demonstrations and remembrances while demanding a referendum to answer once and for all the status of a separate Biafra. However, despite their peaceful methods, IPOB has been targeted by the Nigerian government, with several injuries or deaths caused by the Nigerian military during their crackdowns.

While the Civil Secessions studied here have experienced definitive failures of their political projects to manifest as independent states, the case studies offered for the Long Wars actually succeeded in their goals. While this makes them often an exception, as smaller conflicts started during this period (and in some cases still ongoing) have not reached their goals of independence, both of these case studies can point toward the complexity of the political goal of secession even following the successful prosecution of a secessionist conflict. As noted, both Eritrea and South Sudan emerged victorious in their conflicts. However, simple victory and even the international recognition of their independence did not necessarily answer the immediate questions of transition to civil governance that these victories allowed. In fact, although this volume has argued that the emergence of essentially a system of civil and social governance within these conflicts was a precondition to their victory, in turn the forms and capacity of this governance would lead these two case studies down very different paths following their military successes.

The story of Eritrea's successful secession was essentially one of a disparate population eventually organizing itself into a disciplined society that could sustain and prosecute its long conflict against Ethiopia. Although this took decades, the consolidation of power under the EPLF, the building of a militarized and politically conscious society, and the incorporation of numerous interest groups allowed the EPLF to continue its conflict even during the massive influx of military capacity from the Soviet bloc to the Ethiopian Derg. This same centralized and disciplined organization took the lead in the plebiscite that would help grant Eritrea its independence and then took on the role of the interim government of the new state. During this time the EPLF under Isaias Afwerki promulgated the idea of general elections and a new constitution by 1997, allowing representative government to be established within the new polity. However, this was never carried out. The EPLF renamed itself the People's Front for Democracy and Justice (PFDJ) and established itself as the sole allowed party within the new country, filling the National Assembly with its own members and installing Afwerki as the first, and to this date only, president of Eritrea.

Since then Eritrea has become an increasingly authoritarian state, with the PFDJ exercising extremely oppressive single-party rule. Dissent from this new order has largely been met with brute force and, increasingly, political imprisonment, with Eritrea's human rights record being one of the worst in the world. This oppression of its citizens has been paired with a mandatory national service component for all Eritreans between eighteen and forty, alienating the rising generation of youth who were born or came of age after the liberation struggle.[17] Beyond its domestic authoritarianism, Eritrea's foreign policy has seen it become increasingly isolated. Regionally Afwerki's regime has had both major and minor conflicts, including a conventional war with Ethiopia in the late 1990s[18] and a scuffle with Yemen over Red Sea islands. In the broader international context, the increasingly strident human rights violations of his regime have largely made Eritrea a pariah to all but the most desperate international partners, with Eritrea having been given the moniker of the "North Korea of Africa."[19]

Given these results, it is rather obvious to note that simply winning a secessionist conflict is not a guarantee of effective or representative governance, even for that group which has led the secession. While those members of the EPLF (and later PFDJ) have largely emerged from that conflict with representation and state authority, this is certainly not anything close to a universal experience. Instead, the larger part of the population has found itself within a system of governance that appears somewhat at odds with what had been promised initially: self-determination, representation, larger social caucuses, and the ability to mould a new Eritrea for themselves and their children. Instead, the expansive and disciplined organization, which had proven its strength and resilience in its long war, followed the path of many revolutionary fronts to dictatorship and authoritarianism.

However, in contrast to the EPLF, which emerged as an extremely centralized and robust secessionist front, the South Sudanese case featured a loose organization of numerous fragmented fronts that had only been welded together in the final few years of the conflict. Even then, while John Garang had managed to bring the majority of the fronts under his unified SPLM-Mainstream, his group never necessarily had control of all of the armed groups struggling against the North. Instead, it was far more common for numerous small splinter groups to continue their own struggles or for groups like the Southern Sudan Independence Movement, which themselves splintered even as they made an accommodation with the North. Garang's group had managed to at least create a basic social and political infrastructure beyond that of its rivals, and it was this infrastructure that enabled him and his followers to survive the challenging period following the collapse of the Mengistu government, which had been supplying much of his arms.

However, whereas the Eritrean infrastructure created a firm and powerful force for unification, even if it descended into authoritarianism, the South Sudanese political base would be one that had trouble enforcing its authority over its various constituent parts. This became even more evident during the period between the official cessation of hostilities in 2005 and the plebiscite that would give the South its independence. Shortly after the signing of the ceasefire, Garang was killed in a helicopter crash in July 2005.[20] He was succeeded by Salva Kiir as president, with Riek Machar retaining the vice presidency. Initially beginning their careers on very different sides of the very fractured military landscape of the SPLA, the two would often have trouble seeing eye to eye, and to many they embodied the precarious relationship between the various factions of still-armed fighters, including an ethnic split between the Dinka and the Nuer peoples of South Sudan.[21] Already dealing with the challenge of building a government, the Kiir regime then faced a series of crises as it inched toward independence. In 2010 it fought against an armed rebellion by the South Sudan Democratic Movement, which attracted a series of dissident officers and fighters who felt estranged from the new government.[22] This was followed in 2011 by another group, the South Sudan Liberation Movement, and a series of continuous raids between various pastoralist groups.[23] In all cases the government did its best to suppress or pay off these dissidents, but they represented increasingly alienated constituencies that could only be ignored at the peril of the emerging state.

At the same time, hostilities re-erupted with the North over territory in the Southern Kordofan and Blue Nile provinces, leading to serious bloodshed. While the struggle initially arose primarily because the populations of the two provinces were not included within South Sudan but the SPLA had been active within them, it took on a new cast thanks to the Abyei territory that straddled the Kordofan and Bahr el Ghazal provinces.[24] This territory was particularly oil-rich and was desired by both the North and the South, leading to support to local affiliated groups and eventual direct intervention by both the Sudanese military and SPLM. While eventually the Abyei dispute was quashed with the aid of United Nations peacekeepers, the struggle between SPLM-allied forces in the Blue Nile and Kordofan regions and the North has continued for years. While the South has avoided official involvement in these continuing conflicts, they illustrated the continued challenges and centrifugal forces facing the new and ill-defined nation regarding citizenship, participation, and borders, especially following the end of the long war against the North.

Even entering independence in 2011, South Sudan had extremely limited capacity to maintain a unified governance. The various factions within the SPLM/A remained at odds, numerous smaller armed conflicts were erupting within and without the new country, and the main figures within the government represented far more their individual ethnicized factions than the unified government. Despite the best-intentioned efforts by the international community, led by the United States, Africa's newest country was at best a fractious sovereign territory heading into 2013. In the wake of a rumoured coup attempt, President Kiir began to swiftly reorganize his government, dismissing numerous members of the police, military, and government while trying to position his own loyalists in place. At the same time, he accused his rivals of fomenting the ethnic and political divisions that had characterized so much of the secessionist struggle, heightening tensions within the country. Finally, in July 2013, Kiir dismissed Machar and the rest of his cabinet, dismantled much of the political structure of the SPLM, and indicated his continuing resolution to lead the country.[25]

These actions, occurring as they did within the context of ethnic and political tensions, precipitated a crisis. Following what was characterized as a mutiny in Juba in December 2013, fighting broke out throughout the country. By early 2014 a civil war was in full swing, with rebels led by Riek Machar fighting Bor and Kiir's forces, which were being aided by Ugandan troops that had been deployed in support of his regime.[26] Despite a series of ceasefires and mediation by the Intergovernmental Authority on Development (IGAD) and other parties, the violence continued off and on into 2016, with increasing indications of ethnic cleansing, sexual violence, and the use of child soldiers. By the beginning of 2017 there was continuing political manoeuvring between various ethnic factions and there still was no end in sight despite a threatened redeployment of an aggressive United Nations presence. Finally, in December 2017, the government signed another ceasefire with the rebels after capturing much of their territory through the previous year, and the conflict has momentarily ceased. However, the state itself remains fractured and damaged from the four years of war and the cleavages within its population remain largely unresolved, with the government largely remaining in power through external intervention and support.

While the Civil Secessions ended as formal conflicts but carried on as political causes and the Long Wars saw success in secession but failures in achieving sustainable governance, the newer wave has offered a series of other fascinating lessons. The historical contexts of the Cold War–era conflicts offered a distinct path of rebels versus the state attempting to demand their own sovereignty, which lent itself to the binary of success or failure in their secessionist goals. However, as seen in the earlier attempts, failure in the secessionist conflict did not necessarily end the desire for secession, even though the Cold War support given to sovereign states often precluded further attempts. Interestingly, it was also the end of that support that aided the success of the Long Wars, but in turn the changing nature of the African state meant that the emergent nations would deal with the challenges all other African states were dealing with. Thus, Eritrea found itself isolated while South Sudan found itself born without the capacity to sustain itself. However, this same context would offer an entirely new complexity to the New Wave secessions during and indeed after their conflicts.

For Somaliland the intervening years have not yielded much change from where the case study ended. While the post–Cold War moment has largely seen a weakening and in some cases collapse of state capacity in Africa, Somaliland has managed to not only maintain theirs but grow into its own de facto state during its now over twenty-five years of existence. However, as noted this is only really half the story. Somalia, its notional parent state, has remained a broken polity, and it is this exact collapse of capacity that has allowed Somaliland to flourish as opposed to being forced into an interminable conflict to retain its self-determination. Even long past its collapse in 1991 Somalia has not managed to rebuild itself, having faced a series of internal conflicts with clan-based warlords, the Islamic Courts Union,[27] and now the insurgent group al-Shabaab. Specifically, these latter two have significantly changed the context within which Somalia and thus Somaliland must be understood. The Islamist character of these two movements have compelled both regional and international powers to intervene. With the Islamic Courts Union's rise in 2006, Ethiopia intervened directly in Somalia to overthrow the waxing Islamist group.[28] Following the overthrow of the ICU, a new Islamist threat built around jihadis returning from Afghanistan arose in 2009 calling itself al-Shabaab. Proving itself even more formidable in its struggle against the federal government than even the ICU had been, al-Shabaab triggered an international response, with interventions by Kenya, the African Union, and the United States all occurring to blunt the power of the rising Islamist threat.[29] Following a series of aggressive campaigns during 2011–2014, the Federal Republic of Somalia and its allies managed to crush much of the conventional strength of al-Shabaab, but this simply led the group to adopt more irregular tactics, launching a series of guerrilla and terror strikes both in Somalia and abroad. While al-Shabaab has continued to be a deadly terror group, this has conversely continued the military pressure exerted by the United States as part of its Global War on Terror.

During this period of time and to the present, the federal government of Somalia has slowly built its capacity, but due to the interminable military struggles it has had to undertake as well as the challenges of rebuilding effective governance, it has only been able to promulgate a constitution and build the constituent parts of government within the past five years. However, this has meant that while the South of the country has finally been finding its way and Puntland has slowly been entering negotiations to be part of the new federal government, the de facto state of Somaliland has used its stability to fully flesh out as much of a de jure existence as it can. The informal state has used its position free from the turbulence of Islamists to reach out to its other neighbours and establish, if not formal recognition, at least lasting relationships that have helped continue the economic development of Somaliland.[30] Specifically, its port of Berbera has proven to be an excellent transit port for both landlocked states in the Horn and for trading partners in the Arabian Peninsula, offering Somaliland the status of an increasingly bustling entrepot.

However, beginning in the second decade of the twenty-first century there has been a resurgent challenge that might change the trajectory of Somaliland. The federal government has finally begun gaining enough capacity to press forward its claim as the central government of the entirety of the old state. In a large part this capacity has been aided by its African and increasingly international partners, in particular Turkey. This increasing international aid has been viewed as part of a complex series of alliances tying countries of the Horn into a larger struggle amongst the Gulf Nations, such as the United Arab Emirates, Saudi Arabia, and Qatar.[31] However, whereas Somalia has found itself aligned with Turkey and Qatar, Somaliland has recently signed an agreement involving access and construction in Berbera with Ethiopia and a United Arab Emirates–owned company.[32] This has caused a strain within the equilibrium of the region, as Somalia has formally rejected any authority Somaliland has to enter into such an agreement even as Somalia's patron Turkey has increasingly been placing pressure against the UAE. While Somalia has had little chance to challenge Somaliland since 1991, with its increasing capacity and the support of its newfound allies, a challenge to the actual state apparatus that has been built in Somaliland might not be long in coming.

Finally, in Azawad, the autonomy that was granted following the conflict between Mali and the Kel Tamasheq in the mid-1990s never quite managed to live up the expectations of the Kel Tamasheq, with the local autonomy still not allowing the Kel Tamasheq full access to the resources of the state that they had desired nor integration into the political and military structures of the state. This process was paralleled in Niger, where resources that had been promised to the Nigerien rebels never fully materialized and the integration of fighters into the armed forces under French auspices did not occur in large numbers as desired. From the end of the armed confrontations in 1995 until 2007 there was at best an uneasy peace as the Kel Tamasheq of both countries felt the peace deal they had signed was not being lived up to. This eventually led to a re-eruption of hostilities in 2007 in both countries, as armed groups of nomadic fighters launched attacks against government installations.[33]

The fighting was largely in the Kidal region in Mali and the Agadez region in Niger, with a series of piecemeal offensives by the rebels throwing the government troops in both regions into chaos. This was seen as extremely alarming by international observers, as the Agadez region of Niger held large uranium deposits that, absent formal state control, could very quickly provide fissile material to non-state actors. However, in both countries the response was relatively swift. In Mali the army quickly sent troops to garrison northern towns and launched a diplomatic offensive in the hopes of defusing the new rebellion before it spiralled further out of control. This offensive proved to be effective, as non-rebelling Kel Tamasheq communities put pressure on those fighting to end their conflict, resulting in a new ceasefire toward the end of the year. While several smaller splinter groups of rebels continued the fight and launched several audacious raids deep into Mali, by 2009 these groups had largely been marginalized and driven into Libya, where they found safe haven with Muammar Gaddafi's government. In Niger the conflict raged on for a longer period, with neither the Nigerian forces nor the Kel Tamasheq able to land a decisive blow against the other. By 2009, with the Malian conflict largely over and attempts at broadening their conflict having failed, the Kel Tamasheq forces in Niger split, with some hardliners fleeing to Libya to join their Malian brethren, while the bulk negotiated a settlement along the lines of that reached in Mali. In both cases, the agreements called for amnesty for the rebels, closer integration of the Kel Tamasheq into the government, and the disarmament of the former rebels.

There was also a sideshow of these conflicts that would prove to be a harbinger of later issues. During the conflict, six hostages were taken by a group that would become known as al-Qaeda in the Islamic Maghreb, or AQIM, which had formed in the aftermath of the Algerian Civil War. This group, professing radical Islamist beliefs, was initially confused by onlookers as being part of the larger Kel Tamasheq rebel movements and was seen as heralding a new wrinkle in these struggles. Despite this confusion, AQIM was never formally part of any of the existing Kel Tamasheq nationalist groups but was instead an increasingly capable armed group that professed its own form of radical Islam as a solution to the issues of the Maghreb and claimed connections to the larger international web of Islamist fighters known as al-Qaeda.[34] Ever since the September 2001 attacks on the World Trade Center in the United States, there had been a growing concern amongst international actors that radical Islamist groups would form the vanguard of a new era of instability in the developing world. While the Kel Tamasheq groups were not formally affiliated with AQIM, their involvement in the larger struggle was taken by many to be a warning sign of a possible new vector for Kel Tamasheq grievance.

These fears seemed to be validated with a new eruption of violence in 2012 in northern Mali. The toppling of Muammar Gaddafi's government in 2011–2012 had left those remaining Kel Tamasheq hardliners in Libya without safe haven, leading them to return to northern Mali. However, they had not spent the intervening years idle. Many had served as mercenaries in the service of Gaddafi, gaining new arms and training as well as forging connections with several Islamist groups within the region. With their return to Mali, fighting began anew, but the returning Kel Tamasheq and their allies proved to be too well armed and trained for the Malian army, decisively sweeping them out of the North and seizing Timbuktu and Gao in the opening months of 2012.[35] In turn, the Malian armed forces launched a short-lived coup, crippling the response against the combined Kel Tamasheq and Islamist offensive. However, with the North now firmly in their hands, the newfound allies fell out over arguments of how the North was to be governed. The Kel Tamasheq nationalists, represented largely the National Movement for the Liberation of Azawad (MNLA), wished to see the North finally become the Azawad state they had desired.[36] However, their Islamist allies of the Ansar Dine and the Movement for Oneness and Jihad in West Africa (MOJWA) instead wished to carry on a larger struggle to create a local Sharia-compliant state in the Maghreb. This disagreement eventually led to violent clashes within Gao in late June, leading the MNLA elements to withdraw from the city and its surrounding environs.[37]

The initial partnership had raised concerns that the new drive for ethno-nationalist secession or separatism might find potent new partners in the transnational Islamist fronts that were proliferating in the first decade of the new century. However, the falling out of the MNLA and MOJWA seemed to reinforce the central tension between the ethno-nationalists and the Islamists, where one defined itself via its national identity whereas the other demanded a larger transnational subservience to an ideological form of Islam. This fissure was reinforced as the MNLA actually launched several independent attacks on MOJWA and Ansar Dine positions, including an unsuccessful attempt to regain Gao. The fissure also led to a realignment, as the MNLA forces opened talks with the Malian government, renouncing their claim on an independent Azawad. While this nation-state had initially seemed so close at hand, the nationalists were now caught between strong and aggressive former allies and a national government that was shortly to be receiving massive international aid to put down an Islamist threat. The MNLA thus made the calculations that it would be best to abandon their hopes for Azawad again and instead drive for Kel Tamasheq home rule, an agreement the Malian government endorsed shortly before French and African Union forces arrived to bolster their struggle against the Islamists in early 2013. The French launching of Operation Serval and its supporting AU missions quickly smashed most of the Islamist forces in the North and allowed for the Malian and allied contingents to reassert their control over their territory as quickly as it had been lost the previous year.[38]

This struggle has continued to the present day. While the increasingly fragmented Islamists in the Sahel have kept up their struggle, launching isolated attacks against the government forces of Mali and Niger (as well as the remaining French and United Nations forces), the Kel Tamasheq have largely avoided being swept up into these struggles. While isolated members of their community have found their way into the Islamist camp, the communities have largely continued their struggle for self-rule and separatism within their states. While this has not always been achieved to the degree these communities would have hoped, there has not been another general rebellion by the Kel Tamasheq. and the much-feared alliance between the nationalists and the Islamists has never re-emerged. Essentially, while the ethno-nationalist and irredentist desires of the MNLA and other Kel Tamasheq have not disappeared, they have largely settled for as much autonomy as they can achieve at the moment while trying to avoid being swept into the larger and deadlier conflicts that continue to rage in the region.

A New Dynamic to Secession

Since the success of South Sudan's plebiscite and secession with the unified support of the international community, we have seen a paucity of new secessionist attempts, much less successes. This has largely been due to yet another shift in the international context since the end of the Cold War. This shift is actually revealed within the failure of the 2012 declaration of Azawad by the MNLA and their eventual re-alignment with the Malian state and their French allies. This failure of an almost-achieved de facto secession serves as a central example of the current new dynamics within secession in Africa for the near term. The immediate post–Cold War moment had reopened the question of secession for a number of reasons. The lack of international intervention or consensus had removed much of the threat of either hegemonic or regional-organization interference in secessionist struggles. In addition, there was the question of the legitimacy of the existent state and state governments amongst the international community, opening the intellectual, ideological, and even diplomatic space for possible alternative states on the continent. Simply put, in the absence of the Cold War dynamics forcing competing camps to support the existing balance of states in Africa, there was suddenly a fluidity to sovereignty that hadn't existed before.

However, this changed again in 2001 with the sudden eruption of the Global War on Terror as led by the hegemonic United States and supported by its developing world allies. Suddenly African state governments found a new avenue for international support: to cast themselves as the bulwark against the new wave of Islamist groups that were emerging across the continent.[39] This summoned the same diplomatic, developmental, and defence support that previously choosing a side in the Cold War would have, once again infusing weaker states with the capacity and international support necessary to stabilize their own monopoly on the legitimate use of violence and again largely suppressing the secessionist or separatist movements within their country. This eventually crystallized in many cases into partnerships across regions to suppress the Islamist threat and any other groups that could be construed as furthering those threats. Agreements such as the Trans-Saharan Counter Terror Partnership (TSCTP) pumped money and training into regional military partnerships that then allowed them to more effectively fight back against any illicit groups seen as threats to the sovereign state.[40]

In addition, while the Organization of African Unity had transitioned into the African Union in 2001 and reformed its initial ironclad focus on state sovereignty, particularly in issues of peacekeeping and stability, new dynamics were afoot. Often frustrated with the seeming inability of the OAU to deal with the problems they were facing, the states of the continent largely began forming more effective regional partnerships with the support of the international community. These regional partnerships existed to help stabilize the regional order of their constituent states and as such offered increased capacity to any individual member. Regional organizations such as the Southern African Development Community (SADC) or the Economic Organization of West African States (ECOWAS) offered forums where internal issues could be negotiated but in times of deep instability could also offer entire peacekeeping contingents to help restabilize a region and suppress any internal revolt.[41]

With the new post-9/11 dynamics recasting the African state as the ultimate bulwark against the Islamist threat and the consequent reimposition of hegemonic support for those existent states, the fluidity that had seemed to emerge for the concept of sovereignty disappeared again.[42] While the plebiscite for the secession of South Sudan continued apace with the blessing of the United States, almost all other ambitions for secessionists were dashed, with separatism as the at-best consolation prize for their efforts. Even to the present day, many of those populations with separatist ambitions, whether in the Casamance region of Senegal or in the anglophone region of Cameroon, have found their hopes crushed as their host countries have instead become staunch partners in the expansive and ill-defined Global War on Terror. Africa has thus largely re-entered a period where the official boundaries of states have again become immobile and even separatism remains a rare and often ill-defined quality due to the resurgence of state capacity and the growing regional consensuses on the continent.

Coda

Since the drawing of boundaries on the continent and the devolution of political power to the newborn states, there has been the concept of secession in Africa. The very first attempt happened a mere three days after the independence of the Congo on 30 June 1960, an attempt that would prove to be almost archetypal in its reasons if not its execution. Populations within the continent, defined either through common understandings of political power or through ethnic communities, have desired to exercise their own political and ultimately economic and social autonomy with respect to the nation whose borders were drawn around them. Absent any peaceful way to attempt this separation from their host state, these communities have turned to violent means to secure their separation or autonomy.

Of course, these violent means have in turn been shaped by their political, social, and economic contexts, just as are all forms of warfare. While initial attempts at secession tried to simply declare their separation and fight the conventional wars that might grant them recognition, this was quickly seen to be a pipe dream. Future attempts were more realistic, fighting protracted conflicts intended to maximize the advantages of the secessionists or separatists, who often knew the ground and communities where the struggle would be fought. For a lucky few, these protracted conflicts continued burning until the shock wave of the end of the Cold War undermined so many states on the African continent and allowed these combatants a brief window to achieve their goals of an independent state for their community.

However, for many more secessionists and separatists, the protracted war continues even as their long-time opponents and hosts regain their strength and the concept of secession recedes even further under the surface of a resurgent Africa. While these groups might be able to call upon aid from other dissidents against the new US-centric world order, this has not been enough to truly force the separation that the collapse of Ethiopia or Somalia had or even to draw on a hegemon's aid as South Sudan did. Instead, for the moment these groups can at best survive and hope for a local settlement even as they face new regional orders that deny them their desired autonomy, and the concept of secession seems as remote as it might ever have in the 1980s.

Of course, this all again depends on the current world dynamics, which are underpinned by a state-centric policy supported by a hegemonic United States pursuing a war on terror. While at the moment this might be seen as extending into the foreseeable future, one might have reasonably said that the Cold War would continue indefinitely from their perch in 1984. However, much as the Cold War ended slowly and then quickly, there is no telling how much longer the Western Consensus will last or even if the Global War on Terror will remain the central initiative it has been. Even now revisionist powers such as China and Russia are currently challenging the US-led Western consensus and the political and military establishment of the United States is increasingly looking toward near-peer adversaries and less at Islamist insurgencies. This isn't to say that the current political dynamics that support legacy African states will disappear overnight, but simply that no world order lasts forever and that even now the current global moment might be changing. While secession and even separatism on the African continent might seem remote now, those groups still waging a protracted conflict might find their own opportunity at some future date and establish their own formal sovereignty under the auspices of the nations of Africa.

Notes

Introduction

1. Frontline States is being used as a general shorthand for those African countries engaged in the loose alliance that formed during liberation struggles at any point during those struggles, including Zambia, Tanzania, Angola, Mozambique, and Botswana; however, it is understood that the formal term for the Frontline States did not emerge until later. See Gilbert M. Khadiagala, *Allies in Adversity: The Frontline States in Southern African Security, 1975–1993* (Lanham, MD: University Press of America, 2007), 10.

2. Cuito Cuanavale was a battle fought from mid-1987 to early 1988 in the so-called South African Border War between the South African Defence Force, with their UNITA Allies, and the Cuban/Angolan armed forces. It was the largest conventional battle on African soil since the Second World War, and although a tactical draw, it was strategically a crushing blow for the South Africans and likely led directly to the end of the war. See Timothy J. Stapleton, *A Military History of South Africa: From the Dutch-Khoi Wars to the End of Apartheid* (Santa Barbara, CA: Praeger, 2010), 181–86.

3. The typology that follows is largely taken from Christopher Clapham's introduction in his excellent work *African Guerrillas*. See Clapham, "Introduction: Analysing African Insurgencies," in *African Guerrillas*, ed. Christopher S. Clapham (Bloomington: Indiana University Press, 1998), 6–7.

4. Of course, it is inappropriate to view these particular struggles in a vacuum. While the individual struggles of liberation fronts occurred, they did so within the context of much larger struggles, which led these individual struggles to flow into one another. At a base level, these fronts aided and helped one another across their guerrilla struggles, with groups such as the *Movimento Popular de Libertação de Angola* (MPLA) aiding the South West Africa People's Organization (SWAPO) with their fight in what would eventually be Namibia. In addition, the larger conflicts of the Frontline States against the white settler regimes cannot be disentangled from these guerrilla liberation fronts. Not only did Frontline States such as Tanzania offer material aid and support to these liberation movements, but the larger conventional struggles such as the Border War and the Rhodesian incursions into Mozambique were undertaken specifically to try and neutralize those governments that were supporting the continued guerrilla liberation struggles.

5. Much as with the liberation struggles listed above, while the combatants within RENAMO and UNITA might have viewed their struggles as independent reform insurgencies, these did not exist independently from the other continental

conflicts. Both RENAMO and UNITA were armed and supported by the South African government as part of their larger conventional and irregular conflicts against the Frontline States and were an attempt to undermine the new governments of Angola and Mozambique, both of which were strategically threatening to the South Africans. In fact, UNITA forces fought side by side with conventional South African forces throughout the Border War, and the offensive that culminated in the aforementioned Battle of Cuito Cuanavale was largely intended to help preserve UNITA as a fighting force against the advancing Cuban and Angolan forces. The sustained conflicts that both the Angolan and Mozambican governments undertook against these insurgencies can thus be viewed both as a struggle against a reform insurgency and as part and parcel of a larger conventional war for African liberation.

6   Clapham also identifies a category called "Warlord Insurgencies" in his introduction to *African Guerrillas*, a category this volume will not delve into due to its more recent and specialized existence.

7   This will be covered more extensively in chapter 5.

8   Donald Horowitz, "Patterns of Ethnic Separatism," *Comparative Studies in Society and History* 23, no. 2 (1981): 170.

9   Henry Hale, "The Parade of Sovereignties: Testing Theories of Secession in the Soviet Setting," *British Journal of Political Science* 30, no. 1 (2000): 33–36.

10 Pierre Englebert and Rebecca Hummel, "Let's Stick Together: Understanding Africa's Secessionist Deficit," *African Affairs* 104, no. 416 (2005):400.

11 For more on the "Weak State" thesis, see Joel Migdal, *Strong Societies and Weak States: State-Society Relations and State Capabilities in the Third World* (Princeton, NJ: Princeton University Press, 1988).

12 See OAU Charter, article III.

Part I

1   The lone country left was Poland, which was at the meetings drafting the agreement but was absent at the signing of the charter.

2   This was the second purpose enunciated in chapter I, article 1 of the UN charter.

3   UN charter, chapter 12, article 76, section (b).

4   Henry S. Wilson, *African Decolonization* (London: Hodder Education, 1994), 82–83. This extremely relevant section refers to the manoeuvring of the British during the creation of the UN and the initial struggle of the USSR and China to treat trustee territories and those other "non self-governing territories" as the same in the postwar world.

5   UN charter, chapter XI, article 73, section (b).

6   Which of course were led toward independence since they fell under the jurisdiction of chapter XII as opposed to chapter XI due to their status as former Axis colonies, although Italian Somaliland was given back to Italian administration in 1950 until its joining with British Somaliland in independence in 1960. The story of Eritrea will be covered in its case study in chapter 3 of this volume.

7   Despite the fact that the Sudan was technically a sub-Saharan African nation, its independence was not greeted with any continental cheer for a variety of reasons. The first was the limited greater nationalism the Sudan had displayed—it had no Nkrumah to make its independence a fully African matter. The second was the fact that it was not entirely a British colony in international law, being instead under the joint control of Britain and Egypt, which led to revolutionary Egypt being instead the greater partner in securing the Sudan's independence.

8   Nkrumah served as prime minister for the Gold Coast Colony from 1952 to 1957, helping press forward the independence claims of the colony while also helping form an effective plan for a centralized nation under his political party's control.

9   Prior to this the French had been working within a relationship with their colonies called the French Union, which had been enshrined in the Constitution of the Fourth Republic in 1946. However, following the war in Algeria and the attempted coups in France, the Fifth Republic tried to form a looser but still French-led community called the *Communauté française* or French Community. This construct would have offered France's African colonies a degree of self-rule while keeping them within the French military and economic orbit. Guinea, under its nationalist leader Sékou Touré, refused to accept the 1958 constitution and French Community and thus transitioned to independence.

10 The Salazar government and its successor under Marcelo Caetano firmly believed that the Estado Novo had managed to bring forth the compelling idea of lusotropicalism, the idea that thanks to colonial assimilation there was one indivisible nation that stretched between Europe and Africa. This argument, coupled with their strategic island holdings, which were critical for NATO, would hold Portugal's empire in Africa in place until the Carnation Revolution in 1974.

11 These borders would finally become complete and legitimate following the creation and agreement of the states within the Organization of African Unity.

12 David A. Ijalaye, "Was 'Biafra' at Any Time a State in International Law?" *American Journal of International Law* 65, no. 3 (1971): 551.

13 Ijalaye makes this exact argument in terms of Biafra: Ijalaye, "Was 'Biafra' at Any Time a State in International Law?" 559.

14 Ricardo René Laremont, "Borders, States, and Nationalism," in *Borders, Nationalism, and the African State*, ed. Ricardo René Laremont (Boulder, CO: Lynne Rienner, 2005), 5.

15 Katanga in terms of the *Comité spéciale du Katanga* and Biafra in terms of its previous status as the state of Eastern Nigeria.

16 For more on the waning and waxing legitimacy of ethnic states, the reader is directed to Philip L. White, "Globalization and the Mythology of the 'Nation State,'" in *Global History: Interactions Between the Universal and the Local*, ed. A. G. Hopkins (New York: Palgrave Macmillan, 2006), 257–84. White maintains that following the destructive forces unleashed by nationalism in the Second World War, the idea of the ethnic state fell into disrepute and therefore lost what legitimacy it had gained since the burst of nationalist revolutions in 1848. Ethnic states would not be acceptable in the world community until the fall of the Soviet Union, when the United States began encouraging the ethnic nationalisms of the former Soviet peoples.

17 The South Sudan's complex situation does not fit easily into any category of separatism or secession or even reform insurgency, but it still serves as a useful example in this sense in that its separate administrative boundaries have indeed been used as the basis for its legitimacy as its own autonomous state.

18 A. B. Assensoh, *African Political Leadership: Jomo Kenyatta, Kwame Nkrumah, and Julius K. Nyerere* (Malabar, FL: Krieger, 1998), 79.

19 Assensoh, *African Political Leadership*, 80.

20 This was the party he formed after splitting from the older and more established United Gold Coast Convention (UGCC) in 1949.

21 Interestingly enough, Nkrumah would win this election to lead the first indigenous government of the Gold Coast while in jail.

22 Assensoh, *African Political Leadership*, 46.

23 Initially Kenyatta organized for the Kenyan African Union (KAU) and helped spread its influence across Kenya after his ascension to its presidency in 1947. Assensoh, *African Political Leadership*, 56.

24 Assensoh, *African Political Leadership*, 58.

25 The Kenyan African National Union (KANU) was one of two parties formed during Kenyatta's imprisonment, the other being the Kenyan African Democratic Union (KADU).

26 Assensoh, *African Political Leadership*, 126. Nyerere used this degree to earn a teaching position at St. Francis' School at Pugu, where he earned his nickname of Mwalimu (Kiswahili for teacher).

27 For example, Moise Tshombe was an elected member of the CONAKAT party in the Congo and Ojukwu was the military governor of the Eastern region before its secession from Nigeria.

28 Such figures as Moïse Tshombe and Godefroid Munongo are synonymous with the Katanga Crisis, and it is impossible to separate the figure of Ojukwu from Biafra.

29 For an excellent discussion of the colonial military and police in East and West Africa up to the transition to independence, Anthony Clayton and David Killingray, *Khaki and Blue: Military and Police in British Africa* (Athens: Ohio University Center for International Studies, 1989), offers a still unmatched overview of their structures and usage.

30 For more on the Gold Coast Regiment and the RWAFF, see A. Haywood and F. A. S. Clarke, *The History of the Royal West African Frontier Force* (Aldershot, UK: Gale & Polden, 1964).

31 The standard survey for the KAR is Lt. Col. H. Moyse-Bartlett, *The King's African Rifles: A Study in the Military History of East and Central Africa, 1890–1945* (Uckfield, UK: Naval & Military Press, 2016). However, this only covers to 1945, and it is best supplemented by the excellent Timothy Parsons, *The African Rank and File: Social Implications of Colonial Service in the King's African Rifles* (Oxford: James Currey, 1999).

32 Gerry S. Thomas, *Mercenary Troops in Modern Africa* (Boulder, CO: Westview Press, 1985); and Antony Mockler, *The Mercenaries* (Sugarland, TX: Free Companion Press, 1981).

33 Perhaps the most remarkable aspect of the Biafran War was the almost total mobilization of available adult and adolescent male manpower.

34 Again, see Moyse-Bartlett, *The King's African Rifles*, and Clayton and Killingray, *Khaki and Blue*, for general readings on the tactics, strategy, and construction of the inherited militaries.

35 This of course also tied into the economics of the postcolonial African nations. With little industrial base, it was easier and cheaper to train and equip infantry than it was to import tanks, armoured cars, aircraft, and the expertise to use them. This is not to say that the African armies did not do so, but that the work to make the militaries complete systems did not begin until independence and was generally incomplete at the time of the Civil Secessions.

36 A perfect example is the suppression of the Baluba in Katanga during the period of secession. Jules Gérard-Libois, *Katanga Secession*, trans. Rebecca Young (Madison: University of Wisconsin Press, 1966), 154.

37 This is not to say that guerrilla operations did not occur, but they were the exception and not the rule in these secessions and were generally only used in the pursuit of secondary objectives.

38 Although, as will be seen, part of this was due to support from its former colonial power and part was due to the historical legacy of the administration of the region.

39 While UN Security Council Resolution 169 declared the secession illegal, it was the final extension of several other resolutions, including 161 and 143, all of which will be covered in chapter 1.

40 Again, see chapter 1 for an expansion of this point.

Chapter 1

1. White defines a "civil nation" as one where the sovereign government is obliged to oversee a heterogeneous population with little to no discrimination based upon ethnicity. This is taken from Philip L. White, "Globalization and the Mythology of the 'Nation State,'" in *Global History: Interactions Between the Universal and the Local*, ed. A. G. Hopkins (New York: Palgrave Macmillan, 2006), 260.

2. Catherine Hoskyns, *The Congo Since Independence, January 1960–December 1961* (New York: Oxford University Press, 1965).

3. Jules Gérard-Libois, *Katanga Secession*, trans. Rebecca Young (Madison: University of Wisconsin Press, 1966), 9.

4. Conor Cruise O'Brien, *To Katanga and Back: A UN Case History* (New York: Faber & Faber, 2015), 84; and Gérard-Libois, *Katanga Secession*, 11–17.

5. Gérard-Libois, *Katanga Secession*, 296.

6. Patrice Lumumba, *Lumumba Speaks* (Boston: Little, Brown, 1972), 222.

7. Gérard-Libois, *Katanga Secession*, 85.

8. Hoskyns, *The Congo Since Independence*, 87; and Ernest Lefever and Wynfred Joshua, *United Nations Peacekeeping in the Congo, 1960–1964*, vol. 2: *Full Text* (Washington, DC: Brookings Institution, 1966), 14.

9. When confronted following Independence, Janssens had written "Before Independence=After Independence" on a blackboard while making a speech to the soldiers of the Force Publique. It is often assumed that Janssens was attempting to be deliberately provocative in an attempt to undermine Congolese independence, but there is little direct evidence of this hypothesis.

10. Hoskyns, *The Congo Since Independence*, 98.

11. Hoskyns, *The Congo Since Independence*, 329.

12. Stephen R. Weissman, *American Foreign Policy in the Congo 1960–1964* (Ithaca, NY: Cornell University Press, 1974), 59.

13. Georges Abi-Saab, *The United Nations Operation in the Congo, 1960–1964* (New York: Oxford University Press, 1978), 14.

14. Abi-Saab, *The United Nations Operation in the Congo*, 36.

15. For a revealing description of Mobutu's actions and its results, see Larry Devlin, *Chief of Station, Congo: Fighting the Cold War in a Hot Zone* (New York: PublicAffairs, 2008).

16. In particular, the Eisenhower administration had been viewing him as a Communist agent or proxy since his inauguration and were already working on numerous ways to remove him from power, preferably permanently. See Madeleine G. Kalb, *The Congo Cables: The Cold War in Africa from Eisenhower to Kennedy* (New York: Macmillan, 1982), 128.

17 Hoskyns offers an excellent discussion about this self-declared government in *The Congo Since Independence*, 289–92.

18 This was United Nations Security Council Resolution 161, which urged the UN to immediately take measures to prevent the occurrence of civil war in the Congo, allowing even the use of force. The council also demanded the withdrawal of all Belgian and other foreign military personnel not serving with the UN and that all member states refrain from aiding such personages to enter the Congo. The UN also decided that it would launch an investigation into the death of Patrice Lumumba and his colleagues, promising punishment to the perpetrators.

19 Gérard-Libois, *Katanga Secession*, 148–51.

20 The experiences of the Indian contingent during this period are discussed within B. Chakravorty, *The Congo Operation, 1960–63*, ed. S. N. Prasad (New Delhi: Historical Section, Ministry of Defence, Government of India, 1976), starting at p. 50.

21 O'Brien, *To Katanga and Back*, 132.

22 O'Brien, *To Katanga and Back*, 216–18.

23 Excellent discussions of Operation Morthor can be read in both O'Brien, *To Katanga and Back*, 252–88, and Chakravorty, *The Congo Operation, 1960–1963*, 70–88.

24 This episode is recounted thoroughly in Rose Doyle and Leo Quinlan, *Heroes of Jadotville: The Soldiers' Story* (Dublin: New Island, 2016).

25 There are numerous theories on how this crash actually occurred, from instrument failure to the pilot losing his way in a region that had little air traffic infrastructure. However, there is also evidence that points to foul play, with members of the intelligence services of the United States, Great Britain, South Africa, and France all implicated to various degrees in what is generally held to be an aerial attack that downed Hjammarskjöld's plane. For one of the more popular theories pointing to foul play, see Susan Williams, *Who Killed Hjammarskjöld?: The UN, the Cold War, and White Supremacy in Africa* (New York: Oxford University Press, 2014).

26 UN Security Council Resolution 169, which empowered the UN forces to use even greater force to bring the foreign personnel of Katanga to heel and formally declared the secession illegal.

27 Trevor Findlay, *The Blue Helmets' First War? Use of Force by the UN in the Congo, 1960–64* (Cornwallis Park, NS: Canadian Peacekeeping Press, 1999), 117.

28 Walter Dorn, "The UN's First 'Air Force': Peacekeepers in Combat, Congo 1960–64," Journal of Military History 77, no. 4 (2013): 1406–7.

29 Provisions included the adoption of a federal constitution, the splitting of mining royalties between Katanga and the Congolese central government, unification of currency, absorption of the gendarmerie into the ANC, restructuring of the Katangan government to allow representative government, and an amnesty for

	political prisoners. This information is from Findlay, *The Blue Helmets' First War?* 127.
30	These were largely sourced from South Africa, whose government was sympathetic to the Katangan secession. See Dorn, "The UN's First 'Air Force,'" 1409–10.
31	Gérard-Libois, *Katanga Secession*, 296.
32	Gérard-Libois, *Katanga Secession*, 316
33	For a more complete portrait of Tshombe, see Ian Colvin, *The Rise and Fall of Moïse Tshombe: A Biography* (London: Leslie Frewin, 1968).
34	Gérard-Libois, *Katanga Secession*, 293.
35	Gérard-Libois, *Katanga Secession.*, 294.
36	Gérard-Libois, *Katanga Secession*, 296.
37	Gérard-Libois, *Katanga Secession*, 310.
38	Christopher Othen, *Katanga 1960–63: Mercenaries, Spies and the African Nation that Waged War on the World* (Stroud, UK: The History Press, 2018), 105.
39	Kennes and Larmer estimate about 13,000 gendarmes. See Erik Kennes and Miles Larmer, *The Katangese Gendarmes and War in Central Africa: Fighting Their Way Home* (Bloomington: University of Indiana Press, 2016): 56.
40	Lefever and Joshua, *United Nations Peacekeeping in the Congo*, 104.
41	Lefever and Joshua, *United Nations Peacekeeping in the Congo*, 104.
42	Lefever and Joshua, *United Nations Peacekeeping in the Congo*, 194.
43	Doyle and Quinlan, *Heroes of Jadotville*, 21.
44	Chakravorty, *The Congo Operation, 1960–63*, 141–42.
45	Lefever and Joshua, *United Nations Peacekeeping in the Congo*, 212.
46	Lefever and Joshua, *United Nations Peacekeeping in the Congo*, 220.
47	Lefever and Joshua, *United Nations Peacekeeping in the Congo*, 229.
48	Ludo de Witte, *The Assassination of Lumumba* (London: Verso, 2002), 27 and 46.
49	Abi-Saab, *The United Nations Operation in the Congo*, 100.
50	Findlay, *The Blue Helmets' First War?* 8–9.
51	Charter of the United Nations, chapter XV, article 99.
52	Findlay, *The Blue Helmets' First War?* 23–24.
53	OAU Charter, article III, sections 2 and 3.

Chapter 2

1. The "Dual Mandate" refers to the two missions that British colonialism saw as its central goals: the development of the economy of a colony and the uplift and education of its people, although both of these tended to take forms that heavily benefited Britain. The initial use of the term as well as a useful explanation of its underpinnings is found in F. J. D. Lugard, *The Dual Mandate in British Tropical Africa*, 5th ed. (London: F. Cass, 1965). This work also serves as an excellent introduction to the processes that led to Nigeria taking its colonial and later postcolonial form. For another accessible source on the formation of colonial and postcolonial Nigeria, see Sir Rex Niven, *The War of Nigerian Unity, 1967–1970* (London: Evans Brothers, 1971), although his narrative of the history has a decidedly pro-Federal slant.

2. Interestingly enough, it was this relationship that led Horowitz to use the Igbo as one of his prime examples of advanced groups in backward regions in his work on ethnic secession. See Donald Horowitz, *Ethnic Groups in Conflict*, updated ed. (Berkeley: University of California Press, 2000), 243–79. As will be shown, this volume agrees that there was an ethnic motive for secession but not for the creation of an ethnic state.

3. John de St. Jorre, *The Nigerian Civil War* (London: Hodder & Stoughton, 1973), 110.

4. De St. Jorre, *The Nigerian Civil War*, 31. This is borne out in Major Nzeogwu's speech of January 15, 1966, handily reprinted in Zdeněk Červenka, *The Nigerian Civil War, 1967–1970* (Frankfurt am Main: Bernard & Graefe, 1971), 255–57.

5. Ironically, what was seen as the failure of an "Igbo" coup attempt installed Ironsi, who was himself an Igbo, at the head of the state.

6. De St. Jorre, *The Nigerian Civil War*, 60.

7. Niven, *The War of Nigerian Unity*, 85–86, serves as an excellent example of the more extreme narration of these events in terms of a suspected Igbo coup.

8. This was largely the legacy of the British military construct in Nigeria. Under the Martial Race theories that were prevalent during the colonial era, the Northerners were often largely seen as uneducated but tough and proper material for the rank and file. However, this meant that when transitioning to independence the Northern Muslim populations were often seen as unfit for commissioning and instead Southern populations were heavily recruited for the leadership positions, so that by the mid-1960s Southern populations such as the Igbo were overrepresented in the higher officer ranks while the Northern Muslim groups such as the Hausa were only beginning to catch up.

9. Červenka, *The Nigerian Civil War*, 25–26.

10. It was also marked by protests at the prominent Northern University at Zaria and the town of Kaduna. Červenka, *The Nigerian Civil War*, 26.

11. De St. Jorre, *The Nigerian Civil War*, 69.

12 Červenka, *The Nigerian Civil War*, 29.

13 Červenka, *The Nigerian Civil War*, 32.

14 Col. Yakubu Gowon's speech upon ascension to power, 1 August 1966, reprinted in Červenka, *The Nigerian Civil War*, 261–64.

15 Making matters worse, several of these incidents involved uniformed soldiers of Northern extraction, adding to the Easterners' perceptions that the Federal government would not intercede to halt the violence.

16 The numbers claimed vary throughout the conflict. Initially they were assumed to be somewhat low but climbed as the conflict continued, hitting an almost impossible high of 50,000 in Ojukwu's Ahiara Declaration. See Niven, *The War of Nigerian Unity*, 93; de St. Jorre, *The Nigerian Civil War*, 86, and Červenka, *The Nigerian Civil War*, 37–38, for commentary on the figures.

17 In later years Ojukwu would discuss this direction to Igbos to return north as his greatest regret.

18 De St. Jorre, *The Nigerian Civil War*, 108.

19 "Declaration of the Republic of Biafra," May 30, 1967. For reference, see Červenka, *The Nigerian Civil War*, 291–93.

20 See de St. Jorre, *The Nigerian Civil War*, 148–52, and Niven, *The War of Nigerian Unity*, 115.

21 De St. Jorre, *The Nigerian Civil War*, 153–56.

22 Červenka, *The Nigerian Civil War*, 57.

23 The entirety of this whirlwind mini-campaign and the short-lived Mid-West separatism is very well told by de St. Jorre in his chapter "Ojukwu's Mid-West Gamble," in *The Nigerian Civil War*, 147–75.

24 Onitsha would prove to be the site of several major engagements that also decided the fate of the small mercenary detachments that were working for Biafra.

25 Červenka, *The Nigerian Civil War*, 62; de St. Jorre, *The Nigerian Civil War*, 193.

26 Červenka, *The Nigerian Civil War*, 63. It has been said by many that after the fall of Port Harcourt the war was unwinnable by the Biafrans. The authors agree with this sentiment and regard its fall as the decisive moment of the military operations against Biafra.

27 See de St. Jorre, *The Nigerian Civil War*, 206. Other reminiscences of weapon scarcity may be found in Rolf Steiner and Yves-Guy Bergès, *The Last Adventurer* (Boston: Little, Brown, 1978) and C. E. Arachie, *The Bye-Gone: Horrors of a Crude War; Biafra Experience* (Lagos, Nigeria: C. E. Arachie, 1991), among others.

28 Červenka, *The Nigerian Civil War*, 65. The arms that were delivered had come from the French and were flown into Biafra from the former French colonies of Gabon and Cote d'Ivoire. France's reasons for supporting the Biafran cause will be covered in depth later in this chapter.

29 Červenka, *The Nigerian Civil War.*, 71.

30 De St. Jorre, *The Nigerian Civil War*, 343–44. This is when future President Olosegun Obasanjo took over the 3rd Marine Commando Division, which is discussed in his work *My Command: An Account of the Nigerian Civil War, 1967–1970* (London: Heineman, 1981).

31 A full text of the Ahiara Declaration can be found at http://www.biafraland.com/Ahiara_declaration_1969.htm.

32 This line is often quoted from Gowon's final speech after the Biafran surrender in January 1970.

33 This is somewhat complicated by the fact that Biafra still took aid wherever it could get it, including from South Africa, France, and Portugal, all three of whom had proven less than sympathetic to African self-determination. However, whereas Katanga actively aligned themselves with Belgium and other Western powers, Biafra at most quietly took what aid was offered and put forth little foreign policy aside from its demands to be recognized.

34 Although this conception was based almost solely on the idea that the region produced roughly 50 percent of the income of the nation yet received a much smaller portion of tax revenues and governmental representation.

35 See Biafra's Resolution giving Ojukwu a mandate to declare the separatist state of Biafra, which notes, "WHEREAS in consequence of these [the pogroms in the North] and other acts of discrimination and injustice, we have painfully realized that the Federation of Nigeria has failed, and has given us no protection." See C. O. Ojukwu, *Biafra: Selected Speeches with Journals of Events* (New York: Harper & Row, 1969), 191–93.

36 Niven, *The War of Nigerian Unity*, 28, offers a short and concise recollection of these events.

37 This was done by the Ironsi government following his accession to power in 1966.

38 De St. Jorre, *The Nigerian Civil War*, 132. De St. Jorre pithily notes that both the Somalis and (most importantly in terms of this volume) non-Igbos of the region might dispute that claim.

39 It is estimated that Igbos only made up about 64 percent of the total population of the East. J. N. Saxena, *Self-Determination: From Biafra to Bangladesh* (Delhi: University of Delhi Press, 1978).

40 This sort of ethnic paranoia is illustrated very effectively in Ntieyong U. Akpan, *The Struggle for Secession, 1967–1970: A Personal Account of the Nigerian Civil War* (London: Frank Cass, 1971), 92.

41 Again note the specific language mentioned in note 35. This is repeated in Ojukwu's "Declaration of the Republic of Biafra," where he lays out the claim "AWARE that you can no longer be protected in your lives or your property by any government based outside Eastern Nigeria." Ojukwu, *Selected Speeches*, 193.

42 De St. Jorre, *The Nigerian Civil War*, 39, and Červenka, *The Nigerian Civil War*, 24. Of course there is still today the contentious argument as to the exact constitutionality of Ironsi's investiture of power, with most agreeing it had at best a faint patina of legality. Even a relatively short time later the act was already being criticized by Nigerian intellectuals such as O. Onipede, "Nigeria Crisis," in *Africa Quarterly* 9, no. 3 (1969): 233–63.

43 This is of course complicated by the fact that Ironsi also drew acceptance from the East due to his Igbo heritage, whereas Gowon's Northern heritage meant he faced an uphill struggle to be accepted as legitimate within much of the South.

44 The most commonly available retelling of Ojukwu's life so far is Frederick Forsyth, *Emeka* (Ibadan, Nigeria: Spectrum, 1992). While it is an accurate retelling of the bulk of Ojukwu's life, Forsyth himself was deeply involved in the conflict and can occasionally be a rather biased and inaccurate observer.

45 For example, his interference in the Niamey peace talks of 1969, where his telegram cooled any warm feelings being expressed between the two sides. De St. Jorre, *The Nigerian Civil War*, 227.

46 Steiner, *The Last Adventurer*, and Gerry S. Thomas, *Mercenary Troops in Modern Africa* (Boulder, CO: Westview, 1985), 23.

47 Akpan, *The Struggle for Secession, 1967-1970*, 166.

48 Ojukwu's final statement to his PR firm, Markpress. Quoted in de St. Jorre, *The Nigerian Civil War*, 413.

49 De St. Jorre, *The Nigerian Civil War*, 280.

50 Arachie, *The Bye-Gone*, contains an excellent narrative of the ad hoc training the average recruit underwent, including a "graduation" exercise involving a mock deployment.

51 This figure is taken from the controversial but generally accurate Scott Report (named for its author, Col. R. E. Scott), which was regrettably leaked and printed in the July 11, 1970 issue of the *Sunday Telegraph*.

52 Červenka, *The Nigerian Civil War*, 141.

53 Steiner brazenly lionizes himself and his unit in his own volume, but Thomas offers a more muted response, writing that the utility of the 4th Commando was notably compromised by the friction it experienced with the more traditional Biafran High Command. Thomas, *Mercenary Troops*, 89.

54 De St. Jorre, *The Nigerian Civil War*, 215.

55 This was largely due to French concerns about British influence in the region and to help fragment the powerful anglophone bloc in West Africa, which otherwise could dominate regional affairs beyond the control of the French Community states spread across the region. While there were initially some accusations that this was to gain France access to the Biafran oil resources, both de St. Jorre (210–13) and Červenka (113–15) dismiss this reasoning with strong evidence that

France's actions never were focused on the oil resources of the region, although they were happy to take oil money in return for their arms shipments.

56 De St. Jorre, *The Nigerian Civil War*, 216. This is backed up in Scott's report, although he refers only to "30 large aircraft and a correspondingly large tonnage nightly."

57 Scott Report; also Červenka, *The Nigerian Civil War*, 148.

58 In Arachie, *The Bye-Gone*, the author recounts the creation and use of homemade ordinance against the Federal forces.

59 Scott Report; also Červenka, *The Nigerian Civil War*, 150, and Steiner, *The Last Adventurer*,

60 While this ambush was not of the magnitude expressed in Frederick Forsyth, *The Biafra Story* (Baltimore: Penguin, 1969), 126–27, it was still a notable victory and remained a site of interest to the press for the rest of the war.

61 It does bear noting, though, that much of the support for these secessions came from the secessionist governments leveraging natural resources that had great value to the outside world; copper for Katanga and oil for Biafra. The centrality of these resources for material and political support likely helped dictate a need for military tactics that would hold territory, a consideration that would not be present in the contemporary conflicts in Eritrea and the South Sudan.

62 See such volumes as Susan Cronjé, *The World and Nigeria: The Diplomatic History of the Biafran War 1967–1970* (London: Sidgwick & Jackson, 1972), and Joseph E. Thompson, *American Policy and African Famine, The Nigeria-Biafra War 1966–1970* (New York: Greenwood, 1990).

63 However, Nigeria did let in an international observer team formed by the United Nations to watch for atrocities and assuage international humanitarian concerns. This team's later report served as the largest single blow to the narrative of Igbo genocide.

64 Some also expected the UN secretary-general to bring the Nigerian conflict before the General Assembly under the provisions of article 99, but the secretary-general made his stance that the war was an OAU matter very clear at the Algiers Assembly of that body. See Saxena, *Self-Determination*, 44.

65 For a slightly lengthier synopsis see the invaluable Červenka, *The Nigerian Civil War*, 121–30. Other than this, whole volumes have been written such as the aforementioned Thompson, *American Policy and African Famine*.

66 Again, Červenka, *The Nigerian Civil War*, 103–10; Forsyth, *The Biafra Story*, 141–74; and Saxena, *Self-Determination*, 42.

67 Červenka, *The Nigerian Civil War*, 117–21; de St. Jorre, *The Nigerian Civil War*, 181–84.

68 De St. Jorre, *The Nigerian Civil War*, 210.

69 The reasons for this limited aid tend to be viewed as an attempt at playing both sides. If the limited aid allowed Biafra to win, then France gained its regional goals of fragmenting the anglophone bloc and having Biafra as a strong ally and potential area of economic development. If the limited aid failed to turn the tide, then France would be able to extricate itself from the situation and not lose what standing it had with the Federal Government of Nigeria. See Christopher Griffin, "French Military Policy in the Nigerian Civil War, 1967–1970," *Small Wars & Insurgencies* 26, no. 1 (2015): 114–35.

70 For an excellent overview of this Biafran propaganda campaign, see Roy Doron, "Marketing Genocide: Biafran Propaganda Strategies during the Nigerian Civil War, 1967–70," *Journal of Genocide Research* 16, no. 2/3 (2014): 227–46.

71 In fact, the OAU can only serve as a diplomatic instrument in terms of peacemaking, as lamented in Gemuh E. Akuchu, "Peaceful Settlement of Disputes: Unsolved Problem for the OAU (A Case Study of the Nigeria-Biafra Conflict)," *Africa Today* 24, no. 4 (1977): 39–58.

72 De St. Jorre, *The Nigerian Civil War*, 191.

73 Onyeonoro S. Kamanu, "Secession and the Right of Self-Determination: An O.A.U. Dilemma," *Journal of Modern African Studies* 12, no. 3 (1974): 355–76; David A. Ijalaye, "Was 'Biafra' at Any Time a State in International Law?" *American Journal of International Law* 65, no. 3 (1971): 555–56, and the already-mentioned Akuchu, "Peaceful Settlement of Disputes: Unsolved Problem for the OAU," 42–43.

74 OAU Resolution 51, adopted at the Kinshasa meeting of the OAU, September 1967, section C.

75 Although Ijalaye argues that these recognitions were unjustifiable and illegal under international law and therefore essentially invalid. Ijalaye, "Was 'Biafra' at Any Time a State in International Law?" 556–59.

76 De St. Jorre, *The Nigerian Civil War*, 196.

77 De St. Jorre, *The Nigerian Civil War*, 193.

78 As will be seen in Chapter 3, Ethiopia would break this consensus when the EPRDF took control of the country and gave permission for the Eritrean People's Liberation Front to hold a plebiscite on separation. The plebiscite itself would take place in 1993.

79 See note 55.

80 These would be the foundation of the legend of the Swedish Count von Rosen and his intrepid air force. See de St. Jorre, *The Nigerian Civil War*, 334–39, and Thomas, *Mercenary Troops*, 6.

81 De St. Jorre, *The Nigerian Civil War*, 328

82 Thomas, *Mercenary Troops*, 22. Interestingly enough, this work cites Faulques' contract, which supposedly directed him to raise a Katanga-style army manned by Biafrans but encadred by European mercenaries.

83 De St. Jorre, *The Nigerian Civil War*, 324.

84 One notable exception in this category were mercenary pilots. Modern warplanes required significant technical training to effectively use, and the air war on both sides featured foreign pilots being employed to offer air cover. On the Federal side there were pilots from Egypt and Pakistan flying Nigeria's newly acquired MiG fighters, whereas on the Biafran side there was Count Gustav von Rosen, who repurposed several small Minicon planes to offer close air support for Biafran forces.

85 David Wood, *The Armed Forces of African States* (London: Institute for Strategic Studies, 1966).

86 Červenka, *The Nigerian Civil War*, 138.

87 Scott's report was scathing in this regard and was not greeted with enthusiasm by the Federal High Command.

88 This from Major General Philip Effiong, quoted in de St. Jorre, *The Nigerian Civil War*, 223. Similar sentiments were expressed by Raph Uwechue, Biafra's emissary to Paris (at 224), and N. U. Akpan, the head of the Biafran Civil Service (Akpan, *The Struggle for Secession, 1967–1970*, 13–14).

89 Ojukwu, "Ahiara Declaration": see http://www.biafraland.com/Ahiara_declaration_1969.htm.

90 As discussed in the previous chapter.

Part II

1 The Whampoa Academy would prove to be a political hotbed, producing the majority of the military figures for both the Communists and Nationalists over the next decade.

2 For a good narrative of this period, see Suyin Han, *The Morning Deluge: Mao Tsetung and the Chinese Revolution, 1893–1954* (St. Albans, UK: Panther, 1976).

3 These conflicts were primarily between the orthodox Bolsheviks who believed that the revolution was an urban proletarian occurrence and the dissenters such as Mao who looked toward a rural peasant uprising. See Mao Tse-Tung, "From the City to the Countryside," in *Mao Tse-Tung on Revolution and War*, ed. M. Rejai (Garden City, NY: Anchor Books, 1970), 58–59.

4 Mao Tse-Tung, "On Protracted War," in *Mao Tse-Tung on Revolution and War*, 271–79.

5 Although they did receive aid from the Russians in the form of allowing them to capture the Japanese garrisons and equipment in Manchuria, overall the Chinese Communists gained almost no direct military aid.

6 Yenan had been the Communist capital throughout the Sino-Japanese War. It was retaken by the Communists within a year of the Nationalist victory

7   Translated to English, this means "League for the Independence of Vietnam."

8   Vo Nguyên Giap, *People's War, People's Army* (New York: Bantam, 1962), 48.

9   Interestingly, his statement was made using language borrowed from the American Declaration of Independence. See Ho Chi Minh, "Declaration of Independence of the Democratic Republic of Vietnam (September 2, 1945)," http://www.mtholyoke.edu/acad/intrel/vietdec.htm.

10 Giap, *People's War, People's Army*, 12–15.

11 The United States by this point had become very concerned about the possibility of a Communist government in Vietnam and assumed it would be a puppet of either Russia or China as well as a node for spreading Communism throughout Southeast Asia. Thus, although the US had initially been supportive of an independent Vietnam, the Eisenhower administration changed policy and instead offered significant financial and military aid to the French.

12 Giap, *People's War, People's Army*, 28–30.

13 Henry S. Wilson. *African Decolonization* (London: Hodder Education, 1994), 127–29.

14 Lusotropicalism was a term used to describe what Portugal saw as its "civilizing mission," with the eventual goal of assimilation into Portugal proper. Kenneth W. Grundy, *Guerrilla Struggle in Africa: An Analysis and Preview* (New York: Grossman, 1971), 91–93.

15 As will be discussed briefly, this mandate dates from the end of the First World War.

16 This act was known as the Unilateral Declaration of Independence. See Wilson, *African Decolonization*, 190.

17 Among others, see George M. Houser, *No One Can Stop the Rain: Glimpses of Africa's Liberation Struggle* (New York: Pilgrim, 1989), 199–200.

18 An excellent if brief overview of these struggles may be found in Basil Davidson, *The People's Cause: A History of Guerrillas in Africa* (Burnt Mill, UK: Longman, 1983), 119–38, as well as Thomas H. Henrikson, "People's War in Angola, Mozambique, and Guinea-Bissau," Journal of Modern African Studies 14, no. 3 (1976): 377–99.

19 Portugal received NATO support as both a member state and in return for letting the United States lease the Azores as a base. Houser, *No One Can Stop the Rain*, 160.

20 Janet Cherry, *Spear of the Nation (Umkhonto WeSizwe): South Africa's Liberation Army, 1960s–1990s* (Athens: Ohio University Press, 2012), 14.

21 Houser, *No One Can Stop the Rain*, 257.

22 Timothy J. Stapleton, *A Military History of South Africa from the Dutch-Khoi Wars to the End of Apartheid* (Santa Barbara, CA: Praeger, 2010), 160.

23 Stapleton, *A Military History of South Africa*, 161. The use of "Alone" as the secret name for the forces was intended to confuse the South African security forces as to the formation and numbers involved in the armed liberation forces.

24 Stapleton, *A Military History of South Africa*, 162 and 166. Countries that housed and trained these developing forces included Algeria, Egypt, and, most notably, Tanzania, where both inhabited military camps.

25 Stapleton, *A Military History of South Africa*, 163.

26 Ian van der Waag, *A Military History of Modern South Africa* (Philadelphia: Casemate, 2018), 266.

27 Stapleton, *Military History of South Africa*, 166

28 Houser, *No One Can Stop the Rain*, 248–49.

29 For a full narrative of the ending of the Border War, see Edward George, *The Cuban Intervention in Angola, 1965-1991: From Che Guevara to Cuito Cuanavale.* (New York: Routledge, 2012).

30 Rhodesia was initially Southern Rhodesia; however, the process of decolonization had eventually led to the territory to shorten its name. Initially in 1953 it had joined with Northern Rhodesia and Nyasaland to form the Central African Federation, but the federation fell apart in late 1963 and Northern Rhodesia and Nyasaland claimed their independence in 1964 as Zambia and Malawi respectively. This led to Southern Rhodesia renaming itself simply Rhodesia, although Britain never recognized it as such.

31 Alois S. Mlambo, *A History of Zimbabwe* (New York: Cambridge University Press, 2014), 127.

32 In fact, their hopes for a final confrontation involved a conventional invasion of Rhodesia along several axes, overwhelming the Rhodesian security forces. This invasion was still being prepared as the liberation struggle ended. Paul Moorcraft and Peter McLaughlin, *The Rhodesian War: A Military History* (South Yorkshire, UK: Pen & Sword Military, 2008), 72–77. This focus on conventional warfare is also discussed at length in Jeremy Brackhill, "Daring to Storm the Heavens: the Military Strategy of ZAPU 1976 to 1979," in *Soldiers in Zimbabwe's Liberation War*, ed. Ngwabi Bhebe and Terence Ranger (London: James Currey, 1995), 48–72.

33 Moorcraft and McLaughlin, *The Rhodesian War*, 72–76. This linkage is also talked about in David Martin and Phyllis Johnson, *The Struggle for Zimbabwe: The Chimurenga War* (London: Faber & Faber, 1982), 12. It is also notable that ZANU specifically began working with FRELIMO, who had also used Maoist strategic thought in their own struggle, and that the reconstruction of the ZANU guerrilla forces was considerably helped by both FRELIMO and Chinese trainers in Tanzania and Mozambique.

34 Moorcraft and McLaughlin, *The Rhodesian War*, 74–75, specifically note that the training of their fighters included ideological indoctrination, with the goal of

being able to radicalize the populations they worked with, including discussions of historical grievances.

35   South Africa sent limited military support under the auspices of a police mission after ANC guerrillas were found in the Zambezi Valley along with ZAPU cadres. See Stapleton, *Military History of South Africa*, 163.

36   South Africa never removed all of their support; troops were still deployed in strategic points within Rhodesia until the Lancaster House agreements but were rarely in combat. However, South Africa did choke off much of their economic support beginning in 1976 to try and force a resolution to the question of majority rule. This was done in exchange for the United States once again offering aid to South Africa per the plans of Henry Kissinger. See Moorcraft and McLaughlin, *The Rhodesian War*, 125.

37   This makes sense, given that the Maoist strain of ideology followed by ZANU was intended to mobilize the masses and get them aligned with the political program of the liberation front. This same process will be seen in successful social revolutionary initiatives put forth by the Eritrean People's Liberation Front later in this section.

38   Interestingly, this idea had been enunciated 400 years earlier in Niccolò Machiavelli, *The Prince*, trans. Luigi Ricci (New York: Signet Classics, 1999), 64–65.

39   Mao Tse-Tung, "Problems of Strategy in China's Revolutionary War," in *Mao Tse-Tung on Revolution and War*, 279–80; Giap, *People's War, People's Army*, 87–97.

Chapter 3

1   See Dan Connell, *Against All Odds: A Chronicle of the Eritrean Revolution* (Trenton, NJ: Red Sea Press, 1993), 58. This is also accepted by the account of Richard Sherman, *Eritrea: The Unfinished Revolution* (New York: Praeger, 1980), 73. Other studies sometimes choose 1962 as the starting year of the formal beginning of the conflict, as this was the year the federation was officially dissolved. A prime example of this dating of the conflict is Haggai Erlich, *The Struggle Over Eritrea, 1962-1978: War and Revolution in the Horn of Africa* (Stanford, CA: Hoover Institution Press, 1983). The authors have chosen the 1961 start date, as this book is a study of secessionist conflicts, and thus the beginning of violence marks the beginning of interest.

2   Connell, *Against All Odds*, 53. There has been relatively little work done on the actual service of Eritrean Askaris in the Italian Invasion of Ethiopia, but this service had lasting effects on the relations of the two regions.

3   Connell, *Against All Odds*, 55

4   Sherman, *Eritrea: The Unfinished Revolution*, 21.

5   Sherman, *Eritrea: The Unfinished Revolution*, 23. For the actual resolution, please reference Resolution 390A (V) passed on 2 December 1950.

6   Sherman, *Eritrea: The Unfinished Revolution*, 27. For a concrete representation of this linguistic policy, see Connell's related anecdote in *Against All Odds*, 58–59.

7   Connell, *Against All Odds*, 58.

8   Connell, *Against All Odds*, 57–58.

9   Sherman, *Eritrea: The Unfinished Revolution*, 29. In terms of the threat of violence against the Eritrean Assembly, Connell claims Ethiopian jet fighters were buzzing the city and police had surrounded the assembly while the proceedings were underway. See Connell, *Against All Odds*, 57.

10 Osman Saleh Sabbe has a very unique and complex role in the Eritrean Revolution, one that this study cannot fully explore. Let it suffice to say that he served both major liberation fronts in senior positions before being forcibly removed from each in turn. He then formed his own front to lead, although this was never a major force. While a controversial figure due to his extremely conservative Islamist and Pan-Arab agenda, his strong supply and training connections with Saudi Arabia, Syria, and other Pan-Arab states made him valuable enough for all involved to try and work with him for prolonged periods of time. He finished the struggle as a distrusted and largely irrelevant figure.

11 Sherman, *Eritrea: The Unfinished Revolution*, 74, among others, including Alexander de Waal, *Evil Days: 30 Years of War and Famine in Ethiopia*. (New York: Human Rights Watch, 1991), 41.

12 The United States had been a major patron since the end of the Second World War, rebuilding the Ethiopian military in return for the establishment of the Kagnew listening station in Ethiopia. Ethiopia in turn was an enthusiastic ally, sending troops to support the US-led efforts in the Korean War.

13 Following Haile Selassie's return, the United States became Ethiopia's primary military partner and supplier, with the total amount of aid granted during 1946–1975 equalling approximately US$286.1 million. For a total breakdown of these costs, see Sherman, *Eritrea: The Unfinished Revolution*, 176–77.

14 Sherman, *Eritrea: The Unfinished Revolution*, 43, and Connell, *Against All Odds*, 80. Connell makes the clearest case for the Anseba meeting being the first move of the new radical foreign-trained future leadership in creating a revolutionary front.

15 Connell, *Against All Odds*, 80–82, and Sherman, *Eritrea: The Unfinished Revolution*, 43–44. Both emphasize the contradictory accounts and ephemeral nature of the agreements at Adobha.

16 De Waal, *Evil Days*, does an excellent job discussing the prevalence of these blunt tactics of populace sweeps and random bombing.

17 Villagization is a common counter-insurgency strategy used since the days of the Boer War or even before. It consists of the forced removal of the populace to fortified and controlled villages to both protect them from and limit their contact with the insurgents, thereby cutting off the enemy guerrillas from any popular support. It generally emerged into the popular consciousness during the Vietnam

	War, but in that conflict as in most others the actual effects of the strategy are debatable.
18	Derg is the Amharic word for "Committee" and was the name taken by the new regime.
19	Sherman, *Eritrea: The Unfinished Revolution*, 46. This temporarily ended what has been known as the Eritrean Civil War, although the peace was always uneasy and would be shattered again in the wake of the 1978 Ethiopian offensives.
20	As will be briefly discussed, the TPLF's role in the conflict was pivotal and deserves far greater attention than is given in this chapter. For a more complete overview of their contributions, it would be difficult to do better than John Young, *Peasant Revolution in Ethiopia: The Tigray People's Liberation Front, 1975–1991* (New York: Cambridge University Press, 1997).
21	The Ogaden War began in 1977 with Somalia invading the Ogaden region of Ethiopia to support the irredentist claims of the ethnic Somalis living in the region.
22	Sherman, *Eritrea: The Unfinished Revolution*, 90. This section also deals with the wide array of weaponry involved in the transaction.
23	Sherman, *Eritrea: The Unfinished Revolution*, 90–91.
24	Connell, *Against All Odds*, 154. However, this direct ground intervention seems to have been more due to the recent arrival of the weaponry and subsequent Ethiopian unfamiliarity with it. As to the naval bombardment, it remains a pervasive but unsubstantiated rumour.
25	The numbers given for the Cuban troops vary from approximately 11,000 to over 15,000, with a large number of these being frontline combat troops and not simply advisors and trainers. Tareke notes that at several points it was Cuban armoured formations that formed the backbone of the Ethiopian counteroffensives: see Gebru Tareke, *The Ethiopian Revolution: War in the Horn of Africa* (New Haven, CT: Yale University Press, 2009), 207.
26	Sherman, *Eritrea: The Unfinished Revolution*, 90.
27	Connell, *Against All Odds*, 160–61.
28	For more details on this, see Connell, *Against All Odds*, chapter 10.
29	See De Waal, *Evil Days*, 114. De Waal pinpoints this second offensive as the one that truly broke the ELF, noting, "By continuing to engage the Ethiopian army rather than retreat, it ensured its military defeat."
30	De Waal, *Evil Days*, 115.
31	David Pool, *From Guerrillas to Government: The Eritrean People's Liberation Front* (Athens: Ohio University Press, 2001), 146–47.
32	De Waal, *Evil Days*, 117. The Red Star Campaign remains arguably the largest military campaign waged on African soil by an African nation.

33 De Waal, *Evil Days*, 184.
34 Connell, *Against All Odds*, 228.
35 De Waal, *Evil Days*, 237.
36 For a quick and useful overview of the relations between the two fronts, John Young, "The Tigray and Eritrean Peoples Liberation Fronts: A History of Tensions and Pragmatism," *Journal of Modern African Studies* 34, no. 1 (1996): 105–20, is an excellent choice.
37 De Waal, *Evil Days*, 272–73.
38 G. K. N. Trevaskis, *Eritrea: A Colony in Transition: 1941–52* (London: Oxford University Press, 1960), 5.
39 Trevaskis, *Eritrea: A Colony in Transition*, 5.
40 Sherman, *Eritrea: The Unfinished Revolution*, 7.
41 For an example, see James Bruce, *Travels to Discover the Source of the Nile* (Edinburgh: Robinson, 1790).
42 Sherman, *Eritrea: The Unfinished Revolution*, 12.
43 Sherman, *Eritrea: The Unfinished Revolution*, 13, and Connell, *Against All Odds*, 51.
44 Connell, *Against All Odds*, 52.
45 Sherman, *Eritrea: The Unfinished Revolution*, 15.
46 Sherman, *Eritrea: The Unfinished Revolution*, 15.
47 Connell, *Against All Odds*, 53.
48 Connell, *Against All Odds*, 54.
49 This has been well established in the previous chapters on Katanga and Biafra.
50 The fact that Ethiopia was the host nation in fact made things more complex, both for external political reasons, as Ethiopia remained a symbol to many Africans, and internal ones, as the multi-ethnic composition of the state would cause problems in the philosophical relations between the Eritrean fronts and those housed in Ethiopia.
51 OAU Charter, article II, section 1, and article III, section 6.
52 Against both the Kuomintang government and the Japanese, 1929–1949.
53 Against both the Japanese and the French, 1941–1954.
54 Connell, *Against All Odds*, 80 and 144.
55 Mao Tse-Tung, "On Protracted War," in *Mao Tse-Tung on Revolution and War*, ed. M. Rejai (Garden City, NY: Anchor, 1970), 275.
56 Strategically this difference would also be shown in the Cuban Revolution, where, lacking distances, the revolutionaries became dependent on the difficult terrain of the Sierra Maestra Mountains.

57 Mao Tse-Tung, "On Protracted War," 276.
58 Mao Tse-Tung, "On Protracted War," 278.
59 Mao Tse-Tung, "Problems of Strategy in China's Revolutionary War," in *Mao Tse-Tung on Revolution and War*, 279–80.
60 Mao Tse-Tung, "Problems of Strategy in China's Revolutionary War," 280.
61 Mao Tse-Tung, "The Present Situation and Our Tasks," in *Mao Tse-Tung on Revolution and War*, 285–86.
62 Mao Tse-Tung, "The Present Situation and Our Tasks," 286.
63 It was during this period that the future leadership figures of the EPLF encountered the liberation front, joined, and then were sent to China for training. See Connell, *Against All Odds*, 79–80.
64 Connell, *Against All Odds*, 163–65.
65 Interestingly, positional warfare is almost always avoided under Maoist doctrine, as it removes the advantages of mobility and stealth from the usually weaker revolutionary forces. However, in the case of the EPLF as in the case of the Cuban Revolutionaries, there was not adequate territory to pursue a mobile strategy, so strong positional warfare in mountainous terrain was used to bolster the military strength of the numerically inferior revolutionaries while guerrilla bands roamed behind the Ethiopian lines.
66 A concrete application of Mao's strategic principle number nine, as enunciated earlier in this chapter.
67 The losses incurred in repulsing the counterattacks of 1984–1985 serve as an excellent illustration of the principle that the difficulty of applying Maoist strategy is not in understanding the stages of the conflict but of properly timing the transition between them. In this case (and as the TPLF would continue to maintain) the EPLF prematurely transitioned from a combination of positional defence and guerrilla operation to a conventional mobile offence, thus opening themselves up for losses to a still strong enemy.
68 Connell notes that it took the British two weeks to defeat the Italians at Keren while it took the EPLF a mere four days to defeat the Derg forces. See Connell, *Against All Odds*, 95–96.
69 This comparison was explicitly made by scholar Basil Davidson on the BBC news broadcast of 21 March 1988. It has since been quoted or paraphrased in the majority of the literature on the Eritrean war.
70 Connell provides several excellent anecdotes about the EPLF's spirit of morale and momentum. The most telling example of the shift of power is the EPLF's dismissal of the "Sparta" brigades and their gimmickry. See Connell, *Against All Odds*, 235.
71 These ideas are central to most other revolutionary war theorists of the time, with Vo Nguyên Giap's *People's War, People's Army* (New York: Bantam, 1962) stressing the necessity of popular peasant and proletariat support. Even Che Guevara's

Guerrilla Warfare (New York: Praeger, 1970), put forth the idea of a people's war, although the Cuban Revolution at its heart was based in the bourgeoisie.

72 Sherman, *Eritrea: The Unfinished Revolution*, 98.

73 This split in turn reflects the split within revolutionary theorists, where one camp (represented primarily in the ideas of Mao and Giap) argues that the education and organization of the populace must precede the launching of any armed struggle. This view is opposed by those theorists who feel that the armed struggle is paramount, and that any and all organization and changes are only truly possible after a military victory. Guevara's idea of *foquismo*, where the struggle is sparked by military action first and transformation later, falls into this category.

74 A full accounting of these concepts can be found in article 2, section A of the document "Objectives of the National Democratic Programme of the EPLF," which can be found in a number of publications, including Appendix B of Sherman, *Eritrea: The Unfinished Revolution*.

75 The example of Zagher is a particularly famous one, as it served as a model village for the EPLF and was reported on in both Connell, *Against All Odds*, 109–26, and Pool, *From Guerrillas to Government*, 111–14.

76 See "Objectives of the National Democratic Programme of the EPLF," article 2, section B.

77 "Objectives of the National Democratic Programme of the EPLF," article 2, section E.

78 "Objectives of the National Democratic Programme of the EPLF," article 4, section a, part 8.

79 Pool, *From Guerrillas to Government*, 123–24.

80 Pool, *From Guerrillas to Government*, 124.

81 "Objectives of the National Democratic Programme of the EPLF," article 3, section B, part 1.

82 Connell, *Against All Odds*, 38–39.

83 Sherman, *Eritrea: The Unfinished Revolution*, 104.

84 "Objectives of the National Democratic Programme of the EPLF," article 3, section C.

85 Sherman, *Eritrea: The Unfinished Revolution*, 102

86 "Objectives of the National Democratic Programme of the EPLF," article 4, section B.

87 Notably, the role of women in the aftermath of the success of the FLN has been cited as less than satisfactory.

88 Sherman, *Eritrea: The Unfinished Revolution*, 106.

89 Connell does an excellent job explaining the extraordinary effects that these reforms had on women's lives in Eritrea. His chapter "Destroying Shyness" is an excellent window into the process. Connell, *Against All Odds*, 127–37.

90 Connell also offers an interesting look into the interconnectedness of the revolutionary consciousness with the refusal of poor peasants to consent to the stripping of Eritrean women of their rights, rightly seeing the parallels between their own new-found freedoms and those of women. Connell, *Against All Odds*, 136.

91 Gérard Chaliand, "The Horn of Africa's Dilemma," *Foreign Policy* no. 30 (Spring 1978): 126.

92 Even after the return of Ethiopian troops in the 1978–1985 offensives, the EPLF loyalist areas still resisted the Derg forces and clandestinely aided the EPLF, a decisive factor in the struggle.

93 The current best work on the subject of the TPLF is Young, *Peasant Revolution in Ethiopia*.

94 During this same time period the ELF established closer ties with other Ethiopian dissident groups such as the Ethiopian Democratic Union and the Ethiopian People's Revolutionary Party. These unfortunately did not prove as successful as the TPLF, and during the second Eritrean Civil War the TPLF helped drive the ELF out of Eritrean and Tigrayan territory.

95 Pool, *From Guerrillas to Government*, 149, and Young, "The Tigray and Eritrean Peoples Liberation Fronts," 107.

96 Young, "The Tigray and Eritrean Peoples Liberation Fronts," 108. As mentioned in note 67, this is part of a larger debate as to the timing of the alterations of mode of warfare in the Maoist framework of conflict.

97 Young, *Peasant Revolution in Ethiopia*, 152–54.

98 Young, *Peasant Revolution in Ethiopia*, 154–55.

99 Young, *Peasant Revolution in Ethiopia*, 156–57. This splinter group, the Democratic Movement for the Liberation of Eritrea (DMLE), eventually fell by the wayside and by 1991 only existed abroad.

100 Despite the Ogaden War's conclusion in 1978, Ethiopia and Somalia each maintained significant troop levels in the region and tensions remained high. After a small clash in 1988, the two countries agreed to withdraw their troops from the border region.

101 Interestingly, the TPLF itself began as a separatist insurgency and only later became a reform insurgency by Clapham's definition. The transition left them in an interesting form, as they advocated nationalist separatism but in a federal form under a greater Ethiopian government.

Chapter 4

1. Dunstan M. Wai, *The African-Arab Conflict in the Sudan* (New York: Africana, 1981), 26; Francis Mading Deng, *War of Visions: Conflict of Identities in the Sudan* (Washington, DC: Brookings Institution, 1995), 10; Douglas H. Johnson, *The Root Causes of Sudan's Civil Wars* (Bloomington: Indiana University Press, 2003), 4.
2. Johnson, *The Root Causes of Sudan's Civil Wars*, 5.
3. Hilde F. Johnson, *Waging Peace in Sudan: The inside Story of the Negotiations That Ended Africa's Longest Civil War* (Eastbourne, UK: Sussex Academic Press, 2011), 6–7; Deng, *War of Visions*, 10–11; Wai, *The African-Arab Conflict in the Sudan*, 30–32.
4. Wai, *The African-Arab Conflict in the Sudan*, 35; Johnson, *The Root Causes of Sudan's Civil Wars*, 10–11.
5. Scopas Sekwat Poggo, *The First Sudanese Civil War: Africans, Arabs, and Israelis in the Southern Sudan, 1955–1972* (Basingstoke, UK: Palgrave Macmillan, 2011), 30.
6. Wai, *The African-Arab Conflict in the Sudan*, 34.
7. Robert O. Collins, *The Southern Sudan in Historical Perspective* (New Brunswick, NJ: Transaction, 2007), 51.
8. Johnson, *The Root Causes of Sudan's Civil Wars*, 23.
9. Johnson, *The Root Causes of Sudan's Civil Wars*, 24.
10. Wai, *The African-Arab Conflict in the Sudan*, 39.
11. Collins, *The Southern Sudan in Historical Perspective*, 59–60.
12. Poggo, *The First Sudanese Civil War*, 37.
13. Poggo, *The First Sudanese Civil War*, 42.
14. Poggo, *The First Sudanese Civil War*, 45.
15. Wai, *The African-Arab Conflict in the Sudan*, 74.
16. Johnson, *The Root Causes of Sudan's Civil Wars*, 31.
17. Poggo, *The First Sudanese Civil War*, 63; Deng, *War of Visions*, 139.
18. There is some debate as to how connected the 1955 mutineers actually are to the formation of the Anya-nya. For an alternative viewpoint, see Øystein H. Rolandsen, "The Making of the Anya-Nya Insurgency in the Southern Sudan, 1961–64," *Journal of Eastern African Studies* 5, no. 2 (2011): 212.
19. Deng, *War of Visions*, 140.
20. Wai, *The African-Arab Conflict in the Sudan*, 92.
21. Johnson, *The Root Causes of Sudan's Civil Wars*, 31.
22. Poggo, *The First Sudanese Civil War*, 74–87.
23. Wai, *The African-Arab Conflict in the Sudan*, 97.

24 Wai, *The African-Arab Conflict in the Sudan*, 98–99.

25 Mohamed Omer Beshir, *The Southern Sudan: From Conflict to Peace* (London: C. Hurst, 1975), 5–6.

26 Wai, *The African-Arab Conflict in the Sudan*, 108.

27 Poggo, *The First Sudanese Civil War*, 123.

28 Poggo, *The First Sudanese Civil War*, 171.

29 Poggo, *The First Sudanese Civil War*, 175.

30 Robert O. Collins, *A History of Modern Sudan* (New York: Cambridge University Press, 2008), 103.

31 Collins, *A History of Modern Sudan*, 106.

32 Beshir, *The Southern Sudan*, 110.

33 Matthew LeRiche and Matthew B. Arnold, *South Sudan: From Revolution to Independence* (London: Hurst, 2012), 28.

34 Beshir, *The Southern Sudan*, 32; William H. Dorsey, "Anyanya Leader Joseph Lagu," *Africa Report* 17, no. 9 (1972): 18.

35 Johnson, *The Root Causes of Sudan's Civil Wars*, 41–42.

36 During this period scattered groups of Anya-nya fighters occasionally continued to attack the Sudanese military forces, but this was not as part of an accepted strategy of the South to continue the conflict.

37 For example, Numeiry put up Abel Alier as the sole candidate for president of the High Executive Council, ensuring his election. Collins, *A History of Modern Sudan*, 115.

38 Johnson, *The Root Causes of Sudan's Civil Wars*, 41; Collins, *A History of Modern Sudan*, 114. Part of the reason for this was that the underdeveloped educational system of the South often meant Southern fighters lacked the formal education to qualify for officer positions within the Sudanese military.

39 Johnson, *The Root Causes of Sudan's Civil Wars*, 61; LeRiche and Arnold, *South Sudan*, 58.

40 LeRiche and Arnold, *South Sudan*, 62.

41 Philippa Scott, "The Sudan Peoples' Liberation Movement (SPLM) and Liberation Army (SPLA)," *Review of African Political Economy* 12, no. 33 (1985): 70.

42 LeRiche and Arnold, *South Sudan*, 63.

43 Scott, "The Sudan Peoples' Liberation Movement (SPLM) and Liberation Army (SPLA)," 71.

44 Douglas H. Johnson, "The Sudan People's Liberation Army and the Problem of Factionalism," in *African Guerrillas*, ed. Christopher Clapham (Oxford: James Currey, 1998), 61.

45 Johnson, "The Sudan People's Liberation Army and the Problem of Factionalism," 58.

46 Johnson, "The Sudan People's Liberation Army and the Problem of Factionalism," 66–67.

47 John Young, "Sudan: Liberation Movements, Regional Armies, Ethnic Militias & Peace," *Review of African Political Economy* 30, no. 97 (2003): 424. Young is skeptical of the structure of the civil administration, but notes its existence and ability to keep the region loyal to the SPLM/A.

48 Peter Woodward, *Sudan, 1898-1989: The Unstable State* (Boulder, CO: L. Rienner, 1990), 158.

49 Johnson, *The Root Causes of Sudan's Civil Wars*, 72.

50 Local militias would offer a potent and, most importantly, inexpensive tool to pursue the continuing counter-insurgency campaign.

51 LeRiche and Arnold, *South Sudan*, 72; Johnson, *The Root Causes of Sudan's Civil Wars*, 81–82.

52 Johnson, *The Root Causes of Sudan's Civil Wars*, 85.

53 LeRiche and Arnold, *South Sudan*, 74.

54 As seen in the previous chapter.

55 Johnson, "The Sudan People's Liberation Army and the Problem of Factionalism," 62.

56 Johnson, "The Sudan People's Liberation Army and the Problem of Factionalism," 63.

57 Johnson, *The Root Causes of Sudan's Civil Wars*, 116. As Johnson notes, there had been the assumption that the initial rupture would be between Dinka and Nuer forces, but instead the strong ties of some SPLA forces, which contained both Dinka and Nuer troops, led to a confrontation between two groups of Nuer combatants.

58 Johnson, *The Root Causes of Sudan's Civil Wars*, 99.

59 LeRiche and Arnold, *South Sudan*, 90.

60 Johnson, *The Root Causes of Sudan's Civil Wars*, 102.

61 Johnson, *The Root Causes of Sudan's Civil Wars*, 121.

62 LeRiche and Arnold, *South Sudan*, 99.

63 LeRiche and Arnold, *South Sudan*, 106. This was accomplished with significant Intergovernmental Authority on Development (IGAD) involvement.

64 Manṣūr Khālid, *War and Peace in Sudan: A Tale of Two Countries* (London: Kegan Paul, 2003), 75.

65 Woodward, *Sudan, 1898-1989*, 107.

66 Johnson, *The Root Causes of Sudan's Civil Wars*, 31. Johnson notes that initially at least SANU kept their slogan as "self-determination" to avoid the negative optics of secessionist attempts, but the leadership generally assumed self-determination would lead directly into independence.

67 They did, however, reach out to Southern officers in the Sudanese Army to try and get them to defect to form their own forces. See Poggo, *The First Sudanese Civil War*, 64.

68 The Anya-nya were very lightly armed until 1964, when the Abboud government was in turmoil and more hardware fell to them. The surrender of the Simbas fleeing the Congo also offered a ready store of arms. Johnson, *The Root Causes of Sudan's Civil Wars*, 31.

69 Rolandsen disagrees and makes a convincing argument for a closer relationship between the political and military branches of the struggle. Rolandsen, "The Making of the Anya-Nya Insurgency in the Southern Sudan, 1961–64," 212.

70 Wai, *The African-Arab Conflict in the Sudan*, 100.

71 Johnson, *The Root Causes of Sudan's Civil Wars*, 32–34.

72 Wai, *The African-Arab Conflict in the Sudan*, 110–11.

73 Collins, *A History of Modern Sudan*, 103–6.

74 Collins, *A History of Modern Sudan*, 110–11.

75 Poggo, *The First Sudanese Civil War*, 143.

76 The Soviets would deploy significant forces in both these regions. While they offered military hardware to the North and there are some accusations of the provision of pilots, the Soviet involvement in the Sudan never reached the levels of these two primary conflicts.

77 Johnson, "The Sudan People's Liberation Army and the Problem of Factionalism," 60–62.

78 Collins, *A History of Modern Sudan*, 143.

79 Johnson, "The Sudan People's Liberation Army and the Problem of Factionalism," 64–65.

80 Johnson, "The Sudan People's Liberation Army and the Problem of Factionalism," 65.

81 Johnson, "The Sudan People's Liberation Army and the Problem of Factionalism," 65.

Part III

1 An excellent account of this period can be found written by the hand of Gorbachev himself. See Mikhail Gorbachev, *Perestroika: New Thinking for Our Country and the World* (Norwalk, CT: Easton Press, 1996).

2   A series of interviews and recollections of this coup attempt have been archived online for reading and use, called collectively "Voice from and (Attempted) Soviet Coup," edited by Anya Chernyakhovskaya, John Jirik, and Nikolai Lamm, at https://sites.google.com/site/jiriksoviet/.

3   In stark contrast to the Congo Crisis, where eventually the United Nations intervened to patch the entirety of the Congo back together following the multiple fissures within its territories.

4   See Philip White, "Globalization and the Mythology of the 'Nation State,'" in *Global History: Interactions Between the Universal and the Local*, ed. A.G. Hopkins (New York: Palgrave Macmillan, 2006): 257–84.

5   Michael K. Addo, "Political Self Determination Within the Context of the African Charter on Human and Peoples' Rights," *Journal of African Law* 32, no. 2 (1988): 184–85. Addo notes this left a remarkable narrow and limited definition of what "people" were eligible for self-determination, with members of the OAU essentially being the Namibian people, non-white South Africans, and the Saharaoui people of the western Sahara.

6   See chapter 3 and its ending.

7   As noted in the initial chapter, this idea is largely taken from Pierre Englebert and Rebecca Hummel. "Let's Stick Together: Understanding Africa's Secessionist Deficit." *African Affairs* 104, no. 416 (2005): 400.

8   For a fuller critique of the role of the state in postcolonial Africa, see Basil Davidson, *The Black Man's Burden: Africa and the Curse of the Nation-State* (New York: Times Books, 1992).

9   This isn't to say that there were not several states that rejected this bipolar construct. Led by Nasser in Egypt and Sukarno in Indonesia, a large bloc of the decolonizing world chose to cast itself as non-aligned in the great global struggle and not hew to any particular allegiance. However, the simple fact of the matter was that the vast majority of these countries were economically underdeveloped, and despite the growth and support offered by the non-aligned faction, they still needed the manufactured goods and global markets that the two poles of the struggle offered. While these states did not necessarily accept the global Cold War, they were obliged to still deal with its effects and shape their diplomatic, economic, and military choices around its dynamics.

10 Alicia C. Decker and Andrea L. Arrington, *Africanizing Democracies, 1980–Present* (New York: Oxford University Press, 2015), 2.

11 Frederick Cooper, *Africa since 1940: The Past of the Present* (New York: Cambridge University Press, 2002), 5.

12 Cooper, *Africa since 1940*, 5–6.

13 Jonathan T. Reynolds, *Sovereignty and Struggle: Africa and Africans in the Era of the Cold War* (New York: Oxford University Press, 2015), 30–35 and 38–41.

14 Cooper, *Africa since 1940*, 160.

15   Cooper, *Africa since 1940*, 53.

16   Uganda appears in both lists thanks to the career of Field Marshal Idi Amin, who rose to power in Uganda in 1971 under the patronage of the West and enjoyed warm relations with Britain and Israel. However, by the mid-1970s these patrons had cooled on Amin and were beginning to refuse his demands for robust military and financial support. This led to Amin seeking and receiving Soviet support for his regime, as well as conspicuously dropping his connections to the capitalist powers.

17   Decker and Arrington, *Africanizing Democracies*, 2.

18   Mobutu would briefly attempt some show reforms to continue staying in the West's grace, but these would not last long enough or go far enough to qualify as anything beyond a façade. See Jason K. Stearns, *Dancing in the Glory of Monsters: The Collapse of the Congo and the Great War of Africa* (New York: PublicAffairs, 2012), 64–65.

19   This had also shown some recent non-secessionist success with the victory of Yoweri Museveni's National Resistance Army in the Ugandan Bush War, which brought Museveni to power. Some discussion of his reported methods can be found in his speech to the US Army's Command and General Staff College captured in Yoweri Museveni, "The Strategy of Protracted People's War: Uganda," in *Military Review* 88, no. 6 (2008): 4–13.

Chapter 5

1   Maria Brons, *Society, Security, Sovereignty, and the State in Somalia: From Statelessness to Statelessness?* (Utrecht: International Books, 2001), 245.

2   I. M. Lewis, *Making and Breaking States in Africa: The Somali Experience* (Trenton, NJ: Red Sea Press, 2010), 65.

3   As will be discussed at greater length later in this chapter, the Somali population had been divided between regions controlled by the British, French, Italians, and Ethiopians. During decolonization, only Italian Somaliland and British Somaliland were joined to become Somalia. French Somaliland voted against joining Somalia, although this plebiscite is still looked upon with some suspicion. The Ogaden region, despite being a Somali homeland, was retained by the Ethiopian state per their 1897 treaty with Great Britain. More will be discussed on this region shortly. Finally, a significant Somali population lived in the northeast region of Kenya; this population would later fight the lengthy but ultimately unsuccessful Shifta War through the 1960s to try and effect irredentist goals.

4   The Haud was the extensive grassy lowlands within the Ethiopian-held region of Somali territory. It had commonly been a source of contention, with Ethiopia claiming the Haud but with it bordering Somalia, Djibouti, and British Somaliland.

5   Mark Bradbury, *Becoming Somaliland* (Oxford: James Currey, 2008), 26.

6   Daniel Compagnon, "Somali Armed Movements," in *African Guerrillas*, ed. Christopher Clapham (Oxford: James Currey, 1998), 74.

7   Lewis, *Making and Breaking States in Africa*, 119; Gebru Tareke, *The Ethiopian Revolution: War in the Horn of Africa* (New Haven, CT: Yale University Press, 2009), 187. Tareke goes to great lengths to discuss the coordination between the WSLF and Siad Barre's military regime.

8   Bradbury, *Becoming Somaliland*, 39.

9   Bradbury, *Becoming Somaliland*, 42.

10   Bradbury, *Becoming Somaliland*, 61.

11   Daniel Compagnon, "Somali Armed Movements," in *African Guerrillas*, ed. Christopher S. Clapham (Oxford: James Currey, 1998), 80; Bradbury, *Becoming Somaliland*, 44.

12   Bradbury, *Becoming Somaliland*, 62.

13   Compagnon, "Somali Armed Movements," 80.

14   Beyond that of the Derg regime in Ethiopia.

15   Bradbury, *Becoming Somaliland*, 62.

16   Bradbury, *Becoming Somaliland*, 63; Brons, *Society, Security, Sovereignty, and the State in Somalia*, 211.

17   Brons, *Society, Security, Sovereignty, and the State in Somalia*, 212.

18   Brons, *Society, Security, Sovereignty, and the State in Somalia*, 213.

19   This conflict is most fixed in international eyes through the American-led Operation Restore Hope.

20   Part of the tensions between the north and south had to do with their colonial history. The north had been a British colony and had been administered as British Somaliland; the south had been an Italian colony and administered as Italian Somaliland. These divisions would follow Somalia into its unification and decolonization, where the administrators and soldiers of the former British colony were often marginalized in the new government.

21   Bradbury, *Becoming Somaliland*, 82.

22   Lewis, *Making and Breaking States in Africa*, 151–53.

23   Lewis, *Making and Breaking States in Africa*, 160–61; Bradbury, *Becoming Somaliland*, 89.

24   Bradbury, *Becoming Somaliland*, 89.

25   Brons, *Society, Security, Sovereignty, and the State in Somalia*, 249.

26   Lewis, *Making and Breaking States in Africa*, 169.

27   Brons, *Society, Security, Sovereignty, and the State in Somalia*, 249–50.

28 Bradbury, *Becoming Somaliland*, 98–101; Brons, *Society, Security, Sovereignty, and the State in Somalia*, 250–51.

29 Bradbury, *Becoming Somaliland*, 99.

30 Bradbury, *Becoming Somaliland*, 101.

31 Diya-paying groups are the family groupings that are defined by who would owe the fine for the wrongdoing of a member and thereby form an ad hoc self-contained authority group, as the group has direct responsibility for its members and their behaviour.

32 Lewis, *Making and Breaking States in Africa*, 176–77.

33 Bradbury, *Becoming Somaliland*, 116–17.

34 Bradbury, *Becoming Somaliland*, 121.

35 Bradbury, *Becoming Somaliland*, 122–23.

36 With the death of Aideed, the strongest faction in the south lost its leader and thus any drive for "federalism" was significantly weakened.

37 Brons, *Society, Security, Sovereignty, and the State in Somalia*, 252; Bradbury, *Becoming Somaliland*, 124.

38 Bradbury, *Becoming Somaliland*, 125.

39 The Transitional National Government was set up in the southern part of Somalia in Mogadishu and purported to represent the entirety of former Somalia as the legitimate government. It had been granted wide international recognition upon its formation but had been unable to effectively project its power and authority to all of its claimed territory. The Transitional National Government has since been superseded by first the Transitional Federal Government and now the Federal Government of Somalia.

40 Puntland was another breakaway territory that attained self-government upon the collapse of the central Somalian state. Encompassing the northeastern portion of Somalia, including the tip of the Horn, Puntland managed to form its own government and has largely governed itself since. However, since the rise of the Federal Government, Puntland has been increasingly aligning itself with the central government and has offered no support or recognition to Somaliland.

41 Bradbury, *Becoming Somaliland*, 127.

42 Bradbury, *Becoming Somaliland*, 133.

43 I. M. Lewis, *The Modern History of Somaliland: From Nation to State* (New York: Praeger, 1965), 61.

44 Helen Chapin Metz et al., *Somalia: A Country Study* (Washington, DC: Federal Research Division, Library of Congress, 1993), 14–15.

45 Lewis, *The Modern History of Somaliland*, 130.

46 Lewis, *The Modern History of Somaliland*, 139–40.

47 Bradbury, *Becoming Somaliland*, 31.
48 Lewis, *The Modern History of Somaliland*, 152.
49 Lewis, *The Modern History of Somaliland*, 163–64.
50 Bradbury, *Becoming Somaliland*, 33.
51 Bradbury, *Becoming Somaliland*, 34.
52 Brons, *Society, Security, Sovereignty, and the State in Somalia*, 255.
53 Bradbury, *Becoming Somaliland*, 142–43.
54 Bradbury, *Becoming Somaliland*, 81.
55 Bradbury, *Becoming Somaliland*, 153. It is estimated that Ethiopian trade makes up 30–50 percent of the total trade passing through Berbera.
56 Bradbury, *Becoming Somaliland*, 154.
57 Lewis, *Making and Breaking States in Africa*, 149–50.
58 Said S. Samatar, *Somalia: A Nation in Turmoil* (London: Minority Rights Group, 1991), 25.
59 Lewis, *Making and Breaking States in Africa*, 98–99.
60 Bradbury, *Becoming Somaliland*, 41.
61 Brons, *Society, Security, Sovereignty, and the State in Somalia*, 257–58.
62 Brons, *Society, Security, Sovereignty, and the State in Somalia*, 267.

Chapter 6

1 Priscilla Ellen Starratt, "Tuareg Slavery and Slave Trade," *Slavery & Abolition* 2, no. 2 (1981): 84.
2 Susan Rasmussen, "Disputed Boundaries: Tuareg Discourse on Class and Ethnicity," *Ethnology* 31, no. 4 (1992): 352.
3 Baz Lecocq, *Disputed Desert: Decolonisation, Competing Nationalisms and Tuareg Rebellions in Northern Mali* (Boston: Brill, 2010), 2.
4 Thomas K. Seligman, "Art of Being Tuareg Sahara Nomads in a Modern World," *African Arts* 39, no. 3 (2006): 58.
5 Starratt, "Tuareg Slavery and Slave Trade," 84.
6 Lecocq, *Disputed Desert*, 4.
7 Lecocq, *Disputed Desert*, 4–5.
8 Lecocq, *Disputed Desert*, 5.
9 Lecocq, *Disputed Desert*, 5, and Seligman, "Art of Being Tuareg Sahara Nomads in a Modern World," 59. Seligman proposes descent from Jewish populations that fled to the Sahara, which seems unlikely.

10   Starratt, "Tuareg Slavery and Slave Trade," 88.
11   Starratt, "Tuareg Slavery and Slave Trade," 88.
12   Starratt, "Tuareg Slavery and Slave Trade," 98.
13   Starratt, "Tuareg Slavery and Slave Trade," 98.
14   Baz Lecocq, "The Bellah Question: Slave Emancipation, Race, and Social Categories in Late Twentieth-Century Northern Mali," *Canadian Journal of African Studies / Revue Canadienne Des Études Africaines* 39, no. 1 (2005): 52.
15   Baz Lecocq and Georg Klute, "Tuareg Separatism in Mali," *International Journal: Canada's Journal of Global Policy Analysis* 68, no. 3 (2013): 425.
16   Lecocq, *Disputed Desert*, 33.
17   The OCRS was floated as a concept in 1956–57 but survived as an idea beyond the independence of the French Colonies. However, given the vague issues around border, sovereignty, and trade involved in its conception, the nationalist governments did not find it as appealing as did its architects. See LeCocq, *Disputed Desert*, 41.
18   Lecocq, *Disputed Desert*, 60–61.
19   Lecocq, *Disputed Desert*, 40.
20   This date is generally recognized due to the theft at gunpoint of a native goumier's gun and equipment by two Kel Tamasheq insurgents and the insurgents' subsequent declaration of resistance. See LeCocq, *Disputed Desert*, 151.
21   Lecocq, *Disputed Desert*, 161.
22   Lecocq, *Disputed Desert*, 168.
23   Lecocq, *Disputed Desert*, 168.
24   Lecocq, *Disputed Desert*, 168.
25   Lecocq, *Disputed Desert*, 175.
26   Lecocq, *Disputed Desert*, 177.
27   Lecocq, *Disputed Desert*, 180.
28   Lecocq, *Disputed Desert*, 186.
29   Lecocq, *Disputed Desert*, 158.
30   Ines Kohl, "Modern Nomads, Vagabonds, or Cosmopolitans? Reflections on Contemporary Tuareg Society," *Journal of Anthropological Research* 66, no. 4 (2010): 450.
31   Kohl, "Modern Nomads, Vagabonds, or Cosmopolitans?" 452–53.
32   Lecocq, *Disputed Desert*, 206.
33   Kohl, "Modern Nomads, Vagabonds, or Cosmopolitans?" 450.

34   Lecocq, *Disputed Desert*, 207.

35   Lecocq, *Disputed Desert*, 222.

36   The applicability of the nation-state ideal can be seen through the *Tenekra* creed of "One Country, One Goal, One People." See LeCocq, *Disputed Desert*, 218.

37   Lecocq, *Disputed* Desert, 230.

38   Lecocq, *Disputed Desert*, 233.

39   Lecocq, *Disputed Desert*, 233.

40   At the time the government of Morocco was fighting to retain its control over the region known as the Western Sahara against its indigenous liberation movement, the *Frente Popular de Liberación de Saguía el Hamra y Río de Oro*, or Polisario. The Western Sahara had been annexed by Morocco as part of a tripartite agreement with Spain, who had ruled the region since 1884. However, its local populace believed they had the right to self-determination and had taken up arms to enforce that right. Algeria had been supporting Polisario's efforts against Morocco and had been urging the older Kel Tamasheq leaders to channel the armed support of their followers to aid Polisario's efforts as well.

41   Lecocq *Disputed Desert*, 239.

42   Lecocq, *Disputed Desert*, 243.

43   Lecocq, *Disputed Desert*, 244.

44   Lecocq and Klute, "Tuareg Separatism in Mali," 426.

45   Technicals were the name given to arms platforms used in the Libyan-Chad wars that were constructed out of all-terrain four-wheel-drive pickup trucks with a crew-served weapon in the bed, usually a heavy machine gun or a rocket launcher. These platforms became iconic within these conflicts, combining powerful weaponry with reliable mobility, and their centrality to the Chadian war efforts eventually led to these military operations being called the Toyota Wars after the ubiquitous Toyota Hilux pickup trucks that made up the bulk of their technicals. Many armed groups noted the effectiveness and simplicity of these weapons systems and they were quickly adopted across the developing world.

46   Lecocq and Klute, "Tuareg Separatism in Mali," 426; Lecocq, *Disputed Desert*, 253.

47   Lecocq, *Disputed Desert*, 257.

48   The signatory was Iyad ag Ghali, who would later emerge as the leader of Ansar al-Din in the later rounds of fighting. See Lawrence E. Cline, "Nomads, Islamists, and Soldiers: The Struggles for Northern Mali," *Studies in Conflict & Terrorism* 36, no. 8 (2013): 619–20.

49   Thomas Krings, "Marginalisation and Revolt among the Tuareg in Mali and Niger," *GeoJournal* 36, no. 1 (1995): 61.

50   Lecocq and Klute, "Tuareg Separatism in Mali," 426.

51 Lecocq, *Disputed Desert*, 264.

52 Lecocq, *Disputed Desert*, 265.

53 LeCocq notes that ARLA split off as a group of Kel Adagh that felt that significant reform was needed within Kel Tamasheq society, which had caused tension with the more moderate leadership of the MPA. See LeCocq, *Disputed Desert*, 267.

54 Lecocq, *Disputed Desert*, 269.

55 Krings, "Marginalisation and Revolt among the Tuareg in Mali and Niger," 61.

56 Krings, "Marginalisation and Revolt among the Tuareg in Mali and Niger," 61; Lecocq, *Disputed Desert*, 272–73.

57 Lecocq and Klute, "Tuareg Separatism in Mali," 427.

58 Lecocq, *Disputed Desert*, 281.

59 Krings, "Marginalisation and Revolt among the Tuareg in Mali and Niger," 61.

60 Lecocq, *Disputed Desert*, 285.

61 Krings, "Marginalisation and Revolt among the Tuareg in Mali and Niger," 61.

62 Lecocq and Klute, "Tuareg Separatism in Mali," 427.

63 Alpha Oumar Konaré was a scholar and political activist in Mali during the administrations of President Keita and General Traoré. Following the arrest of General Traoré by his Presidential Guard in 1991, Konaré participated in the transition to a representative democracy and won election to the presidency in 1992.

64 Scott Straus, *Making and Unmaking Nations: War, Leadership, and Genocide in Modern Africa* (Ithaca, NY: Cornell University Press, 2015), 170.

65 Lecocq and Klute, "Tuareg Separatism in Mali," 428; Lecocq, *Disputed Desert*, 307.

66 For additional information on the Ganda Koy militias and their role before and after the amnesty, see Marc Andre Boisvert, "Failing at Violence: The Longer-Lasting Impact of Pro-Government Militias in Northern Mali since 2012," *African Security* 8, no. 4 (2015): 272–98.

67 Jennifer C. Seely, "A Political Analysis of Decentralisation: Coopting the Tuareg Threat in Mali," *Journal of Modern African Studies* 39, no. 03 (2001): 504–5.

68 See again Lecocq, *Disputed Desert,* 161.

69 Krings, "Marginalisation and Revolt among the Tuareg in Mali and Niger," 61.

70 With both these organizations being represented by a singular figure in Iyad ag Ghali, as noted earlier.

71 Lecocq, *Disputed Desert*, 267.

72 Lecocq, *Disputed Desert*, 281–83.

73 Seely, "A Political Analysis of Decentralisation," 516.

74 Jibrin Ibrahim, "Political Exclusion, Democratization and Dynamics of Ethnicity in Niger," *Africa Today* 41, no. 3 (1994): 21.

75 Ibrahim, "Political Exclusion, Democratization and Dynamics of Ethnicity in Niger," 24.

76 Ibrahim, "Political Exclusion, Democratization and Dynamics of Ethnicity in Niger," 25.

77 Lecocq, *Disputed Desert*, 243.

78 Lecocq, *Disputed Desert*, 244.

79 Krings, "Marginalisation and Revolt among the Tuareg in Mali and Niger," 60.

80 Krings, "Marginalisation and Revolt among the Tuareg in Mali and Niger," 60.

81 Lecocq and Klute, "Tuareg Separatism in Mali," 426.

82 Krings, "Marginalisation and Revolt among the Tuareg in Mali and Niger," 62.

83 Krings, "Marginalisation and Revolt among the Tuareg in Mali and Niger," 62.

84 Krings, "Marginalisation and Revolt among the Tuareg in Mali and Niger," 62.

85 Lecocq, *Disputed Desert*, 244.

86 Krings, "Marginalisation and Revolt among the Tuareg in Mali and Niger," 62.

Conclusion

1 As noted, this form of warfare often took a specifically Maoist cast, hence the use of the term "protracted warfare"; however, these sorts of conflicts were waged across much of the world in very similar ways throughout the 1950s and 1960s, with additional military and political thought being imported from other revolutionary places such as Cuba, Algeria, and even Yugoslavia.

2 In this case, specifically the premises laid out in the United Nations charter, with the most relevant pieces being chapter I, article 1, and chapter XII, article 76.

3 Henry S. Wilson, *African Decolonization* (London: Hodder Education, 1994), 72–74.

4 Wilson, *African Decolonization*, 81–83.

5 Wilson, *African Decolonization*, 92–93.

6 Jules Gérard-Libois, *Katanga Secession*, trans. Rebecca Young (Madison: University of Wisconsin Press, 1966), 316.

7 Baz Lecocq and Georg Klute, "Tuareg Separatism in Mali," *International Journal: Canada's Journal of Global Policy Analysis* 68, no. 3 (2013): 425.

8 Frederick Cooper, *Africa Since 1940: The Past of the Present* (New York: Cambridge University Press, 2002), 5.

9   A good overview of these powers and their roles is in Elizabeth Schmidt, *Foreign Intervention in Africa: From the Cold War to the War on Terror* (Cambridge: Cambridge University Press, 2013), 18–29. The remainder of the book also offers several well-researched case studies illustrating the role of these international patrons in African conflicts.

10 In some cases these were issues of humanitarian interest, as noted in Alicia C. Decker and Andrea L. Arrington, *Africanizing Democracies, 1980–Present* (New York: Oxford University Press, 2015), 2; for others, as noted, the new perceived threat of Islamism was cited as a deep concern, as noted in Schmidt, *Foreign Intervention in Africa*, 214.

11 Now the Democratic Republic of the Congo.

12 The evolution of the Katangan Gendarmerie is captured in Erik Kennes and Miles Larmer. *The Katangan Gendarmes and the War in Central Africa: Fighting Their Way Home* (Bloomington: Indiana University Press, 2016).

13 Shaba was the new name given to Katanga during Mobutu's period of Zaireanization.

14 Schmidt, *Foreign Intervention in Africa*, 187–88.

15 Their website is still active and discusses their activities. See MASSOB, http://massob.biafranet.com/.

16 For example, see James Eze, "Biafra: Enugu police arrest 15 MASSOB members," *Premium Times*, 22 May 2018, https://www.premiumtimesng.com/regional/ssoutheast/269353-biafra-enugu-police-arrest-15-massob-members.html.

17 See C.L., "The National Service in Eritrea: Miserable and Useless," *The Economist*, 10 May 2014, https://www.economist.com/baobab/2014/03/10/miserable-and-useless.

18 "Q&A: The Horn's Bitter Border War," BBC.com, 7 December 2005, http://news.bbc.co.uk/2/hi/africa/4041073.stm.

19 Nathaniel Myers, "Africa's North Korea," *Foreign Policy*, 15 June 2010, https://foreignpolicy.com/2010/06/15/africas-north-korea/.

20 "The Death of John Garang," *The Economist*, Print Edition, 4 August 2005, https://www.economist.com/middle-east-and-africa/2005/08/04/the-death-of-john-garang.

21 Salva Kiir is Dinka and Machar is Nuer.

22 "South Sudan Democratic Movement, Army," *Sudan Tribune*, http://www.sudantribune.com/+-SSDM-A-South-Sudan-Democratic,483-+ .

23 "South Sudan Liberation Movement/Army," *Sudan Tribune*, http://www.sudantribune.com/spip.php?mot355.

24 James Copnall, "Sudan: Why Abyei is Crucial to the North and South," BBC, 23 May 2011, https://www.bbc.com/news/world-africa-13502845.

25   Simon Tisdall, "South Sudan President Sacks Cabinet in Power Struggle," *The Guardian*, 24 July 2013, https://www.theguardian.com/world/2013/jul/24/south-sudan-salva-kiir-sacks-cabinet.

26   Patrick McGroarty, "South Sudan's Kiir Says Uganda Helping to Fight Rebels," *Wall Street Journal*, 16 January 2014, https://www.wsj.com/articles/south-sudan8217s-kiir-says-uganda-helping-to-fight-rebels-1389876829.

27   The Islamic Courts Union was a reaction to the continued violence of the warlord conflicts. The ICU arose as a stern but pacifying force in the south of Somalia and rapidly gained support and legitimacy. See "Profile: Somalia's Islamic Courts," BBC.com, 6 June 2016, http://news.bbc.co.uk/2/hi/africa/5051588.stm.

28   Said S. Samatar, "The Islamic Courts and Ethiopia's Intervention in Somalia: Redemption or Adventurism," *Chatham House*, 25 April 2007, https://www.chathamhouse.org/sites/default/files/public/Research/Africa/250407samatar.pdf.

29   Stig Jarle Hansen, *Al-Shabaab in Somalia: The History and Ideology of a Militant Islamist Group* (New York: Oxford University Press, 2016).

30   For example, Somaliland continues to get glowing international profiles, such as in Joshua Keating, "When Is a Nation not a Nation? Somaliland's Dream of Independence," *The Guardian*, 20 July 2018, https://www.theguardian.com/news/2018/jul/20/when-is-a-nation-not-a-nation-somalilands-dream-of-independence.

31   Rashid Abdi, "A Dangerous Gulf in the Horn: How the Inter-Arab Crisis is Fueling Regional Tensions," International Crisis Group, 3 August 2017, https://www.crisisgroup.org/middle-east-north-africa/gulf-and-arabian-peninsula/dangerous-gulf-horn-how-inter-arab-crisis-fuelling-regional-tensions.

32   Bashir Ali, "How an Unrecognized State's Port Deal Could Shift Dynamics Across the Horn," *African Arguments*, 1 May 2018, http://africanarguments.org/2018/05/01/how-an-unrecognised-states-port-deal-could-shift-dynamics-across-the-horn-berbera-port-dpworld-somaliland/.

33   Angel Rabasa et al., "The Tuareg Insurgency in Mali, 2006-2009," in *From Insurgency to Stability,* vol. 2: *Insights from Selected Case Studies*, ed. Angel Rabasa et al. (Santa Monica, CA: RAND, 2011), 124.

34   Rabasa et al., "The Tuareg Insurgency in Mali, 2006-2009," 128.

35   Adam Nossiter, "Qaddafi's Weapons, Taken by Old Allies, Reinvigorate an Insurgent Army in Mali," *New York Times*, 5 February 2012, https://www.nytimes.com/2012/02/06/world/africa/tuaregs-use-qaddafis-arms-for-rebellion-in-mali.html.

36   "Mali Tuareg Rebels Declare Independence in the North," BBC, 6 April 2012, https://www.bbc.com/news/world-africa-17635437.

37   Peggy Brugiere, "Backed By Popular Support, Mali's Islamists Drive Tuareg from Gao," *France24*, 29 June 2018, http://observers.france24.com/en/20120629-mali-backed-popular-support-islamists-drive-tuareg-separatists-north-city-gao.

38 Michael Shurkin, *France's War in Mali: Lessons for an Expeditionary Army* (Santa Monica, CA: RAND, 2014), 13–24.

39 Schmidt, *Foreign Intervention in Africa*, 213.

40 This is covered in Schmidt, *Foreign Intervention in Africa*, 216, but a lengthier study of the structure and goals of the TSCTP is Lesley Anne Warner, *The Trans Sahara Counter Terrorism Partnership: Building Partner Capacity to Counter Terror and Violent Extremism* (Washington DC: Center for Complex Operations, 2014).

41 ECOWAS, for example, sent contingents with increasing ability to stabilize the civil wars in Liberia and Sierra Leone in the late 1990s, while SADC intervened in Lesotho and helped organize the Force Intervention Brigade in the Democratic Republic of the Congo.

42 Schmidt, *Foreign Intervention in Africa*, 213.

Bibliography

Abdi, Rashid. "A Dangerous Gulf in the Horn: How the Inter-Arab Crisis Is Fueling Regional Tensions." International Crisis Group, 3 August 2017. https://www.crisisgroup.org/middle-east-north-africa/gulf-and-arabian-peninsula/dangerous-gulf-horn-how-inter-arab-crisis-fuelling-regional-tensions.

Abi-Saab, Georges. *The United Nations Operation in the Congo, 1960–1964*. New York: Oxford University Press, 1978.

Adam, Hussein M. "Formation and Recognition of New States: Somaliland in Contrast to Eritrea." *Review of African Political Economy* 21, no. 59 (1994): 21–38

Addo, Michael K. "Political Self Determination within the Context of the African Charter on Human and Peoples' Rights." *Journal of African Law* 32, no. 2 (1988): 182–93.

Adebajo, Adekeye. *Curse of Berlin: Africa After the Cold War*. New York: Oxford University Press, 2014.

Akinrade, Sola. *Africa in the Post Cold War International System*. Washington, DC: Bloomsbury Academic, 1998.

Akpan, Ntieyong U. *The Struggle for Secession, 1966–1970: A Personal Account of the Nigerian Civil War*. London: F. Cass, 1971.

Akuchu, Gemuh E. "Peaceful Settlement of Disputes: Unsolved Problem for the OAU (A Case Study of the Nigeria-Biafra Conflict)." *Africa Today* 24, no. 4 (1977): 39–58.

Ali, Bashir. "How an Unrecognised State's Port Deal Could Shift Dynamics across the Horn." *African Arguments*, 1 May 2018. https://africanarguments.org/2018/05/01/how-an-unrecognised-states-port-deal-could-shift-dynamics-across-the-horn-berbera-port-dpworld-somaliland/.

Arachie, C. E. *The Bye-Gone: Horrors of a Crude War; Biafra Experience*. Lagos, Nigeria: C.E. Arachie, 1991.

Arnold, Matthew B. "The South Sudan Defence Force: Patriots, Collaborators or Spoilers?" *Journal of Modern African Studies* 45, no. 4 (2007): 489–516.

Assensoh, A. B. *African Political Leadership: Jomo Kenyatta, Kwame Nkrumah, and Julius K. Nyerere*. Malabar, FL: Krieger, 1998.

Azikiwe, Nnamdi. *Origins of the Nigerian Civil War*. Apapa: Nigerian National Press, 1969.

Badmus, Isiaka Alani. "The Quest for Security After the Cold War: Africa's Security Concerns." *Review of International Affairs* 60, no. 1133/34 (2009): 25–47.

Bahadur, Jay. *The Pirates of Somalia: Inside Their Hidden World*. New York: Vintage, 2012.

Bassil, Noah R. *The Post-Colonial State and Civil War in Sudan: The Origins of Conflict in Darfur*. London: I.B. Tauris, 2013.

BBC. "Profile: Somalia's Islamic Courts," 6 June 2006. http://news.bbc.co.uk/2/hi/africa/5051588.stm.

BBC. "Q&A: Horn's Bitter Border War," 7 December 2005. http://news.bbc.co.uk/2/hi/africa/4041073.stm.

Benjaminsen, Tor A. "Does Supply-Induced Scarcity Drive Violent Conflicts in the African Sahel? The Case of the Tuareg Rebellion in Northern Mali." *Journal of Peace Research* 45, no. 6 (2008): 819–36.

Bereketeab, Redie, ed. *Self-Determination and Secession in Africa: The Post-Colonial State*. New York: Routledge, 2016.

Beshir, Mohamed Omer. *The Southern Sudan: From Conflict to Peace*. London: C. Hurst, 1975.

Bhebe, Ngwabi, and Terence Ranger. *Soldiers in Zimbabwe's Liberation War*. London: James Currey, 1995.

Boas, Morten, and Kevin C. Dunn. *African Guerrillas: Raging Against the Machine*. Boulder, CO: Lynne Rienner, 2007.

Boisvert, Marc Andre. "Failing at Violence: The Longer-Lasting Impact of Pro-Government Militias in Northern Mali since 2012." *African Security* 8, no. 4 (2015): 272–98.

Brackhill, Jeremy. "Daring to Storm the Heavens: the Military Strategy of ZAPU 1976 to 1979." In Bhebe and Ranger, *Soldiers in Zimbabwe's Liberation War*, 48–72.

Bradbury, Mark. *Becoming Somaliland*. Oxford: James Currey, 2008.

———. "Sudan: International Responses to War in the Nuba Mountains." *Review of African Political Economy* 25, no. 77 (1998): 463–74.

Bradbury, Mark, Adan Yusuf Abokor, and Haroon Ahmed Yusuf. "Somaliland: Choosing Politics over Violence." *Review of African Political Economy* 30, no. 97 (2003): 455–78.

Brons, Maria. *Society, Security, Sovereignty, and the State in Somalia: From Statelessness to Statelessness?* Utrecht: International Books, 2001.

Bruce, James. *Travels to Discover the Source of the Nile*. Edinburgh: Robinson, 1790.

Bulhan, Xuseen Cabdillahi. "A Self-Portrait of Somaliland: Rebuilding from the Ruins." Somaliland Centre for Peace and Development Xarunta Nabada Iyo Horumarinta Soomaaliland, War-Torn Societies Project, 1999.

C.L. "The National Service in Eritrea: Miserable and Useless." *The Economist*, 10 March 2014. https://www.economist.com/baobab/2014/03/10/miserable-and-useless.

Červenka, Zdeněk. *The Nigerian War, 1967–1970: History of the War: Selected Bibliography and Documents*. Frankfurt am Main: Bernard & Graefe, 1971.

Chabal, Patrick, and Jean-Pascal Daloz. *Africa Works: Disorder as Political Instrument*. Bloomington: Indiana University Press, 1999.

Chakravorty, B. *The Congo Operation, 1960–63*. Edited by Sri Nandan Prasad. New Delhi: Historical Section, Ministry of Defence, Government of India, 1976.

Chaliand, Gérard. "The Horn of Africa's Dilemma." *Foreign Policy*, no. 30 (Spring 1978): 116–31.

Cherry, Janet. *Spear of the Nation (Umkhonto WeSizwe): South Africa's Liberation Army, 1960s–1990s*. Athens: Ohio University Press, 2012.

Cissoko, Joachin F. "A Third-World Country Facing Indigenous Insurgencies: The Malian Touareg Insurgency." Master's thesis, US Command and General Staff College, 2011.

Clapham, Christopher, ed. *African Guerrillas*. Oxford: James Currey, 1998.

Clayton, Anthony. *Frontiersmen: Warfare in Africa since 1950*. London: UCL Press, 1999.

Clayton, Anthony, and David Killingray. *Khaki and Blue: Military and Police in British Colonial Africa*. Athens: Ohio University Center for International Studies, 1989.

Cliffe, Lionel. "Peace in the Horn This Year?" *Review of African Political Economy* 30, no. 97 (2003): 497–504.

———. "Regional Dimensions of Conflict in the Horn of Africa." *Third World Quarterly* 20, no. 1 (1999): 89–111.

Cline, Lawrence E. "Nomads, Islamists, and Soldiers: The Struggles for Northern Mali." *Studies in Conflict & Terrorism* 36, no. 8 (2013): 617–34.

Collins, Robert O. "Africans, Arabs, and Islamists: From the Conference Tables to the Battlefields in the Sudan." *African Studies Review* 42, no. 2 (1999): 105–23.

———. *A History of Modern Sudan*. New York: Cambridge University Press, 2008.

———. *The Southern Sudan in Historical Perspective*. New Brunswick, NJ: Transaction, 2007.

Colvin, Ian. *The Rise and Fall of Moïse Tshombe: A Biography*. London: Leslie Frewin, 1968.

Compagnon, Daniel. "Somali Armed Movements." In Clapham, *African Guerrillas*, 73–90.

Connell, Dan. *Against All Odds: A Chronicle of the Eritrean Revolution*. Trenton, NJ: Red Sea Press, 1993.

Cooper, Frederick. *Africa since 1940: The Past of the Present*. New York: Cambridge University Press, 2002.

Copnall, James. "Sudan: Why Abyei Is Crucial to North and South." BBC, 23 May 2011. https://www.bbc.com/news/world-africa-13502845.

Cristiani, Dario, and Riccardo Fabiani. "The Malian Crisis and Its Actors." *International Spectator* 48, no. 3 (2013): 78–97.

Cronjé, Suzanne. *The World and Nigeria: The Diplomatic History of the Biafran War, 1967–1970*. London: Sidgwick & Jackson, 1972.

Davidson, Basil. *The Black Man's Burden: Africa and the Curse of the Nation-State*. New York: Times Books, 1992.

———. *Modern Africa: A Social and Political History*. New York: Routledge, 1994.

———. *The People's Cause: A History of Guerillas in Africa*. Burnt Mill, UK: Longman, 1983.

Dayal, Rajeshwar. *Mission for Hammarskjöld: the Congo Crisis*. Princeton, NJ: Princeton University Press, 1976.

De St. Jorre, John. *The Nigerian Civil War*. London: Hodder & Stoughton, 1973.

———. "Nigerian Civil War Notebook." *Transition*, no. 38 (June–July 1971): 36–41.

De Waal, Alexander. "Counter-Insurgency of the Cheap." *Review of African Political Economy* 31, no. 102 (2004): 716–25.

———. *Evil Days: 30 Years of War and Famine in Ethiopia*. New York: Human Rights Watch, 1991.

———. *War in Sudan*. London: Peace in Sudan Group, 1990.

De Witte, Ludo. *The Assassination of Lumumba*. New York: Verso, 2002.

Decker, Alicia C., and Andrea L. Arrington. *Africanizing Democracies: 1980–Present*. New York: Oxford University Press, 2015.

Deng, Francis Mading. *War of Visions: Conflict of Identities in the Sudan*. Washington, DC: Brookings Institution, 1995.

Devlin, Larry. *Chief of Station, Congo: Fighting the Cold War in a Hot Zone*. New York: PublicAffairs, 2008.

Dorn, Walter. "The UN's First 'Air Force': Peacekeepers in Combat, Congo 1960–64." *Journal of Military History* 77, no. 4 (2013): 1399–1425.

Doron, Roy. "Marketing Genocide: Biafran Propaganda Strategies during the Nigerian Civil War, 1967–70." *Journal of Genocide Research* 16, no. 2/3 (2014): 227–46.

Dorsey, William H. "Anyanya Leader Joseph Lagu." *Africa Report* 17, no. 9 (1972): 17–19.

Doyle, Rose, and Leo Quinlan. *Heroes of Jadotville: The Soldiers' Story*. Dublin: New Island, 2016.

Drysdale, J. G. S. *Somaliland: the Anatomy of Secession*. Hove, UK: Global-Stats, 1992.

———. *Stoics Without Pillows: A Way Forward for the Somalilands*. London: HAAN, 2000.

Elmi, Afyare Abdi. *Understanding the Somalia Conflagration: Identity, Political Islam and Peacebuilding*. New York: Pluto Press, 2010.

Emerson, Stephen A. "Desert Insurgency: Lessons from the Third Tuareg Rebellion." *Small Wars & Insurgencies* 22, no. 4 (2011): 669–87.

Englebert, Pierre. *Africa: Unity, Sovereignty, and Sorrow*. Boulder, CO: Lynne Rienner, 2009.

Englebert, Pierre, and Rebecca Hummel. "Let's Stick Together: Understanding Africa's Secessionist Deficit." *African Affairs* 104, no. 416 (2005): 399–427.

Erlikh, Hagai. *The Struggle over Eritrea, 1962–1978: War and Revolution in the Horn of Africa*. Stanford, CA: Hoover Institution Press, 1983.

Eze, James."Biafra: Enugu police arrest 15 MASSOB members." *Premium Times*, 22 May 2018. https://www.premiumtimesng.com/regional/ssouth-east/269353-biafra-enugu-police-arrest-15-massob-members.html.

Farah, Ahmed Y., and Ioan M. Lewis. "Making Peace in Somaliland." *Cahiers d'Études Africaines* 37, no. 146 (1997): 349–77.

Findlay, Trevor. *The Blue Helmets' First War? Use of Force by the UN in the Congo, 1960–64*. Cornwallis Park, NS: Canadian Peacekeeping Press, 1999.

Forrest, Joshua B. *Subnationalism in Africa: Ethnicity, Alliances, and Politics*. Boulder, CO: Lynne Rienner, 2004.

Forsyth, Frederick. *The Biafra Story*. Baltimore: Penguin, 1969.

———. *Emeka*. Ibadan, Nigeria: Spectrum, 1992.

Franke, Richard W. "Tuareg of West Africa: Five Experiments in Fourth World Development." *Antipode* 16, no. 2 (1984): 45–53.

George, Edward. *The Cuban Intervention in Angola, 1965–1991: From Che Guevara to Cuito Cuanavale*. New York: Routledge, 2012.

Gérard-Libois, Jules. *Katanga Secession*. Translated by Rebecca Young. Madison: University of Wisconsin Press, 1966.

Giap, Vo Nguyên. *People's War, People's Army*. New York: Bantam, 1962.

Gibbs, David N. "Dag Hammarskjöld, the United Nations, and the Congo Crisis of 1960-1: A Reinterpretation." *Journal of Modern African Studies* 31, no. 1 (1993): 163–74.

———. "The United Nations, International Peacekeeping and the Question of 'Impartiality': Revisiting the Congo Operation of 1960." *Journal of Modern African Studies* 38, no. 3 (2000): 359–82.

Gilkes, Patrick. "Somalia: Conflicts within and against the Military Regime." *Review of African Political Economy* 16, no. 44 (1989): 53–58.

Gorbachev, Mikhail Sergeevich. *Perestroika: New Thinking for Our Country and the World*. Norwalk, CT: Easton Press, 1996.

Gordon, David F., David C. Miller Jr., and David Wolpe. *The United States and Africa: A Post–Cold War Perspective*. New York: W. W. Norton, 1998.

Grant, J. Andrew, ed. *The New Regionalism in Africa*. Burlington, VT: Ashgate, 2003.

Griffin, Christopher. "French Military Policy in the Nigerian Civil War, 1967–1970." *Small Wars & Insurgencies* 26, no. 1 (2015): 114–35.

Grundy, Kenneth W. *Guerrilla Struggle in Africa: An Analysis and Preview*. New York: Grossman, 1971.

Guevara, Che. *Guerrilla Warfare*. New York: Praeger, 1970.

Hailu, Solomon. "A New Start for African Security." *International Journal on World Peace* 26, no. 4 (2009): 63–73.

Hale, Henry E. "The Parade of Sovereignties: Testing Theories of Secession in the Soviet Setting." *British Journal of Political Science* 30, no. 1 (2000): 31–56.

Han, Suyin. *The Morning Deluge: Mao Tsetung and the Chinese Revolution*. St. Albans, UK: Panther, 1976.

Hansen, Stig Jarle. *Al-Shabaab in Somalia: The History and Ideology of a Militant Islamist Group*. New York: Oxford University Press, 2016.

Hashim, Alice Bettis. *The Fallen State: Dissonance, Dictatorship, and Death in Somalia*. Lanham, MD: University Press of America, 1997.

Haywood, A., and F. A. S. Clarke. *The History of the Royal West African Frontier Force*. Aldershot, UK: Gale & Polden, 1964.

Henriksen, Thomas H. "People's War in Angola, Mozambique, and Guinea-Bissau." *Journal of Modern African Studies* 14, no. 3 (1976): 377–99.

Hopkins, A. G. *Global History: Interactions between the Universal and the Local*. New York: Palgrave Macmillan, 2006.

Horowitz, Donald L. *Ethnic Groups in Conflict*. Updated ed. Berkeley: University of California Press, 2000.

———. "Patterns of Ethnic Separatism." *Comparative Studies in Society and History* 23, no. 2 (1981): 165–95.

Hoskyns, Catherine. *The Congo Since Independence: January 1960 –December 1961*. New York: Oxford University Press, 1965.

Houser, George M. *No One Can Stop the Rain: Glimpses of Africa's Liberation Struggle*. New York: Pilgrim, 1989.

Hughes, Matthew. *The Central African Federation, Katanga and the Congo Crisis, 1958–65*. Salford: European Studies Research Institute, University of Salford, 2003.

Ibrahim, Jibrin. "Political Exclusion, Democratization and Dynamics of Ethnicity in Niger." *Africa Today* 41, no. 3 (1994): 15–39.

———. "Political Transition, Ethnoregionalism, and the 'Power Shift' Debate in Nigeria." *Issue: A Journal of Opinion* 27, no. 1 (1999): 12–16.

Ijalaye, David A. "Was 'Biafra' at Any Time A State in International Law?" *American Journal of International Law* 65, no. 3 (1971): 551–59.

International Crisis Group. "Negotiating a Blueprint for Peace in Somalia." International Crisis Group, 2003. http://www.crisisgroup.org/en/regions/africa/horn-of-africa/somalia/059-negotiating-a-blueprint-for-peace-in-somalia.aspx.

———. "Somaliland: Democratisation and Its Discontents." International Crisis Group, 2003. http://www.crisisgroup.org/en/regions/africa/horn-of-africa/somalia/066-somaliland-democratisation-and-its-discontents.aspx.

Islam, M. Rafiqul. "Secessionist Self-Determination: Some Lessons from Katanga, Biafra and Bangladesh." *Journal of Peace Research* 22, no. 3 (1985): 211–21.

Johnson, Douglas H. *The Root Causes of Sudan's Civil Wars*. Bloomington: Indiana University Press, 2003.

———. "The Sudan People's Liberation Army and the Problem of Factionalism." In Clapham, ed., *African Guerrillas*, 53–72.

Johnson, Hilde F. *Waging Peace in Sudan: The Inside Story of the Negotiations That Ended Africa's Longest Civil War*. Eastbourne, UK: Sussex Academic Press, 2011.

Johnson, Michael, and Trish Johnson. "Eritrea: The National Question and the Logic of Protracted Struggle." *African Affairs* 80, no. 319 (1981): 181–95.

Jok, Jok Madut. *Sudan: Race, Religion and Violence*. Oxford: Oneworld, 2007.

Jok, Jok Madut, and Sharon Elaine Hutchinson. "Sudan's Prolonged Second Civil War and the Militarization of Nuer and Dinka Ethnic Identities." *African Studies Review* 42, no. 2 (1999): 125–45.

Jørgenson, Thomas. "Sovereignty of States in The Post–Cold War Era: Implications for Sub-Saharan Africa." *Scientia Militaria – South African Journal of Military Studies* 32, no. 1 (2004): 96–119.

Kalb, Madeleine G. *The Congo Cables: The Cold War in Africa from Eisenhower to Kennedy*. New York: Macmillan, 1982.

Kamanu, Onyeonoro S. "Secession and the Right of Self-Determination: An O.A.U. Dilemma." *Journal of Modern African Studies* 12, no. 3 (1974): 355–76.

Kapteijns, Lidwien. *Clan Cleansing in Somalia: The Ruinous Legacy of 1991*. Philadelphia: University of Pennsylvania Press, 2012.

Keating, Joshua. "When Is a Nation Not a Nation? Somaliland's Dream of Independence." *The Guardian*, 20 July 2018. https://www.theguardian.com/news/2018/jul/20/when-is-a-nation-not-a-nation-somalilands-dream-of-independence.

Keenan, Jeremy. "Terror in the Sahara: The Implications of US Imperialism for North & West Africa." *Review of African Political Economy* 31, no. 101 (2004): 475–96.

———. "Turning the Sahel on Its Head: The 'Truth' behind the Headlines." *Review of African Political Economy* 33, no. 110 (2006): 761–69.

———. "Uranium Goes Critical in Niger: Tuareg Rebellions Threaten Sahelian Conflagration." *Review of African Political Economy* 35, no. 117 (2008): 449–66.

———. "US Militarization in Africa: What Anthropologists Should Know about AFRICOM." *Anthropology Today* 24, no. 5 (2008): 16–20.

Keita, Kalifa. "Conflict and Conflict Resolution in the Sahel: The Tuareg Insurgency in Mali." *Small Wars & Insurgencies* 9, no. 3 (1998): 102–28.

Kennes, Erik, and Miles Larmer. *The Katangese Gendarmes and War in Central Africa: Fighting Their Way Home*. Bloomington: Indiana University Press, 2016.

Khadiagala, Gilbert M. *Allies in Adversity: The Frontline States in Southern African Security, 1975-1993*. Lanham, MD: University Press of America, 2007.

Khālid, Manṣūr. *War and Peace in Sudan: A Tale of Two Countries*. London: Kegan Paul, 2003.

Kisangani, Emizet F. "The Tuaregs' Rebellions in Mali and Niger and the U.S. Global War on Terror." *International Journal on World Peace* 29, no. 1 (2012): 59–97.

Kohl, Ines. "Modern Nomads, Vagabonds, or Cosmopolitans? Reflections on Contemporary Tuareg Society." *Journal of Anthropological Research* 66, no. 4 (2010): 449–62.

Krings, Thomas. "Marginalisation and Revolt among the Tuareg in Mali and Niger." *GeoJournal* 36, no. 1 (1995): 57–63.

Laremont, Ricardo René. "Borders, States, and Nationalism." In *Borders, Nationalism, and the African State*, edited by Ricardo René Laremont, 1–31. Boulder, CO: Lynne Rienner, 2005.

Lecocq, Baz. "The Bellah Question: Slave Emancipation, Race, and Social Categories in Late Twentieth-Century Northern Mali." *Canadian Journal of African Studies / Revue Canadienne Des Études Africaines* 39, no. 1 (2005): 42–68.

———. *Disputed Desert: Decolonisation, Competing Nationalisms and Tuareg Rebellions in Northern Mali*. Boston: Brill, 2010.

———. "Unemployed Intellectuals in the Sahara: The Teshumara Nationalist Movement and the Revolutions in Tuareg Society." Supplement, *International Review of Social History* 49, no. S12 (2004): 87–109.

Lecocq, Baz, and Georg Klute. "Tuareg Separatism in Mali." *International Journal: Canada's Journal of Global Policy Analysis* 68, no. 3 (2013): 424–34.

Lefebvre, Jeffrey A. *Arms for the Horn: U.S. Security Policy in Ethiopia and Somalia, 1953-1991*. Pittsburgh: University of Pittsburgh Press, 1992.

———. "Iran in the Horn of Africa: Outflanking U.S. Allies." *Middle East Policy* 19, no. 2 (2012): 117–33.

Lefever, Ernest W., and Wynfred Joshua. *United Nations Peacekeeping in the Congo, 1960-1964: An Analysis of Political, Executive and Military Control*, vol. 2: *Full Text*. Washington, DC: Brookings Institution, 1966.

Legum, Colin, and Bill Lee. *Conflict in the Horn of Africa*. New York: Africana, 1977.

Lemarchand, Rene. "The Limits of Self-Determination: The Case of the Katanga Secession." *American Political Science Review* 56, no. 2 (1962): 404–16.

LeRiche, Matthew, and Matthew B. Arnold. *South Sudan: From Revolution to Independence*. London: Hurst, 2012.

Lewis, I. M. *Making and Breaking States in Africa: The Somali Experience*. Trenton, NJ: Red Sea Press, 2010.

———. *The Modern History of Somaliland: From Nation to State*. New York: Praeger, 1965.

Lugard, F. J. D. *The Dual Mandate in British Tropical Africa*. 5th ed. London: F. Cass, 1965.

Lumumba, Patrice. *Lumumba Speaks: The Speeches and Writings 1958–1961*. Boston: Little, Brown, 1972.

Lusk, Gill. "Democracy and Liberation Movements: The Case of the SPLA." *Middle East Report*, no. 174 (Jan.–Feb. 1992): 30–31.

Lyons, T. "Post–Cold War U.S. Policy toward Africa." *Brookings Review* 10, no. 1 (1992): 32.

Machiavelli, Niccolò. *The Prince*. Translated by Luigi Ricci. New York: Signet Classics, 1999.

Mao Tse-tung. *Mao Tse-Tung on Revolution and War*. Edited by M. Rejai. Garden City, NY: Anchor, 1970.

Markakis, John. *National and Class Conflict in the Horn of Africa*. New York: Cambridge University Press, 1987.

Martin, David, and Phyllis Johnson. *The Struggle for Zimbabwe: The Chimurenga War*. London: Faber & Faber, 1982.

McGroarty, Patrick. "South Sudan's Kiir Says Uganda Helping to Fight Rebels." *Wall Street Journal*, 16 January 2014. https://www.wsj.com/articles/south-sudan8217s-kiir-says-uganda-helping-to-fight-rebels-1389876829.

Metz, Helen Chapin. *Somalia: A Country Study*. Washington, DC: Federal Research Division, Library of Congress, 1993.

Migdal, Joel S. *Strong Societies and Weak States: State-Society Relations and State Capabilities in the Third World*. Princeton, NJ: Princeton University Press, 1988.

Mlambo, Alois S. *A History of Zimbabwe*. New York: Cambridge University Press, 2014.

Mockler, Antony. *The Mercenaries*. Sugarland, TX: Free Companion Press, 1981.

Moorcraft, Paul L., and Peter McLaughlin. *The Rhodesian War: A Military History*. South Yorkshire, UK: Pen & Sword Military, 2015.

Moyse-Barlett, Lt. Col. H. *The King's African Rifles: A Study in the Military History of East and Central Africa, 1890–1945*. Uckfield, UK: Naval & Military Press, 2016.

Museveni, Yoweri. "The Strategy of Protracted People's War: Uganda." *Military Review* 88, no. 6 (2008): 4–13.

Myers, Nathaniel. "Africa's North Korea." *Foreign Policy*. https://foreignpolicy.com/2010/06/15/africas-north-korea/.

Niven, Rex, Sir. *The War of Nigerian Unity, 1967–1970*. London: Evans Brothers, 1971.

Obasanjo, Olusegun. *My Command: An Account of the Nigerian Civil War, 1967–1970*. London: Heineman, 1981.

O'Brien, Conor Cruise. *To Katanga and Back: A UN Case History*. New York: Faber & Faber, 2015.

Ojukwu, C. O. *Biafra: Selected Speeches with Journals of Events*. New York: Harper & Row, 1969.

Onipede, O. "Nigeria Crisis." *Africa Quarterly* 9, no. 3 (1969): 233–63.

Othen, Christopher. *Katanga 1960–63: Mercenaries, Spies and the African Nation that Waged War on the World*. Stroud, UK: The History Press, 2018.

Parsons, Timothy. *The African Rank and File: Social Implications of Colonial Service in the King's African Rifles*. Oxford: James Currey, 1999.

Poggo, Scopas Sekwat. *The First Sudanese Civil War: Africans, Arabs, and Israelis in the Southern Sudan, 1955–1972*. Basingstoke, UK: Palgrave Macmillan, 2011.

Pool, David. *From Guerrillas to Government: The Eritrean People's Liberation Front*. Athens: Ohio University Press, 2001.

Prunier, Gérard. "Rebel Movements and Proxy Warfare: Uganda, Sudan and the Congo (1986–99)." *African Affairs* 103, no. 412 (2004): 359–83.

Rabasa, Angel, et al. "The Tuareg Insurgency in Mali, 2006-2009." In *From Insurgency to Stability*, vol. 2: *Insights from Selected Case Studies*, edited by Angel Rabasa et al., 117 56. Santa Monica, CA: RAND, 2011.

Rasmussen, Susan. "Disputed Boundaries: Tuareg Discourse on Class and Ethnicity." *Ethnology* 31, no. 4 (1992): 351–65.

——. "Ritual Specialists, Ambiguity and Power in Tuareg Society." *Man* 27, no. 1 (1992): 105–28.

Reid, Richard. "The Challenge of the Past: The Quest for Historical Legitimacy in Independent Eritrea." *History in Africa* 28 (2001): 239–72.

Renders, Marleen. "Appropriate 'Governance-Technology'? – Somali Clan Elders and Institutions in the Making of the 'Republic of Somaliland.'" *Africa Spectrum* 42, no. 3 (2007): 439–59.

Reno, William. *Warlord Politics and African States*. Boulder, CO: Lynne Rienner, 1999.

Reynolds, Jonathan T. *Sovereignty and Struggle: Africa and Africans in the Era of the Cold War, 1945–1994*. New York: Oxford University Press, 2015.

Rolandsen, Øystein H. "The Making of the Anya-Nya Insurgency in the Southern Sudan, 1961–64." *Journal of Eastern African Studies* 5, no. 2 (2011): 211–32.

Samatar, Said. "The Islamic Courts and Ethiopia's Intervention in Somali: Redemption or Adventurism?" *Chatham House*, 25 April 2007. https://www.chathamhouse.org/sites/default/files/public/Research/Africa/250407samatar.pdf.

———. *Somalia: A Nation in Turmoil*. London: Minority Rights Group, 1991.

Sangmpam, S. N. "Neither Soft nor Dead: The African State Is Alive and Well." *African Studies Review* 36, no. 2 (1993): 73–94.

Saxena, J. N. *Self-Determination: From to Biafra to Bangladesh*. Delhi: University of Delhi, 1978.

Schmidt, Elizabeth. *Foreign Intervention in Africa: From the Cold War to the War on Terror*. Cambridge: Cambridge University Press, 2013.

Schraeder, Peter J. "From Irredentism to Secession: the Decline of Pan-Somali Nationalism." In *After Independence: Making and Protecting the Nation in Postcolonial and Postcommunist States*, edited by Lowell W. Barrington, 107–40. Ann Arbor: University of Michigan Press, 2006.

Scott, Philippa. "The Sudan Peoples' Liberation Movement (SPLM) and Liberation Army (SPLA)." *Review of African Political Economy* 12, no. 33 (1985): 69–82.

Seely, Jennifer C. "A Political Analysis of Decentralisation: Coopting the Tuareg Threat in Mali." *Journal of Modern African Studies* 39, no. 3 (2001): 499–524.

Seligman, Thomas K. "Art of Being Tuareg Sahara Nomads in a Modern World." *African Arts* 39, no. 3 (2006): 56–79.

Sherman, Richard. *Eritrea: The Unfinished Revolution*. New York: Praeger, 1980.

Shurkin, Michael. *France's War in Mali: Lessons for an Expeditionary Army*. Santa Monica, CA: RAND, 2014.

Spears, Ian S. "Reflections on Somaliland & Africa's Territorial Order." *Review of African Political Economy* 30, no. 95 (2003): 89–98.

Stapleton, Timothy J. *A Military History of South Africa: From the Dutch-Khoi Wars to the End of Apartheid*. Santa Barbara, CA: Praeger, 2010.

Starratt, Priscilla Ellen. "Tuareg Slavery and Slave Trade." *Slavery & Abolition* 2, no. 2 (1981): 83–113.

Stearns, Jason K. *Dancing in the Glory of Monsters: The Collapse of the Congo and the Great War of Africa*. New York: PublicAffairs, 2012.

Steiner, Rolf, and Yves-Guy Bergès. *The Last Adventurer*. Boston: Little, Brown, 1978.

Straus, Scott. *Making and Unmaking Nations: War, Leadership, and Genocide in Modern Africa*. Ithaca: Cornell University Press, 2015.

Sudan Tribune. "South Sudan Liberation Movement/Army." http://www.sudantribune.com/spip.php?mot355.

———. "South Sudan Democratic Movement, Army." http://www.sudantribune.com/+-SSDM-A-South-Sudan-Democratic,483-+.

Takeuchi, Shin'ichi. "Political Liberalization or Armed Conflicts? Political Changes in Post–Cold War Africa." *The Developing Economies* 45, no. 2 (2007): 172–93.

Tareke, Gebru. *The Ethiopian Revolution: War in the Horn of Africa.* New Haven, CT: Yale University Press, 2009.

Taylor, Ian. *The International Relations of Sub-Saharan Africa.* New York: Bloomsbury Academic, 2010.

Tekle, Amare. *Eritrea and Ethiopia: from Conflict to Cooperation.* Trenton, NJ: Red Sea Press, 1994.

Thomas, Gerry S. *Mercenary Troops in Modern Africa.* Boulder, CO: Westview, 1985.

Thompson, Joseph E. *American Policy and African Famine: The Nigeria-Biafra War, 1966–1970.* New York: Greenwood, 1990.

Trevaskis, G. K. N. *A Colony in Transition: 1941–52.* London: Oxford University Press, 1960.

Van der Waag, Ian. *A Military History of Modern South Africa.* Philadelphia: Casemate, 2018.

Vries, Lotje de, Pierre Englebert, and Mareike Schomerus, eds. *Secessionism in African Politics: Aspiration, Grievance, Performance, Disenchantment.* New York: Palgrave Macmillan, 2019.

Wai, Dunstan M. *The African-Arab Conflict in the Sudan.* New York: Africana, 1981.

Walls, Michael. "The Emergence of a Somali State: Building Peace from Civil War in Somaliland." *African Affairs* 108, no. 432 (2009): 371–89.

Warner, Lesley Anne. *The Trans Sahara Counter Terrorism Partnership: Building Partner Capacity to Counter Terror and Violent Extremism.* Washington DC: Center for Complex Operations, 2014.

Weissman, Stephen R. *American Foreign Policy in the Congo, 1960–1964.* Ithaca, NY: Cornell University Press, 1974.

White, Philip L. "Globalization and the Mythology of the 'Nation State.'" In *Global History: Interactions Between the Universal and the Local*, edited by A. G. Hopkins, 257–84. New York: Palgrave Macmillan, 2006.

Williams, Susan. *Who Killed Hammarskjöld?: The UN, the Cold War and White Supremacy in Africa.* New York: Oxford University Press, 2014.

Wilson, Henry S. *African Decolonization.* London: Hodder Education, 1994.

Wood, David. *The Armed Forces of African States.* London: Institute for Strategic Studies, 1966.

Woodward, Peter. *Crisis in the Horn of Africa: Politics, Piracy and the Threat of Terror.* London: I.B. Tauris, 2013.

———. *Sudan, 1898–1989: The Unstable State.* Boulder, CO: L. Rienner, 1990.

Young, John. *Peasant Revolution in Ethiopia: The Tigray People's Liberation Front, 1975-1991*. New York: Cambridge University Press, 1997.

———. "Sudan: Liberation Movements, Regional Armies, Ethnic Militias & Peace." *Review of African Political Economy* 30, no. 97 (2003): 423-34.

———. "The Tigray and Eritrean Peoples Liberation Fronts: A History of Tensions and Pragmatism." *Journal of Modern African Studies* 34, no. 1 (1996): 105-20.

Index

Achuzie, Joseph "Hannibal," 85
Addis Ababa, 91, 117, 131, 143, 152, 173; Sudan agreement, 167–168, 169, 180
Afwerki, Isaias, 274
Aguiyi-Ironsi, Johnson, 69, 70, 80, 81
Ahiara Declaration, 76–77, 82, 96, 97
Aideed, Mohamed Farah, 205, 207, 208, 216
Algeria, 194, 231, 232, 238, 240, 242–243, 245, 254, 258, 261; Kel Tamasheq haven, 240–241, 244, 259; liberation struggle 4, 55, 104, 119; mediation 248, 256
Ali, Muhammed, 131, 158
Angola, 3, 5, 13, 104–105, 106, 107, 111, 182, 193, 197, 272; Cabinda region, 13, 18, 199
Anya-nya, 20, 164, 165, 167–168, 169, 170, 177, 178, 179–180, 186
Anya-nya II, 20, 169, 170, 172, 174, 183
Azania Liberation Front (ALF), 165
Azawad, 22, 149, 231, 245, 249, 253, 255, 257, 261, 280, 282, 283

Babangida, Ibrahim, 197
al-Bashir, Omar, 172, 174, 175, 176, 185–186
Belgium, 8, 39, 40, 41, 42, 44, 52, 57, 59, 62, 91, 265; aid to Katanga, 42, 47, 55, 56, 57–58, 78, 88; colonialism, 52, 53
Berlin Conference, 27, 29, 131, 193, 258
Biafra, Republic of, 14, 23, 53, 67, 74, 75–78, 81, 82, 87, 95–97, 99, 129, 130, 134, 149, 152, 179, 180, 189, 226, 267, 268, 272–273; administrative state, 29, 79, 241; as nation state, 79 80; declaration of independence, 72; international recognition, 35, 74, 91–93, 263
Biafran army, 73, 74, 76, 83–86; Biafran Organization of Freedom Fighters, 83, 85; 4th Commando Brigade, 83, 85, 94; Mid-West offensive, 73; *ogbunigwe*, 75, 84; struggle for Onitsha, 73–75; supply issues 83–84; strategies and tactics 84–86
Border War, 107
Burco, 206, 209, 210, 211, 215, 216

Cabral, Amilcar, 105, 135
China, 19, 90, 100, 101, 103, 108, 120, 135, 145, 286; first republic, 100; civil war, 101, 135, 140
Cold War, 12, 29, 51, 128, 182, 191–192, 195, 232, 252, 253, 254, 256, 261, 264, 267–270, 272, 277–278, 284, 286; African dynamics, 14, 22, 39, 64, 186, 189, 192–194, 257; end of, 20, 94, 174–175, 184, 187, 190, 195, 197, 199, 203, 207, 256, 269, 283
Confédération des associations tribales du Katanga, (CONAKAT), 17, 40, 41–42, 52, 53–54, 55
Congo, 5, 11, 14, 30, 35, 39, 41, 54, 61, 81, 87, 88, 97, 99, 130, 179, 192, 272, 285; crisis, 17, 39, 42, 44–45, 49, 56, 62, 64, 94, 180; Democratic Republic of, 21, 193, 197; First Congo War, 272; Free State, 52; relations with Belgium 26, 40, 43, 48, 52, 57, 59, 91, 93; Second Congo War, 272; Zaire, 20, 21, 197, 198
Coordination de la résistance armée (CRA), 260
Cuito Cuanavale, battle of, 3, 107

Diori, Hamani, 258

Effiong, Philip, 77, 79, 82
Egal, Mohammed Ibrahim, 212, 213, 214, 215, 216, 217, 218, 222
Elisabethville, 41, 45, 48, 49, 51, 54
Enugu, 72, 73
Eritrea, 5, 111, 115, 121, 123, 126, 128, 134, 139, 140, 147, 181, 186–187, 224, 226, 264, 273; development under Italians, 116, 131–132, 220–221; early nationalism, 117–118; federation with Ethiopia, 116–117; historical separation from Ethiopia, 53, 130–131, 133; independence referendum, 115, 129, 152, 270; post-independence authoritarianism, 274–275, 278; relations with Sudan, 174–175, 185; war with Ethiopia, (1998–2000), 2

341

Eritrean Liberation Front, 116, 118, 122, 123, 126, 135, 141, 143, 144, 150; internal dissent, 119–120; military strategy, 119, 121, 125, 139–140
Eritrean Liberation Movement, 118
Eritrean People's Liberation Front, 19, 120, 121, 124, 125, 126, 183, 274–275; agricultural reforms, 144–145; Battle of Afabet, 128, 142; Battle of Nacfa, 127, 140, 141; education policy, 146–147; gender relations, 147–148; health policy, 147; industrial reforms, 145–146; military strategy, 19, 125, 128, 129, 135, 139, 141, 143; People's Front for Democracy and Justice, 274; relations with TPLF, 122, 128, 129, 150–151; siege of Keren, 125; social revolution, 126, 127–128, 129, 143–144, 148–149; split with ELF, 120–121
Ethiopia, 2, 3, 5, 19, 20, 92, 115, 117, 118, 121, 124, 128, 129, 130, 133, 134, 150, 152, 162, 172, 173, 175, 182, 183, 185, 189, 193, 204, 209, 211, 217, 220, 223, 226, 274, 286; Derg Government, 5, 122, 123, 128–129, 141, 150, 151, 170, 172, 183, 204–205, 270, 274; first Italian invasion, 131, 220; "Red Terror," 122; second Italian invasion, 116, 132, 220; use of Berbera, 224, 279
Ethiopian military, 50, 118–119, 120, 121, 122, 124–125, 126, 127, 128, 135, 139, 142, 143, 205; aid from United States, 119; intervention in Somalia, 227, 278; Peasants' Crusade, 123, 151; Red Star Campaign, 127, 141, 151; siege of Massawa, 124; Soviet aid, 124, 125, 195, 197, 205
Ethiopian People's Revolutionary Democratic Front, 128–129, 152, 183, 223
Equatoria Corps, 159, 161, 162

Faulqes, Roger, 55, 94
France, 32, 47, 88, 193, 196, 233, 241, 250, 256; decolonization, 25–26, 29, 222, 235, 265; empire 4, 102–103, 220; Operation Serval, 282; support for Biafra, 78, 84, 90–91, 92, 93–94
Front populaire de libération de l'Azawad (FPLA), 249, 251, 255
Front populaire pour la liberation du Niger (FPLN), 259

Ganda Koy, 251, 252, 257
Garang, John, 169–170, 172–176, 183–185, 275
Global War on Terror, 22, 262, 279, 283, 285, 286
Gorbachev, Mikhail, 189, 190
Gowon, Yakubu, 71, 72, 77, 78, 80, 82
Great Britain, 25, 68, 89, 93, 132, 221; decolonization, 26, 32, 108, 109, 222; empire, 4, 26, 29, 67–68, 105, 108, 158, 220, 265; stance towards Biafra, 75, 88–89
guurtis, 209–210, 211, 212, 213

Hammarskjöld, Dag, 49, 60, 61, 62
Hargeisa, 206, 214, 215, 216, 227

Igbo, 10, 18, 67–68, 69–72, 75, 77, 78–81, 83, 96
Indigenous People of Biafra (IPOB), 273
Islamic Courts Union (ICU), 227, 278

Jadotville, siege of, 49, 56

Kahin, Dahir Riyale, 218, 219
Kasavubu, Joseph, 40, 41, 43, 44, 46, 53, 59
Katanga, 13, 14, 17, 18, 23, 29, 35, 44, 51, 62, 64, 79, 81, 86, 95, 97, 129, 134, 149, 192–193, 226, 241, 253, 266, 269; Comité spéciale du Katanga, 30, 40, 52, 80, 130; declaration of independence, 42; European population, 35, 41; International recognition, 263, 267; gendarmerie, 44, 46, 47, 48–49, 50, 55–56, 57 58, 60, 94, 272; negotiations with Congolese government 45–47, 50, 99; province of the Congo, 13, 30, 40–41, 53; relations with Belgium, 43, 47–48, 57–59, 78, 87–88, 93; Union minière du Haute Katanga, 57, 58
Keita, Modibo, 235, 236, 237, 239, 240, 249, 253
Kel Adagh, 242, 245, 246, 249, 254, 255, 258
Kel Tamasheq, 194, 242, 243, 253–257, 262, 266, 280, 283; Alfellaga (first revolt), 239–242, 244, 245, 254; alliance with Islamists, 281–282, 283; in independent Mali, 236–239; in Libya, 245–246, 281; in Niger, 258–260, 280; origins, 232–233; second Malian revolt, 246–252, 254, 255; social structure, 233–235
Kenyatta, Jomo, 30
Khalil, Adbullah, 162, 177
Kiir, Salva, 275, 276, 277
Kountche, Seyni, 258, 259

Lagu, Joseph, 166, 167, 170, 172, 180, 182, 183
Léopoldville, 5, 42, 44, 45, 46, 60, 61
Libya, 2, 3, 26, 124, 231, 232, 242, 243, 245, 258, 259, 261, 280, 281
Lumumba, Patrice, 40, 41, 43, 45, 53, 59, 88; assassination, 44, 45, 59, 60, 267

Machar, Riek, 173, 174, 275, 277
al-Mahdi, Sadiq, 171, 183
Mahgoub, Mohamed Ahmed, 166
Mali, 21, 22, 193, 231, 236, 238, 243, 253–255, 257, 260, 262, 263, 280, 281; coup, 250, 256; elections, 252; independence, 235, 237; Mali Federation, 235–236; rebellion (2007), 280–281; rebellion (2011), 282–284; relations with Algeria, 241
Menelik II, 115, 131, 220
Mengistu Government, 20, 123, 124, 129, 139, 142, 143, 152, 170, 175, 183, 184, 185, 204, 205, 275; Mengistu Haile Mariam, 122, 127, 223
mercenaries, 17, 32, 47, 48, 49, 50, 55, 57, 58, 62, 81, 87, 93, 94, 272, 281
Mobutu, Joseph, 39, 44, 59, 88,
Mobutu, Sese Seko, 20, 197, 198, 272
Mouvement de libération de l'Azawad (MLA), 245
Mouvement populaire de liberation de l'Azawad (MPLA), 248, 255, 259
Movement for the Actualization of the Sovereign State of Biafra (MASSOB), 273
Mozambique, 3, 4, 5, 104, 105, 106, 107
Munongo, Godefroid, 41, 47, 53, 54, 55

National Movement for the Liberation of Azawad (MNLA), 282, 283
Niger, 22, 74, 194, 231, 242, 243, 245, 258, 259, 260, 261, 262, 280, 282,
Nigeria, 10, 18, 26, 29, 35, 67, 68, 72, 77, 78, 80, 82, 87, 88, 91, 92, 197, 263, 267, 273; Eastern region, 67, 68, 72, 80, 92; first coup, 69–70, 80, 81; independence, 68, 79; Mid-West region, 67, 72; Niger Delta, 13, 68, 75; Northern region, 21, 68, 80; second coup, 70–73, 79, 80; Western region, 67, 68, 72
Nigerian army, 75, 76, 89, 94; 1st Division, 73, 77; 2nd Division, 73; 3rd Marine Commando Division, 74, 76, 77; battle for Onitsha, 74; capture of Port Harcourt, 74; capture of Umuahia, 76; expansion, 95; international arms support, 75, 89
Nkrumah, Kwame, 26, 30
al-Numeiry, Gaafar Mohammed, 166, 167, 168, 170–171, 180
Nyerere, Julius, 3, 31, 93; recognition of Biafra, 92

O'Brien, Conor Cruise, 48
Ogaden, 2, 3, 123, 124, 151, 204–205, 206, 220, 221, 222, 223
Ojukwu, Emeka Odumegwu, 18, 72, 76, 77, 79, 81, 82, 83, 86, 94, 95, 96, 97
Organisation commune des regions sahariennes (OCRS), 236, 242, 253, 258
Organization for African Unity (OAU), 14, 35, 63, 74, 88, 92, 97, 134, 152, 163, 178, 180, 182, 227, 284; Charter, Article III, 63, 91, 134

Portugal, 26, 78, 104, 265; decolonization conflicts, 4, 104–105, 135
Puntland, 217, 226, 227, 279
protracted war, 3, 5, 6, 7, 8, 18–19, 103, 104, 109, 110, 129, 134–135, 137, 138, 151, 157, 165, 181, 264, 285; strategic defense, 135, 139; strategic offensive, 136, 141–143; strategic stalemate, 136, 140

Quinlan, Patrick, 56

Rhodesia, 3, 4, 48, 51, 55, 78, 106; Unilateral Declaration of Independence, 4, 104, 108; liberation struggles, 3, 108–109; Zimbabwe African National Union (ZANU), 4, 108–109, 111; Zimbabwean African People's Union (ZAPU), 4, 108–109, 111

Sabbe, Osman Saleh, 118
Selassie, Emperor Haile, 116, 117, 121, 122, 132, 140, 141, 150, 167, 204, 220, 221, 222
al-Shabaab, 227, 278–279
Siad Barre, Mohammed, 123, 204, 205, 206, 207, 209, 212, 215, 222, 225,
Somali National Movement (SNM), 204, 205, 207, 208, 221, 223, 225,
Somalia, 2, 3, 21, 123, 124, 151, 174, 193, 203, 204, 206, 207, 208, 210, 212, 215, 219, 220, 222, 223, 224, 225, 226, 278, 286; Federal Republic of, 217, 227, 279; "Greater

Somalia," 194, 204, 205; Transitional Federal Government, 227; Transitional National Government, 217, 227

Somaliland, 8, 21, 53, 203, 204, 208, 210, 211, 212, 215, 216, 217, 218, 219–228, 278, 279; Berbera Port Authority, 214; Borama Conference, 212, 213'; National Charter, 209, 212, 213, 214, 215; Sanaag Regional Peace Charter, 213,

South Africa, 3, 4, 6, 104, 105, 106, 107, 108; apartheid, 4, 104, 106, 107

South African liberation struggles, 106, 107; African National Congress, 4, 106, 107; Pan-African Congress, 4, 106; Poqo, 106; Umkhonto we Sizwe, 106

South Sudan, 20, 53, 111, 149, 157, 176, 186, 187, 226, 264, 271, 273, 275, 276, 278, 286; decolonization, 161–163; plebiscite, 162, 176, 177, 186, 187, 283, 284; separate administration, 159–161

Southern Sudan Liberation Movement, 167, 180

Southern Sudan Provisional Government (SSPG), 165, 167, 179

Soviet Union, 11, 12, 24, 108, 123–124, 128, 151, 182, 195, 204; collapse, 14, 20, 189–191, 205, 270

Stanleyville, 5, 44, 45, 46, 60, 61

Steiner, Rolf, 81, 83, 94

Sudan, 20, 26, 30, 92, 123, 126, 128, 130, 139, 157, 158, 159, 160, 170, 172, 174, 175, 177, 177, 179, 183, 185, 189, 220, 221, 226, 270; Abboud Government, 163–164, 177–187; Declaration of Principles, 175; First Civil War, 161–168, 180, 182; Second Civil War, 169–176, 182; "September Laws," 171

Sudanese African National Union (SANU), 163, 164, 165, 178, 179

Sudanese People's Liberation Movement (SPLM/A), 20, 169, 170, 171, 172, 173, 174, 175, 176, 183, 184, 185, 186, 187, 276, 277

Tamanrasset Accords, 248, 249, 250, 255, 256

Tenekra, 244, 245, 254, 261

Thant, U, 49, 60, 62–63; U Thant Plan for National Reconciliation, 50, 51

Thyssens, Georges, 47

Tigray People's Liberation Front (TPLF), 20, 122, 123, 126, 128, 129, 150, 151, 152

Torit mutiny, 161, 169

Toure, Amadou, 250, 256

Traore, Moussa, 248, 249, 250, 256

Treaty of Ucciali, 131, 133

Tse-Tung, Mao, 5, 8, 18, 101, 103, 135, 136, 137, 138, 140, 143, 149,

Tshombe, Moise, 17, 42, 43, 45, 46, 47, 48, 49, 50, 53, 54, 55, 57, 58, 60, 87, 272

Tuareg. *See* Kel Tamasheq

Uganda, 2, 3, 5, 32, 162, 175, 185, 196, 197

United Movements and Fronts of Azawad (MFUA), 250, 251, 256

United Nations, 14, 17, 25, 26, 35, 39, 43, 51, 57, 59, 61, 62, 63, 91, 97, 99, 115, 116, 117, 129, 134, 176, 178, 182, 191, 193, 194, 221, 226, 265, 266, 267, 269, 270, 276, 277, 282; chapter XI, 25, 26; chapter XII, 25, 26

United Nations peacekeeping, 43, 45, 47, 56, 58, 88, 192, 208, 227; Operation Grand Slam, 50, 60–61; Operation Morthor, 48, 49, 58, 60; Operation Rum Punch, 48, 58, 60, 61; Operation UNOKAT, 49, 60

United Nations Security Council, 43, 45, 61, 62; Resolution 143, 43, 57, 60; Resolution 145, 43, 57, 60; Resolution 146, 43, 57; Resolution 161, 57, 60

United States, 20, 24, 30, 101, 103, 132, 189, 191, 192, 193, 194, 195, 197, 208, 269, 270, 278–279, 281, 283, 286; military aid to Ethiopia, 116, 119; policy in the Congo, 42, 43, 44, 58–59; policy towards Nigeria, 88, 89, 93; policy towards Sudan, 175–176, 182, 184, 185, 275, 284

Vietnam, 88, 100, 104, 135, 181; Indochina War, 102–103, 142

Yoruba, 13, 67, 68, 73

www.ingramcontent.com/pod-product-compliance
Lightning Source LLC
Chambersburg PA
CBHW041438300426
44114CB00026B/2930